16.95

The Limits of Law

The Limits of Law

by Antony Allott

M.A., Ph.D., Professor of African Law,
School of Oriental and African Studies,
University of London

London · Butterworths · 1980

| England | Butterworth & Co (Publishers) Ltd |
| London | 88 Kingsway, WC2B 6AB |

Australia	Butterworths Pty Ltd
Sydney	586 Pacific Highway, Chatswood, NSW 2067
	Also at Melbourne, Brisbane, Adelaide and Perth

| Canada | Butterworth & Co (Canada) Ltd |
| Toronto | 2265 Midland Avenue, Scarborough M1P 4S1 |

| New Zealand | Butterworths of New Zealand Ltd |
| Wellington | 77–85 Customhouse Quay |

| South Africa | Butterworth & Co (South Africa) (Pty) Ltd |
| Durban | 152–154 Gale Street |

| USA | Butterworth (Publishers) Inc |
| Boston | 10 Tower Office Park, Woburn, Mass 01801 |

© Butterworth & Co (Publishers) Ltd 1980

ISBN Casebound 0 406 55242 8
      Limp   0 406 55243 6

Typeset by Butterworths Litho Preparation Department
Printed in Great Britain by Billing & Sons Limited
Guildford, London and Worcester

Introduction

Of the making of books about the nature of law there is no end. 'What is law?' is one of the most popular questions on the lips of the academic, though not the practising, lawyer. From Plato and Aristotle down to Hart, Fuller and Dworkin, not to mention the Scandinavians and all the other jurists toiling away at answering the great unanswerable question, the list stretches, like Banquo's line of kings, to the crack of doom. And this is to ignore the work of the historians, the political scientists, the philosophers, the moralists, and (most notably today) the sociologists and social anthropologists. These latter tend to be answering a related question, 'How is law?'; but they stray, like everyone else, onto the broader, richer-seeming, and ultimately less nourishing alps of 'What is law?'.

There are books, too numerous to count, about the making of law: who makes the law; what is the role of the judges; and so on. There are books, again too numerous to count, about who enforces the law, and who breaks the law. But there is a great gap, to which one may respect-fully point, in all these studies — and that is an investigation of the usefulness and uselessness of law, about the *limits of law*. Race Relations Acts are passed to change the way we think and behave — do they succeed? African countries seek a way out of under-development by use of the legal weapon — can it work? The statute book grows, so that the average motorist would have to fill his back seat with statutes and commentaries on motoring law as well as with tools and spare wheel if he wishes to be safe — to what end?

Codification, law-making in a systematic way, is all the rage; the Law Commissions of England and Scotland, in their quiet ways, illustrate this trend. The European Economic Communities attract blame, not for their lavish spending on butter mountains so much as for their spending of time and paper on laws and regulations, the jural mountain.

It is in reaction to all this that I write. I started off with a concern with African customary laws, legal systems in which the community makes law, and changes it by its changing practice without help from the legislator. I carried on into a study of law and development, and the desperate attempts of Third World countries to spend their way out of poverty and into riches by over-reliance on legislation: social engineering through law. Then I developed a comparative concern with the role of the ordinary people, the subjects of the law, not only in the making of the law through representative institutions and the like, but also in the unmaking of the law through ignorance, passive resistance, or institutional means such as trial by jury. The law clearly has limits of effectiveness and even of existence: what are they, and what are the causes of them? To discover and dissect the working of such limitations could surely do nothing but good, both to the legislator tempted by the legislative option and to the citizen fearing yet more law. Maybe the legislator today is searching for the new Philosopher's Stone, the alchemy which will set everything right, searching for ways to Eldorado, that golden land where all is tidy and regulated by law. Is there a path which leads to this goal?

In pursuing this theme I am, I believe, to a certain extent innovating.[1] Certainly there has been no previous attempt to pull together and analyse the resultant composite of data from many different societies in which law prevails, works, and does not work. But, outside the legal sphere, this investigation seems to me to resemble other developments in meta-scientific thinking (by 'meta-scientific' I mean thinking about science, rather than thinking or doing science). Physicists stop in their work of exploring and defining the structure of the physical universe and ask themselves the question, 'Can we really know?'. Heisenberg among others answers, 'No, you cannot.' Doctors stop in their work of building more hospitals, devising ever more costly and elaborate machines for diagnosing or treating patients, or of inventing ever more powerful wonder-drugs, and ask themselves, 'In the end, is it worth while? Will it work? Will the bugs eventually be immune to every wonder-drug; will

1. In her very recent study of *Dispute and Settlement in Rural Turkey* (Leiden, 1978), which looks at the way in which a Turkish village deals with legal conflicts in the light of its ancient customs, the rules of Islamic law, and the precepts of the applied Swiss Civil Code, Professor June Starr comprehensively (and, with respect, correctly) summarises the state of play so far as studies of legal transformation of society are concerned:

    'Laws are being passed in almost every modernizing country of Asia, Africa, and Latin America with the intent of changing behavior and attitudes of the less modern sectors of society (the Turkish Village Law of 1924 is one example). Yet, except for initiating statistical records on the cases heard in courts and agencies, there has been little attempt in any country to evaluate how a specific law affects those individuals who come under its jurisdiction. Particularly neglected is the empirical investigation of how diverse ethnic groups and rural populations in a country are reacting to legal innovation. Research on how new laws and procedures alter the behavior and attitudes of groups – especially those which are not members of the modern sector of the country – would seem necessary if governments and their advisors are to assess correctly the impact of their programs.' (at pp. 3–4)

    To which one can only add a very loud Amen!

the machines and the treatments cause disease and disorder rather than cure them?'

We live, then, in an era of healthy self-doubt, when the former certainties yield to introspective enquiry. The doubt is healthy, because there is nothing which is ultimately more dangerous than to rely on a technique or an analysis or a treatment which will not work, or which will finally cause harm. 'The operation was successful, but the patient died', is a common medical quip; 'the Rent Acts worked to protect the tenants, but the tenants disappeared', might be a legal parallel. Obsession with law-making seems a twentieth-century phenomenon, product of the prolonged Age of Enlightenment which stretches down from the eighteenth century to the present day, fed by Bentham and Napoleon, watered by the Germans, and now spreading over all, everyone, and everywhere, like a great green mould.[2]

The causes of this spread are open to speculation. The humanist sentiment that 'Man is the master of all things', even of himself and his companions, Victorian optimism and faith in science, has had something to do with it. But top of the list as cause of legislative spreading I would put, not authoritarian governments (whether of the pseudo-democratic or frankly dictatorial varieties), or even exuberant rationalism, but the mechanical means of producing laws. The printing press, the typewriter, and now the Xerox machine have a great deal to answer for. You want to prevent soil erosion in Africa? Nothing easier. You don't have to hire a single soil expert; all you need do is slip a piece of paper in the legislative typewriter, headed 'Soil Erosion Eradication Decree. 1980'. send it along to the appropriate legislature – if there is one. It will be passed, and the job will be done. Almost equally responsible must be the great academies. Laws need lawyers to devise and press them. Law schools and universities spew out lawyers who are potential draftsmen or operators of the laws they produce; while the devil gives work for idle academic hands by stimulating them to invent new and resounding projects for reform of the law. Each is more ambitious than the last; each has sound arguments to support it; each will reach the statute book – and then? Will it work? The answer is often, No, it won't. The limits of the effectiveness of the law have been reached; but by then the legal reformer, the law-maker, is on his next draft law, like the heart surgeon on his next patient; and he is unlikely to pause in his headlong progress to see what happened to his last effort.

I begin my enquiry into the limits of law by looking at the theoretical nature of law, and asking whether there is anything in the nature of

2. Readers who think that this view is exaggerated, or peculiar either to the author or the United Kingdom, should consult a very recent article by Roger Granger, discussed in the *Guide to Further Reading* at p. 294, which tells exactly the same story of the lawyer and the citizen being 'suffocated' by an excess of legislation in contemporary France.

law which limits its effectiveness and makes it incapable of being fully applied. Discussions of the nature of 'law' have, I believe, been confused by the inadequacies of the available terminology. Pre-eminently unsatisfactory, because used in several different senses in juristic writing, has been the term 'law' itself. *One* term will not do to cover all the functions without confusion of thought and analysis: I accordingly propose *three*, distinguished typographically as LAW (law in the abstract), *Law* (an existing legal system), and law (a particular rule or provision of a *Law*). Rejecting the possibility of ever determining the essence of LAW in the abstract (a task I abandon to the metaphysicians), I look at *Law* as an actual functioning system.

Law I see as a *communications system*, and hence subject to the same problems of transmission and reception of messages as any other communications system. The distinctive character of *Law* is in its being a function of an autonomous and distinct political society or community. It is generated by, or authenticated by, those who have competent and legitimate authority in that community, as possessing positions of power or influence. A legal system comprises not only norms, but also institutions (including facilities) and processes.

In analysing 'laws' (= the rules or norms of a particular system), which are the messages of the legal communications system, a distinction is made between *articulated* and *inarticulate* norms. An inarticulate norm is *latent*, if it has not yet been articulated but provokes *acts of compliance*. In this it is distinguished from *phantom norms* ('norms?' never emitted by any authority) and from *frustrate norms*, norms emitted in valid form but attracting minimal or zero compliance.

From the formal point of view, normative statements (i.e. statements articulating norms) are seen as hypothetical-conditionals; and application of a norm involves the 'matching' of the actual fact-situation to the model fact-situation specified in the 'If' part of the statement. From its nature such matching cannot be accurate. Can we say that facilities and institutions, processes, constitutive acts, and implementing orders within a legal system are 'norms'? How does one distinguish legal from other norms? What are the respective spheres of *Law*, morality, religion and mores? All these are important questions if one is to identify legal norms and their sphere of operation, as well as possible reasons for their ineffectiveness. 'Sanction' is not seen as a defining characteristic of a legal norm, but as a possible means of ensuring compliance. Legal norms are such, not because they are 'binding' (the term is rejected as having no correspondence with any actual phenomenon) or create 'obligations', but because of their source, their context, and their aim. They are seen as essentially *persuasive*.

In discussing limits on the effectiveness of *Law*, we are firstly impeded by the difficulty of measuring effectiveness quantitatively. Effectiveness is assessed in terms of the degree of *compliance* with legal norms; there are problems in deciding what is the measure of compliance for permissive, as well as for mandatory or prohibitory, norms. Sources of weakness and non-compliance in the emitting, transmission and reception of norms are identified. A principal weakness lies, naturally, in the language, in the statement or expression of a norm. In contradiction of jurists who adopt the position that linguistic terms have fixed meanings or point to particular 'things' in the real world, I treat the question, 'How should I use a given term in an English sentence?', as requiring the specification of the *function* of the item in its *verbal* and *social contexts;* this is the 'meaning' of the item. No term, and not merely no legal term, has a fixed and determinate function.

An equal source of weakness is seen in the deficiencies of *monitoring* the reception and implementation of norms, due to the absence of sufficient *feedback* in legal systems.

There has been considerable juristic discussion of the limits of *Law* imposed by the nature of the society in which it operates. Are there societies which are too small or too unorganised to have *Law*, or to have express mechanisms for the making of *Law*? This is the problem of so-called 'primitive' societies. These and related questions are seen as examples of *applied juristics*, that is, the study of the *Laws* in operation, with which the rest of the book is concerned. Hart's hypothetical treatment of a society too small and primitive to have legislature, courts and legal officials of any kind, so that it has only primary, and not secondary, rules of obligation, is measured against the observed facts of simpler societies. I conclude that Hart's theoretical strictures (and those of Ross) that the rules in such societies would be uncertain, static and inefficient, or indeed that such societies lack functional equivalents of law-makers, law-enforcers, and role-bearing institutions, are contradicted by the evidence, and that this casts doubt on his theoretical assumptions at this point. (Similar allegations against international law — often made by positivist lawyers — could have been, but are not, analysed from want of space.) If there are weaknesses, it is legal systems of the English type that come out worse from the comparison. One reason is that the ambitions of the legislators are less extreme in traditional societies; another is that there is much greater reinforcement of the legal message by the concurrence of moral and conventional precepts.

If we pursue our investigation of the effectiveness of *Law* into English society, a grave condition of *anomia*, or lack of knowledge of and responsiveness to *Law*, is diagnosed. Unknown law is ineffective law. English *Law* is little known by its subjects, as there is no effective communication of its requirements and innovations to the citizens at large, and little understanding of *how* and *why Law* is. This state is seen as unnecessary, avoidable, and remediable. Non-compliance with the *Law* is partly due to unwitting failure to comply, partly to deliberate defiance. Industrial relations law is a prime example of the latter case, demonstrating a tenuous respect for *Law* as a controlling mechanism.

But there are many other examples: road traffic law, street offences, divorce law, squatting. This widespread non-compliance must be partly attributable to the non-democratic nature of present legislative realities in Britain. What would happen if there were much greater popular involvement in the making of law, one wonders; almost certainly one result would be less law, another would be fuller compliance.

Laws do not work well if they are out of fit with their social context. In a country like England such lack of fit may be due to *who* made the law, *when* the law was made, and *to whom* the law applies. The adjustment of the *Law* to changing social conditions is partly the work of the *courts*, through their *re-definition of instrumental legal terms*, like the 'reasonable man' in *British Railways Board v Herrington,*[3] and through *contextual interpretation of statutes*, like 'family' in the Rent Acts as re-interpreted in *Dyson Holdings Ltd v Fox.*[4] *Legislation* too is naturally used to adjust *Law* to changed social conditions, though in a step-wise fashion. The *people* too adjust *Law* to their views of what is right and reasonable, and to their ways of living, through *catanomic* (law-conforming) and *paranomic* (law-disregarding) transactions and arrangements, in other words by using their law-making power to make new institutions. Popular disregard of laws does not repeal them directly (except for customary *Laws* properly so called), but it exerts an osmotic pressure on the agents of law-administration in the direction of variation or non-application.

One of the most fascinating examples of popular law-making is currently under way in England, with the development of the relationship of 'common-law wife', which I have christened the 'house-mate'. Developed in parallel with legitimate marriage, and originally in defiance of the norms of morality, convention and *Law*, the house-mate system is now achieving increasing recognition from courts and legislature. Eventually it may emerge as a separate legal status, in which case the triumph of custom as a generator of effective law will be complete. Legislated law is usually treated as excluding or limiting the effect of custom; but custom, as this example shows, can limit the effect of law.

When one turns to the phenomenon of *translocation of laws* (the shifting of a complete legal system or part of it from its home country to new ground), it is predictable that there should be a lack of fit between *Law* and society. African countries formerly under British colonial rule are prime examples of such translocation (though many countries in the Third World got their *Law* in this fashion, and there is now translocation of laws between developed legal systems as well as from them). Such translocation goes far back in time, as with the spread of Roman *Law*. It can be dramatic in its social effects, as with the translocation of Swiss *Law* to Turkey; or it can be more cautious and insidious, as with the

3. [1972] AC 877, [1972] 1 All ER 749, HL.
4. [1976] QB 503, [1975] 3 All ER 1030, CA.

domestication of English *Law* in Africa, where the translocated law had to compete with indigenous customary *Laws*.

Does justice limit *Law*? An old question, but worth looking at afresh, in view of the contradictions between the view (put forward by the positivists) that it is not the business of the *Law* to legislate morality — hence the attack, inspired by Bentham and Mill, on laws which seek to lay down private morality, however generally it may be accepted — and the evident attempt to legislate the new morality (of non-discrimination against races, sexes or religions) into law. If justice, or striving towards justice, is part of the essential definition of a legal system, this is a severe limitation on the possibilities and the validity of *Law*.

My own view is that such a definition is a confusion of levels of analysis. *Law* is an observable fact; the compulsions (or better, persuasions) of the *Law* are social facts. We judge whether *Law* exists, or a norm exists, not as a question of value but as a question of fact. Since we have discarded the notion of the 'binding' quality of *Law*, we do not have to answer the question, 'Can a formally valid but "immoral" (in the eyes of the questioner) law be binding?' A formally valid law is valid and persuasive. Whether its recipient is persuaded, or ought to be persuaded, is conditioned by evaluation at a quite different level, and within a different system, that of morality. A sentence can be grammatical but be a lie; a law can be valid but unjust.

What is the relation of religion and *Law*? Each has at different times, as systems demanding obedience, competed for the allegiance of their subjects or adherents. The new wave of Islamic traditionalism in countries like Pakistan and Iran revives the old questions, and destroys the assumption (again too often made by modern western jurists) that *Law* is now and must be a secular phenomenon. Blasphemy trials in England are the dying gasp of a similarly religiously-inspired system of laws.

Nowhere is the crisis of conscience of the citizen more acute, in deciding whether to respect or disregard a law, than when the whole legal system appears unjust, or even, because it lacks what we call *legality*, any claim to be a legal system. Imagine a society where there are no fixed rules of law, where decisions by 'courts' are based on uncontrolled discretion: is this a society with *Law*? Or must one accept the possibility of the 'no-law state'? This accusation has been directed against the Soviet Union by Solzhenitsyn; but though the use of power, dictate and discretion instead of predictable and rationally applied rules of *Law* is more pronounced there, analysis suggests that there are similar features, posing similar juristic problems, elsewhere. Within the context of a legal system, might *is* right. The foundation norm for a society may be power, however acquired or exercised. But any *Law*, whether founded on might or not, eventually depends for its effectiveness on compliance; and the people have the power, by disregard or failure to comply, of rendering any law ineffective and frustrate, even in an absolute polity. *Legalism*, adherence to the formally valid rules of *Law*, requires compliance at its level; *legality* — a critique of the fairness of aim and provision of laws — authorises non-compliance at a higher level.

Lastly we come to legislators who, though ambitious or overweening, are not necessarily vicious. They seek to procure the social transformation of their society, in whole or part, and to do this use the resources of the *Law* to create and impose radically new patterns of behaviour. Mostly the legislator will do this through *codification*. Some codes have aimed only at *technical transformation* of the laws; though even here there may be major unintended social consequences. Other codes are bolder, and aim at *social transformation*. There are two main ways of procuring such a transformation. The first is slower, more cautious, less assertive, by the creation of *models* which the people may adopt and accept if they choose. Voluntary schemes of land reform, the option of monogamous marriage, parallel provision for conveyancing with written documents, the making of written wills, even marriage itself, and the setting up of framework-laws for co-operatives, friendly societies, corporations, trade unions and the like, can all be seen as model-making laws, where the model is encouraged by the law-maker but adopted voluntarily. These laws are transforming in that these models will, if adopted, radically change the inner ordering and the content of substantial legal relationships.

Such modelling is too slow or uncertain for impatient legislators. Instead they seek to impose a *programme* of compulsory change. The Turkish Civil Code destroyed the old Ottoman family law; Tanzanian legislation has tried to limit private ownership of resources; the Kenya land reforms abolished customary tenure; the Indian codifications seek to impose a uniform, secularist, pattern of family life; British legislation on race relations seeks to transform people's behaviour and attitudes towards citizens of a different ethnic origin or colour. Two legal revolutions hit Ethiopia: the first, under the Emperor and mediated by the Ethiopian Civil Code, sought to transform the country through uniform, secularizing, French-inspired law, displacing customary and religious normative systems; the second, after the revolution which overthrew the imperial system, is transforming the private-enterprise system into the collective economy. All such attempts, whether to offer models or to impose programmes, raise questions about the uses and uselessness of *Law*. Can one, should one, use *Law* to reconstruct a society and its social relations? Can it work; and what reinforcements, by way of education, guidance or feedback, are needed to make it work?

The answer, for those of an anarchical temperament, is mildly comforting. Model laws seem to work better than programmatic ones. Popular resistance can destroy or weaken even the most cast-iron laws, however punitively they may be administered. Paranomic (not law-abiding) practices and institutions grow up 'or continue' to weaken allegiance to those prescribed by the formal law.

The reader may notice two things about this book. The first is that at many points it reflects the influence of numerous living and dead jurists, whose thoughts and analyses have been woven into the texture of this particular study. The second is that acknowledgment of this fact is rarely made. The reasons for these two facts should be given.

It is quite impossible to write a book on legal theory, even if it is on an aspect which seems as yet not to have been fully covered, without building on the work of one's predecessors. These are too numerous to mention. Many have been influential on me, and many approaches used here will be reminiscent of earlier work. No modern thinker-out of jurisprudential problems can avoid the influence of Hart; if it would not be impertinent to enlarge on the point, one would say that his *Concept of Law* is a model of what a fundamental book in legal theory should be: clear, short, sharp, incisive, realistic. One writes in his shadow. After that, the work of the Kelsen school, the Scandinavians and their various forms of realism (especially Ross), Dworkin's percipient extensions of existing theory, John Austin himself, writers on linguistic theory and analysis and communications theory, comparative lawyers, students of ethnojurisprudence or legal anthropology — have all contributed their flashes of insight, their useful terminology, their convincing breaking down of the phenomena.

But Hart and Ross and others are models in a different sense. I believe most strongly that a work on legal theory is not to be composed or written like a textbook on the sale of goods. It is not to be a patchwork of citations and of other men's opinions, but a coherent account of one person's attempt to get to grips with legal phenomena. Hence the paucity of footnotes and of acknowledgments of others' work. What I have tried to do conscientiously is to think through my own opinions and to create my own internally consistent analysis. There may be points of novelty in this analysis, there may be old and accepted juristic chestnuts; but in many cases I have put down how I see it first, and then found out that others look at the matter the same way, rather than the other way round. I therefore do not rely on the authority of other and greater thinkers to support my own analysis, which must stand or fall by the conviction which it may carry as such to the reader.

Antony Allott

February 1980

Acknowledgments

The ideas which this book contains and develops have formed over the course of years of teaching and discussing the law with both colleagues and students. The opportunity to learn from them, not merely important facts about other systems but also how to see those facts, has been of the greatest value to me. I accordingly thank them, and dedicate the present work to my past and present colleagues, both in the Department of Law at the School of Oriental and African Studies and in many universities overseas, with whom I have had the pleasure of collaborating. The influence of my colleagues (and not only my legal colleagues but those who teach anthropology, linguistics and similar disciplines) will be manifest; I hope that I have successfully reflected the learning and perception which are theirs. The inestimable advantage of working at a multi-disciplinary centre such as the School will, I hope, be evident in the approach which I take to legal phenomena.

I especially thank colleagues who read and commented on all or part of the present text, in this or a previous form — notably the Department of Anthropology at the School; Professor I. M. Lewis; Professor L. Neville Brown; Professor William Butler. None of the errors which may be found in my book can, of course, be attributed to them. I also thank Philip Baker, who has helped with the preparation of the Index, and Robin Allott, who assisted with the reading of the proofs.

A number of paragraphs in the present work previously figured (in the present or an abridged form) in an article by myself entitled 'The people as law-makers: custom, practice, and public opinion as sources of law in Africa and England', which appeared in the Journal of African Law, at [1977] JAL 1. The pages of the present text which incorporate this material comprise pp. 85–88; 90–94; 101–104; and 261–264. The School of Oriental and African Studies, as publishers of the Journal, and its Editorial Board, are thanked for permission to make use of these passages. Oxford University Press are thanked for permission to quote from *Colour and citizenship: a report on British race relations*, ed. E. J. B. Rose, 1969.

The co-operation and encouragement of the editorial staff of Butterworths should not be allowed to pass without a special mention.

Lastly, and most importantly, I have to thank the authorities of the School of Oriental and African Studies for giving me time off from my academic duties during the session 1978–79, which enabled me to complete the writing of this work.

A. N. A.

Contents

Table of legislation

Table of cases

B. OTHER COUNTRIES

Canada

India

Nigeria

Pakistan

Rhodesia

Uganda

United States

1 Limits arising from the nature of law

Let us consider first the proposition that

Law from its nature cannot be fully applied or effective.

Is there something in the nature of law which imposes necessary limitations on it and its effectiveness?

It was said in the introductory remarks that 'What is law?' is an unanswerable question, and that investigation of the nature of law is bound not to succeed; it may therefore seem both a bold and a self-contradictory initial step to see whether law has something in its essence or nature which prevents it ever being fully applied or effective. The contradiction may, however, disappear on further analysis. This analysis must fall into two parts: the first will deal with an explanation of 'Law', and the isolation of the perceived or alleged items of its nature which might impede or prevent effectiveness. The second must discuss 'effectiveness': what does this mean, and what are the measures of effectiveness of law?

A THE NATURE OF LAW

When we ask the question, 'What is law?', we must decide what sort of a question we are asking. Are we seeking —

*Metaphysical understanding	— the nature of LAW as an abstraction?
*Social understanding	— the functions of *Laws*, i.e. actual legal systems?
*Linguistic understanding	— the meaning of 'LAW', '*Law*', or 'law'?

The use of three different forms of typography is not accidental. It is my argument that all discussion of law heretofore has been confused by the linguistic poverty and ambiguity of English; when we speak about law we do not know if we are meant to be talking about law as an

1

abstract conception, or as an observable social phenomenon in a given society. To try to reduce this source of ambiguity, I propose to use three distinct words to refer to three different phenomena:

LAW = the general idea or concept of legal institutions abstracted from any particular occurrence of them

Law = a coherent, total, particular legal system prevailing in a given community or country

law = a particular normative provision of a *Law*; a rule or norm of a given legal system.

We can then see that our single question, 'What is law?', has three different meanings according as we use one or other of the three words LAW, *Law,* or law in the question. Previous enquiries have tended to concentrate on LAW, though with periodic and often uncharted deviations to *Law.*

What is LAW?

LAW by definition is an *abstraction* from reality, from particular *Laws* or laws. No question of the form, What is X?, is answerable. There is no way in which one may delimit the boundaries of the unbounded. There is no way in which one can dissect the abstraction and expose the essence at its core. When we use an abstraction, or to speak more precisely an abstract term, we are mentioning by reference the component observables from which we derive the abstraction. I, the user of the abstraction, do so, and define it so, because of characteristics which *I* perceive in the particulars and which seem to me to be (a) typical, and (b) common.

Abstractions therefore are idiosyncratic. But, since their use is not only in analysis but in communication with others, I must so use the abstraction as to convey some meaning to my hearers. It may not be the same meaning, as I may well discover on further investigation of what they have received, and what *they* perceive. What is LAW, or a *Law,* or even a law, is a matter of individual choice, then; but if our usage diverges too far from what other people do and is thereby unintelligible or unacceptable to others, our communication fails. We shall be talking to ourselves in a literally *idiotic*[1] fashion or language. So, though it is our own choice what is LAW, and each may follow his own predilection, exchange of views with others becomes impossible if we speak only our private language (unless we can persuade them of the superior utility of the language we have adopted).

LAW is an abstraction. When we cease to think about it, it ceases to exist. It is not a platonic ideal form, expressed in the world of reality through *Laws* or actual legal systems, because there is no empirical

1. 'Idiotic' in its original etymological meaning from the Greek *idiotes*, a private person, an individual.

evidence to support the notion of the pre-existence of such ideal forms, and in fact such an approach exactly reverses the way in which humans derive more from less abstract conceptions.

Laws or actual legal systems are a social reality. A given society will continue to be governed and controlled by its *Law* even though we cease to think about it. *Law*, as we shall soon see in greater detail, has abstract qualities as well as a concrete substrate. Its perception as a system, and the extent of the phenomena covered by that system, depend on a process of abstraction by an observer. Its mixed character is shown by the literal device we employ: the *L* or capital implies the abstract which springs from and controls the concrete or *aw*.

Because LAW is an abstraction from particular *Laws*, it is useless to attempt to define it or elucidate its abstract and general meaning before looking at the particular on which it rests. We must therefore start with the particular = the actual legal systems or *Laws*. There is an analogy here with LANGUAGE, which is an abstraction from natural or actual *Languages*. Linguistic studies must start with, and be anchored in, the actual *Languages* used.

It will surely be objected that one cannot examine or analyse, or even identify, particular legal systems unless one has a pre-existing general concept of LAW. How do you recognise something unless you have a picture or description to guide you? This objection is both *true* and *false*. It is *true* in that one cannot go fishing without a net. But the fish are there (and the legal systems are there), whether you go fishing or not. It is *false* in that what you find out about particular legal systems must decide your understanding of LAW in general. The fish are the *Laws*, and not LAW.

The situation therefore is that, as with physical science, one starts with a *working hypothesis*, usually based on insufficient evidence or analysis (or it would not need to be a hypothesis). One is willing to amend this hypothesis, or even abandon it, if the facts do not fit. There is two-way feedback between the particular and the general. Imagine for a moment a totally virginal and unsophisticated person (the sort of person who in former times might have qualified as a 'noble savage', though we now realise that this epithet is out of place, seeing the savagery of our own superior civilisations). The person is virginal because he has never allowed his mind, up to this moment, to be sullied or infected by abstract thoughts about LAW. He lives in a traditional, customary, non-literate, peasant society and is therefore naturally subject to its *Law*. He is definitely aware of its laws, which tell him what to do or not to do in a variety of situations, though he may not have worked out that all these laws together constitute a unique *Law* of that society, a system. Tell this virginal jurist, firstly that his society has a *Law*, and then that he must go and find some more *Laws* elsewhere in other societies. He visits neighbouring societies, discovers that they all seem to have laws, that he can recognise a *Law* in each, although it differs in detail from his own. Now let him make a quantum jump, to the United States Supreme Court or some similar institution of the developed western world. Does he see a *Law* here? Can he recognise volumes of statutes as expressive of laws? He may find the imaginative effort too much, and deny that they are really *Laws* or laws.

Exactly the reverse happened in the history of western jurists and their encounter with African customary legal systems. Equipped with their knowledge of western *Laws* at different points in time, they had constructed an abstract LAW, which to them expressed the essence of LAW. They came across customary legal systems, found they did not match with western *Laws* in various ways, and concluded that therefore they were not LAW, or that these societies did not have or recognise LAW. The original western hypothesis was applied to and worked in regard to the small area from which it drew its data; was then applied to a larger area, and found not to work — just like Newtonian physics, which could not meet the challenge posed by Einsteinian space and physics. The scientific response was a new and broader working hypothesis. The response of some western jurists was similarly to elaborate a new and broader construct of LAW. They had revised their hypothesis. It was not a question of LAW changing its nature, but of the users of the term admitting new referents or new characteristics in the *Laws* upon which their use of LAW was based.

The main function of a working hypothesis is to work. The work that such a hypothesis does is *heuristic*, i.e. it assists in the discovery of new facts, new systems, new perceptions of connexion, new perceptions of the function of those systems. A juristic hypothesis with low heuristic value needs discarding — it is not effective. LAW as a term is thus effective only in this sense.

The limits of juristic analysis

Are the theoretical discussions we have already mentioned, and those which are to follow or are found in other authors, arguments about the nature of LAW or about the use of the English language? Thus Hart:

'Many nice linguistic questions may arise over such cases: we might properly say that the gunman *ordered* the clerk to hand over the money and the clerk obeyed, but it would be somewhat misleading to say that the gunman *gave an order* to the clerk to hand it over.'[2]

He uses a factual model to discuss what is an order, and how a legal command may differ from it; he uses the resources of the English language to bring out shades of discrimination.

There is a simple test to decide whether we are arguing about something fundamental in the nature of LAW or are discussing a fine point

2. *The concept of law* (Oxford, 1961), p. 19. Similar sorts of linguistic shading and discrimination are to be found in Hart and other writers *passim*.

of English usage: translate the queried sentence into several foreign languages, preferably not near ones such as French or German but remoter ones such as Chinese or Swahili; does the purported discrimination or argument still stand up? If it does not, it suggests that the argument is a linguistic one about English usage.

This test is particularly important in this connection because other languages, with a completely different grammatical and verbal structure from English, may not have items like 'ought' in their vocabulary, or represent the function in a quite different verbal way. The Bantu languages, for instance, have imperatives — usually the bare or stem form of the verb for direct commands; and may use infixed particles (mu-*zi*-ona = you-must-see, Cewa) or subjunctives (usom*e* = you must or should read, where -*e* is the subjunctive marker; u-*si*-som*e* = do not read, where -si- is the negative subjunctive marker, Swahili) or invariable forms (*lazima* in Swahili, which can be treated sometimes as an adjective, 'necessary, or it is necessary or obligatory', and sometimes as a mood-marker, 'necessarily or obligatorily': *lazima* usom*e* = it is necessary that you read, you must read).[3]

What is *Law*?

A *Law* or 'legal system' is a *system of communication*. That is, it is a member of the same super-genus as a *Language*. The features of a *Law* are thus the same as those of any communications system. The questions one must ask are therefore also the same:

1. *Who* is communicating?	— *Emitter*
2. To *whom*?	— *Recipient*
3. What is the *method* of communication?	— *the Code*
4. What is the *content* of the communication?	— *the Message*
5. *How* is the message *received*?	— *Receiving apparatus, detector*
6. *What is the purpose* of the message?	— *Function*
7. What are the *obstacles* to communication?	— *Noise, interference*
8. *How* may the communication system be *adapted* or *developed:* (a) to transmit different messages or different types of message; (b) to make it more efficient at communicating?	— *Potentiality, variability, adaptive mechanisms*

In our analysis of 'What is *Law*?', we must therefore look at these eight aspects. Before doing this, though, we must justify our use of the phrase, 'a legal system'.

3. This point is discussed more fully below at pp. 41 ff.

A legal system

How far systems are inherent in the phenomena, and how far they are constructs in the eye of the beholder, are philosophical questions into which one cannot delve too deeply now, without leaving insufficient opportunity to develop the more interesting aspects of our topic. When we say that something is a 'system', we can mean firstly that it is visibly interconnected: the interior parts of a watch are a system, as we see as soon as we take the back off, in that all the cogs, gears and springs are inter-connected for the performance of a particular function, viz. to measure physical movements at a constant rate, which are analogically converted to perceived time on the watch face.[4]

Secondly, a system may be imposed on the phenomena. An artist's painting, whether of a landscape or anything else, is an imposed system.

Man, as the *Gestalt* philosophers constantly and rightly remind us, is a pattern-seeking animal, the most important of his mental characteristics, along with curiosity. Man will therefore see system where there is none in nature; he will look for system in everything.

Is a legal system natural or contrived, pre-existent or imposed? Like many of the essentialist questions one has to pose in this study, the answer, unsatisfactorily, is 'both'. A legal system is composed of many elements or items, some of which appear in the real world, like policemen, judges, prisons, lawyers, law-books; while some appear to exist only in a meta-world, a mental world floating in the air over the real world, which yet has the capacity to influence what happens in the real world: such abstractions as rules, principles, standards, institutions, norms. *Law* has abstract elements as well as tangible elements. As a complete system it continues to function (as already remarked) even if no one is thinking about it, even if no one set out consciously to design and operate it as a system. In this sense it is natural. But what one brings within the system depends partly on the *Law*-maker: he can extend the range of the system or insert new elements in it, and partly on the critical observer. (The new school of criminal sociologists may well feed into their definition of the legal system many elements which the traditional jurist would never have thought of, for instance.)

Of what is a Law a system?

The short answer conventionally given is that *Law* is a system of rules; and that, in the juristic world in which we now move, those rules are restricted to rules about behaviour; and that, to avoid over-extension of the term *Law,* the behaviour meant is the behaviour of persons in a political society; and that, to avoid legitimating the illegitimate, only

4. I speak, of course, of the old-fashioned spring-driven watch. The same principle applies naturally to the electronic watch, but the inner workings are not so easily understood by the casual observer!

rules made by a competent and legitimate authority within that society may be called rules of *Law*.

All of these elements are challenged. Dworkin, among others, argues that a *Law* includes principles, policies and standards (as defined by him) as well as rules. The legal sociologists tell us that *Law* includes institutions and relationships as well as rules (or that rules themselves are merely one type of such institutions). Pospišil would argue that *Law* cannot be restricted to a political society, and that any subgroup of a society can have its law.[5] On this view *Law* would extend to rules imposed by the Mafia or the IRA on their members.

Since this study is not confined to the nature of LAW or *Law* as such, these tempting paths cannot be followed. This is not to say that they are not worth exploring; but merely that the argumentation by which I arrive at my present position cannot be displayed here. I shall be obliged therefore to state my view categorically:

A *Law* or legal system comprises norms, institutions and processes. The norms include rules of law, as well as principles (in Dworkin's sense). The rules include both *primary rules*, which directly prescribe behaviour, and *secondary rules,* which govern the application of the primary rules and the functioning of the institutions and processes of the system, including the process for adding to or varying rules.

The institutions of the *Law* comprise both the *facilities* (e.g. judges) for the operation of the processes and the application of the norms, the *statuses* and the *relationships* identified and controlled by the norms, i.e. the relationships on which the norms operate.

The processes of the *Law* describe the norms and institutions in action. Adjudication is one process of the law; making a contract is another.

A *Law* or legal system is a function of an autonomous and distinct society or community, that is, an organised body of persons. To say that the society is autonomous is not to say that it is independent in a formal sense, but that it has its own system of regulation. Thus a tribal group having its own customary *Law* within a modern state is autonomous to the extent that it generates and applies its own system of norms. Although it is theoretically possible to include in such a society one which is illegal or unrecognised by a superior order in the larger society of which it is part, it appears convenient to introduce some notion of *legitimacy* into our definition of a society which, though autonomous, is politically part of a larger whole. Our amended version would then read, 'an autonomous *and legitimate* society or community'. We do this because otherwise we face logical problems. The *Law*? of the IRA is not a *Law* in Northern Ireland, because it, and the community of which it is part, is illegitimate when tested by the

5. L. Pospišil *Anthropology of law: a comparative theory* (1971, New York),

Law of the larger society of which it unwillingly forms part. If we accept that IRA *Law*? is *Law,* then to that extent the *Law* of Northern Ireland, so far as it is contradicted by the *Law* of the IRA, is not *Law.* The *Law* of the IRA would thus become part of the *Law* of Northern Ireland.

We say that the relevant society or community must be 'distinct' because a disorganised class or set of persons does not cohere. *Law* is a principle of coherence or organisation in a society; in fact, the society will have other principles of coherence too: perhaps a shared language, shared ethical beliefs, shared history, physical situation or isolation.

To mention 'society' is question-begging; but it is a question that is frequently begged by sociologists and others. In any event, we have asserted the right of the analyst to beg questions in performing his act of analysis.

It was said earlier that the institutions of the *Law,* or at least some of them, exist in the real world. A policeman is tangible. But when we say that the police are one institution of the *Law,* we mean that the *Law* has created or recognised them as an institution. The body of men who are police are only an institution of the *Law* to the extent that they carry out the function or role attributed to them by the *Law.* Analysts are sometimes tempted to forget that real people are present there behind the roles or institutions; when a policeman arrests you, it is not a role or institution which is arresting you but a man. Discussion of the limits of law must necessarily bring in a consideration of the limitations imposed by the non-institutional aspects of the role-bearer.

Similarly with relationships functioning as institutions of the *Law.* The *Law* can take an existing relationship, e.g. the family group, and recognise or define it as a legal institution. Or the *Law* can invent an institution, which, though it has some physical connexions or implications (without these it could not operate in the real world), is an abstraction: a limited liability company springs to mind. All relationships defined as legal institutions are thus abstract with real connections.

A *Law* consists partly of norms. We examine the nature of norms in greater detail in answering the question, What is law?, below.[6] A legal system is *normative* in character, in that it tells people what to do, or how to do it, in regard to some aspect of their life in society. In so far as the system is, or consists of, norms, it may be thought to be non-factual; as we shall see, normative legal statements are couched in the conditional, and not the indicative, mode. But at the same time *Law* and its norms have a factual, existential character, in that it and they are predicated *both* on the existence of the society and the manner in which its members conduct themselves, *and* on the hypothetical existence of given fact-situations which attract or 'fire' its relays (the hypothetical-conditional statements of the *Law*). A legal system presents itself to those subject to it as articulated norms, or as inarticulate norms and

6. See pp. 16 ff.

principles. This presentation, when articulated, is necessarily articulated in linguistic dress, in verbal form; but the form is not the substance.

So a *Law* or legal system *is a fact,* in the sense that the existence of legal systems is open to experimental observation and confirmation; *is not a fact,* in that its laws/rules/norms do not describe what has happened, but prescribe what is to happen, and which in fact need not happen.

A *Law* — if we define it by what it is not — is
— not a sociological statement of facts only;
— not all control systems (it deals only with certain forms of control);
— not purely theoretical (one can no more have a purely theoretical *Law* not tied to reality than one can walk on air: a purely theoretical *Law* is not anchored to the earth);
— not the regulated application of physical force in a society,[7]
because, as the examination of *Laws* in simpler societies will show, legal norms are not necessarily obeyed because they have physical force lurking behind them.

1. The emitter of Law

The ordinary subject of a *Law* in a society perceives and receives, not *Law*, but laws, i.e. norms which purport to guide his behaviour. Who emits these laws or norms? Western jurists of the positivist school, Austin and after, would answer: the determinate sovereign in that society. Verbal contortions have to be performed to identify such a sovereign in a federal state, in a dyarchy, or in a society ruled by customary *Law*. The effort is not worthwhile; the 'sovereign' is a lay figure manipulated by the analyst, a construct.

If we start at the opposite end, and consider an act of legal communication in a real society, preferably one devoid of lawyers and jurists, the recipient of the normative statement perceives that it is transmitted to him by the fellow-members of his society generally, as at a tribal meeting; by the members of his local community, as at a village moot or meeting; by the fellow-members of his family or kinship group, whether or not they are in authority over him; by those who are recognised as official spokesmen or enunciators of the norms, such as judges or other members of courts, arbiters, diviners, oracles, priests. Most of the normative statements are *transmitted,* not *originated,* by the emitter/enunciator. In other words, the emitter of the norm does not claim to be its originator; the people say that they are quite literally transmitting or handing on the customs of the ancestors. Some normative statements will be, or can be, referred by their emitters to an identifiable source; in response to the question, 'Who says so?', they will answer: 'The chief says so; or the court said so; or the assembly said so'. In fewer cases the emitter will himself (or themselves collectively) be and claim

7. *Contra* Ross, Olivecrona.

to be the originator of the norm: 'You will do this, and so will others in like case, because I say, or said so [and it is the chief who is speaking]'.

The jurist will be tempted to allocate some of these norms to 'customary law', some to 'judicial law', some to 'legislated law'; but it is he who is doing the allocating, and not the subjects of the law. The form of the normative statement, though it may vary in particularity, will be the same or of the same types whatever the identification of the original emitter of it.

Norms do not have to be precisely articulated to have an effect on the behaviour of those who receive them, but the act of articulation is important, and the constituted power of articulation is part of the institutions of the legal system. It will immediately be seen that, to the recipient, what matters is whether he thinks he has received a normative message. If he conforms his conduct to it, and sufficient of his fellows do likewise, then when a context arises in which a norm might be articulated to cover the case, there is a likelihood that the articulated norm will reflect the inarticulate assumption. In other words and as usual paradoxically, a recipient can receive a normative message which has not been generated by an emitter, but which can be converted into an accepted norm by its formal emission at a later date. This is what is meant when we say, or are tempted to say, that habitual practice or usage can generate customary law. Literally speaking, this is impossible. The shift from mere habit to abstract norm involves a change of category. But here we describe behaviour and not categories.

As society develops, and especially as it becomes both more self-conscious and more specialised, so classes of persons who are specialist transmitters and workers-over of norms appear. It would be a foolish error to think that one must wait for the appearance of professional lawyers, still less of university law schools, for this development to occur. Most societies empirically known include persons who are or hold themselves out to be, or are recognised by the society as being, special authorities in the handling of normative statements. African customary *Laws* often recognised the role of 'spokesman' or enunciator of norms, and of judicial experts skilled not only in sifting and trying cases but in manipulating the normative system to do so. However, it is undoubted that in the modern world (globally and not only in the west these days) lawyers, jurists and judges, as well as draftsmen, have systematically introduced more refinement, complication and analysis into the normative system and into the form of particular normative statements.

2. The recipients of Law

Lawyers may not like to be told this, but these are the all-important people in legal communication. Lawyers tend to think that in legal systems it is the lawyers who matter: they make the law, apply it, and improve it — the job of those subject to the *Law* is to be available to the jurist, so that he can purport to explain how law works in its application to them; and then their job is done. But since a *Law* is a set of acts of communication directed to a particular purpose, it is that purpose which must govern; and the purpose is to affect the behaviour of its recipients, those subject to the *Law*.

If I broadcast a message over the radio, the class of persons who receives it may not be co-extensive with the class of persons to whom I directed it. Some of those at whom I aimed the message may never get it, for one reason or another; while many of whom I have not thought will receive the message as well if they are tuned in. Similarly, some of the intended recipients of *Law* or of particular laws may not receive the message, or may receive it only in garbled form, or may misunderstand what has been sent — here is a potent source of the ineffectiveness of law. At the opposite pole one finds the unintended recipient; in legal terms this class includes persons in situations not intended by the norm-emitter to be covered by the norm, and all those who in the subsequent history of the *Law* may be brought within the embrace of the norm through judicial interpretation or social development.

When we turn from theory to practical examples, we shall have to look at the character and disabilities of recipients of legal communications. That no one can receive a communication, legal or otherwise, in full and precisely as transmitted is the fault, not so much of the recipient, as of the nature of communication. We discuss these points at 7. below.

Although there is not a sharp logical distinction between the two categories, one may divide recipients of legal messages into (i) the subjects of the *Law,* whether generally or some special class thereof; (ii) those who are subject to the secondary rules of the system, and for whom the messages are instructions to apply or modify or create the primary rules of the system, and to operate or supervise the institutions and processes of the *Law.* The latter class of recipients, in the developed legal systems, includes judges who try cases, legislators who make laws, policemen or officials who apply laws. These are, of course, also subjects of the law in the general sense. These we may call 'operators' or 'agencies' of the *Law.* The importance of the distinction is that any analysis of *Law* in terms only of rules or norms supported by sanctions does not adequately cover the sorts of norm directed to the latter class of recipients. We would find it difficult to conceive that the legal message to a judge, say, in English law is: 'Apply the primary rules of the system to this-and-this case before you, or else . . .!', because what is the 'or else'? We do not threaten judges to make them judge.

3. The Code: the method of transmission

In behavioural control not every act of control needs to be verbalised. Rather than saying, 'Stop that!', an irate parent may hit his small child who is doing something he disapproves of. If this sequence is repeated, behavioural shaping will take place without the intervention of the spoken or written word. A certain amount of legal control is carried on like that; the citizen's idea of the power of the police is derived more from encounters with police in controlling situations than from studying manuals of police law.

But sooner or later, and especially if the matter is contested, verbalisation, what I have called overt articulation, must take place. The articulated norms are encoded in verbal form. We cannot go into the semantic consequences of this here, but the struggles of judges with the interpretation of statutes in England will sufficiently demonstrate the gap between intended and perceived meaning. Some of the lexical items in which norms are encoded have a specialised function in legal contexts, or are unknown outside a legal context. The problems caused by these intrinsic linguistic weaknesses are examined under 'Effectiveness' below.

4. The message

We study the nature and types of legal messages when we discuss *What is law?*. i.e. how do norms present themselves?, below. The *Law* as a system has no message, but it comprises a series or set of messages.

5. The receiving apparatus

How do the subjects of the law receive or perceive normative messages within the legal system? In Chapter 3 we look at limits imposed by difficulties of acceptance, reception or communication. We note too that while in pre-literate societies the ear is the main receptor, the eye plays the major part in modern societies. We think of *Law* as written, although much *Law* is received in practice as drama — the drama of the court proceeding, the drama of the consultation with the legal adviser, the drama of the arrest or challenge to one's rights.

6. The function of law

While the ultimate function of *Law* is invariable, viz. the shaping of behaviour in society to correspond to the goals set by those having influence within it, the function of particular laws can vary according as the law seeks to impose a primary rule of conduct, establish an institution, or regulate a process. We owe to Hart particularly the insight that law = *Law* offers facilities as well as commands or directives. *Law* can be creative or protective, as well as mandatory or prohibitory. The legal message is transmitted to perform any one or more of these functions; although couched in the abstract, the message operates in the concrete world.

7. *Noise or interference*

Engineers assess the effectiveness of a communications system with reference to the signal-to-noise ratio. 'Signal' is the message; 'noise' the extraneous elements which interfere with its reception.

What is the signal so far as a *Law* is concerned, and what the 'noise'?

It is easy to identify the signal: it is each discrete emission of a legal norm or instruction of some kind or another, and this signal bears the message intended by its emitter. But finding what is the noise that interferes with reception of the signal is a more difficult task. To help us, let us remind ourselves of the noise which one finds in a physical transmission of radio signals. First, there is the noise generated at the transmission end by reason of design faults or inherent limitations of the transmitting equipment, which may emit spurious or distorted signals. Then there is the noise in the medium through which transmission is made, and which is received, along with the signal, at the reception end. This noise is of two main kinds: competing signals bearing messages other than the one we are talking about, as with transmissions from other stations; and background static due to a variety of atmospheric and other causes, which creates 'white noise', i.e. noise which extends over many frequencies and which cannot be separated into discrete signals. Lastly there is noise at the receiving end, generated or induced by imperfections in the receiving equipment.

Legal noise in the emission equipment. The originator or emitter of a legal norm may have only an imperfect idea of the action he wishes to provoke, the mechanisms by which to cause it, the context in which it must operate, or the design limitations of his norm-emitting equipment — the linguistic formulations of his norm. All verbal formulations are subject to the defects of every linguistic message, which are inherent in the nature of LANGUAGE, i.e. in every *Language*. Semantic blur, the fuzziness in the definition of the meaning (=function) of particular verbal items (=words, phrases), is the main such defect. Lack of adjustment between transmitter and receiver is equally an inherent fault (they are 'not on the same wavelength', we say). There is no way in which norm emission equipment, e.g. an Act of Parliament, can do a perfect job. The remedy for this is to try to reduce, though one cannot remove, the imperfections. In a physical system one does this in three ways: through improved design of a system, through redundancy, and through feedback. Improved design of law-transmitting equipment means a study of the ways in which laws are formulated and transmitted. Redundancy means the sending of more signal or message than one strictly need do; if only 50 per cent gets through, the message may be fully understood. All natural *Languages* are heavily redundant, containing many sounds and items not absolutely necessary for communication — think of a formal letter and a telegram. Legal redundancy implies more than one way of transmitting the same normative instruction. Lastly, feedback. A communications system can be induced to improve its own performance through positive or negative feedback. That is, the output or reception of a signal is monitored and compared with a standard; if the signal quality falls below the standard, the feedback loop causes adjustments to be made in the sending apparatus. We do this automatically when we speak instructions to someone in the open air; if we see that he is not complying, the visual feedback of his non-compliance will cause us to raise our voice and shout at him, or alternatively to constrain him physically. The history of penal law especially is replete with examples of feedback. Where the aim is deterrence, monitoring of compliance will show the norm-emitter that his norm is not succeeding in its aim; he will intensify the signal — raise the penalty, perhaps.

Legal noise in the medium. Parliament speaks: who listens? Parliament's message, as found in its statute, must reach the intended recipients, whether of the general or the operator class. Noise, and the attenuation of the legal signal, may get in the way of effective reception. We have explained that the function of *Law* is the shaping of behaviour in society; legal norms, when perceived by their subjects, are received and interpreted as referring to behavioural shaping; but not every message carrying normative instructions about behaviour is a legal message. The recipient is receiving messages from a variety of sources telling him what he 'ought' to do: messages from his religion; ethical messages; messages from those he regards as authoritative in matters of conduct, such as leader-writers in newspapers, and television or radio commentators; messages from his work-mates, his neighbours, his family, his friends; messages from the past. Can the legal message override all these competing messages (where they do not reinforce each other, as they often do not)? The legal message has a special interest and importance for its recipient, because it says to him that this is what his society, or persons with authority in that society and over that society, command or suggest he should do.

Between emission and reception there is often a great gap. In modern English terms we may call this 'ignorance of the law'. The ordinary person is deeply ignorant of most of our modern law; that is why he has to engage professional lawyers to find out what it is for him. And yet the nominal addressee of the legal message, when it is not directed to an intermediate operator, is that same ordinary person. The legal message can easily lose its way if, to change the metaphor slightly, the conduit through which it flows is broken at any point, so that the message leaks out. Most ordinary persons in our society do not have legal advisers, still less advisers permanently tuned in to messages from above.

Legal noise at the receiver. The receiver, then, in developed societies is most imperfect. Improvement of it might include systematic instruction in *Law,* and training in the reception and implementation of legal norms. British education is almost completely deficient in both respects; Soviet and Chinese education is more concerned, at least with the second aspect. In traditional societies governed by customary *Law* we may find fewer deficiencies at the receiving end. This is for various reasons: the societies and their affairs are simpler; what they do or seek to do is comprehensible to every adult member; the societies are smaller, so that interactions are multiplied exponentially; the system of norm-transmission is more accessible to the ordinary person, who may be able to attend a meeting or a court as a regular practice; there are fewer specialised roles and agencies ('operators' in our language) who intervene in the process of norm transmission, so that the signal is less attenuated.

The reaction of the modern jurist might be to say: 'That's all very fine, but you surely don't expect modern societies to conduct themselves like peasant or tribal societies? They can do it because they are simple and close to nature; we, in our complex and vast societies, cannot'. But why does one have to accept defeat in one area of life only? We do not say that because our society is more vast and complex, therefore people must put up with worse health, or worse nutrition, or more imperfect transport. Quite the contrary: we say that, *because* our society is complex and large, we can afford better and more effective medical care, food, transport, and so on. In what is law different?

8. Potentiality, variability, and adaptive mechanisms of the Law

All legal systems contain within themselves the potentiality of change. Even the *Laws* of the Medes and Persians can change. The old-fashioned idea that customary *Laws* were changeless and immutable has been shown to be empirically inaccurate. Customary *Laws* have as much potentiality for change as other types of legal system; indeed, they have often changed faster in this century than the statutory systems to which they have been yoked.

The possibility of making a legal system more efficient has already been discussed in at least one sense: viz. making sure that the legal signals get through. But there are other senses in which we can talk about the efficiency of a legal system. If a *Law* is seen as a system with a purpose, the extent to which the purpose is realised is the measure of the efficiency of the system.

Laws can vary, not just by adding or subtracting particular norms or institutions, but by changing their format or even their nature. A *Law*, or a law, can cease to be oral and customary, and be made statutory and written, for instance. Codification of *Law* is thus one type of variation. Whether codification leads to less or more efficiency is something which must be reserved until we look at the general problems of codification. No *Law* can change unless either: (in the negative) it contains no impermeable barrier to adaptive change produced by the environment, or otherwise than by directed change; or (in the positive) it contains mechanisms for purposive and self-regarding adaptation. It would be wrong to think that a *Law* can only change if there is some express mechanism (e.g. Law Reform Commission + legislature) built into the system; otherwise how comes it that a customary *Law* ever managed to evolve into a non-customary system? But systems are by their nature conservative of themselves, or they would rapidly disintegrate and cease to be systems. The conservatism of law is notorious, of non-legislated law even more so; resistances to change are thus built into most legal systems.

What is law?

We remind ourselves that 'law' is used to mean the particular normative provisions of a *Law* or legal system. 'Norms' includes rules and principles and policies; the institutions and processes which with norms make up the legal system are also normative, though in a different sense.

It is amazing to think, and a compliment to a thinker writing before the Reform Act 1832 gave us even a 19th-century, let alone a 20th-century parliament, that most discussions start off, whether overtly or not, with John Austin and his imperative explanation of LAW. Laws were seen by him as a species of commands. Subsequent jurists have hastened to embroider this formulation, challenge its main features, or re-work it into something which is new, and yet still akin to Austin's approach. LAW as command, or laws as commands, still dominates our thinking. After argument about who is doing the commanding, the modern realist tendency is to drift to 'independent imperatives', which are like spinning bullets fired from no gun, commands without commanders. Calling these — are they 'things', 'social facts', abstractions, or what? — norms, directives or what have you does not alter the case substantially: it is clear that we are still talking about instructions in the imperative mode. The difficulty has been created because the concentration of attention has been on the emitter of the imperative, rather than on its recipient. If you get a ringing in your ears, you can hear a sound which 'is not there'; if you get a norm in your head, you can receive an instruction which was never sent.

A norm is not a pattern of behaviour in the sense of an empirically derived statement of observed behaviour: 'At 9 a.m. every weekday thousands of people habitually stream across London Bridge to work in the City' is a description, based on multiplied observed instances, of patterns of behaviour among City workers; it is not a norm. It is not a command; it is not an imperative; it is not perceived by those who stream across as an imperative. They may think it 'necessary' for the earning of their daily bread; they would not say, 'I must do it' in answer to a question, 'Why?'. So one cannot have a pattern of actually observed behaviour as 'binding'. It is wrong (a confusion of categories, as already observed) to say that a customary practice 'becomes' a customary legal rule without alteration of its character.

A norm 'is' a pattern of behaviour in a quite different sense. The pattern of behaviour is the protasis of a conditional statement (the 'If' clause), of which the apodosis (the 'Then' clause) is the affirmation of an intended (not a predicted) consequence.

Normative statements are thus in the imperative, and not the indicative, mode; but they are not simple commands. A normative statement may therefore be analysed as a 'hypothetical-conditional', in which the hypothesis or assumption represents a pattern or model of behaviour or action or events, which, if it had occurred in the real world and was not governed by 'if', would be descriptive of reality; while the conditional specifies an assigned consequence. Since the first part of the normative statement is hypothetical, the whole statement is hypothetical, and hence in this sense is not descriptive of reality. The statement as an act of communication can, of course, exist in the world of reality.

Norms are not necessarily legal. Any norm of behaviour may be analysed as a hypothetical-conditional. Legal norms are distinguished by the identification of the emitter of the norm, and the nature of the consequence specified by it.

A norm in action 'works' when a fact-situation occurs which may be capable of being 'matched' (i.e. of being compared and found to correspond) with the hypothetical portion of a normative statement. If a sufficient matching can be made, then the norm is potentiated. Whether the consequence specified in the conditional follows is a measure of the effectiveness of the norm.

The 'consequences' of a normative hypothetical-conditional may be expressed with the use of such modal verbs as 'must', 'ought', or with a formulation which can be transformed into such a modality. What the normative statement cannot do is to specify a fact as a consequence of a hypothetical; otherwise it ceases to be a norm and becomes a statement of a physical law.

Norms and other imperatives

What are the defining characteristics of a legal norm? This is another way of expressing the question with which we are concerned in this section: 'What is law?'. We remind ourselves that no definition can be absolute, and that 'characteristics' does not relate to a hidden essence of the item to be defined; if the item is a linguistic one, then 'characteristics' means the observable features of presentation and function of that item; if the item is a non-linguistic one, the 'characteristics' are such as we attribute to it in the light of our orientation and analysis. Among the array which we must try to separate out are: (i) universal imperatives versus singular imperatives; (ii) elements of a legal system which contain imperatives to do or not do something (mandatory and prohibitory norms) and those which create facilities or institutions.

(i) It was commonly assumed (following Austin) that LAW and legal norms contained some essential implication of the universal or general: it and they set prescribed patterns of behaviour, either for the community at large or some class or section of it. This approach would mean that commands addressed to an individual, whether the command related to some legally constitutive act such as the appointment of the Lord Chancellor, or was a private Act of Parliament for the reconstruction of a sewage works (i.e. creating facilities), would not be classed as legal imperatives, because they lack the essential flavour of universality or generality. Later juristic opinion has managed to include such individual pseudo-norms within the definition of legal norm by the simple device of prescriptive definition: it is so because I say it is so.

(ii) It was hard to see how a norm-creating act such as the constitution of a legal agency or the creation of a facility, such as marriage or bankruptcy, could be construed as a command backed by sanctions. Thus Hart says:

'. . . there are other varieties of law [= "law" in our vocabulary], notably those conferring legal powers to adjudicate or legislate (public powers) or to create or vary legal relations (private powers) which cannot, without absurdity, be construed as orders backed by threats.'[8]

Universality

As already remarked (one must regretfully repeat the point here), since this is not a study of general legal theory so much as of one aspect of LAW/*Law*/law (viz. what are the limits on the effectiveness of law?), one cannot discuss the intermediate arguments and the answers to the points raised by various jurists in detail; it is only possible to state the categorical conclusion. As to (i), the word 'law' (and its cognates at different levels) induces in the hearer/user a notion of *regularity* or even of universality. This is a fact of linguistic behaviour, borne out by the etymological connexion between 'rule' and 'regular'. One can also discern some of the explanations for this usage. LAW is thought of as of universal application, because the laws of nature or physical laws are by definition without exception. If there is an exception, then this is to be built into the rule: the exception does not prove, but forms part of, the rule. This meaning of LAW derived from the physical sciences, in which the conditional statements of a law, though hypothetical in the sense that they relate, not only to past occurrences but to possible future

8. At p. 77.

occurrences as well, do not have a modal verb in the Then clause; the consequence of the compliance with the given conditions is stated either as an affirmative couched in the universal present: 'If water is heated to 100°C, and other conditions are satisfied, the water boils', or as a prediction capable of verification by experiment: 'If . . ., then the water will boil'; coupled with an explanation of what is intended, inter alia, by 'boil' in such an affirmation. If water is so heated, and the water fails to boil, we would not say that the law was ineffective, but that it was incomplete, or wrongly formulated, or plain erroneous. All scientific laws are in this sense universal.

The physical meaning of LAW, derived from physical laws, helped to determine the intended meaning of LAW, as conceived in reference to juristic *Laws* and laws. There was thus an illegitimate corruption of (juristic) *Laws* and laws as terms to be used in the analysis of legal systems. The process can be set out graphically:

Physical occurrences $\rightarrow$ (physical) laws$_1$ $\rightarrow$ LAW$_1$ $\rightarrow$ (juristic) LAW$_2$ $\rightarrow$ laws$_2$

Here we use LAW$_1$, etc, to mark out physical laws from juristic LAW$_2$, etc.

The law relating to the Sovereign in Britain, a law to naturalise one person or formerly to divorce a couple by private Act of Parliament, a law to validate retrospectively a ministerial act, and an administrative act (e.g. a planning decision made under the relevant legislation) under the law do not pretend to universality and yet in common parlance would be said either to be 'laws' or at least a feature of the *Law*. Either our definition of *Law* and law is at fault; or the requirement of universality of application must go and a *Law* does not consist solely of universal or general rules. The examples we have just cited have the following features: they either *create* and prescribe the function of *an institution* in the *Law*, or they use the *form* in which laws of general application are made in order to achieve a particular singular result, or they are in *implementation* of a norm. In the result, we should correct our language pragmatically to give a sufficient description of the components of a *Law*. This brings us on to our second point.

Are facilities, institutions and processes in a Law *'norms'?*

Are acts to create or regulate such elements norms? Are they imperatives of any kind? Are they 'orders backed by threats' (Hart)? Are they commands made legal by being supported by sanctions? The 'absurdity' to which Hart refers cannot refer to the 'order' part: since one answers the question, 'How does one create a legal facility?' by the response, 'By ordering that it shall or may be so'. Therefore the absurdity must lie in the presumed sanctioning 'threat'. Let us take some examples of constitutive acts and implementing orders, and analyse them.

Two parties in a dispute (in a customary-*Law* society) choose an *arbiter*:

'Let X decide!'   Statement 1

This is a constitutive act, constituting the arbiter an agency in the legal system, with a limited function, it is true. The statement is grammatically in the imperative mode; semantically and functionally it is also imperative — it is a willed result, the addressees of which are the two parties mutually, and the bystanding potential arbiter.

An authority in a legal system appoints a *judge*:

'Let Y be a judge.'   Statement 2

This is also a constitutive act, though of a more general character, no longer made by two participants in a legal system, but by a person or agency already operating as an institution in a legal system. It also, perhaps more evidently than Statement 1, is in the imperative mode. It is a prescription addressed to all whom it may concern; it has ambitions to generality.

Neither Statement 1 nor Statement 2 is linguistically/grammatically in the form of a hypothetical-conditional. There appears to be no hypothetical to be satisfied, and no conditional consequence to follow on the fulfilment of the condition. But each constitutive act can be analysed as *implying*, referring, or relating to a set (which may be open and hence capable of being added to hereafter) of hypothetical-conditional norms. E.g.:

'If { the arbiter decides { the case, then his decision will
      the judge   a case
be treated as valid within the legal system.'   Statement 3

'If an order of the judge, within his competence, is disobeyed, then the person disobeying shall suffer the following consequences . . .'
                                                        Statement 4

So the constitutive act is an assertion about an element in norms. Thus in a norm of the form:

'If a judge decides, his decision is final.'   Statement 5

a further statement will specify that the term *judge* must bear the following meaning(s) (=functions):

'If a question arises about who is a judge, for the purposes of the norm found in Statement 5, then the following, inter alia, is such a judge: Y . . .'   Statement 6

In other words, Statement 2 may be *transformed* and *extended* into Statement 6. Statement 6 is imperative, despite the 'is' in the conclusion, because that 'is' functions semantically as an instruction or command, and could be replaced by a modal phrase such as 'shall be'.

Now let us look at an authority in a legal system (remember that we
have not yet specified who is an authority) issuing an implementive
order:

'Leave this house.'   Statement 7

Is this an order; a norm; a rule of law? It does not appear to be a rule of
law because it has no ambitions to regularity, generality or universality.
It is set in the here-and-now, and addresses one situation and one
recipient only. It is clearly an order; it is framed as an order, and in
fact tells someone to do something. But is it a norm within a legal
system?

The first point to dispose of is, who is the order addressed to? The
sanctions school of legal theorists, to whom the only legal norm is one
which imposes sanctions for non-compliance, may try to 'save the
appearances' by treating this as an imperative directed, not to the
apparent recipient, but to the appropriate executive agency in the legal
system:

'If the person addressed does not leave this house upon receipt of
this my order, then you [= the court bailiff, the police . . .] shall
impose the following sanctions on him.'   Statement 8

This is because, for those of the Kelsen/Ross persuasion, the addressees
of legal normative messages are not the subjects of the legal system, but
its institutions or executive agents. I prefer the quite straightforward
approach that the analytical recipient of this order is the actual recipient
of it, the apparent addressee. It is true that if the agencies of the *Law*
are not alerted, then or later, or activated, the order may remain
unfulfilled; but separate norms exist for the alerting and activation of
enforcement agencies at the instance of the court or of parties.

Statement 7 is normative, to the extent that it compels or directs
someone to a particular course of behaviour willed by the *Law* or its
recognised agencies. It meets, then, the required element of behavioural
shaping. Does it meet the formal requirement of being a hypothetical-
conditional? There is no spoken '. . . or else', which is the grammatical
form of a sanction; but there may be an implied '. . . or else'. What is
implied may be determined by the context in which Statement 7 was
uttered. Thus:

'Leave this house, { or be executed.'   Statement 9
                   { or . . .

Or it may imply further *implementive* hypothetical-conditionals:

'If you do not leave this house, then . . .'   Statement 10

It should be noted that Statement 10 is not the same as Statement 7.
Formally it is not the same: we do not usually or necessarily command
someone in the form set out in Statement 10. Functionally it is not the

same; we cannot know, without further knowledge of the legal system, what the content of any statement of the form of Statement 10 should be merely by receiving the message of Statement 7.

To specify the context of the utterance of Statement 7, we should need to know if it was:

A judge giving a possession order against the occupier of a house.

The owner of a house telling a trespasser to leave.

A father telling his erring daughter to quit the parental home.

A government department compulsorily acquiring land.

We therefore conclude that orders, whether constitutive or implementive, may in the alternative be cast into the hypothetical-conditional mode, or imply a set of such hypothetical-conditionals; and that such hypothetical-conditionals are normative.

So far as institutions and processes in the legal system are concerned, these cannot be stated or cast in the form of norms; but they are normative because:

— they imply norms, in the senses that they rest on norms for their meaning or function, and are themselves for the implementation of norms; and

— they require norms for their validation or effective action.

Are principles norms?

Legal principles are normative, in the sense that they command or shape the behaviour, whether of the subjects of a *Law* or the agencies of the *Law;* but are they norms? They appear to lack the normative structure of hypothetical-conditional. Let us take one example:

'No man may [?=should] profit by his wrong.'[9]   Statement 11

This may be transformed into a 'super-norm' which says:

'If a man does something, or omits to do something, that is contrary to a mandatory or prohibitory legal norm [and is in consequence liable in *Law* to remedial action activated by another injured by that wrong] , then he shall not make a gain which he otherwise would not do, by reason only of the application of some other norm embodying a normal consequent of that act or omission.'   Statement 12

A typical example would be that of a man with a life assurance policy who commits suicide. This involves the prima facie application of a norm of the type of:

'If a man has taken out an insurance policy, and the peril against which he has insured occurs, then he or his successor in title is entitled to receive the sum assured against the occurrence of the peril.'   Statement 13

9. From Dworkin.

Statement 13˙ is a sub-case of a more general set of norms relating to contracts in general.

Application of super-norm 11/12 to Statement 13 implies the following:

'If the hypothetical events mentioned in Statement 13, or in any other norm of the set to which Statement 13 belongs, occur, then the consequent mentioned in the Statement of Norm shall not occur if the result would be that the norm set out in Statement 12 would be infringed.'   Statement 14

From all these examples we see that norms are of different types; that some elements in a legal system are normative while not themselves having the shape of a norm; and that norms come in sets or hierarchies. A norm may appear on its face to refer to behaviour of subjects of the law; or it may concern the behaviour of agencies or institutions of the law; or it may refer to and control the operation of norms subordinated to it. Each step seems to be a further regression from norms controlling conduct to norms controlling norms. A norm which controls a norm, a meta-norm or super-norm, though in appearance different from what one may call a first-order norm, is not so in reality. The reason is that a *Law* is a system; it is a system with feedback; each element in the system pre-supposes and depends on many other elements. It is unreal, and analytically absurd, to attempt to abstract one norm in isolation from those others which relate with it and give it meaning or control its operation. A simple norm apparently directed to the behaviour of individual subjects of the *Law* implies many norms, of which the most general is:

'Let there be a legal system!'[10]   Statement 15

A simple norm without implementing norms is and must be ineffective. Implementing norms will often consist of instructions to and about the institutions and processes of the law; what we would otherwise call meta-norms. The circle is a closed one.

Legal norms and other norms

Legal norms are norms in a legal system. But we have pointed out the difficulties which may be experienced by a recipient in determining whether a given statement, which he receives in the form of a norm, is actually a legal norm. We suggested that the legal message is one which the recipient receives as coming from his society, or from persons with

10. This Statement could be amplified to:

'If you wish to live in a society, let there be a legal system!'

In other words, a statement of conditional form which expresses the basic norm.

authority in his society, and commanding or suggesting what he is to do in certain hypothetical circumstances. We have spoken of a 'society', without making our words precise; what is intended is a political society, though this formulation also is imprecise. We have further required that the society should be autonomous. It need not be a state in the modern western sense (unless we are prepared to job backwards and say that every autonomous political society is a state). The Bushman bands living in the Kalahari Desert of South Africa were autonomous, and they each formed a society for our definitional purposes, though only the boldest political theorist would call these groups 'states'! The separate tribal groups of homoeonomic[11] ethnic groups like the Nuer of southern Sudan were autonomous, and their regulatory structure was a *Law*.

A received norm or an implementing order may operate in the legal system, as part of it; or it may be outside the *Law*. To be inside the legal system, a norm or order must satisfy the following conditions:

α — The *authority* emitting the norm, or making the order, must be an institution within the legal system, or derive his authority so to do from an institution within the legal system.

β — He must have *constituted power* to issue norms or make orders of the type in question.

γ — For the *purpose of implementing* the purposes of the legal system, or of particular norms of the legal system.

δ — And the *conditions* for the exercise of the power are satisfied in the given case.

Any other imperative is outside the legal system:

Love your neighbour   — moral precept
Eat up your pudding   — domestic arrangement
Dinner jackets will be worn — conventional practice or indication.

Much needless difficulty is caused by the fact that there is an overlap, which goes so far as to become a confusion on occasions, between legal norms and other imperatives. Thus the religious and/or moral precept of 'Thou shalt not kill' overlaps with the legal norm which creates and defines the crimes of murder and manslaughter and the penalties for them. To say that a norm is a legal norm is *not* to say that it is not at the same time also a moral precept, or a conventional practice, or corresponds to an actual domestic arrangement.

In the modern society, Case (i), the spheres of law and morality are not concentric nor even of the same size. Indeed, a more exact picturing of the situation would show the sphere of morality as not one but many; there is no longer a societal morality. Different circles of morality would overlap to different extents with the sphere of law, which remains one. The circles of each of these areas are not separated by a boundary, but overlap. To represent this by a Venn diagram in the case of morality and *Law*:

11. 'Having similar laws'.

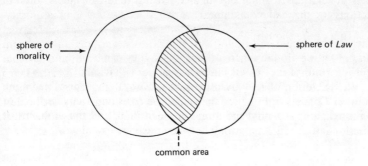

Case (i): modern society

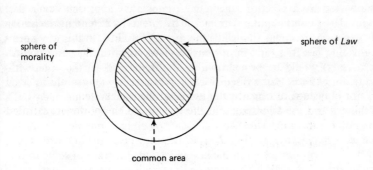

Case (ii): traditional society

In the traditional society, Case (ii), such as the old Kikuyu, Nuer or Bushman societies already mentioned, there is a societal morality. The area of law is entirely located within the sphere of societal morality.

Whereas in the modern society there is much morality which is not expressed as *Law,* and much *Law* which does not correspond to any moral imperative, in the traditional society the two spheres are not co-extensive, but they are concentric.

Concentricity and concurrence of spheres of morality, convention and *Law* mean *reinforcement* of the legal message. In a Case (ii) society it may be harder to say 'This is a legal norm', if what is meant is, 'This is solely a legal norm, and not a moral norm'; but it is easier to say, 'This is a norm, which one must comply with.'

The trouble occurs when a society in Case (ii) is forced to move into Case (i). Modern customary societies in Africa have been placed in exactly this position, and the exponents of their *Law* have been required to state whether a given norm is legal or not. The only test which helps is to ask whether the norm represents, or is felt to represent, the demands or requirements of society. Normally these demands or requirements relate to the external performances of a member of the society, i.e. his acts in relation to some one or more of his fellow-members. Interior actions commanded by an imperative, e.g.:

'Think pure thoughts!'

do not fall within the sphere of *Law* unless they can be monitored from outside, or until they emerge in some exterior behaviour.

The exclusion of *Law* by other normative systems is discussed more fully in Chapter 5, in which the respective roles and characteristics of *Law*, religion, morality and mores are identified, and the problems of discrimination and competition between them are examined.[12]

The notion and utility of 'sanction'

The crude Austinian approach would say that a law is a command supported by a sanction; the refined imperative approach would deal with Hart's point about orders backed by threats by extending the notion of sanction or threat to include the threat of nullity. In this way norms providing facilities (and in our analysis laws constituting institutions or processes) would be brought within the framework of the order-with-sanction pattern. Hart's discussion[13] argues cogently that surely a person is not obliged to obedience to a norm setting out the requirements of a valid will or a valid contract solely or necessarily by the threat of nullity or non-recognition. The two cases are, of course, not necessarily the same. Whereas the English *Law* in disputes deals mainly with failed wills, i.e. a purported act in the law which fails for want of some formal requirement, it deals with many contracts where the parties have to be told that they have made a binding legal agreement which they were perhaps unaware of. In the former case, contrary to a party's hope or expectation, an intended legal result is not achieved; in the latter case, a legal result he or they did not expect is imposed on their voluntary conduct.

This agonising, whether of the pro-sanction or the anti-sanction faction, arises because 'sanction' has been used as a formal marker of a legal norm. If one seeks a formal analysis of a legal norm, as I have argued already, it is to be found in the form of the statement which expresses it. That statement is in two parts: a hypothetical condition precedent, and an imperative conditional consequent. The hypothesis is not a sanction or threat: it is a mentioning, qualified by *If,* of a possible sequence of events. The consequence is not a sanction, though it *may* be: it says that the following re-arrangements in the *Law* are to (=ought to) occur. Such a re-arrangement may be a threat, menace or punishment; or it may be a benefit.

12. See pp. 121 ff.
13. See pp. 33 ff.

Talk about sanctions is not wrong; it is misplaced. The proper place for their mention is not in the formal requirements for a valid legal norm, but in discussion of the later stage: how effective is this norm in controlling or guiding behaviour? In other words, it concerns *implementation* of norms; and the implementation of a norm may be procured, sometimes by orders or processes which are a detriment, and sometimes by orders or processes which give effect to the course of action or re-arrangement specified in the hypothetical-conditional. Implementation is the provision by which *compliance* with norms is secured. Our discussion of effectiveness will therefore be a discussion of compliance.

To repeat, the formal analysis of a legal norm is not a *sufficient* description of the preconditions for existence of a legal norm. There are other requirements, such as the existence of a society, legitimate authority within that society, a legal system. But sanctions are not *necessary* elements of legal norms. Where imperative analysts have gone wrong is in this: they have sought a 'pure' theory of law, a purely fomal analysis of LAW, which does not need a mention of anything actually subsisting in the real world; there are or should be no existential implications of their analysis. But with their explanation of 'sovereign', the supreme author or commander of legal norms, as the person to whom the subjects are in a state of habitual obedience, they force an enquiry into whether a proposed sovereign is actually obeyed. So Hart:

'The question how many people must obey how many such general orders, and for how long, if there is to be law, no more admits of definite answers than the question how few hairs must a man have to be bald. Yet in this fact of general obedience lies a crucial distinction between laws and the original simple case of the gunman's order.'[14]

Kelsen too dirties the pure definition of LAW by bringing in existential facts:

'A norm is not considered to be valid when it is never applied. . . .'
'A norm is considered to be valid if, and only if, it belongs to a system of norms and to a system which, moreover, is generally efficacious.'[15]

Put another way, these statements are statements not about LAW but about *Law*. One does not object to a recognition of the fact that analysis of LAW as such will never get anywhere; but equally one must insist that there is a distinction between the formal marks of legal norms on the one hand, and the extent to which there is compliance with them on the other. We can sensibly say of a proffered example of a norm: 'That is a legal norm, but it does not appear to be an effective legal norm, because . . .' (specifying empirical information about the extent of compliance with it).

14. At pp. 23–24.
15. Cited from Finch's summary of Kelsen's position in his *Introduction to legal theory*, p. 129.

B. THE EFFECTIVENESS OF *LAW*: INHERENT LIMITATIONS ON ITS EFFECTIVENESS

What is it, in the characteristics of *Law* or laws, that determines and limits it or their effectiveness? To answer this question, we must have a definition and a measure of effectiveness.

To recapitulate: a *Law* or legal system is a purposive system existing in a society; a general test of its effectiveness will therefore be to see how far it realises its objectives, i.e. fulfils its purposes. Two objections must be mentioned. The first is that the effectiveness of the whole legal system is rarely in question; it is rather a question, if one discovers the total ineffectiveness of the system as a whole, of the *existence* of the legal system. The *Law*? of Utopia looks like *Law*; but there is no system corresponding to the *Law*?. The second point is that the apparent personification of the legal system could be objected to. It could be objected to in regard to legislated law, in that who is to determine, and by what tests, the 'purpose' of the legal system? Is it a declared objective, or one which one speculatively derives by induction from the presumed intentions of the *Law*-maker? The personification could be objected to in a non-legislated *Law* (e.g. customary system), because 'purpose' must imply a person or persons with an intention; and a person-less purpose seems no more acceptable logically than a commander-less command.

And yet, if one poses to the persons within such systems the question, 'What is the purpose of the *Law*?', this is not a question which is on the face of it meaningless, and which they would consequently refuse to try to answer. Jurists have not only been willing, they have been eager, to answer such a question. Ordinary people too would respond with something like: 'It would be absolute anarchy otherwise'; or 'Who would protect us from criminals?'. We have explained the purpose of *Law* analytically as the shaping of behaviour in society in conformity with the goals of those having influence within it; and this shaping can take place in societies without a single distinct commander or legislator. Nor are those responsible for such shaping, the persons who habitually emit norms of behaviour and whose 'authority' in so doing is recognised, either silent or unaware always of what they are doing. They may be reflective, and say that 'in our society we must try and do such and such'. They have 'authority' in that others listen to what they say and tend to conform to or adopt their view; but this authority may be persuasive rather than imperious.[16]

The main objective or objectives of a society would be differently formulated by different members of the society; and still other purposes

16. For a good illustration of such norm-formers with authority in a chiefless African society see the Kikuyu of Kenya, whose traditional institutions are described by H. E. Lambert in his *Kikuyu social and political institutions*. The Kikuyu recognised the role of *muthamaki*, a leader with qualities of leadership and authority in enunciating norms and settling cases.

might be discerned by external observers. But to us, as jurists, the main purpose of a legal system is to give and express the structure of a society, and to permit the harmonious working of that structure. Activities which threaten the continuance of the structure or its harmonious working or the basic assumptions of the society will be disapproved of and repressed. Harmonious working implies institutions: institutions for the allocation of property, for the attribution of responsibilities, for the settlement of quarrels. Disharmony, disagreement with the way in which allocation, attribution or settlement takes place, will be evidence of ineffective functioning.

Measures of effectiveness of laws

If we turn to the component elements in a legal system, it is often easier to isolate their purposes and hence to measure their effectiveness. The description we have given above of a *Law* as a communications system consisting of many parts showed that the legal system, like any system, is subject to various inbuilt sources of weakness which cannot be entirely eliminated, whatever we do. Our first step is therefore, like a systems engineer, to examine the system for 'bugs', and to 'debug' it so far as possible. One must detect points of weakness in the system, faulty parts, bad connections, teeth missing from gears. We turn therefore to norms, their making, communication and execution, to see the possible points of weakness.

If we wish to measure the effectiveness of medical treatment, we can see how far it is, as the case may be, *preventive* = eliminating a disease or pathogen; or *curative* = restoring the patient to full health and activity. We can tell if a machine is effective by seeing whether it works, i.e. does the job it is designed for. The machine should not break down at all, or at least not frequently; if it does, it must be possible to repair it easily. The machine should be adaptable, so that it can be used in a variety of circumstances.

So far as a norm or a law is concerned, we can tell if it is effective if, its purpose being *preventive,* its existence and application prevent the conduct disapproved of. If its purpose is *curative,* to remedy some deficiency or disorder, its effectiveness is measured by the extent to which the deficiency or disorder disappears. Effective laws should generally do what they are designed to do; if some failure occurs, there should be the possibility and means of easy rectification. If the necessity comes to apply the law in different or new circumstances, the law should be sufficiently adaptable.

The account of efficacy of norms will be made clearer if the vocabulary is made richer and more precise. The following terms and meanings are proposed for this purpose:

Latent norm	— A norm which has not yet been articulated, but which provokes what may be considered acts of compliance. (See the discussion of inarticulate and articulated norms at p. 10.)
Phantom norm	— A norm? which has not actually been emitted by any authority. (Cf. in English law: 'trespassers will be prosecuted'.)
Frustrate norm	— A norm or law emitted in due form, a valid norm with zero or minimal compliance. (Reasons for non-compliance are discussed below.)
Valid norm	— A norm which is formally correct, having been made in due form.
Effective norm	— A valid norm which secures a high degree of compliance; i.e. one which is actually complied with.
Compliance	— Action (or inaction) as the case may be which implements the purpose of a norm.

Our vocabulary does *not* make the definition of a 'valid norm' depend on its efficacy, or compliance as we call it. This usage does not agree with that adopted by some, according to which a norm is not valid unless complied with. Note also that 'compliance' has no necessary connexion with 'sanction'; compliance may be *secured* by a sanction, but the sanction, when applicable, is not the compliance.

Modes of compliance

The matter is worth pursuing further, with examples. Let us start with penal laws, always remembering that, although jurists often use these as their only explanation of the operation of norms, for us this is only one type of norm among many. Let us suppose that in Country X there is a law against homicide, and a law against burglary. Is a high conviction rate for, say, homicide, and a low conviction rate for, say, burglary, evidence of a high degree of compliance with the law against homicide, and a low degree of compliance with the law against burglary? To pose the question as starkly as this may seem an absurdity; but if the conviction rates for homicide go down, and the rates for burglary go up, should one feel glad or sorry in each case? Commentators on criminal statistics can find no agreement about the point.[17] One can

17. See, for example, Nigel Walker's very useful *Crimes, courts and figures: an introduction to criminal statistics,* 1971, and esp. pp. 110 ff. 'Nobody has yet contrived to assess the absolute efficacy of a penal measure, and the difficulties of doing so are obvious' (p. 110). A 1958 experiment by L. T. Wilkins to compare the result of imposing probation as compared with other measures is described; as to the results, Walker comments (p. 112) that 'His [Wilkins's] results are equally consistent with the hypothesis that the absolute efficacy of probation is considerable and with the hypothesis that it is very low, or nil.' [!]

only say that the conviction rate by itself does not measure the rate of compliance; one would have to know (i) the relative stringency of definition of each offence; (ii) the occurrence rate of each type of crime; (iii) the detection rate similarly; as well as (iv) the conviction rate. And, since legislation against crime is presumably both preventive and curative, one would have to know whether the low conviction rate for burglary was followed by an increased rate of occurrence, and vice versa with homicide; in other words, are the norms helping to prevent the conduct disapproved of?

What is the compliance for norms which regulate institutions of the *Law*, such as courts and other agencies? What is the purpose of the norms which set up and regulate such institutions? These norms are not preventive directly — they do not prevent the institutions doing something. Quite the contrary: they are meant to enable the institutions to do something. The ulterior purpose of the institutions is for the implementation of other norms; the measure of success must be the extent to which the institutions succeed in securing compliance with these other norms. Some of the institutions are curative, their ulterior purpose being to remedy some deficiency or disorder, such as a legal conflict between two subjects of the law. To the extent that the institutions succeed in thus remedying the deficiency or disorder, so they are complying with the norm which establishes them.

The *Law* provides facilities; to take the most obvious instance, it may recognise a relationship of marriage, and regulate the state and the consequences of it. What is the mode of compliance with the norms which create and regulate such a facility? Not that every possible person who might get married is married and remains married! Not that those who fail to comply with the norms of marriage shall be punished by divorce, so that divorce is the sanction of marriage! Compliance with the norms means fulfilling the purposes of the norms; the norms both regulate the parties to the marriage, and protect the relationship as against other persons. Compliance for the parties is conformity with the regulations, the responsibilities, imposed by the relationship; compliance for third parties is respect for the relationship. Divorce is the failure of the marriage, and may be due to non-compliance of third parties with the normative requirement of respect for the relationship; in other words, divorce may be treated as evidence of non-compliance.

Is a low rate of take-up of the facility evidence of lack of effectiveness? Suppose that fewer and fewer people actually get married: does this mean that the constitutive norms of marriage, and the protective norms, are to that extent becoming less effective? One can imagine a situation where there is a low rate of marriage, and a very low rate of divorce; while Ireland seems such a case, a better one was pre-revolutionary Ethiopia, where divorce was forbidden to adherents of the Coptic Church, and where the marriage rate under Coptic law was also lower than it might have been. This might suggest that both marriage and divorce failed to meet some social need. We are tempted to say that a facility which is not used is 'useless'. This goes beyond the question of compliance, or opens up a new perspective of it. Exactly the position instanced at the beginning of this paragraph is beginning to occur in developed western countries, e.g. Sweden, the United States and Britain, as marriage gets less popular or is postponed to a later age. In its place we find new non-normative institutions such as the 'house-mate' system, wrongly called 'common law marriage', and referred to in legal contexts as cohabitation. This non-normative institution is forcing itself into the normative array, as we describe in detail in a later chapter.[18]

Sources of weakness and non-compliance

The weaknesses of the norm-emitting, transmission, and implementation system have already been briefly mentioned or hinted at; now it is time to pull these observations together and present them under the appropriate heads. The weaknesses can be identified as due to:

1. *Transmission losses* — failures in transmission and communication.
2. *Inappropriateness of norms and institutions* — weaknesses in the character of the norms, the statements or expression of them, their fit with other components of the legal system, or with the social context in which they are to operate.
3. *Failures in application or implementation.*
4. *Failures in scrutiny or monitoring.*

1. Transmission losses

These are failures in the system of communication, about which something has already been said in discussing the features of communications systems. At the point of generation and transmission of norms and institutions, there are failures in form: thus a norm may not be validly made in accordance with the prerequisites of the legal system; or the norm may be merely latent, and not yet given precise form and expression. Is promulgation to those purportedly affected by a norm an essential requirement of its validity? This cannot be answered in the sphere of LAW; it can be answered in the sphere of *Law* only by looking at the requirements of that *Law*. If the *Law* makes promulgation necessary for validity, then that is a precondition of validity, and a norm not duly promulgated is invalid to that extent. If it does not so provide, there is nothing in the nature of norms that requires promulgation; but there is something in the nature of effective communications that requires transmission of a message to the intended recipient to be actually carried out if it is to be effective. The untransmitted norm will then be valid but ineffective; its ineffectiveness

18. See Chapter 8, at pp. 259 ff. below.

may be cured retrospectively if compliance with it is subsequently monitored (see 4.) and remedial action undertaken.

A norm may be duly made, promulgated if so required, and yet not received by the intended recipient. In our examination of the praxis of legal communication we shall see several examples of laws which have not been effectively received for a variety of reasons.[19] Lack of reception may be due to absence of reinforcement of the message, or to competing signals; or the message may be received and misunderstood. Cynical English lawyers might say that this last case is the common case with judicial interpretation of statutes; but ordinary subjects of the law can as easily 'get the wrong message'.

2. Inappropriateness of norms and institutions

Weakness in the character of norms. By this we mean or include such matters as: imprecision of aim or expression of the law; internal ambiguities of purpose.

Weaknesses in the statement of or expression of a norm. A norm, if it is expressly made ('emitted'), must use the resources of *Language* to convey its message or meaning. It is a common complaint that a law cannot cover every possibility; it deals in the general or usual or expected case. But when the unusual or unexpected case crops up, it may be said that if the legislator wanted to deal with this, he should have said so expressly. How can he win in these circumstances? Which shall he choose, generality or particularity? Some legislators, e.g. some continental codifiers, choose generality; they lay down a general principle, i.e. a widely and vaguely expressed norm, and challenge the subjects and the appliers of the principle to make it fit the actual case, if they can. In effect, in such an instance the legislator is emitting *two* norms, one primary and one secondary. The primary contains his general principle; the secondary tells the applying agencies to modify or extend the primary norm so as to fit the actual case.

Other legislators, e.g. the contemporary British Parliament, express themselves in generalities but indicate that they wish them to be taken as particularities. For the applier of the norm to start writing his own subsidiary norm to meet the actual case would be taken as a usurpation of a competence attributed solely to the legislator: 'We can't have judges making laws! The judge's job is to apply the law made by Parliament, no more and no less' — and similar exhortations. But in the latter case the judge must also 'make his own law'; in performing the act of matching the actual case, the one he is trying, to the hypothetical case instanced in the norm as the first half of the normative hypothetical-conditional,

19. See Chapter 3, pp. 73 ff. and 207 ff., below. And see previous discussion at pp. 11, 12–15.

the judge must stretch and distort the hypothetical to make it fit the actual. Repeated acts of interpretation and application leave the hypothetical case permanently stretched or distorted; or, as we would say in the language of English *Law,* 'an Act of Parliament means what the words of the Act, as authoritatively interpreted from time to time by the courts, say it means'; in other words, a valid Act = norm + interpretation.

A separate or related problem applies to all utterances, and not merely those which contain norms of conduct. We have long abandoned the notion that words 'have a meaning', still less that 'they stand for or represent a concept'. Many words and morphemes, if we take English as an example, are functional forms which 'stand for' no thing and no 'concept'; what do 'but' and 'in' and '-ly' stand for in the world of reality? It is quite wrong, and desperately naive, to analyse an utterance word by word; words fall into groups: 'I must go' is three words in English; the same notion can be expressed in, say, the African language Cewa by what is written as one word: 'ndiziyenda'. It is for this reason that one must take issue with the approach adopted by Stone in his discussion of the problems of defining 'law':

'For what is meant by the word "law" is not an entity with fixed boundaries of meaning, like the words "hydrogen", "man", or "tree".'[20]

Either 'law' is an entity (whatever that means! perhaps it means that LAW is an abstract entity?), in which case 'hydrogen', 'tree' and 'man' are also entities; or none of these is an entity. If Stone is asking for guidance as to how to use the word 'law', then it is an error, one may respectfully suggest, to slide away from the verbal and onto the ontological level. The answer to the question, 'How should I use "law" (or "tree") in an English sentence?' requires a specification of the functions of the mentioned items in their verbal and social contexts in English utterances. Examination of these functions will show that no word or item in a *Language* has 'fixed boundaries of meaning' (where meaning = function in context). The word 'hydrogen', to take one of Stone's instances, does not receive a complete specification of all its functions in English merely by mentioning the chemical formula for it — the phrase, 'the hydrogen bomb', shows the item 'hydrogen' receiving from its context, verbal and social, a much more extended and indeed vaguer function (the bomb is *not* made from hydrogen: this would not be a sufficient description either of the bomb or of the function of 'hydrogen' in the phrase).

Where the error comes from can perhaps be inferred from a later passage from Stone's book, when he discusses 'the elucidation of legal concepts'. He observes:

'in recent jurisprudential discussions, traditional methods of definition

20. *Legal system and lawyers' reasonings* (London, 1964), p. 173.

of legal terms, as if these terms corresponded to some *thing,* like a table or a tree, have been ably and properly challenged.'

Yes: legal terms do not correspond to 'things'. But neither do they correspond to 'entities'. In this they do not contrast with, but are on the same footing as, terms which according to Stone (and many others) correspond to 'things'. A study of the meaning (=function) of 'table' and 'tree' (i.e. the words in question) is not an identification of *table* and *tree,* whether as an entity or a thing. There is no 'thing' which corresponds to the word 'tree'.

A moment's examination of English utterances including the item 'tree' will demonstrate this point. To point to a tree is to point to a thing, certainly; but it is not to explain or lay down precisely how one should use the expression, 'a tree', still less 'tree', in English. A tree is not all members of the class, 'tree'. Even if it were, what is included in the class 'tree' is not specified by things but by a process of abstraction and attribution. But such an abstraction does not exhaust the mention of the uses of the term 'tree' in English sentences. One can cite many utterances where 'tree' does not point to any 'thing' — a logical tree in logic; a decision tree in computers, for instance; a family tree. These cases are not to be met by saying that these do not represent the 'real' meaning of 'tree', but are only attributive uses. Who are we to lay down prescriptively what are the 'real' uses of 'tree' or any other word in the English language; and even if we had the authority, how do we exercise it? *All* uses of 'tree' are attributive. Nor is the list of such uses closed.

To put it another way, analysis of utterances, and explication of the functions of items in them, is a task at one level; pointing at trees, or doing anything else to or with them, is an operation at a quite different level. We can accept that use of a term such as 'tree' can be explained as being provoked by phenomena in the world of reality. We can accept that every term in a natural *Language* relates back in some sort of way to some aspect of reality at some stage, or else our conversation would have no function in real terms. Even 'abstract' terms like 'tort' or 'trust' relate back to events in the world of reality in some sort of way; but the nature of the relation cannot be satisfied by pointing; and the analysis of the use of 'tree' or 'trust' in English sentences is not a description of trees and trusts in English life. We are not describing reality by defining 'trees' or 'trusts', any more than we are contemplating reality by looking at a photograph.

In the result, every term in a natural *Language* has a literally unlimited range of functions. If we think we have restricted its function prescriptively, or that its function is restricted 'essentially', today, our view can easily be falsified tomorrow. The first person who used 'tree' to refer to a family tree, or by extension to the cross on which Christ died, falsified the notion that 'tree' refers to a thing and a fixed and

1. Op. cit., p. 206.

defined thing at that. But even today 'tree' has no precise meaning: Is a seedling a tree? Are the roots part of the tree? Is a dead tree a tree, and does it stay a tree when it is cut up? The questions could be endless.

We conclude that *no* item in a *Language* has a fixed, determinate meaning. The indeterminacy will be greater with items which are more remote from reality, like 'tort' or 'wrong'; but the indeterminacy applies to *every* item in a *Language* – simple items such as 'get' or '-ly' have indeterminate functions. There is no special mystery about legal terms. Study of uses of terms shows, though, that for each term there is a cluster of meanings or functions, or several such clusters. At the centre of each cluster there is a core of easily perceived meaning; round the core there is an indeterminate penumbra, shading off into obscurity, of function. Such indeterminacy is intrinsic to every message in a *Language*. It is intrinsic too to every legal message, including every message which expresses a norm or establishes an institution. This conclusion may seem a longwinded way of stating the obvious, viz. that legal formulations are open to doubt and to controversies of interpretation; but it is important to reach that conclusion by the right road; and the right road is a perception of the indeterminacy of every message, and of every linguistic item within the message.

Lack of fit of norms with other components of the legal system. There is no reason to dwell on the principles of this at this stage, as we shall look at the practice in later chapters. It seems quite obvious that a new norm should fit with the existing normative structure if it is to work successfully. But a new norm may contradict, obviously or less obviously, other existing norms. Indeed, it is the function of reforming legislation to make new norms which contradict old ones; and in a revolution old norms, or even the whole normative system, may be swept away. But norms may also be inoperable because they are self-contradictory. We are familiar with the case where one provision of a statute does not seem to fit with another; and English courts have worked out various rule-of-thumb techniques for dealing with such contradictions. What the courts have done in reality is to emit their own super-norms to guide themselves in the task of resolving such contradictions.

Lack of fit with the social context. A norm, to work, must operate within a given social system. If the norm cuts across the grain of that social system, it is less likely to be effective, or may even be a total failure. A quite obvious observation; and yet how often does one see in practice instances where governments, and other norm-emitters, have flagrantly and perhaps wilfully disregarded it! The reason why governments disregard the principle may be a feeling that they should be masters in their own house, and not the norms or the society which they purport to control. But the examples where governments have failed to be the masters tell us a great deal about the limitations of law as a weapon of mastery; which is why we study some such examples in detail in later parts of this work.

3. Failures in application or implementation

The norm is valid; it is made in due form; it is communicated; but it does not work — it is not implemented, or there is not a sufficient degree of compliance. Why? First, there may be a lack of suitable and sufficient implementing norms/orders/institutions/processes. This may be due to oversight, or to a fundamental misunderstanding by the norm-emitter of what is required to make an effective law. Many of the weaknesses we shall examine in effectiveness of laws, especially but not solely in developing countries, are explained by a lack of suitable machinery for implementation. Take a simple instance: a law to register title to land is passed; twenty years later it is clear that it is ineffective — why? It may be that there was no sufficient machinery instituted for the initial investigation of title, or the recording of subsequent devolutions of title (e.g. Kenya). Or another simple instance: a law is passed to regulate trade unions and to prevent illegal strikes; a few years later it is clear that the law has almost completely failed in these respects. The reason may be that the courts were given insufficient powers to implement these norms, or that the agencies carrying out the implementing orders of the courts were themselves frustrated by resistances outside their control or which there was no will to control (e.g. United Kingdom).

There may be implementing norms, etc, but they do not work because of a lack of zeal or efficiency on the part of the institutions charged with implementing them. The Ethiopian Penal Code was passed during imperial times to provide a complete and comprehensive code of criminal law for Ethiopia. In principle it was the sole source of penal law, and was general and imperative in its character. And yet, just before Haile Selassie fell, it was reported that the Penal Code was rarely applied, or even consulted, outside the capital, Addis Ababa. A lack of zeal, rather than a lack of implementing norms, seems to have been the explanation. This was contributed to by a failure of monitoring, which we mention below.

Lack of application may be due to lack of reinforcement. We have seen that in ordinary communications systems the probability of the message successfully getting through and being acted upon is increased if the signal is reinforced. In legal terms, what would such reinforcement be? A publicity campaign to bring the terms of the new law to the notice of all those affected by it, perhaps; show-trials of persons breaching the new law to get the message across; parallel provision; denial of legal efficacy to other consequences or other acts which relate in some way to the legal consequences or acts prescribed or covered by the new law. As I write, the British government is trying to reinforce the efficacy of its non-statutory and theoretically non-normative (in the legal sense) incomes policy by imposing parallel consequences on those who flout the 'policy', e.g. by denying government contracts to firms who pay wage increases in excess of the 'norm'.

4. Failures in scrutiny or monitoring

To launch a new norm into the world without satisfactory provision for monitoring its effectiveness is like buying a new car and never looking inside the bonnet to see if the engine needs servicing. Scrutiny of how the law works in practice, and monitoring equipment which includes the possibility of remedial action (e.g. by further norm-emission), are normally essential if one wants to make sure that a norm is effective. The remoter the norm-emitter from the norm-receiver, the more necessary and more elaborate and institutionalised such feedback must be. In a simple face-to-face society one has a situation of almost instant feedback. If there is not immediate compliance, the fact will be obvious to the emitter of the norm at once; and new action — if this is socially possible — can be initiated at once. The inertia of the norm-emitter is thus a potent factor in rendering a norm ineffective.

Again these are truisms; and yet how few makers of norms seem to have regard to this aspect of the efficient legal system! In a developed society, such as that of Britain, one could almost imagine the adoption of a working practice, whereunder no law-maker would content himself with issuing the new norm; he would issue a statement in three parts: first, the formal norm(s); secondly, the description of the implementing mechanisms; thirdly, a specification of the arrangements for monitoring compliance and rectifying non-compliance. It is not only the governments of the undeveloped world who gaily launch a shining new law, like a child's balloon, into their society, to float over it and out of it without affecting what lies beneath it; recent legal history is full of such examples.

Effects of non-compliance

To use the vocabulary proposed at the beginning of this section, a norm? which has not actually been emitted by a competent authority within the society is a mere *phantom norm*. It is not designed to shape behaviour, since by definition it is not designed. How does the subject of the law discriminate between a phantom norm and a merely *latent norm*? In a certain sense all valid norms have latency, in that the extent and terms of the articulation of a norm are not settled once and for all at the moment of its first emission. Apart from that, the subject of a *Law* must, to conform to our prescriptive definition, have executed acts of compliance with the latent norm, or must be considering whether to comply with it, having seen that others have purported to comply with it. Such a person may ask himself: am I alone in complying with this norm? If no one else has done so, it suggests that it is not a norm of the society. If it is a question of possible compliance in the future, the person is not alone. He has the means of communication with his fellows, or of consulting some authority. He can ask them; he can discuss with them whether there is a norm, and if so what its terms might be. Too much of the discussion of compliance (sub nom. 'obedience') with the *Law* seems to assume a lonely figure wrestling all by himself with the task of sorting out the real from the phantom norms. The societal dimension and explanation of *Law* are essential ingredients of the legal system; so the responses of members generally to the question, Is this a valid norm?, are all-important in practice. If it is a question of discriminating between legal and other norms, the person can, in a society with a clear definition of authority to emit norms, go to such an authority to ask; failing which, he must fall back on the test already proposed.[2]

A norm which has no, or practically no, compliance is a *frustrate norm*. There is no absolute measure of the required degree of frustration of a norm for it to fall into this category. The frustrate norm fails in its purpose; this may not matter much to the body or person originating it, or it may matter a great deal. But a legal system with too high a percentage of frustrate norms within its total normative array is thereby weakened. A norm, if legal, is one which purports to demand or expect (depending on the kind of end served) compliance. The likelihood of compliance is increased if the subjects of the *Law* assume that in general they should conform their behaviour to the requirements of valid legal norms. It is diminished if they see that, because of large areas of non-compliance, formally valid norms are often ineffective and there is no attempt, through monitoring of compliance, to ensure greater effectiveness. This is a short statement of a characteristic psychological response. Since all law is in a sense a confidence-trick ('Do this!' – 'Why?' – 'Because I say so.' – 'But that is not enough.' – 'Well, then, because you've got to.') in which the norm-emitter as originator expects compliance even if he has no physical power to ensure it, confidence diminishes or disappears if the *Law* is cast into disrepute through the non-observance of its laws. This general failure of conviction or confidence in *Law* is now widespread in Africa on the part of subjects of the *Law*; but in developed countries also there are large areas of life where *Law* has lost its credibility (industrial law in England; tax law in France; speed-limits everywhere).

2. See pp. 25–6 above.

CONCLUSION

'Binding' and 'obligation'

Nothing has been said in this analysis of *Law*/law, and of compliance with it or its effectiveness, about the 'binding' character of norms. Nothing has been said about what 'binding' means, what makes a norm binding, or what makes a person perceive a norm as binding on him. Nothing has been said about 'obligation'.

The reason that nothing has been said is that, in my opinion, nothing need be said. The notion of the binding or non-binding character of norms is unnecessary for an analysis of norms, and is unnecessary for an analysis of compliance, as the account just given, which has not had to use the term 'binding', demonstrates. Nor is the abstract noun 'obligation' necessary for an analysis of the character of norms or of the degree of compliance with them. If we use the translation test suggested earlier,[3] there are *Languages* which lack any lexical item which translates or could be taken to be translated by 'obligation'. Juristics would be impossible in such societies if we accepted that 'obligation' was a necessary element in the analysis of *Law* or law.

To spell the point out categorically, a legal norm is not a norm because it is 'binding'. People do not comply with norms because they 'are' 'binding'. People comply with norms either because they perceive it to be to their advantage to do so, or because they have formed the habit of doing so, or (and these are not mutually exclusive) because the appropriate authority in the legal system has taken steps to secure compliance by one or other of the means mentioned. The 'binding' aspect of a legal norm is not like the suckers on an octopus, gripping the subject to the norm; there are no such suckers. Nor do people comply with norms because 'they have an obligation' to do so. The phrase, 'they have an obligation', is merely an alternative formulation of 'they ought'. Reification of 'obligation' is both unnecessary and unjustifiable. The statement:

> 'People ought to obey the law because they have an obligation to do so.'   Statement 16

transforms into the statement:

> 'People ought to obey the law because they ought to do so.'
> Statement 17

— an unimpeachable but meaningless observation.

One has the feeling that 'obligation' functions in juristic analysis like the ether used to function in the explanation of radio transmissions. Radio signals must be transmitted in and through *something*, some

3. See p. 4 above.

medium, it was thought; this is an invisible, undetectable medium, it is true, but it must exist or we cannot explain how radio signals are transmitted or conveyed; let us call it 'ether'. Legal norms 'force' people to do something [they don't!] ; what is this mysterious potency inherent in the norms? It must be an 'obligation'. Modern scientists have discarded the notion of the undetectable, immeasurable, hypothetical ether; they believe that they can give perfectly satisfactory accounts of the way in which radio waves are propagated and received without it. Modern jurists should discard the notion of 'obligation' similarly. What is unnecessary for analysis can and should be discarded.[4]

Most of the difficulties, not just of jurists but of practical lawmakers too, arise because *Law* is a quite different sort of 'thing'/system/ operation from a description of past events (history; observational science). *Law* (we personify only for brevity here) seeks to control the future rather than to describe the past. Inevitably in such a case it will often not succeed in its aim; indeed, it is probably inherent in it that it should never fully succeed.

Nominalism, anti-nominalism, and linguistic analysis: a surrejoinder

Jurists who make the analysis of 'obligations' the basis of their study of a legal system, and use the idea of 'binding' as the key to finding out why law is obeyed or what defines a law, are not happy with the nominalist position that these terms are superfluous and/or do not correspond to any real phenomenon. Their rejoinder is to show that lawyers, and especially legal theoreticians, constantly use words like 'obligation' and 'duty' in spelling out the content of legal norms and their effect — the appeal to usage; and to assert that the nominalists so-called are talking nonsense, because words, whether abstract or not, do not correspond to real 'things', and so this is not an objection which can be made against such terms in particular — this is the appeal to basic philosophical principles.

Before we deal with these objections, let us just remind ourselves what is the nature of the enterprise upon which we are engaged. My personal task is not to write a manual of theoretical or speculative legal philosophy, but to try to answer the questions: 'What limits are there on the effectiveness of *Law* and law? And what are the explanations for these limitations?' This is in itself a limited task. These questions imply a subsidiary question, 'What is it that induces a subject to comply with a law?' The analysts of whom we speak tend to answer, 'The subject complies *because he has an obligation* to do so'; and 'When I say "obligation", I mean some (thing) that "binds" the subject in a way that non-legal imperatives do not do.'

4. Ockham.

The implications of usage. My answer to this sort of approach was to say that it conveys no information; nor can one find any function for these items in the analysis of legal behaviour. One can certainly find that they function in legal discourse; but this is not the issue. In making their criticisms, the anti-nominalists are perhaps attacking an animal which does not exist. What I may call the 'moderate nominalists', a group to which I would affiliate myself, are not committed to the view that nothing has any reality, and that no words expressing general 'concepts' have any meaning, because they quite clearly do have such a meaning [= function] as used in the language of jurists or others. One would certainly oppose the crude notion that 'words stand for things' (and an attack on that notion has been made already at pp. 34 ff.); but so, I believe, would the enlightened jurists of the opposing class we are just discussing. Where we differ, apparently, is in the existential implications of categorising terms. To use a word, a term, a lexical item is not to make any implication as such about what exists in the 'real world'. It is no answer, therefore, to show that lawyers habitually use the word 'obligation' in their analysis or their arguments, nothing that corresponds to, or can be identified with, 'obligation' is necessarily to be presumed to exist thereby. The patron saint of nominalists, William of Ockham, did not say that we should not recognise *any* entities; he said that they should not be multiplied *without necessity*. There is a necessity for using terms of a general nature if we find that this assists our analysis, and provided we do not deceive ourselves as to whether 'things' corresponding to these terms actually exist. The test, that is, is a purely pragmatic and functionalist one; and I submit that these two terms fail this test. They do not assist our analysis, they obscure it.

Many statements incorporating the word 'God', or its equivalents in other languages, have been made since the dawn of history; it would be an extremely simple way of proving the existence of a deity if the fact of such use could be taken to have existential implications. We habitually talk about the sun 'going down' in the evening or 'rising' in the morning; we continue to do so though the geocentric view of the universe has been long abandoned. There is no scientific implication in our statement that 'the sun is setting', provided we always bear the scientific realities in mind. The appeal to juristic usage will not serve, then.

The limitations of linguistic analysis. It is a popular technique of the linguistic analysis school to take a variety of sentences in the English language and tease them this way and that, to say that in one circumstance one could say A, and in another circumstance one could say B but not A: what are they doing, these linguistic analysts, when they tell us this? Are they telling us some philosophical truth, or teaching us how to use the English language? The normative effect of legal prescriptions can be conveyed in many different formulations. Thus one might tell someone:

'You have an obligation (to do some act, etc)'
'You have a duty to . . .'
'You are obliged to . . .'
'You are obligated to . . .' (American)
'You must . . .'
'You shall . . .'
'It is required that . . .'
'You ought . . .'
'It shall be mandatory for . . .'
'You are under a liability to . . .'

and so on.

Do these variations have significance, not just in the linguistic code of English *Law*, but transcendentally and universally? If they are only significant for English usage and English *Law*, then they have no place in a book on general legal theory; if they have universal significance, one has to explain how the accidents of English idiomatics can reveal the universal truths of axiomatics. Jurists (English-speaking) spend much time trying to distinguish the significance of 'You have an obligation to . . .' from that of 'You are obliged to . . .'. Whole books could be written, and *have* been written,[5] on 'Obligation' and linguistic discriminations of this kind. Writers may triumphantly show that, say, the word 'obliged' could be used in an English context when there is no suggestion of legal duty or compulsion: 'I was obliged to get out of the car to remove something from the windscreen'; whereas 'I was under an obligation to get out of the car to remove something from the windscreen' differs in its implication in that (a) it suggests the pre-existence of a legal rule or norm under which I acted; (b) it does not imply, as the first sentence does, that I actually got out of the car and did remove something from the windscreen. A very neat indication of the use of two English words — but does it help us to understand why I did or did not in the second instance actually comply with the law? No, it does not. 'I was under an obligation . . .' (in *English,* and in the mouth of a lawyer) probably means (though not necessarily — it might have been a moral obligation or a social obligation) that (i) there was in existence a legal norm; (ii) that norm had something to do with keeping one's windscreen unobscured; (iii) in my given case the facts of my situation matched the model facts of that norm; (iv) if I failed to comply with that norm, and was detected in my non-compliance, then a penalty might be imposed upon me by an agent of the *Law*, acting according to another norm directed to him and telling him what to do in circumstances like these.

5. E.g. by J. C. Smith *Legal Obligation* (London, 1976).

I come back to the translation problem, and the translation test. It is by no means probable that I shall find a single term in another language and another *Law* which would function like 'obligation' in this set of sentences, and which would convey to the hearer the same set of meanings. Nor, to revert to English, does the statement 'I was under an obligation . . .' represent anything more than a convenient way of saying that there was a norm which applied to me; such a thought could be conveyed in many different grammatical forms, some of which would be by way of verbs and not nouns. We have an incurable habit in English of using abstract nouns to say things which could as easily be said through verbs: what happens to the fine discussion of the noun if we eschew its use?

2 Limits from the nature of the society

We move now from legal theory, which, if not pure, is at least general in character, to legal fact, from what one may term *juristics* to that special branch of it that we can, by analogy, call *applied juristics*. Pure physicists tend to look down on applied physicists; pure mathematicians the same; but of all the disciplines the pure jurist can least afford to look down on his applied jurist colleague. Law (= *Law* and law) is about real people living in real societies; its sole justification as a subject of study is that it relates to, and is by intention related to, the facts of real life. And yet applied juristics (which is partly referred to when earlier writers spoke about 'the science of legislation') is the relatively neglected sister of her purer and more celebrated sibling. For criminal law and procedure the criminologists have made all the running; there are no equivalent 'civilologists'.

What we must look at, then, is the sociology of the laws in operation. There has been work in the sociology of law, but most of it, for reasons not unconnected with the dominance of social anthropologists, has tended to be concentrated in the study of the simpler societies. If not that, then it has tended to be generalised and speculative, rather than observational and analytical. Weber is the model here of all that it is right, and much that is wrong, with legal sociology as previously practised. Before getting down to the particular examples which illustrate the theme of the limitations on law, examples which we shall see as cutting across the categories and the analysis of problems dealt with in Chapter 1, there are one or two further general and preliminary remarks which must be made.

Law cannot compel action

The first observation is that a law cannot compel action. No one can be forced to do anything merely by a law. No law can compel any particular course of action, even if the law if accompanied by a sanction. All that a law can do is to try to induce someone, by order or by persuasion or by suggestion, to a certain course of action. The inducement may, as we have seen, take various forms — punishment, reward, non-disapproval. So a law which commands its subjects not to murder (a negative command) does not stop persons committing murder; it merely punishes them if they do so. A law which commands someone to do something (a positive command), e.g. to take out a licence, merely says that without the appropriate licence some action will be *invalid*, and/or an offence may have been committed. Even physical compulsion is not enough: in such a case one cannot say that the law has compelled someone to do something. Thus an order, 'Leave the country immediately, or be deported', does not compel someone to leave the country. If he fails to leave, the position does not change if the person is physically deported, that is, dumped over the frontier. Why he has left the country is because of his physical removal, and not because of the compelling force of the law.

Classification of laws

The classification of laws into those which command, those which prohibit, and those which permit, seems on the face of it to be exhaustive and adequate. The Islamic jurists, who devoted much thought to such questions, classified human acts, as seen through the eyes of the Islamic religious *Law*, into five categories:

(i)   Expressly commanded
(ii) Recommended or desirable
(iii) Permitted or indifferent
(iv) Reprobated
(v)   Absolutely forbidden or abominable.

Not all of these acts are expressly commanded or forbidden by the *Law*. Some are matters of religious obligation only, or matters of morality, good manners or convention.

Both schemes suffer from limitations. The main weakness in each case lies in the category of 'permitted' actions. As various jurists, including Stone,[1] have helpfully pointed out, an action may be permitted by the *Law* in two distinct senses and ways: either the *Law* expressly declares a particular action to be permitted; or the *Law* fails to express any rule either way on the matter, i.e. it is 'neutral' or non-committal. (In the latter case, there must be an assumption of the legal system, corresponding to a super-norm, that what is not expressly forbidden is permitted.)

But the main weakness of these schemes seems to me to be that they appear to relate solely to the *formal* aspects of the *Law*: does the *Law* on the face of it command, prohibit, or permit some action?; and they

1.   See his *Legal system . . .*, p. 197.

do not have regard to or analyse the *commitment* or interest of the legislator: what is the commitment or purpose of the legislator in making this particular law? If we have regard to this extra dimension, the scheme must be broadened. We must distinguish cases where the law-giver, the commander, positively and strongly wishes that which is commanded, intrinsically, because it corresponds to the life-picture or life-style supported by the law-giver, from those cases where he must make an ad hoc or arbitrary choice between various solutions of practical problems. The law-giver in the latter case is intrinsically indifferent to the pattern chosen before it is chosen; but commands it when chosen so as both to affirm the validity of the action required and to secure its effectiveness.

A simple example of the former case is the law against murder. It is still the case in a country such as Britain that the law-giver intrinsically reprobates the deliberate and unjustifiable killing of one person by another; the law implements this prior commitment. We may call this a *strong imperative*. A simple example of the latter case is the law requiring one to drive on a given side of the road (on the left in England, on the right in France). So far as one can tell, the legislator in each country was indifferent *before* the choice was made and the law enacted; he is not indifferent to compliance with the law *after* it is made, of course. We may call this sort of command a *weak imperative*.

A similar division may be made as regards prohibitory laws. A *strong prohibition* is one contained in a law where the law-maker strongly desires to see the act prohibited not carried out because it contradicts his life-picture; a *weak prohibition* carries no such prior commitment.

In the area of actions permitted by the law, a *strong or hortatory permission* is one where the law-giver is interested in encouraging the result aimed at or permitted, without making it mandatory; an example, perhaps, is with the law providing for the franchise, and perhaps still in England (though not in Sweden) with the law providing for marriage. One finds it difficult to imagine cases where the law-giver has a strong interest in the result of the permission, and yet does not express this interest through a positive law. Failure to enact a law against marriage, for instance, would not be taken as a strong permission to get married. A *weak or neutral permission* is one where the law-maker is uninterested in the result, i.e. does not positively desire it. Such permission may extend to *inaction* (the law does not require one to do something positive) as well as *action* (the law does not forbid one to do something). Sometimes the law-maker gives permission by not making a law or by repealing an existing law; thus the law-maker in England has given a permission to persons to commit suicide or indulge in prostitution, or engage in homosexual acts in some circumstances, through repeal of the laws which formerly prohibited such acts; but one must presume that the legislator (even the most progressive elements within this term) did not imply by the repeal of these laws that the formerly forbidden acts were now to be encouraged. It is not clear whether marriage is falling gradually into the same category as suicide or prostitution: we give you no positive encouragement to get married, but we will not stop you, and if you want to do it, this is the permitted way. This situation would arrive if the present protections for the relationship of marriage were further dismantled, and if alternative forms of relationship were officially recognised. This has already happened in Sweden, where the law is now indifferent between couples who marry and those who live together without formal marriage.

A weak or neutral permission may be exactly that, a token of weakness, when the indifference of the legislator is to be explained by his inability to do otherwise. He cannot enforce a law to command or prohibit, so he tolerates. The existence of weak or neutral permissions of various forms of action is thus a mark or feature of the limits of the effectiveness of law, and of the means of enforcing compliance with it.

We may also wish to make a distinction between *preventive law* and *affirmative law*. Preventive law is on the face of it a law commanding one *not* to do something. Compliance with it can be assured by inaction on the part of those subject to it. A law against murder can be complied with by not murdering anyone; a law against driving on the wrong side of the road can be complied with either by driving on the right side of the road, or by not driving at all. Affirmative law seems the opposite; one must do something positive to comply with it: an example would be the income tax law; compliance with that requires filling in and submitting one's forms correctly, and then paying the right tax as and when demanded. A morally less neutral example is the responsibility of parents to look after and maintain their children.

From the purely logical point of view one might argue that a preventive law does by implication affirm the contradictory of that which it commands or prohibits; the law against murder affirms and requires a non-murdering pattern of life; the law against driving on the wrong side of the road requires a driving-on-the-right-side-if-at-all pattern of life; and so on. But this is to misstate the pragmatic and socio-psychological differences between the two types of law, the strong and the weak. The weak prohibition does not imply the positive affirmation on the part of the law-giver of a particular life-style or set of values; while the strong prohibition does. The affirmation is by the 'legislator'. This term is a shorthand way of referring to the views and actions of a number of persons concerned with the formulation and emission of a norm in diffᵉrent kinds of society, a matter which we look at below. We note now that the 'legislator' may in some way, when making an affirmative law, express the convictions of the society in which he functions; or he may be at odds with it; or the society may have no clear and settled view to express.[2] We may note further that in less developed societies the legislator may *be* the society in an

2. See pp. 67 ff.

important sense.[3] We finally note that even in developed societies the society may eventually make law *against* the wishes of the formal legislator and in affirmation of its own values.[4]

So much by way of preliminary. There are two aspects which will be considered in turn to the question, Does the nature of a society impose any special limits on the operation of law? The first aspect touches the kinds of society in which *Law* may or may not be found; the second concerns the ambitions and intentions of the legislator within different kinds of society. (For purposes of comparison with western societies, we shall make reference almost entirely to African traditional societies. The reasons for this are the wealth of literature on them and their laws, and my personal familiarity with that literature; but it must be said emphatically that similar statements and conclusions could be made on the basis of customary *Laws* in other parts of the world, which have an underlying family resemblance.)

A LIMITS ON LAW FROM THE NATURE OF THE SOCIETY

Are some societies too small or too unorganised to have *Law*, or to have express mechanisms (= a legislator) for the making of *Law*? This fundamental question implies a number of subsidiary questions, about the role of custom, the need or otherwise for overt legislation in the making of *Law*, the efficacy of sanctions, the role of 'courts', and so on.

Two broad challenges must be met and answered. These can best be spelt out (contrary to our normal practice) by the citation of statements by eminent jurists which pose such challenges. Hart in his *The Concept of Law* has a special section on 'Legal limitations on legislative power',[5] in which he rejects the imperative theory of LAW that there must be a sovereign, and a legally unlimited one at that, for one to be able to say that there is *Law* in that society:

'The objection to the theory as a general theory of law is that the existence of a sovereign such as Rex [Hart's imaginary proto-sovereign] in this imagined society, who is subject to no legal limitations, is not a necessary condition or presupposition of the existence of law. To establish this we need not invoke disputable or challengeable types of law. Our argument therefore is not drawn from systems of customary law or international law, to which some wish to deny the title of law just because they lack a legislature.'[6]

And then, when discussing the elements of law, Hart goes on:

'It is, of course, possible to imagine a society without a legislature, courts or officials of any kind. Indeed, there are many studies of

3. See pp. 53 ff., and pp. 68–70.
4. See Chapter 8 generally.
5. At pp. 64 ff.
6. At pp. 66–7.

primitive communities which not only claim that this possibility is realized but depict in detail the life of a society where the only means of social control is that general attitude of the group towards its own standard modes of behaviour in terms of which we have characterized rules of obligation. A social structure of this kind is often referred to as one of "custom"; but we shall not use this term, because it often implies that the customary rules are very old and supported with less social pressure than other rules. To avoid these implications we shall refer to such a social structure as one of primary rules of obligation.'

Hart sees three main defects in such a society lacking what he calls 'secondary' rules, i.e. rules about rules. The first is:

'. . . if doubts arise as to what the rules are or as to the precise scope of some given rule, there will be no procedure for settling this doubt, either by reference to an authoritative text or to an official whose declarations on this point are authoritative. For, plainly, such a procedure and the acknowledgement of either authoritative text or persons involve the existence of rules of a type different from the rules of obligation or duty which *ex hypothesi* are all that the group has. This defect in the simple social structure of primary rules we may call its *uncertainty*.'

The second defect 'is the *static* character of the rules. The only mode of change in the rules known to such a society will be the slow process of growth, whereby courses of conduct once thought optional become first habitual or usual, and then obligatory . . .' and where obligatory rules gradually decay.

The third defect 'is the *inefficiency* of the diffuse social pressure by which the rules are maintained. Disputes as to whether an admitted rule has or has not been violated will always occur and will, in any but the smallest societies, continue interminably, if there is no agency specially empowered to ascertain finally, and authoritatively, the fact of violation.'[7]

Then Alf Ross:

'We speak of *customs* when the correspondence between directives and social facts arises not through legislation but spontaneously as a product of an organic and unconscious evolution, a slow process of adaptation under the pressure of forces whose nature we little understand. In the case of custom, no operative role in the social pattern of events is played by the directive itself, or rather by any verbal expression and promulgation of the directive. There exists no authority whose function it is to enunciate the directive; anyone's account of the directive is correct and justified so long as it corresponds with the social facts which exist independently of any actual formulation of the directive.

7. At pp. 89–91.

Customs are *legal* and constitute *customary law*, if there are judicial authorities established to exercise organized sanctions in case of violation of the implied directives. Otherwise, customs are *conventional*.

The transition from customary law to legislation is immensely important in the evolution of any society. Customary law is conservative; it relies on traditional and static patterns of behaviour. Those bound by it act as their fathers did. This does not mean that customs are unchangeable, for they may be adapted to changing conditions; this adaptation is slow and unplanned, lacking calculation and rational understanding of the requirements of a change in conditions.'[8]

Societies without legislators?

The first challenge is this: it is asserted or implied that the word 'law' in its total meaning may only be applied to a society if that society possesses a distinct 'legislature' (Hart) and/or 'courts' (Ross). In other words, 'law' is what 'officials' deal with, and for the existence of which officials are necessary.

The second challenge is that: if a society only has custom or even customary law, the norms of behaviour of a type which we might otherwise call legal will be characterised by being uncertain, diffuse, static, lacking effectiveness in application, and being ill-adapted to the society through want of planned, rational, reflective articulation and alteration of norms.

The counter-challenge which one must proffer to these assumptions and assertions is that they do not correspond in any way with the empirical evidence of how societies in, say, traditional Africa actually function or functioned; and that they fundamentally ignore, or misrepresent, the character and efficiency of the legal normative system in such societies. The reason why there is such a lack of correspondence between reality and analysis in such treatments as this is because the societies which the authors purport to portray are merely theoretical constructs of the speculative imagination, dummies put up to be knocked down again. Unfortunately, jurists who are faced with this counter-challenge will be tempted to reply, 'I don't really mean it! I was just saying: let's pretend. There are no such societies'. Such mythical, manufactured societies then become merely one element in the logical advancement of a juristic theory; their existence or non-existence does not weaken the argument, which is about the nature of LAW. Unfortunately, this response may be difficult in Hart's case, as his introductory words seem to tie up the imaginary societies without legislature, etc, with 'many studies of primitive communities', i.e. hard, tangible evidence. He would, one presumes, assert that such studies show societies without legislature, courts, and officials; and on the face

8. In his *Directives and Norms* (London, 1968), p. 97.

of it it seems that he may be right in respect of a few of such societies. Maybe; but if for 'legislature' one substitutes 'approved or recognised emitter of legal norms'; and for 'court' one substitutes 'approved or recognised persons or institutions with authority to settle cases'; and for 'officials' one substitutes 'persons having a socially approved and defined role in the administration of a society', then every society empirically known has every one of these. Without them the society could not function. We are playing, then, with definitions rather than with substance.

In all African societies except the smallest, there can be no doubt about the matter. There are judges, if by that we mean persons who specialise in deciding disputes which concern legal norms and their implementation. There are legislators, even though the role of overt legislation is more reduced in such societies than in modern western societies. In societies without chiefs (e.g. the Kikuyu in what is now present-day Kenya), legislation was made by the councils of elders, who among the Kikuyu took office as the turn of their generation came, and who, in a way reminiscent of the classical Roman praetor, laid down the laws that they proposed to enforce during their term of office. In societies with chiefs, like the Tswana of southern Africa, it was the chief or principal ruler of a tribe who made laws in a tribal assembly and with the consent of his subjects. There is a variety of officials in such societies concerned with administration of the *Law*, the allocation of rights in land, the enforcement of the rulers' decisions, and so on.

It is only in the very smallest societies that there could be a doubt, in, say, the Bushmen of the Kalahari Desert in southern Africa, or the pigmies who inhabit the forests of central Africa. Some of the observers of such tiny societies (albeit observing them at a very late, and to some extent degenerate, phase of their history) have been tempted to deny that such peoples 'have law'. It is not the failure of such people to conform to the norms of their society which causes such observers to deny that there is law among them; quite the contrary, it is the rarity of any contestation, whether of the norms or of their application, that suggests, or causes analysts to assert, that 'they lack law'. This approach would clearly and swiftly lead to an unacceptable paradox: a society which is completely law-abiding, and indeed is so law-abiding that there are no occasions for argument as to what is the relevant norm in any particular circumstance, would be deemed to be anarchical and lawless! It may be riposted that there is an alternative, viz. that such a society is what we may term a completely 'discretionary' society; i.e. there are no fixed and premeditated rules or norms of behaviour; each member of the society does what he wishes to, or thinks best in the circumstances; in other words, an outside observer could detect no regularities of behaviour in such a society. But this is not the case with such small societies in Africa; no one asserts that the Bushmen or the pigmies lived in a social organisation like that; it contradicts what we have just described as the predominant characteristic of such societies, and is in any case a formal impossibility. Imagine a completely formless assembly of persons, e.g. four friends who have decided to go for a day's outing to the seaside in England. If those four are to reach the same spot on the coast at the same time, then there must be means of decision of disputes which may arise; in a completely discretionary society each would go his own way. So much for a single expedition; if the friends habitually went on such expeditions, a practice for deciding where to go, how to pay for it, and so on would soon establish itself.

The Bushmen and the pigmies both live in environments which are hostile, and where mutual association for protection and the getting or gathering of food is essential to survival. In such circumstances there is the strongest of motives for the avoidance of disputes, which would divide and perhaps destroy the group. In other words, it is asserted that even for such tiny societies there are norms of behaviour; these norms are infrequently referred to or invoked (any more than the conventions observed by passengers on Tube trains are either formally emitted, referred to, or frequently invoked). Since norms do not make themselves, what makes them is the willingness of those subjected to them to conform their behaviour to these latent norms. Occasionally there may be reinforcement and overt formulation of such norms if a problem arises. There is no court, in the sense of a formal structure staffed by wigged and learned gentlemen; but it would be an absurdity of the comparative method to deny a similarity of perceived social function to any institution differing from our own. There are ways, in other words, in which disputes may be settled, rare though they are; the persons with the socially approved and defined role in the settlement of disputes will be the leader(s) of each band or group, aided by the adult members of it. The head of the group has a role in the administration of his tiny society, limited though this is.

In such tiny societies almost totally, and in larger traditional societies to a large extent, there is no formal legislation, if by that we mean self-conscious and express formulation of norms designed to be of general future application. Does this mean that if we subtract such legislation, even giving the term an extended sense, the rest of the putative legal norms are 'not really *Law*'? That 'custom' is king, and that custom is not law? The argument seems to turn around the absence of a defined legislator, that is, a socially recognised emitter or declarer of general norms, an authority with power to 'make law'. There is no such legislator, the circular argument goes, because there are no secondary rules which specify who has such authority or power.

This conclusion, and the justifications for it, must both be categorically denied. Our reasons for this denial are to be sought in empirical observation of actual societies, which have such equipment. That the legislator and his mode of operation do not present themselves in the same form as we are accustomed to in the 20th century should not disturb us one whit; it is the function and not the form that counts. Hart, and those who adhere to his analysis at this point, would doubtless reply that in that case such societies do not fall within the theoretical description of 'social structures with primary rules of obligation only' with which Hart commences his treatment of the question. This point has already been dealt with above; if the hypothetical societies do not 'really' exist or correspond to anything in the known world, then one is wasting one's time in discussing them. However, in case this is not the correct way to dispose of this argument, and to avoid the attachment by innuendo of allegations of imperfection to customary legal systems generally, something must be said about the processes by which norms are emitted and identified (= legislation) in such societies. That there are latent, if not express, norms available in such societies can easily be tested by any observer who conducts a field-work investigation there; if he asks his informants in such a society what their rules are in respect of a particular matter of conduct in society, his informants are generally prepared to reply immediately with an expression of the relevant norms; or to say in rarer cases that they are not sure; or that the matter has never arisen as yet but if it did then the decision might go such-and-such a way. In what way is this different from asking professors of law in western societies about the norms of *Law* in such societies? They too might reply that such-and-such norms are settled; in other cases there might be a doubt, because, say, of the conflict of two principles; and in yet other cases they might respond that the question has not yet arisen, so that any determination would be speculative. There are norms 'in the air', then; but many of them are not in the air, and firmly anchored to the ground by reason of their having been enunciated and relied on in legal disputes within living memory.

The shaping of the norms owes much to the behaviour of those in the society who are potentially affected by them; the expression of them in more precise form owes much to persons involved in disputes, and especially those having socially recognised authority to attempt to settle disputes. The fact that such persons with authority may include (e.g. among the Kikuyu or other acephalous societies) partisans of one side or another is neither here nor there; society is always waiting to give its support or lack of support to the determination of rights and norms; and the fact that the parties participate in 'making law' is of no greater moment than the fact that parties to a contract or an industrial dispute in England do likewise. What matters is the social recognition and approval of the result.

The 'weaknesses' of customary Law

We turn now to the second challenge. Customary *Law*? may exist, but it is said that it lacks many of the necessary requirements of an effective legal system: it is not fixed and certain; it is not sharp and precise in its application; it is not adaptable; it is not effectively complied with because there are no effective sanctions.

What must surprise a scholar specialising in the study of such systems is that each of these accusations could be counterbalanced by a mirror-image alleged weakness in the opposite sense. Alien observers of customary *Law* have in the past sometimes attacked it on the grounds that: (i) it was too fixed in its formulation; (ii) it was too mechanical and rigid in its application (no 'equity'); (iii) it was so flexible and adaptable to different social circumstances and problems that it could not be said to have fixed rules; (iv) it was effectively complied with because it relied on social sanctions (e.g. ostracism, banishment from the group) or supernatural sanctions (the curse or taboo) which were much more effective than modern western secular sanctions.[9]

Which set of assertions, if either, is right? The answer is, both or neither. Each exaggerates; and the charges in each wing of the attack could as well be brought against modern western law.

Let us take each of the allegations in turn.

Lack of certainty. There is in such 'primitive' societies, it is averred, a lack of fixity or certainty in the normative rules of behaviour. This is because there is no authoritative person, text or procedure to which reference can be made in case of doubt. This is self-proving, because if such an authority exists, then there are secondary rules and the society does not fall into Hart's class of societies with rules of primary obligation only. Ross goes further: 'anyone's account of the directive is correct . . .'. The Hartian attack relates only to his presumptive 'primitive' societies; Ross's relates to all societies in which there are customs, if there is no 'judicial authority'. Since some of the obloquy rubs off from the mythical primitive societies onto the rest, we shall treat this as a general assault on societies in which customary rules are the sole or main form of law.

To repeat a point, one is struck in investigating this kind of society by the readiness of adult and aware members of the community generally to cite norms which they take as well settled. The difficulty is not about the general existence, certainty and citability of norms, but about the way in which such norms are applied in the society. A different criticism sometimes levelled is that the normative rules are of such a general character as to provide no sure guide to the solution of any particular dispute, and that what is lacking is detailed rules of application (quite apart from questions of enforcement and sanctions). The citations from the literature to contradict these points could be multiplied; to

9. Space does not allow a documented history of each of these (sometimes mutually contradictory) assertions; but by way of example one may refer to Brandford Griffith CJ's, well-known assertion about Ghana (Gold Coast) customary law that it had no fixed rules and 'It generally consists of the performance of the reasonable in the special circumstances of the case'.

avoid emphasizing the obvious, such citations will be taken solely from accounts of *Law* in societies which these critics might argue lack 'judicial authorities'. It must be strenuously emphasized that we have to rely in large measure on late accounts by anthropologists and others working in the colonial and post-colonial periods, the reconstruction of the way the *Law* was when these societies were unaffected by western ideas and demands is necessarily to a certain extent tentative. Western rule and legal influence have had many effects on the indigenous customary *Law*; the most serious are that (i) the western colonial legal system introduced a competitive system of *Law* which its subjects might choose in lieu of customary *Law*; (ii) customary *Law* was made subject to the formal and substantive requirements of an alien legal code; (iii) the traditional authorities who proclaimed and administered the customary *Law* were changed, restricted or abolished; (iv) the life-styles of these subject to the *Law*, and the economic background, were both radically altered by outside influences; (v) there was a wearing away of the ordinary person's knowledge of, and respect for, the traditional *Law*. In the result, we are in the presence of a decaying legal system when we look at modern African customary *Law*.

The American legal anthropologist Sally Falk Moore summarised the general position in regard to anthropological investigations of African customary *Laws* thus:

'In many courts and in many cases there are wide choices to be made by judges among applicable norms, and suitable ones could be found to rationalize a variety of decisions. Norms are often general and subject to a considerable range of interpretation. Even where the applicable norm is clear, alternative decisions are often possible on the ground of the adequacy or inadequacy of the evidence. There is also in the background the possibility of judicial innovation. All these complicate the process of decision, and make norms something less than automatic guides to decision. But whatever the *real reasons* for a judicial decision, norms are frequently explicitly cited or referred to by implication to support decisions. Often this is taken at face value. It is assumed that the norms cited by judges determine their choices. But the place of norms in judicial decisions is much more complex than that.[10]

Moore is speaking of 'judges' here, but she is using the term in a broad sense, inspired by a discussion by Gulliver of dispute-settlement among the Arusha of Tanzania, who were a chiefless and ? judgeless society. What she has to say will not shock or surprise us: it fits in exactly with the thesis put forward in Chapter 1. This is that every judge or person called on to apply a norm does so by a process of 'matching' of the hypothetical model situation and the actual facts of the case. This matching is inevitably crude. A further looseness is introduced by the

10. 'Politics, procedures and norms in changing Chagga law' (1970) 40 Africa 321, at p. 323.

inherent ambiguities and limits of the language in which a legal normative statement is expressed. A norm purports to be a general prescription; unavoidably it cannot exactly fit any particular case; unavoidably there must be clash or conflict between two or more norms whose ambit appears to extend to the given case. This is nothing novel; the superior courts in England have to cope with the problem of competing norms every day of the week, as a glance through the English law reports will show. Which norm is to take precedence when a trespassing child is injured on property on which he has no right to be? − 1. A person who goes on property on which he has no explicit or implicit right to be cannot complain of harm that he suffers as a result. 2. The owner or occupier of land must use reasonable care to avoid harm being caused to those who may use that land. 3. Children are in a special category so far as the law is concerned, and special protective measures must be undertaken for them.[11]

So let us look at the Arusha of Tanzania, as described by Gulliver.[12] The Arusha, an offshoot of the Masai group of peoples of East Africa, abandoned their pastoral ways and settled down to agriculture on the slopes of Mount Meru in the 19th century. The Arusha lacked chiefs or judges in the sense in which these terms are applied to other African peoples, though they had a kinship and age organization, and they had recognised 'spokesmen' who were something of legal experts and who could speak for their groups (rather like QCs retained by two big commercial concerns in a commercial arbitration in England, save that the spokesmen were from within the group, and not professional outsiders). Gulliver's findings on norms among the Arusha are summarised by him as follows:

'... I shall content myself by asserting that among the Arusha there are, as in any society, commonly enunciated and accepted norms of behaviour. Arusha speak of *embukunoto*, pl. *imbukunot*. These norms are well known, and each is similarly enunciated everywhere in the country. Not all transgressions of norms precipitate disputes, of course; only those which seem to a person to injure his interests or welfare are, or at his volition can be, made subject to regulatory procedures ...

The norms themselves were invariably quoted during dispute discussions and this confused me further. I noted that the Arusha themselves were not worried by this gap [between the applicable norms and the actual decision in a case]; indeed they seldom commented on it, although it was sometimes large. After beginning to appreciate Arusha concentration on compromise, which would provide a mutually acceptable resolution of a dispute, I was almost inclined to describe them as cynical opportunists. If by that is meant "unprincipled", it is

11. *British Railways Board v Herrington* [1972] 1 All ER 749, HL. See below, at pp. 101 ff.
12. *Social control in an African society* (1963).

a wrong description of the Arusha in these matters. Clearly they recognise norms, and they hold them in great respect: they are what make Arusha different from other peoples with whom they come into contact. In their modern opposition to outside influences, and their desire and attempt to preserve their distinct way of life, they have in fact come to emphasise these norms, rather than passively take them for granted.[13]

The limitations on the application of Arusha legal norms, then, are *not* to be found in imprecisions or lack of certainty, but in the processes of bargaining by which actual disputes are settled. This arbitral element in Arusha dispute-settlement no more invalidates the notion that there are Arusha norms than the settlement of many if not most actions in the High Court in England out of court implies that there are no settled rules of *Law* in England. The disputes are the 'trouble-cases', as Llewellyn puts it, where the *Law* and the parties are in difficulties; we must not forget the much greater number of instances where there is conformity with norms and hence no dispute.

Are the Arusha unusual in African customary societies? No. Meek describes the Ibo of Nigeria, another mostly chiefless and 'judgeless' (in the crude sense) society or group of societies.[14] He comments briefly, at the end of his book which sets out the principles of Ibo *Law*, and which is replete with clear and sharp expressions of normative rules of behaviour, that:

'It is quite clear from our studies that even in days long antecedent to the spread of European influence the Ibo-speaking peoples were, in the widest sense of the term, a law-abiding people. They had well-established norms of conduct maintained by numerous institutions framed for the express purpose of preserving order and harmony within their immediate group, as well as a measure of equilibrium with neighbouring groups.'

Again, Meek shows that in traditional Ibo *Law* the settlement of disputes was as much as an arbitration as a trial, and that the so-called 'judges' had the function of collecting and expressing the general public opinion on the merits of the case, which was possible because of public presence and participation in the hearing of a dispute. 'Trials, therefore', says Meek, 'were often nothing more than an organized expression of public opinion' — a quite reasonable definition of '*Law*', one might think!

The Tiv of Nigeria are another acephalous society fairly recently described by Bohannan.[15] They too can be said to have traditionally no judges in a narrow sense (without conceding the point whether they

13. At p. 241.
14. C. K. Meek *Law and authority in a Nigerian tribe* (1937), at p. 336.
15. P. Bohannan *Justice and judgment among the Tiv* (1957).

have judges in the broader sense advocated here). Bohannan denies that
the Tiv have a 'corpus juris', as he describes it, by which he means a
body or discipline of law specially 'resystemized' for use by professional
judges in court. However, Tiv have norms and rules of *Law*:

'Among Tiv, the *jir* [= proceeding for settlement of dispute, meeting]
settles disputes. The judges or *mbajiriv* [= men of the *jir*; also *mbatarev*,
or elders] do so in terms of their knowledge of Tiv institutions; . . . The
"rules" in Tivland are the norms of institutions . . . There are only laws
and the norms of institutions . . .'[16]

[So far as proceedings concerning marriage are concerned] 'These
rules are not merely implicit in the cases, but are very often made
explicit by the Tiv themselves. They are rules of the sort that Llewellyn
and Hoebel have called "legal norms".[17]

(But this should be contrasted with an observation by Bohannan at
another place, apparently in conflict with the above, that 'The decision
[in a *jir*] seldom overtly involves a point of law, in the sense that we
think of a rule or a law.'[18])

As for the Kikuyu, an acephalous tribe of Kenya, in old Kikuyu law
there was, says Lambert,[19] a code of law:

'. . . the widely held view that Africans have not yet evolved a code of
law requires some qualification. Every tribe has a code, but it is a code
of general principles, not of detail. Every judgment must conform to
it, though the principles are applied with a latitude unknown in
European law . . .'

'. . . case law is a potent factor in the assessment of individual decrees.
A *muthamaki* or *mugambi* [two terms for an indigenous legal expert, an
elder specialising in deciding cases] depends for his judicial reputation
very largely on his knowledge of the principles on which the judgements
in previous cases have been based, and this, though theoretically it only
strengthens or reiterates early principles of common law and custom, in
practice tends to codify the detailed findings in celebrated cases into
precedents which acquire the force of law.'

Again, for the removal of doubts it must be said that the Kikuyu
traditionally did not have 'judges', though they did have legal experts
who assisted with the arbitration or settlement of cases.

There is no need to multiply the African instances: the message is
clear. There are well-known and settled norms of *Law*; there are
procedures for determining what they mean, through the opinions of

16. At pp. 96–7.
17. At p. 96.
18. At p. 19.
19. H. E. Lambert *Kikuyu social and political institutions* (1956), at pp. 118 and
    120.

authorities or experts and through popular decision or consensus. The process of fixing the ambit of such norms is a slow one, and is never completed; but exactly the same is true of the well-accepted norms of English common law. The norms are often more general in character than some of the precise rules contained in, say, the English Companies Act, so that they appear to fall within the category of 'principles' rather than 'rules' in some instances. But to admit this must not lead to a failure to notice the very many rules of African *Laws* which are as precise and detailed as any pedantic Chancery lawyer could ask for. Such rules may, for instance, specify in great detail the precise compensation to be paid for various kinds of injury; such rules may precisely lay down how one may get married, or divide an estate on death, or acquire entitlement to land, or assert a claim in court.

Static quality. The notion that customary *Laws* are ancient and immutable is contributed to by some of the verbal phrases and assertions of persons subject to those *Laws*. When such peoples claim that their customary *Law* is 'the law of the ancestors' or 'the law of long ago', they seem to give support to the thesis of Hart and Ross. Yes, *some* of their *Law* is traditional; some may even be ancient (on an African time-scale); but there are three things which must be said about the consequent implication that their *Law* is unchanging and static. The first is that a general principle of their *Law*, e.g. that proper respect must be shown to elders and persons in authority, may well be handed on from the past; but the meanings of such a principle, and the specific norms of behaviour which flow from it, can and will alter as the circumstances of the society alter, and as new ideas and practices develop. Exactly the same is true of some of the ancient principles of English law and equity. The procedure for the settlement of disputes in African societies (with its ready adaptation of the norms to changing circumstances, and the availability of a socially sanctioned and sanctioning authority – the respected chiefs or elders, the population in attendance) is well fitted to the development of the *Law ambulando*, as one might say. Secondly, customary *Laws* have in the past changed, and continue to change, rapidly and radically to meet new circumstances. From pre-colonial times one can cite, as just one example, the fundamental change in the property law of the Arusha; in modern times customary *Laws* have fundamentally altered in so many respects that it is not possible to isolate more than one or two instances here: e.g. radical changes in the law of marriage and divorce; completely new forms of land-holding, and new rules applying to old forms. Thirdly, the possibility of legislation – of frank and overt law-making – is present in every society. In all but the simplest, there was usually a recognised authority or set of authorities with institutional power to declare and amend laws. Every people we have mentioned in the discussion above had such an institution. In the very simplest and smallest societies, this function was performed by the head of the domestic group, or the religious functionary (if he was different), with the consensus of the group. No one familiar with the processes and pace of change in customary *Laws* in Africa (*not* due to the colonial incursion only) could accept for a moment the statement that the process of change was 'slow', or that those bound by them necessarily 'act as their fathers did'.

Still less would one accept the proposition that the changes, such as they were and are, were unthinking, 'unplanned, lacking calculation and rational understanding of a change in conditions' (Ross). This would be an excellent prescription for the making of an ill-adapted, and hence ineffective, law. Exactly the reverse is to be observed in African customary societies, for a very clear and simple reason. Such societies were much more 'marginal' than our own, by which I mean that they lived nearer to the margin of existence or non-existence. There are two ways in which such a society might cease to exist as it was: either the means of existence themselves (land, water, seeds) might be depleted if due regard was not paid to the exigencies of the environment; or the existence of the society as a single coherent group could be destroyed if fissiparous tendencies were reinforced or created. We, in our rich, resourceful, modern societies can afford the occasional error in our law-making, even if it causes social tension or uses up scarce resources; Africans living in their societies could not. The purpose and effect of any change, or indeed of any existing provision, would thus be closely scrutinised and rationally considered. That the understanding of members of such societies was not the same as our own goes without saying — after all, they lacked most of our scientific knowledge; that their idea of what is rational varies from our own is also patent; but, in terms of their own understanding and reasoning, any change had to be well thought out. Sometimes, because of the marginality of existence, chances could not be taken with innovations; to that extent I suppose one could say that there was a tendency towards keeping what one had got; but a similar conservative policy has not yet been proved to be a bad strategy in our own world too. In other words, openness to change does not mean acceptance of any proposal for change without close attention to the feasibility of what is proposed.

It is not the case, and many documented accounts of African *Laws* show this, that change in the customary *Laws* was only through 'the slow process of growth' (Hart). On the contrary, to repeat an earlier point, facilities for legislation in the overt sense are generally found. Organic growth and decay also occur; but then this is a characteristic too of developed western systems. We accordingly reject the proposition that customary *Laws* were, and necessarily were by their nature, static.

The ineffectiveness of customary law. This objection is a purely book objection. It derives from a concern with sanctions as well as with the alleged lack of authoritative institutions for the administration of the *Law*. One does not want to recoil from the picture of a so-called *Law* which is never observed or effectively enforced only to step back into the pit of the mechanical and automatic observance of custom, a story with which an earlier generation of writers used to regale us: unthinking automata went about their business, moving in response to the binding force of custom: Custom was King.

Effectiveness of the *Law* is measured by compliance with it. Could the impartial observer say, when comparing a traditional African society with a modern western one, that there was less compliance in the former than the latter? Sidestepping the question of how one quantifies the degree of compliance with any legal system, and remaining only at the impressionistic level, one could not come to such a conclusion — quite the reverse. Take only penal law as an example. The long queue of offenders waiting to pass through the English courts (literally in their millions per annum) cannot be matched by similar millions of offenders in traditional Africa. The offender, and his offence, are in Africa the disturbing exception rather than the norm. Nor in Africa was there a dark mass of unreported, undetected or unconvicted crime, as there is in England with, say, burglary (less than 10 per cent conviction rate) or rape.

The reasons for this difference are not far to seek. Small village communities in Europe have much less crime than the national average; there are islands off Scotland which have neither crime nor policemen. The reasons are the same as explain the paucity of infringements in small African societies which occur or which go undetected or are not dealt with: they are that in a small community it is difficult in the first place for someone to do something without the rest of the community soon being aware that it has been done, and who has done it. Unexplained occurrences, e.g. the theft of cattle, a hut destroyed, a girl attacked, are much easier to investigate, and it is much easier in the small, closed society to find out who is responsible. The offender may be able to avoid retribution only by removing himself from the community altogether by flight; in this case the primary objective of the legal system, the preservation of harmony within the community, will have been achieved. Anonymity and largeness (the two go together) are the enemies of effective *Law*. Many small communities traditionally had special means of finding out who was responsible for unattributed harm and of punishing those responsible. These means comprised the use of conditional curses or spells on the unknown malefactor, oracles and divination, and the like. The invocation of the supernatural may seem to us irrational; that it was and is effective is evidenced by all the literature and by personal observation. It works because people believe it will work — exactly the same reason why *Law* works in modern societies![20] To use supernatural means which have been proved to be

20. Cf. p. 39 above.

effective to detect or punish crime or prevent its recurrence is at least as rational as to use policemen, criminal trials or prison to detect, punish and prevent crime in Britain (all proved to be in some measure ineffective).

In societies like the Bushmen or the Nuer, which are split into a large number of autonomous units, it may happen that a crime occurs, e.g. a wounding, or a kidnapping of a woman, where the person responsible comes from outside the unit. Such a crime is not within the domestic or municipal legal system at all. It is an 'international' wrong. The customary equivalent of international law must then be relied on for its remedying. Retaliation, feud or arbitration leading to payment of compensation may be the methods used to obtain redress or a counterbalancing penalty. It is freely conceded that some of these methods may be unsuccessful on occasion, that might may triumph over right; the same is naturally and only too frequently true of international wrongs between States in the modern world. But the fact cannot be used to impugn the effectiveness of the domestic, internal *Law*.

The effectiveness of detection of wrongdoing within the customary community is not the end of the story. The probability of a satisfactory settlement of the resultant dispute is much higher. Again the reasons are fairly obvious once they have been pointed out. Two factors work in the direction of a successful outcome. The first is the will of the wrongdoer to make amends. He may deny or bluster about the particular grievance to begin with; but most wrongdoers at the end of the day wish to be re-accepted into the community, and to meet the necessary requirements which will allow them to be so accepted. The second factor largely explains the first; it is the effectiveness of social pressures radiated from the rest of the community who in one sense are not partisan in the conflict, though highly committed in another sense to a peaceful settlement. Harmony within the group is a paramount good; respect for its norms is of equal importance. The two principles operate in counterpoint — sometimes one, sometimes the other will dominate. This explains the references, for instance in the passages from Gulliver and Lambert quoted earlier,[21] to the Arusha 'concentration on compromise', even at the expense of the settled norms, and to the fact that the traditional Kikuyu arbitration applied the principles of *Law* 'with a latitude unknown in European law'. Lying behind the persuasiveness of the community members, who can participate in the procedures for the settlement of a dispute, there is both an appeal and a threat. The appeal is to the parties to abandon their dispute on terms acceptable to both sides; the threat is that, if one or the other side obstinately refuses to come to terms, there may be a partial or total withdrawal of community support from them, both physical (no help with labour or in time of famine) and psychological, maybe leading to sending to Coventry or even expulsion.

21. See pp. 57 and 59.

Now for sanctions and enforcement procedures. It would be quite wrong to ignore the evidence that in many African customary *Laws* there have been problems with enforcement. The usual picture presented is of judicial or arbitral proceedings for the settlement of disputes, in which the decision of the proceeding is that X should do or pay such-and-such, but there is no efficient enforcement mechanism to compel him to do or pay what is ordered. In response to this possibly damaging assertion, one can begin by eliminating those societies where there were chiefs − centralised authorities equipped with agents and power to secure compliance with their orders. We are left only with some of the chiefless societies, typically ruled by councils of elders so far as local or clan communities are concerned, or by family heads and councils in the case of family and lineage groups. Here the warning given earlier about the dangers of jobbing backwards from the modern era into the traditional pre-colonial era becomes especially relevant. The effect of colonial rule was to remove many of the sanctions which had traditionally existed. When warfare and raiding (for slaves or property) were endemic between communities, an outcast from a particular community was in every sense an 'outlaw': there was no *Law* to protect him. To be cast out of the community was almost equivalent to a sentence of death. Colonial rule brought 'peace, order and good government' and the suppression of such a powerful sanction. If one is cast out of a community today, one can move to another, or go to the city for work. Secondly, customary *Laws* recognised many forms of supernatural and social sanctions, whose effectiveness we have already mentioned; many of these in their turn have been suppressed by colonial legislation, which declared, say, that practising witchcraft was a major criminal offence, so that preventive or protective use of spells might be a crime rather than a means of dealing with crime. Forcible seizure of a wrong-doer's property and its devastation by order of the elders − one typical sanction − became, in terms of the imported *Law*, a lawless act. This is not a treatise on traditional customary procedure, so no complete documentation on all these practices can be given here; but the interested reader can have a look at some of the practices and the texts mentioned in a footnote.[1]

1. Cf. the Kikuyu and Kamba *king'ole*: for which see Lambert, op. cit., 79, and D. J. Penwill, *Kamba customary law* (Kampala, 1972); this was the use of the warriors by the elders to round up and kill a heinous criminal. For seizure of property in execution of judgments or punishment of offenders, see, e.g., for the Kikuyu, Lambert, 129 and 138; for the Ibo, see Meek, op. cit., 209. For the use of supernatural means of enforcement, see, for the Kikuyu, Lambert, 122 ff.; for the Tiv, see Bohannan, op. cit., 68 (elders threaten to withdraw supernatural protection of offender against witchcraft); for the Ibo, see Meek, 340; for the use of ostracism and outlawry, see, for Ibo, Meek, 209 (exile in case of homicide), 217 (use of public ridicule as punishment for thief); for the Tiv, Bohannan, 126 (ridicule of thief); for the Kikuyu, Lambert, 129 (ceremonial form of ostracism imposed to deal with continued failure to comply with order of arbitral bench), 114 (expulsion of habitual offender from clan).

Quite apart from all these forms of enforcement procedure, two common features of African customary *Laws* greatly increased compliance with norms and with implementing orders made under them. The first of these was the recognition of *self-help*. Self-help, or self-right-enforcement, means that the injured party, armed with an order of a court or proceeding, or otherwise entitled under the norms of his society, ensures compliance by the wrongdoer through his own (i.e. the enforcer's) act. In this form of right-enforcement the injured party may often have his family group, kin, or age-group to help him. Self-help was a very common remedy in all types of African society, though many chiefly societies discouraged it as tending to interfere with the chief's monopoly of coercive power. Self-help is not lawlessness; it is the socially (=legally) approved enforcement of a right by the right-holder himself, alone or aided by other members of the community. In such circumstances the self-helper is an agent of society and an institution of the *Law*.

Self-help is sometimes thought of by jurists as a primitive form of procedure, which is found only in undeveloped legal systems and which marks out those systems as being in some way deficient. Modern systems by contrast, it is assumed, do not need (or even positively prohibit) such self-help, as contradicting the notions of law and order and the function of the community as guarantor of them. But this appears to be an inadequate analysis. If we take the whole course of a proceeding for the enforcement of a right, from the first occasion when the right-holder finds his right challenged to the final assertion of his right by remedial action against the challenger, the correct question to ask is, 'At what stages are a personal initiative and personal action by the right-holder required if his right is to be asserted and protected?'. Phrased in these terms, the question relates as much to the initiation of proceedings as to their conclusion. Now it is a quite obvious point that, without an initial complaint or even more positive action by an injured party, no civil action and very few criminal actions would be commenced in England and English *Law* today. Even after the initiation of proceedings, if the complainant or the plaintiff as the case may be fails to prosecute his charge or claim the proceedings will fail – the court and other agencies of the state will do nothing to help him if he is idle. The criminal case before a magistrates' court (as most are) will be dismissed if the prosecutor fails to appear, or fails to marshal enough evidence; the civil action will be dismissed for want of prosecution. The initiator of legal proceedings must in England move swiftly if he wants a remedy: within six months for summary charges, within the limitation period (six years for tort and contract claims) in civil proceedings.

Let us assume the complainant wins. Whereas in criminal cases the court (acting for the state) now takes over responsibility for enforcement of, say, a fine awarded by the court, in civil proceedings the initiative continues to rest with the plaintiff. If there is no compliance with the order of the court, the plaintiff must move the court or nothing will be done. At every stage, then, the injured or complaining party must 'help himself'; if he does so in the correct form, the state will give him support and validate his action. It is just the same with self-help in traditional African societies.

The second feature of traditional African *Laws* to which we call attention as being a major contribution to effectiveness of the norms is *group responsibility* and involvement in legal proceedings. It is the normal case that in African customary *Laws* a person's family or kinship group was responsible for his actions, or at least habitually participated in any proceedings which called those actions in question. Vicarious responsibility of this kind, demonstrated most clearly in homicide cases where the dispute was often between the family groups of the killer and the slain, led to the imposition of collective sanctions on the group responsible. Such a sanction might consist of the payment of compensation, or, where this was not possible or acceptable, of possible feud or retaliation against the persons or the property of the offender's group. A family group would also customarily participate in the prosecution of a claim by one of its members. This double reinforcement greatly added to the effectiveness of procedures, and at the same time increased the degree of public participation and public concern in the achievement of a satisfactory outcome.

What is so clearly missing from modern English law is any comparable feature. Even less than many other 'civilised' systems of law, English *Law* fails to recognise any vicarious liability by one group or person for the act or omission of another. Our surviving bits of vicarious liability are almost entirely outside the family sphere, and do not touch the local community sphere; they concern instead the liability of an employer or a principal for the deeds of his employee or agent. In a way insurance companies in modern England are involved, like the family groups of traditional Africa, in the settlement of claims; but for them to be involved there must first of all have been a voluntary initiative on the part of the offender, through his having taken out appropriate insurance. It may be that a large part of the ineffectiveness of modern English *Law* can be attributed to this gap.

Our conclusion on this point can therefore be simply and categorically expressed. Traditional customary *Laws* on the whole achieved much fuller compliance than modern western *Laws*. The sanctions, if we are interested in them, were generally more effective. If there is to be a comparison, modern systems of *Law* come worse out of it. It is not the case that 'disputes always occur ... and continue interminably' in customary societies (Hart); fewer disputes occur than in western societies, and although it may well be that more community time is spent on discussing them than in modern England, the results are usually more satisfactory and the *Law* proved more effective. There are effective means for dealing with violation of (mandatory or prohibitory) norms.

The case against customary *Laws* and against the existence or efficacy of legal norms in small societies is not made out. The smallness of a society does not limit either the existence or the effectiveness of *Law*, though the smaller and simpler the society, the less *Law* there will have to be.

B LIMITS FROM THE AMBITIONS OF THE LEGISLATOR

Judged purely by volume, then, there are fewer norms, i.e. less *Law*, in such simpler societies; and the norms may (as previous quotations suggest) be less detailed in their prescriptions. Is there something which inhibits the law-maker in such societies from making norms, or from making norms of the detailed kind we are familiar with in the west?

Yes, the legislator in such societies has inhibitions, and these may prevent him from making laws as freely as he would do in a modern state. To explain and discuss this thesis, we must go back to our discussion of affirmative law, of strong and weak commands, prohibitions, and permissions, and to the observations on the relationship between the law-maker and society which were made in this connexion.[2]

It was said (at p. 48) that the legislator, when making an 'affirmative' law, may in the alternative (i) express the convictions of his society; or (ii) be at odds with the society; or (iii) be inspired by no settled view in the society, either for or against his proposed law. Where the legislator expresses by his law the convictions of his society, he secures greatly increased reinforcement for his legal message; where his law contradicts the view of society, he weakens it. There is a great temptation in modern societies for the legislator to be at odds with his society, or to attempt to impose on his society through law a view which it does not yet hold. If we quote Britain to begin with, it is generally accepted that the law abolishing capital punishment for murder would be repealed tomorrow if the law expressed the convictions of society (c. 80 per cent in favour of hanging). It is the same with many other modern British laws (e.g. giving privileges to trade unions). The enactments on race relations and on equal opportunities for women can be seen as an attempt by a legislator to impose his view of society on a society without a formed view, or perhaps with contradictory views in the matter.

The picture is no more encouraging in underdeveloped countries. Radical changes in, say, family and marriage laws have been made by a wave of the legislator's wand: one of the most extreme examples has been in the Ivory Coast, where the legislator purported to abolish completely the customary systems of marriage and the family, substituting solely a system of monogamous marriage and the small, parent-dominated, nuclear family. An equally extreme example was the

2. See pp. 46–9.

legislation abolishing inferior legal and social status for 'untouchables' in India.[3] Legislators in under-developed countries constantly seek to produce a new society by legislation; Tanzania has sought to impose a 'socialist' family and economic structure on the people through its *ujamaa* laws and practices.[4] There are uncountable other examples.

It will be part of the general thesis of this book that, although some laws of this kind may eventually succeed, more will fail; and that, through failing, they will tend to weaken the *Law* of which they form part. The main reasons for their failure will include (though not being confined to) the lack of agreement between law-maker and society.

What this means is that the modern legislator has developed ambitions which take him beyond the limits set by the nature of *Law* in earlier societies, and the constraints which that nature imposed on overt law-making. Laws are dangerous weapons, as devastating and as apparently powerful in their effects as the sub-machine guns of the professional criminal. The loss of inhibitions by the modern legislator in the more activist governments serves to highlight two things: first, the nature of the inhibitions which operate in simpler societies; and secondly, the existence of new reasons for limits on the effectiveness of *Law*. We must look now at these inhibitions in the context of the general relationship between law-maker and society in customary societies. Again, we shall take Africa as our source of examples.

The inhibitions on the legislator in a traditional society largely governed by customary *Law* consist first in the fact that in a number of different ways *the society itself* may be the law-maker. Norms, as we have described them, have a certain latency, especially in such societies, until they have been sufficiently acted upon and invoked or formulated by those with recognised authority to enunciate them. The strengthening and fixing of norms in this way take place partly through the actions of persons who thereby comply with these norms, and partly in their express emission in appropriate situations, whether of conflict or otherwise. In each type of event members of the society play a full, indeed a major, part. The persons called on in some of the chiefless societies we have already discussed have as their role the enunciation of the common conviction of the community, rather than the imposition on that community of their personal views. This is not to say that such 'spokesmen' (as they are in more senses than one) can never take the legal initiative, either by reformulating and amplifying old norms or even by proposing a new one; indeed, reports from many such societies say that leaders who can do this sort of thing thereby acquire their reputation for wisdom and understanding of the *Law*. But if the spokesman, as arbiter, judge, or formulator of norms, emits a norm which already conforms to the general acceptance of the community, then he does not innovate in a way which contradicts the view of society; on the

3. See pp. 214–7 below.
4. And see p. 195 below, and also at p. 302.

contrary, he expresses it. If he emits a normative statement which is new, it will be of no effect unless the community concurs in it. He is 'proposing' law rather than making it.

This type of activity goes on mostly in judicial or arbitral proceedings where rights have to be considered and claims adjusted; the community's participation, and the parties' acceptance, are law-making. But there is also overt law-making in non-conflict situations. In chiefless societies it is often the elders who perform this role. Surely this gives them a chance as legislators to behave like modern European law-makers, and seek to impose their view on society? Now authority is a well-accepted concept in African society, and this means that the right and power of those having authority to exercise it are conceded. Elders in such societies obtain their authority either by their own personal qualities (which may be recognised by some special ceremony or form of acceptance) or by their status, e.g. that they are the members of the now-ruling generation, or that each is the senior in his family grouping. With such authority the elders can command behaviour from those subject to them; but it is not an unlimited and absolute authority. Often the importance of popular acceptance is demonstrated by a customary requirement that a new law should be formally and publicly accepted by those to be subjected to it: thus among the Embu (close relatives of the Kikuyu) Lambert tells us that:

'. . . acceptance of a new law is demonstrated on such occasions [at a customary religious ceremony] by a slow and rhythmical clapping of hands by the public present.'[5]

Authority is recognised, then, in the acephalous, elder-governed, societies as well as in the chiefly ones. A person with authority can propose or even seek to impose new norms on those responsive to his authority; to a certain extent such actions demonstrate that he has authority, and is prepared to exercise leadership. But the constraints which hold back the would-be legislator are many. First, there are the constraints of the society and its economic setting. Then there are the constraints set by the need for effectiveness; nothing, quite obviously, destroys authority and the right to command quicker than the perception that the commander's wishes are not complied with. Now, when we compare traditional African societies with modern western societies one of the features which must strike us is that the linkages and gearing between social authorities and those subject to them are much tighter and more numerous in them than in modern societies. The feedback loops are there, attaching to the commander and his commands. By contrast, in western society the legislator, and indeed the court, is detached; what feedback there is, if there is any, is indirect, low-geared, and ineffective. This is most obvious with western courts, where

5. Op. cit., p. 138.

strenuous attempts are made specifically to detach judges from social pressures in the interests of their impartiality. The contempt law, the constitutional principles which help to preserve the independence of the judiciary, and the absence of any mechanism for the feeding in of the popular view on the law so as to modify its operation in practice, such as one constantly finds in traditional African society, all serve to insulate, isolate, and detach the judges from the people.

This is not to ignore the ways in which popular influence on law can be exercised in Anglo-American *Laws*. We consider these in detail in a later Chapter of this work.[6] The most notable of them is the institution of the jury; through it the ordinary people, by their refusal to convict, can effectively veto a criminal law which they dislike. But the jury does this in despite of, and not through, the formal rules of the *Law*, which obliges them, by the jurors' oath, to 'faithfully try the several issues joined between Our Sovereign Lady the Queen and the prisoner at the bar and give a true verdict according to the evidence'. By this oath the jury must 'faithfully' try the case, that is, in accordance with the law of the land, and give a 'true' verdict, which must mean a verdict on the facts as proved to them and as a result of faithfully applying the current law of the land to those facts. The oath does *not* license the jurors to disregard a law of which they disapprove. Contrariwise in African customary *Law*, in which the people participating in the trial of a case help to *make* the *Law*, or show their assent or dissent to any rule or principle put forward by those in authority. This is not a breach of their *Law*, but an essential feature of it. Nor of course does western *Law* permit what is common practice in many African *Laws*, viz. the constructing of a new law in the course of a case by dialogue between court, parties, and people.

In modern democratic societies with constitutions on the Westminster or liberal models, one might think that there is a nexus between legislator and people, and a feedback mechanism, represented by the people's right to elect or refuse to re-elect its law-makers from time to time. However, if we look only at the modern British constitution, which after all has been evolved by the law-makers rather than by those subject to them, one might almost say that it has been expressly designed so as to reduce any such feedback to a minimum. First, the feedback is generalised and diffuse; it is not particular to any given law. If the people do not like a new law, there is no immediate comeback for them, other than a refusal to observe it. Secondly, the feedback is delayed: unless there is a revulsion of feeling in Parliament, which leads those who normally support the government of the day to withdraw that support, then the unpopular law-maker with his unpopular law will not be turned out of office until the statutory life of Parliament is ended. Even then, the law-maker will be willing to take his chance that by then

6. See pp. 90 ff. below.

the objection will have been forgotten, or that the electorate may be willing to waive it in the interest of securing some other promised good.

There is, in the British constitution, no provision for referendums on new projects of law; no retrospective referendums for the repeal of existing laws; no right of recall, by which the electorate can demand that their representative should expose himself again to election to see if his actions are supported. The whole consultative machinery, of Green Papers, White Papers, Royal Commissions, public inquiries and the rest, does not bind the government of the day to make or unmake law. Often they can be cynically disregarded, fixed in advance, or shelved. To ask that such feedback features should be inserted in the British constitution (or at least considered for insertion) is not to demand the impossible or the unworkable; such procedures are already part of many modern constitutions, from Switzerland to California. The humblest peasant society in many parts of the world treats their equivalents as self-evidently necessary.

What concerns us here is the consequence of this tremendous gap in the functioning of the British constitution. We find it a classic case of power without responsibility. 'Responsibility' means 'answerability'; if we are responsible, we must answer for our actions. If we are legislators with power to make laws delegated to us by the people, we must answer to the people for the laws we make or do not make. 'The privilege of the harlot down the ages' corrupts those who exercise power unchecked by any immediate reactive control. The corruption of the British legislative class is demonstrated by their works: not that those works are all or necessarily evil or wrong in themselves — that is not the question; but that those works are imposed by persons in authority conscious of their authority and conscious of the fact that there is no effective control over that authority. It is an irony that, in the modern would-be egalitarian and democratic system which Britain now possesses, overweening elitism has a freer hand than it did in the aristocratic England of the 18th and 19th centuries, when Dukes exercised political power as to the manner born.

The contrast between modern Britain and traditional African societies can best be put graphically.

The spread of social attitudes in a given society is marked by the upper and lower limits: progressive and conservative. It slowly changes against Time. We thus get the band, broader or narrower, shown on the graph. Customary law-making (broken line) operates within this band. Sometimes it wanders somewhat to the progressive side, sometimes to the more conservative; but it does not step outside the limits of the band itself.

Law-making in modern Britain (dotted line) moves in a series of step-wise developments. Left to itself, the *Law* will gradually lag behind social attitudes, falling below the conservative limit. Law-making tends to take the *Law* above the band of general social attitudes,

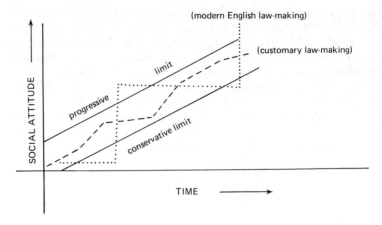

the law-maker hoping that the social attitudes will eventually catch up with his law. There is no necessary reason why they should do so. A law, whether it is above or below the band of societal attitudes, has nothing to lean on but itself. Now the elitist legislator, even if ultra-progressive in his attitudes, may be said to fall within the band of social attitudes; and so it may be argued that this presentation is defective, and that *all* legal change, save where it is imposed by an incoming alien conqueror, must spring from existing social attitudes, however few people may share them. In one way this is true; our visual presentation is necessarily crude. But the message we want to convey is that the elitist legislator may hold attitudes outside the *common* range of *general* social attitudes in his society; and the band should be interpreted in this sense.

3 Limits of communication, reception, or acceptance

An enquiry into the ordinary Englishman's perception of Law

A LAW THE UNKNOWN

There is no need to recapitulate the points sufficiently made in earlier Chapters, that a law can only be effective if communicated, and that there are various obstacles to effective communication and reception of law. We have seen that in traditional African, and other customary small-scale, societies there was generally an efficient communication and reception of laws; the inadequacies of the ordinary English person's acquaintance with law have also been mentioned. Now it is time to look in greater detail at the limits of the knowledge, which is to say the limits of the ignorance, of the *Law* in England and Wales. I do not discuss the situation in other countries, because their situation is generally unknown to me; as for African and other countries directly influenced by English *Law*, these will be the subject of a separate enquiry, because they represent examples of the phenomenon of *translocation of laws*, where a legal system has been exported from the society which gave it birth, and imposed on another (and almost certainly quite different) society. The ignorance we are now after is that which is endogenous. Alongside illiteracy and innumeracy, the inability to understand or work with words or numbers, we must now set *anomia*, the lack of *Law* or lawlessness.[1]

A society which is anomic or the bulk of whose members are anomic cannot function well, just as modern technological society depends on a sufficiency of literate and numerate people to run it, or even to respond to its road signs. It is therefore a grave condition in a society, such as that of England, if it appears that anomia is the predominant state of its members. Knowledge of, and consequent responsiveness to, the *Law* is not an optional extra for life in society. We can put forward the proposition that *unknown law is ineffective law*.

---

1. I use a form closer to the Greek, rather than 'anomy' or 'anomie', which have acquired secondary meanings of disorder rather than simple lack.

How far, in England and Wales, do the law-making processes provide for communication of their output to their subjects? How deep are the knowledge and understanding of the existing laws? Is there any popular awareness of the processes by which laws are made or administered? These are the questions which must be considered.

In answering them I shall not draw to any extent on empirical research into popular knowledge and understanding of laws. There are two reasons for this: an institutional one, and a personal one. The first reason is vital — there is little or no empirical research by sociologists, or sociolegal experts, into perceptions of *Law* in England. A certain amount of work has predictably been done in the criminal sphere; practically nothing, so far as I know, on the civil side. The second reason is that I personally am unfamiliar with scientific enquiries into the extent of the knowledge of the law in England, though I am familiar with similar enquiries into knowledge of customary *Laws* elsewhere, and I have been personally concerned in attempts to discover how far the ordinary citizen in an African country is aware of the non-customary laws which purport to regulate his life. I suspect that the reason for my unfamiliarity is the already mentioned lack of such studies. However, in various capacities, including that of Justice of the Peace, I have endeavoured to note from time to time the extent of knowledge of the *Law* shown by the ordinary citizen, and to make appropriate enquiries. My feelings and conclusions are thus to some extent subjective and unquantifiable. That this is so is a supporting argument for proper organised research into popular understanding and knowledge of *Law*. Setting up such a project (or set of projects, for this is what is required) is not a difficult task;[2] similar investigations are constantly made of a variety of other forms of knowledge or ignorance, of which we can mention just two. First, there are the various public opinion polls, which test the voter's awareness of current political controversies and problems, or his acquaintance with the names of the current rulers of Britain. The common message which comes out of such investigations is often the alarming ignorance of the ordinary person, and still more of the ordinary schoolchild; large numbers do not know the name of the Prime Minister, or the constitutional function of the Queen. Then there are the market research surveys, investigating perhaps the readiness of the consumer to take a new product, or his awareness of existing products.

2.   Some time ago I had the privilege of assisting a Norwegian research student who was making a sociological investigation of this very matter in English *Law*; the problems caused by attempting this research came mainly from its novelty, and from looking for an easy way of obtaining suitable informants. A native member of the society has only to investigate his friends and neighbours to begin with (*not* the proverbial taxi-driver!) to discover what is known and unknown in the legal field.

What we propose is another form of consumer research. The subjects of the *Law* are its consumers. Commercial concerns feel that it is worth their while to lay out millions of money to ascertain whether a product is acceptable or a facility is known. The law-maker should have a similar concern and a similar readiness to spend.

The law-making process and publicity

If we take (which would be wrong) law-making to be what happens in Parliament, then in theory 100 per cent publicity attends the process, as both newspapers and radio can now report verbatim what happens there. But this would be a complete misstatement of the way in which the media actually handle parliamentary news, as well as a complete misunderstanding of the nature of the law-making process. The newspapers read by the masses contain no parliamentary news, or, if they do, what they retail are trivialities and personalities, confrontations and conflicts, not the meat and substance of laws in the making. The 'quality' papers are little better; they may have parliamentary reports, but set them beside Hansard and one sees immediately that these reports do no more than lightly skim the surface of things. Anyone relying on newspapers to keep him abreast of the laws would be disappointed. At the most, he might learn that a new law had been introduced; it is certain that he would not learn exactly what the law provided, or, more important, how it meshed in with the existing legal system.

If the enquiring citizen turned to Hansard (and the difficulty is that he does *not* enquire), his situation would be little better. I remember well when the Community Land Act 1975 was going through its various parliamentary stages in both Houses, and when I tried to find out, through Hansard, the state to which the proposed law had come at different phases of this process — disentangling this from Hansard was an almost impossible task, even for the expert. When the Bill becomes an Act, if it does, the average citizen is less likely to see a copy of it than to climb Mont Blanc; if he could get hold of it, it is written in an abstruse language of which he can make out little; nor can he tell what effect it will have on him, or on the rest of the law. Even the expert lawyer must admit some bafflement when confronted with a statute such as the Community Land Act, the Rent Act, or the latest Finance Act. By an *a fortiori* argument, one can readily see that the ordinary citizen will be left in almost total darkness as to the meaning and effect, or even the very existence, of a new law. And this argument relates solely to overt and frank law-making by the body officially charged with this task; what about the covert law-making by courts, or by administrative bodies exercising their discretions?

The process of law-making attracts practically no publicity; what there is is ineffectual to convey any message to the intended recipients.

There the matter would rest unless other efforts were made to publicise the meaning and effect of laws. These are now examined, first, in regard to official publicity and propaganda, and secondly in regard to unofficial publicity.

Official publication of new laws

It is a relatively new phenomenon for the government, or one of its ministries or agencies, to publicise a law which has just been made (allegedly) by the legislative arm. In time of war laws requiring conscription, or registration, or other similar mobilisation of persons or goods, will be publicised through advertisements or leaflets. In peacetime such publicity is rare, and was (the conjecture requires verification) unheard of. In the last few years there has been an increase in the amount of government propaganda about new laws. In part this reflects the welfare revolution, and is an attempt to make people aware of their welfare rights; in part this reflects the workings of the bureaucratic or 'nanny' state. But from time to time a government department unleashes a volume of propaganda about a new law; the means it may use include radio and TV messages (exploiting the BBC's preparedness to carry official government messages though not private advertising), advertisements in newspapers, leaflets (especially those exhibited in Post Offices), and door-to-door circulars. It is instructive to see the topics to which this propaganda relates; in the last two or three years they have included:

- welfare rights – especially rights of 'claimants' to various new allowances, pensioners' allowances;
- housing law: rights of tenants under new protective legislation;
- race relations law;
- equal opportunities law;
- industrial and labour law;
- consumer credit law – here the advertisements are directed mainly not at the beneficiaries of the new law, as are most of the other categories of law advertised, but at the groups on whom new obligations are imposed, e.g. to register if in the business of lending money;
- other consumer protection.

Examination of this list helps to define the constituency to whom the advertisements are directed, as well as the kind of law which it is sought to publicise. Broadly the persons at whom the publicity is aimed are those without ready access to legal advice, and for whose benefit protective legislation has been enacted. These are the dependants of the welfare state, as defined by modern bureaucratic centralising socialistic law-makers. An even-handed publicisation of a new law would take an all-round view, and tell everyone – landlords, for instance, as well as tenants — what they should know of a new law for their own advantage. There is no suggestion of such an even-handed approach in our examples. In other words, what is being communicated is not a new law, but selected rights acquired under a new law.

By the side of this small amount of new law officially publicised by the government and its agencies we must set the vast amount of new law which receives no such publicity. What is *not* publicised? The short answer is, practically the whole of the statute book. Nor is there any attempt to publicise existing law, whether statutory or non-statutory. There is no publicity for facilities for marriage, although this might seem to be a welfare benefit accorded by the state legal system, no advertisements which say:

'You can get married! This is the procedure: do it now!'
There is no advertisement which spells out the citizen's power to make contracts:

'Make a contract today!'
Why not?

One answer might be that there is nothing novel about marriages or contracts; the possibility of using or creating these legal facilities is well known and requires no publicity. Another answer might be that there is already a high voluntary take-up of such facilities, so that no reinforcement is needed. And yet the citizen's knowledge of the intricacies of the marriage law, for instance, is minimal; it would certainly be to his (and in this case her) advantage to know them in detail before embarking on matrimony; the need for knowledge is there, and why should the government not satisfy it? As for contract, citizens may have a vague idea about agreements; but not one citizen in a hundred probably appreciates when he is making a valid binding contract, or what his rights and responsibilities under it may be. In this case, his situation is even worse than it is with marriage, where at least he generally has a fairly shrewd idea that he has got married! The production of babies is neither novel nor in need of official explanatory propaganda to secure a supply; but the fact that it is not novel nor unnatural has not prevented totalitarian and other governments with social objectives from publicising the need for babies and new laws which reinforce that publicity.[3] There

3. One of the earliest recorded attempts at social engineering, which involved the enactment of laws for the encouragement of marriage and the production of babies, was made by Augustus, who with two laws (the lex Julia, 18 BC, and the lex Papia Poppaea, AD 9) penalised unmarried adults and childless persons by making them incapable of benefiting under a will. Adult unmarried persons between the ages of 25 and 60 for males, and 20 and 50 for females, lacked the *ius capiendi* and took nothing under a devise or bequest; a married male without a child (*orbus*), and a married female with less than the full quota of children prescribed (four), took ½ share only. To avoid cheating, Nero enacted that a potential beneficiary could not get round the law by adopting a child or children! Whether the law was successful in its aim one does not know; but what is striking is the use of economic penalties to secure social ends.

is, in other words, nothing in the subject-matter of a given branch of the law which interdicts the use of governmental propaganda for publicising it or explaining it. 'Good wine needs no bush' is thus at best a partial explanation; though the saying might lead one to ask why the wine is good in this case, and why less good in other cases.

What is it about the branches of law which *have* been officially publicised that they, rather than their recipients, have in common? A cynic might be tempted to argue that there appears to be a direct correlation between the degree of official publicity required for a new law and its unacceptability, uselessness, or complication. But this would not be wholly fair, though it certainly applies to much new law, like that of consumer credit or VAT. The bureaucratic complications of the new law do not provoke the publicity; it it the will of the legislator, his commitment to ensuring compliance (even when what is offered is to be accepted voluntarily) that induces him to advertise. At the same time, it is the novelty of the legislation, when compared with existing laws, which means that there is little likelihood of unaware voluntary compliance with it. The administrative superstructures and complications of definition, regulation or administration which so often accompany such novel laws are largely demanded by the novelty of what is sought to be achieved. If the legislator is trying to remake society to his image, then he feels that he must have a powerful and complicated regulatory machine to ensure that his objective is attained; nowhere is this better illustrated than in the towering structures of race relations and equal opportunities. The cruel paradox is, however, built into the system, that the creation of such elaborate and intricate regulations and machinery may be the best possible way of preventing understanding, reception or acceptance of the new law, and of making the new law unworkable. The legislator is thus drawn onto a self-defeating course.

Unofficial publicisation of new laws

It is a new phenomenon, and one worthy of remark, that agencies and organisations in the welfare field, often these days with a strong crusading tinge to their work, also share in the publicisation of new laws — usually laws of the same type as those publicised by government, and directed at the same sort of constituents. Handbooks and journals, and inspired articles in newspapers, are the main forms of such publicity. Thus one finds handbooks on social security benefits, children's 'rights', women's rights, race and immigration legislation, and so on. Consumers' rights are extensively covered by such bodies as the Consumers' Association.

Compared, then, with the position 10 or 20 years ago, there is now a wealth of explanatory material on the laws, or rather on certain very specific aspects of them; but the gaps are still more prominent than the areas covered. An inventory of such material would make interesting reading.

Knowledge of existing laws

Some of the material put out relates mostly to the existing law; this is especially true of the Consumers' Association publications, as it is of the many textbooks which seek to describe either the English legal system in general or one quite specific aspect of it (e.g. the law relating to teachers). This material reflects two new concerns: the first is the attempt to teach *Law* formally in schools and colleges for A and O level courses; the second is the expanding market for works on *Law* at a popular level.

The formal teaching of law, other than at the university/polytechnic or professional level, is still in its infancy. It only touches a minute proportion of all the subjects of the law. Even those who study law by these means may not gain much from the study. One should ask oneself why anyone should study law. There appear to be two main reasons. The first is to gain a general insight into the way in which *Law* and legal institutions function in a society (our own society, mostly); in this perspective *Law* is one of the factors of society, requiring understanding on the same basis as the political and social history, or the economic structure. Now the general works which provide courses in law (?=*Law*) for schools and colleges do not seem to be designed with this aim in mind, or to achieve such an effect in the students, if one may judge from discussions with those who have been through such courses. Some of the courses emphasise 'rights' rather than laws — as already remarked, rights are only part of the legal system, and duties and structures must be of at least equal importance. The second objective is at the practical level, to enable the student to operate within the legal system. Popular works on law thus fall into the same category as, say, motorcar maintenance handbooks or Do-It-Yourself books on 'how to build a house'. The school textbooks entirely fail in this aim (and perhaps their authors would say that they do not possess it); the practical works are sometimes very useful, though necessarily they cannot take the place of, or supply the information available from, professional advisers.

But these books and pamphlets do not go very far in correcting what is now apparently the normal condition of the ordinary Englishman, namely, an almost total ignorance of his laws. However, one must take some account of media exposure of *Law*, from police series and court-room dramas on television to the phone-in programmes on radio which answer listeners' queries. A barrister in a wig is now a common sight in the ordinary British home, nearly as usual as a policeman in a Panda car. To see barristers in your living room does not of itself give an understanding of the law and legal process, unfortunately; though one is fascinated to detect the feedback when the ordinary citizen comes to court, say on a motoring charge. He is no longer completely ignorant, for instance, of cross-examination of witnesses (though the whole process of giving evidence, and the restrictions on its reception, still have to be explained constantly to the citizen as defendant or witness). Certain expressions or concepts now appear in the courts: everyone seems to have heard of the 'common-law wife', which is strange in that this status is not recognised in English *Law*![4] Many have heard of 'citizen's arrest', another Americanism. To have watched TV presentations of criminal cases does not give the viewer a permanent understanding of his criminal law; and it leaves untouched his massive ignorance of civil law. Nor does advice (often full and adeptly presented) from a radio expert by itself educate the listening public, any more than a consultation with a solicitor would by itself have a permanent residual effect on a person's knowledge and understanding of *Law*.

We are back, therefore, to the superficial, to acquaintance with a bit of jargon, which is positively inimical to a proper reception and understanding of the legal system generally or in its particular aspects. To test the popular understanding or lack of understanding of *Law* possessed by the man-in-the-street, the simplest method of investigation is to go into the street, to stop the passer-by, and to question him about the *Law*. Such an investigation quickly shows that the average man knows very little about the *Law*, and that what he knows is mostly wrong. Thus he will tell you confidently that:

'Trespassers will be prosecuted', or that

'It doesn't matter if you don't do any damage', or that

'An agreement is not binding if you haven't signed it', or that

'A dog is allowed its first bite', or that

'Possession is nine-tenths of the law', or that

'An Englishman's home is his castle'.

— or any number of similar aphorisms which at best are half-true, and at worst are highly deceptive.

Where the ordinary person's ignorance is most profound, however, is about the structures and the processes of the *Law*. Knowledge of *Law* is more than a knowledge of individual rules of law; the rules must be fitted into a system, and the working of that system, and of the institutions and agencies through which the rules can be applied, must be understood as well. If one considers that the institutions of the *Law* govern the daily lives of those subject to it, the extent of misunderstanding about them is alarming. We can start off with the police; the police themselves rely on the ignorance of the general public for the effectiveness of their work. Many of the interrogatory techniques used would be invalidated if a citizen invoked the strict norms which govern such interrogation. This cannot be a healthy situation. If the *Law* as at present in force is unworkable, then the remedy is to change the *Law*, not to leave its subjects in total and vulnerable ignorance of it. Ignorance

4. See Chapter 8 below, for a discussion of the 'common-law wife', among other odd conceptions which are now penetrating English *Law*.

of courts, both what they are and how they work and the limits of their powers, is equally profound.

Our conclusion is short and stark: the ordinary Englishman's perception of, understanding of, his *Law* is minimal, his ignorance maximal. The question is whether this state is necessary or avoidable — is it the case that in any modern legal system the citizen should be so ignorant? Now no one suggests that legal advisers and specialists can be done away with; many of the complexities of modern legislation are justifiable (though this is not to say that some could not be done away with if the sphere of operation and the ambitions of legislation were restricted). But one can have a general knowledge and understanding of a subject without having a technical knowledge; the millions of music-lovers in the United Kingdom, who know the classical composers and enjoy their works without knowing anything about musical theory, show what is possible. Citizens do not have a knowledge of the *Law* comparable to the music-lover's knowledge of music. Is this unavoidable? I would answer, No. The reason for the situation is mostly because the government, as law-emitting authority, has generally failed to appreciate its responsibility to ensure effective communication of the *Law*. This has been left to the latest stage, as if no dietetic or health advice were given to ordinary people, who would only learn that they should have avoided certain foods or substances when they were taken to hospital gravely ill. This is the position with the laws at present. On the criminal side, the citizen learns from the policeman's hand on his shoulder, or the summons in the post, that he should not have done something. He learns from the anguished expression on the solicitor's face, or on that of the Citizens' Advice Bureau adviser, that he should have avoided some civil-law catastrophe much earlier, and would have done if only he had known sufficient about the *Law* and legal processes.

B ACCEPTANCE OF LAW

If one does not know that a law exists, one cannot voluntarily comply with it. One may comply accidentally, because one would have conformed one's behaviour to the same norm anyhow; or one may comply because one is forced to do so by some other agency. Legislation which cuts across existing mores, attitudes and expectations is unlikely to achieve accidental compliance. Much modern legislation falls into this category, at least in the protective state, or in one which practises social engineering.

Non-compliance with the *Law* can thus be sub-divided into *unwitting failure to comply* and *deliberate defiance* of the *Law*. We concentrate our attention now on the second aspect, and ask how far law is accept-able and accepted. Observation is the crucial tool of investigation, observation of people's actual behaviour, observation enriched by a survey of their attitudes which explain their behaviour. What would such an investigation show in modern England?

We can start with the optimistic, one might almost say traditional or official, view, expressed (slightly surprisingly) in a piece by Sir Otto Kahn-Freund. In his article on 'Labour law' in the collection called *Law and Opinion in England in the Twentieth Century*,[5] published in 1959, he wrote:

'My third general observation is even more general, and it may sound very platitudinous to anybody who has had no opportunity of looking at the British scene from outside: It is the remarkable respect, not indeed for the lawyers, but for the law among the British people, and in particular among the working classes.'

And he goes on to illustrate this respect by the conduct of the workers during the General Strike of 1926.

An opposite view, also about labour law, can be extracted from another writer (writing in 1976), M. Whincup. He wrote in his book on *Modern Employment Law*[6] that:

'In a more or less free society like ours the law is powerless unless most people are willing to be bound by it, and recent history suggests that certain unions are not so willing if the law is not to their liking.'

Whincup cites the case of the *Ford Motor Co v AEF*[7] and the experience with the Industrial Relations Act 1971. He goes on to say:

'The resulting impotence of the law was duly demonstrated by a number of immensely damaging strikes, the ultimate effect of which was to bring down the lawfully elected government.

... the unions, once so oppressed, have fought for and now achieved the right to break or to lead others to break any contract they like ... But would the individual employee think it equally right to break his own word and thereby injure someone else as and when he thought fit, or would he agree that other people — employers, shopkeepers, bus conductors, car dealers, house sellers, etc. — should be free to do the same to him? If he would not, why should his union alone be above the law?'[8]

Industrial law

Let us examine a little more closely the attitudes of the organised working class (or at least substantial sections of it) to *Law*, as demonstrated by recent experience in the field of labour law. In the oscillations of

5.   Ed. M. Ginsberg (London, 1959) 215 at p. 226.
6.   At p. 20.
7.   [1969] 2 All ER 481.
8.   At pp. 20–21.

official law regulating the activities of trade unions and the right to strike, the general drift of the law in the 20th century had been towards extending the recognition and the privileges of trade unions in the legal field. This extension was cut back in the aftermath of the General Strike of 1926; and the Industrial Relations Act 1971, brought in by a Conservative government but which expressed principles which had been adopted by the preceding Labour Cabinet, sought further to regulate by legal process the constitution and activities of unions and the right of workers to resort to industrial action. As is well known, the Act failed; it failed because of the all-out defiance of the law by the trade unions and by other groups of workers. What lesson do we learn from this failure?

Kahn-Freund in a more recent writing[9] learns the lesson (or attempts to teach other, especially potential law-makers, the lesson) that this Act was a futility, that it was 'disruptive' (i.e. interfered with pre-existing practices), and that in short:

'Everywhere the effectiveness of the law depends on the unions far more than the unions depend on the effectiveness of the law. The effectiveness of the unions however depends to some extent on forces which neither they nor the law can control.'[10]

He concludes:

'The failure of the Industrial Relations Act has re-inforced our insight that neither the legislature nor the courts should attempt to burden the law with tasks which it cannot fulfil.'[11]

If the failure, or deliberate sabotage, of the Industrial Relations Act 1971 teaches us anything, it is that the British working class, if it ever had a remarkable respect for the law, has it no longer, at least so far as industrial action is concerned. Is Kahn-Freund further, and more generally, correct when he says that the legislature should not burden the law with tasks which it cannot fulfil? And, if a law mistakenly creates such a burden, is it the correct response for the *Law*, like a snail which has met an unpleasant obstacle, to retreat into its shell, and even accord more extra-legal privileges to those who have defied it than they would have had anyhow? My argument would be that Yes, no law should attempt the impossible; Kahn-Freund is right. Many of the laws which remain dead letters in the Third World exactly fall into this category, though they have nothing to do with industrial relations. Perhaps race relations laws are in the same category? Laws can impose an impossible burden, not just because they command what is clearly unacceptable to the majority and which is likely to excite violent opposition, but because they require such a burdensome

9. *Labour and the Law* (1977, 2nd edn).
10. At p. 10.
11. At p. 276.

machinery of enforcement and supervision that they cannot effectively be administered.

But to accept Kahn-Freund's thesis — which is only an echo of the ancient maxim by which our legislative interpreters have guided themselves, that *Lex non cogit ad impossibilia* — is not the end of the enquiry. The further tasks remain, first to discover why what is commanded would be impossible, or too heavy a burden; and secondly, to consider whether there is any way in which the impossible might be made possible, or the burden lightened. Whincup is both right and wrong in saying that 'the law is powerless unless most people are willing to be bound by it'; he is right in that at the end of the day popular acceptance is the key to effective administration of the laws; he is wrong in implying that, provided the majority accept or acquiesce, all will be well. The frightening lesson one learns, not only from the Industrial Relations Act but from many other instances, is that defiance by a resolute minority can be effective in destroying a law. Defiance by a few Sikhs of the motor-cycle helmets law led to amendment of the law, rather than punishment of those defying it. The resolute minority can succeed in this way because the majority, or the rulers, are irresolute or are inhibited by other considerations.

There is nothing in the nature of industrial relations that would make a law such as the Industrial Relations Act 'impossible'; it was merely that at that time and place, and given the nature of the forces opposed to it, including Her Majesty's Opposition, the forces pro could not match the forces anti without resorting to compulsion which public opinion would not accept. At another time, for instance when Kahn-Freund wrote in 1959, the Industrial Relations Act might have succeeded. As for the Sikhs, governmental inhibitions about apparently being beastly to coloured immigrants of a different religion prevented the maintenance of the law as it was (even though the assertion that it was contrary to the Sikh religion to wear crash-helmets was strongly controverted by expert opinion). The Industrial Relations Act might become possible again if the balance of social, economic and political forces changed, as it may well do with a collapse of the British economy and a fundamental change in public attitudes (which up to now have been of the 'spare me the public turmoil and the private deprivation that a strike would bring! so please settle quickly, whatever they want' variety).

In other words, changes in attitude can be all-important, whether these are the attitudes of government, work-force, or the public at large. Such changes can occur as the result of unplanned and undirected events, or they may be consciously sought through education and direction. Here we come back to the earlier point about the public ignorance of *Law*; it is not merely ignorance *of Law*, it is ignorance of *why Law* is vital, and the ends which it serves. A major educational effort could revolutionise popular attitudes to, and respect for, *Law*, if coupled with a serious attempt to involve the public more in the making of it.

Other law

Is it the case that industrial law is unique in its degree of unacceptability to the public? There are obviously special reasons why dissatisfaction with regulatory law controlling employment, strikes, picketing and so on is likely to be more effective in negating law than similar dissatisfaction with other branches of law. Employment generally leads to concentrations of large numbers of persons in the same place at the same time; to some extent, control of them through law faces the same difficulties as the control of any other crowd (say at a football match). Secondly, employment, whether in manufacturing industry or in service industries, contributes directly to the daily life of the nation, what it eats and how it lives. Suspension or disruption of this work has an immediate and large-scale effect. And thirdly, employment in groups offers those with a particular line to sell of industrial or political agitation a ready and easy field of operations, which a dispersed work-force would not offer. These ideas are easily tested by comparing dissatisfaction with, say, the law of divorce, which affects small units or households taken separately, where action which is against the law (e.g. by leaving home and living in sin) provides no problem of crowd control, where the individual units are much less amenable to agitation designed to promote or exploit dissatisfaction, and where failure to accept or comply does not disrupt the life of the nation.

But industrial law is not the only legal area where there is major difficulty with compliance. The road traffic laws, for different reasons, face the same sort of problem. If there is one thing one can be sure about in modern England, it is that the 30 mph speed limits are broken by 90 drivers out of every 100. There are other branches of the law which are frequently disregarded, and where the effect of disregard has been dramatic. We may start with the use of highways.

Parking on the highway. Public roads, or roads over which the public have the right of passage, are 'highways' under the common law. The essential characteristic of a highway is that it is solely for the purposes of the public passing to and fro. As Halsbury's *Laws of England,*[12] cited in *Hubbard v Pitt,*[13] puts it:

'The right of the public is a right to "pass along" a highway for the purpose of legitimate travel, not to "be on" it, except so far as their presence is attributable to a reasonable and proper use of the highway as such.'

12. Vol. 19, p. 73, para. 107 (see now 4th edition, vol. 21).
13. [1975] 1 All ER 1056 (QBD) at 1060.

Although the common-law public right of passage over a highway might (except where it was for foot-passengers only) extend originally only to the use by the public of horses, and of carts and coaches drawn by horses or oxen, as new forms of vehicle have appeared, so has their use been recognised as within the permission; so that today cars, lorries and other vehicles freely make use of roads set aside for their use. Obstructing the highway is a wrong committed against the owner of the sub-soil on which the highway runs; and the owner has an action in trespass on this account. An obstruction or misuse of a highway may be a public injury, a 'public nuisance', if by a wrongful act a person prevents the public from freely, safely and conveniently passing along the highway or any portion of it. Modern law recognises as the only excuse for such an obstruction that it was minimal and reasonably incidental to the main purpose of highways, viz. their use for movement of persons or goods passing or repassing.

So prima facie a motorist who stops on the highway, and thereby creates an obstruction, however fleeting, may commit a private wrong (of trespass) against the interest of the owner of the soil, and a public nuisance or injury against the right of the public. Motoring would be impossible if this were taken too strictly and literally; so an exception is allowed if the motorist has to stop to repair a breakdown, or to set down or take up passengers or goods. What about parking on the highway? It is notorious that motorists have a propensity to park, and indeed to leave their cars immobile for long periods; in theory every such motorist would be committing some wrong by so doing. The law, however, works on the *de minimis* principle, i.e. not to object to trivial breaches of the law. But that the exception to the principle is truly slight is demonstrated by another case, that of *Nagy v Weston*[14] in 1964. This case related to a criminal prosecution (not a private claim in trespass, nor even an action for public nuisance) for breach of section 121 (1) of the Highways Act 1959, the relevant consolidating statute. This section makes it an offence for a person who

'. . . without lawful authority or excuse, in any way wilfully obstructs the free passage along a highway . . .'.

The defendant, Mr Nagy, achieved legal fame by parking his motor van in St Giles Street, Oxford, for the purpose of selling hot dogs from it. He was there on the particular occasion only 5 minutes before he was arrested for obstruction under the section. He was convicted and ordered by the Oxford magistrates to pay a fine of 40 shillings. He appealed by way of case stated on a point of law, it being argued on his behalf that he had not made an unreasonable use of his right to stop by stopping and selling food. The magistrates were of the view that it was an unreasonable use of the highway to park a van on it even for 5

14. [1965] 1 All ER 78 (QBD).

minutes. The Queen's Bench Division agreed that on the given facts this was a valid interpretation of the law, that this was an obstruction, and that it was not reasonable and hence not justifiable.

Statute law creates a number of offences dealing with obstruction by motor vehicles; but these wrongs are in addition to, and not in substitution for, liability under the law of trespass and public nuisance. Under these laws, if strictly enforced, practically every motorist would be liable to prosecution − the point of mentioning this instance here is that very few motorists are in fact prosecuted. The law is disregarded by a tacit understanding between police and public; the general disregard by the public of the letter of the law is ignored by the prosecuting authorities. Only where the obstruction is blatant or aggravated will police prosecute. All this represents a victory for popular practice over the letter of the law. Popular practice has effectively repealed the law.

A similar process is now going on to legitimise parking on the pavement; in many areas the police turn a blind eye to this practice, but in other areas the driver will be prosecuted. Will a new custom entitling someone to park on the pavement be established similar to that which already legitimises parking on the roadway? − the outcome is uncertain.[15]

Street offences. Off-the-course cash betting was illegal; most such betting took place in the street. Police prosecutions of bookmakers and their runners took up a great deal of police time and did not stop the practice. The universal disregard of this law led to its change: a sort of deal was done with public opinion and practice. The law which allowed the setting up of betting places (betting shops) off the racecourse legalised betting face-to-face; betting in the street ceased to be necessary. Popular practice had defeated the law, and led to its change. There is a similar history in regard to the law against prostitution.

Divorce law. Under the divorce law up to 1969, divorce was an adversary procedure; collusion between a husband and wife wishing to separate from each other permanently (unless all they sought was separation and not divorce) was fatal to the chances of either of them obtaining a divorce. Contrived or arranged divorces between partners wishing to

---

15. Sections 36A and 36B of the Road Traffic Act 1972 make it an offence for a person to park heavy and other vehicles on footpaths adjoining urban roads; the offence is prosecutable at the instance of the local authority. Section 36B, which deals with vehicles other than heavy commercial vehicles, is just about to be brought into operation. Theoretically, therefore, any practice of parking on the pavement will be contrary to the law − but will this stop the practice? After all, the 30 mph speed limit does not stop speeding, and police in practice do not prosecute unless the vehicle exceeds the limit by 10 mph; obstruction of the road by a vehicle is already an offence under various laws − and yet urban roads are constantly and completely obstructed with impunity.

dissolve their marriage were however not uncommon: the husband would 'provide evidence' of adultery for the divorce court by arrangement with his wife; the court machinery would operate on this fiction; and the collusive divorce was obtained. The law showed itself powerless to cope with this disregard of one of its fundamental principles. It was the law that was changed.

Squatting. To enter another's house and live therein is undoubtedly a civil wrong or trespass against the house-owner; it is or may be also an offence against the criminal law. A sort of custom of squatting, in the definition of which there participated the police, the local authorities, and the pressure of public opinion and practice, was emerging. The question was whether the new custom of 'squatting' would eventually be sanctified by being enshrined in legislation. In 1977, after two reports from the Law Commission, the answer emerged, in the shape of the Criminal Law Act 1977. Contrary to what one might have predicted, the result has been to cut back the legitimate scope of squatting rather than to extend it. The Act, by section 6, protects possession as such, whether lawful or not, by enacting that it is an offence for someone to use 'violence' for the purpose of securing entry into premises against the will of someone present on the premises at the time − and this applies whether or not the person in occupation is lawfully there or wrongfully in occupation; yet the exception made for the 'displaced residential occupier' is so great as to diminish the former protection given by the law to squatters in occupation. It is, by section 6 (3), a defence for a person accused of so using violence to show that he was a displaced residential occupier. At the same time, the section naturally penalises squatters who have gained entry in the first place by violence. Similarly with the new offence created by section 7, of 'adverse occupation of residential premises', which consists of failing to leave premises on which one is present as a trespasser when required to do so by a displaced residential occupier.

The movement towards a new custom of squatting has thus been arrested; but the custom still remains in being so far as squatting in premises which are not residentially occupied is concerned. Furthermore, with the many other calls on police time, and the political embarrassment it may cause to the police or other authorities to move against squatters in any given case, there is a reluctance to enforce the letter of the law in most cases. The squatters therefore remain in occupation; and the main thesis put forward here remains untouched, that general or widespread resistance to or disregard of a law produces in practice the repeal of that law, *de facto* or *de jure*.

Examples could easily be multiplied. The easiest way to find them is to scan the list of enactments which are from time to time repealed as being obsolete. This process of spring-cleaning the statute-book of Acts which have fallen into disuse has now gone very far, so that we have fewer odd medieval survivals than we did at one time; but theoretically the mere fact of the periodical removal from the *Law* of the country of enactments which have been effectively repealed by disregard or disuse significantly supports our thesis, because the theory of the matter in English *Law* is that every Act of Parliament remains in force until expressly or impliedly repealed by another Act of Parliament; and the doctrine of desuetude has no place in English *Law*. Theory and practice do not match. What are the consequences of this mismatch?

The first consequence is to discredit the notion that English people are characterised by a surprising degree of respect for existing laws. There are too many laws, civil and criminal, that they disregard to make this picture a credible one. The second consequence of any successful disregard of laws is to weaken all the other elements of the legal system. Disregard of industrial law, or rejection of the role of law altogether in industrial disputes, weakens both respect and the place for *Law* in other spheres of life. If we seek the causes of the modern tendency to anarchy in British life ('anarchy' to mean the conscious rejection of *Law*, as contrasted with *anomia*, the lack of law, whether through ignorance or otherwise), it is an interesting question whether the rejection of law in industrial relations is a reflection or a consequence or a cause of the rejection of law elsewhere. It is commonly asserted, at the impressionistic level, that the widespread disregard of motoring law on the one hand, and resentment at the action of the police in attempting to enforce it on the other, provoke in the ordinary motorist, and hence in the ordinary person (because the two groups are the same, more or less), a reaction against and a tendency to play down the acceptability of laws generally. Similarly there has been, over the last ten years or so, an increasing rejection at the popular level of respect for the police and police processes. It is no use arguing that the police have, through their misdeeds, earned this disrespect; because it is a demonstrated feature of social life that a body of persons which is rejected by the rest of society tends to conform itself to the image imposed on it by society.

More and more laws enacted and imposed on the citizen body; more and more complexity in those laws; more and more ambitious attempts at remaking the minds as well as the behaviour of those subject to those laws — all this on the one hand, while on the other hand there is para- doxically an ever-increasing rejection of the acceptability and uncontroverted authority of laws. Are the two linked? Whether they are linked or not, what is the answer for a legislative authority which seeks to impose laws and make them effective? Not only, as already noted, is education needed, but a fundamental reform of the legislative authority's own attitude to its work, and an acceptance, where there is now a lack, of the necessity for the involvement of the public generally in the making, as well as in the observing and even the breaking, of laws. The effects of such an involvement are worth charting here. However, before the effects of popular involvement in the formal making of laws are discussed, I should like to draw attention to the informal means by which the people at large already participate in the making, shaping and definition of laws. There are three aspects which we must consider: the role of the jury; the role of justices of the peace; and social drag on the police in the performance of their functions.

The role of the jury

As far as one can go back in English legal history, even to Anglo-Saxon times before the Norman Conquest in 1066, one finds that the lay element in the administration of justice has been an important one. The gradual appearance of professional judges in the 12th and 13th centuries to replace the earlier worthy men of substance and courtiers of the King who had been called upon to try cases was matched by an ever-increasing involvement of laymen in the work of the courts. Not, as in customary African societies, as spectators, even if participant at times (as we have seen), but as judges of guilt and innocence in criminal trials, and as adjudgers of title and wrong in civil cases too.

In criminal trials before the higher courts on assize or in London, trial by a jury of twelve men has been a feature of English law since the early 13th century. For many centuries those empanelled on juries doubtless represented only a certain section of the community, those with a substantial property stake in the district; and doubtless again injustice was often done by corrupted or frightened juries in the 15th to 18th centuries. But two sovereign principles have remained to this day to protect the accused in an English criminal trial: that the court starts off with a presumption of the innocence of the accused, which can only be displaced by evidence establishing guilt beyond a reasonable doubt; and that 12 ordinary men (and now women) must be convinced of the guilt of the accused before he can be punished, where the offence is an indictable one. (Of course, since the Criminal Justice Act 1967, a judge is entitled to accept a majority verdict of the jury in certain circumstances, but these circumstances are limited, and at least 10 of an eleven or twelve-member jury must be convinced of the guilt of the accused before the verdict can stand.)

In our present context, though, we must see the requirement of jury trial not as a means of protecting the accused, but as a way (unintended, to be sure) by which the jury make law in the process of applying it or refusing to apply it. In *Bushell's Case* in 1670, after the abolition of the Star Chamber, it was held that judges could not punish jurors who refused to convict an accused person. Judges in the 17th and 18th centuries nevertheless resorted to extreme means, such as locking up the jury without food, light or heat, to compel them to come to a verdict. Today refusal by a jury, and still more refusal by a series of juries, to convict for particular types of offences effectively repeals the law which establishes those offences. In the field of prosecutions for obscenity and the like this has recently been fully demonstrated since the *Lady Chatterley's Lover* case; but the possibility that juries will override the law is constantly present wherever strong minority views are held, as in trials which can be represented to have political overtones. The recent generalisation of liability to jury service, which means that practically everyone of voting age may serve on a jury, is highly relevant here. Coloured minorities; those who follow an alternative life-style; Welshmen dealing with nationalists on trial; those who adhere to extremist left-wing or right-wing politics — the list of potential dissentients is almost endless. If there are more than two such dissentients on a given jury, it may be impossible, even with the provision for majority verdicts, to secure a conviction. The jury's power (and it is now the power of the people or a section of it) to refuse to convict gives the people the power of disallowance of criminal law; but there is no similar positive power, of course, to create new offences.

The jury now lacks, except in the field of defamation, a similar law-making or law-destroying power in civil matters, by reason of the virtual disappearance of jury trial in civil cases in England and Wales. (The situation may well be different in the United States; but I have not investigated this aspect of our theme empirically there.)

This aspect of trial by jury — of the jurymen making or disallowing law — has not met with judicial disapproval; on the contrary, it has been seen as part of the immemorial rights of the citizen. As Lord Denning said his memorable words in *Ward v James:*[16]

'Let it not be supposed that this court is in any way opposed to trial by jury. It has been the bulwark of our liberties too long for any of us to seek to alter it. Whenever a man is on trial for serious crime, or when in a civil case a man's honour or integrity is at stake, or when one or other party must be deliberately lying, then trial by jury has no equal.'

And the report of the commissioners appointed to inquire into the superior courts of law at Westminster added their own words, a century earlier in 1853, to the case for juries. The jury, said the commissioners, brings along to the trial 'a varied stock of information which the judge cannot be expected to possess, and which is of the most essential advantage in the administration of justice'. What is more, the jury tempers the strict letter of the law which a judge might otherwise adhere to; the jury has the opposite tendency, 'to take a more enlarged and liberal view, according to the morality and equity of the case ... The knowledge of this tends to keep harsh and discreditable cases out of court.'[17]

16. [1966] 1 QB 273, CA.
17. *Second Report of the Commissioners Appointed to Inquire into the Process, Practice and System of Pleading in the Superior Courts of Law at Westminster,* 1852–3, p. xl.

Naturally there are disadvantages — from the point of view of those who must administer the law — attaching to this feature of the jury system. Juries may acquit through fear or sympathy, on racial or religious or political grounds, so that a just verdict is not arrived at. But whenever in England there has been a proposal to cut down the scope of jury trial, there has been vigorous protest from civil libertarians — which suggests that with all their faults juries have perceived advantages as protectors of liberty, that liberty being defined by the people and not by the small elite who formally make the laws.

The role of justices of the peace

Less serious criminal cases are tried in England before magistrates' courts, which in the vast majority of instances are composed of lay magistrates. Despite their being advised by a professionally qualified clerk, magistrates' courts have the sole power to decide at the end of the day whether or not a particular kind of behaviour was a crime, and if so how it should be dealt with. The lay justices' interpretation of the law effectively creates as well as disallows law, especially when such all-purpose charges as those of 'obstruction' and 'conduct whereby a breach of the peace may be occasioned' are brought before them. Their effective law-giving power is only partially restrained by the appellate and supervisory powers of the superior courts, since the vast majority of cases do not go to appeal; and although, where the court has mis-directed itself on the law, an appeal by way of case stated may be had, the opportunity for this rarely arises and is yet more rarely taken advantage of. So far as I am aware, there has been no study of the law-making power of magistrates' courts to date; this would make an ideal topic for practical work in legal sociology.

There are those who would argue that lay magistrates are not the people, but represent what one might call the conventional establishment, that they are precisely the *legales homines*, or worthy law-abiding citizens of substance, who functioned as justices and jurors in the early Middle Ages. Be that as it may, there is now a conscious attempt to broaden the basis of selection of the Bench; and, what is more, justices in their daily lives are open to all the popular and extra-judicial influences represented by their circles of friends and contacts, and by what they see in the papers and on television, so that, at second and third remove, the views of the people at large impress themselves on them. My own experience indicates that justices frequently take what one may describe as a common-sense, popular, robust view of the *Law*, and that in this they differ fundamentally from the professional judge. Their views, and those of jurors too, are thus *not* those of the law-making establishment; they constitute a populist approach which is in dialectic with establishment views. The disapproval of a law by justices may be unconsciously expressed, not only by a reluctance to find the charge proved, but by a mitigation of any penalty that is imposed if a conviction is ordered.

Social drag on the police

I have already said a good deal about the reluctance of police to prosecute various kinds of offences.[18] This reluctance may extend to the Director of Public Prosecutions and the Attorney-General himself, when his fiat is required for a prosecution. If we analyse why police may be reluctant to prosecute, we can identify several causes, among which one includes (i) where there is a low chance of conviction, due to the unwillingness of juries to convict for that type of offence, or to accept police evidence relating to it; (ii) where the police feel that they would make themselves needlessly unpopular or in confrontation with a large or important section of the community as a result of enforcing the law strictly; (iii) where the duties involved in detecting and pursuing that type of crime are unattractive; (iv) where there is a conscious decision to make a better use of police time by pursuing other types of offence. The obscenity (and formerly the blasphemy) laws are examples of (i); prosecutions for unlawful picketing in industrial disputes illustrate (ii). Hostile or uncooperative reactions from the public constitute a form of 'social drag' on the police in the performance of their duties and the full implementation of the laws. No penal law can be effective (despite the provision for private prosecutions in England) unless the detecting and prosecuting authorities are determined and active in their implementation of it. Again there is scope for a full-scale sociolegal investigation of cases of social drag influencing the implementation of laws, which I cannot pursue here without further research and an abbreviation of other aspects which equally call for attention.

From this negative aspect we can now move to the positive, which at the same time will be more speculative, viz. the more direct involvement of the people in the making of laws.

Effect of popular involvement in the making of law

Involvement of the public in the making of law might lead to various consequences which the present law-making elites might find unappealing. For a start, there might well be *less law*. If every law were submitted to the popular test of requiring at least 50% affirmative opinion before it was retained, how many laws would survive the test? Secondly, the laws which survived might be diametrically opposed to present laws; and this would doubtless be found unacceptable by the dominant intellectual elite which has usurped the function of prescribing approved

18. See, e.g., p. 87.

patterns of thought and behaviour for the majority. Some laws, e.g. on homicide, might be toughened up; others, e.g. on race relations, relaxed or abandoned. Penalties for certain types of criminal offence might be made more severe and draconian; imprisonment might be made less of a soft option. Many of the 'progressive' penal reforms of the last decade might be set at nought. But, before we yield to the anguished shrieks of the outraged reformists who have been responsible for these changes, we might well ask them to exhibit their credentials and their authority. 'By what authority', one might ask them, 'do you impose laws on people which the people themselves, if left to themselves, would indignantly reject?' It is no use the law-making minority appealing to higher standards or principles to justify their actions; in a really democratic, as opposed to a pseudo-democratic, polity their authority to legislate derives from popular mandate; otherwise it is no more than platonic absolutism; and since they are a self-appointed legislature in the latter case, they can appeal to no democratic principle to validate their activity.

Once we have flushed out the non-democratic or anti-democratic nature of present legislative realities in Britain, the legislative elite might make rejoinder by showing the harmful consequences of treating the democratic nature of our society seriously. 'To allow the people to make law would not merely put unenlightened attitudes on the statute book', they might say, 'but it would substitute for what you call the "tyranny of a minority" the far worse state of a "tyranny of the majority". It cannot be the case', they might argue, 'that a majority legitimates what is fundamentally wrong; such a majority could easily ride roughshod over individual and minority rights and interests; and in our book a true democracy is one which respects the opinion of the majority, *provided that* that opinion respects the rights and interests of minorities.' Fine! But to accept this argument leaves us still perplexed: how is one to define the rights and interests of minorities; how to decide whether they have been impugned by any particular legislation; what remedial action should be undertaken by whom if the legislation affects minority rights injuriously? In other words, who are to be the *censors* of the law? And if such censorship is desirable in itself as a matter of principle, why is it not already in operation, so as to censor the legislation promoted and introduced by this minority which is now complaining?

Americans, and every country with a written constitution and a constitutional court, might legitimately say that they are far in advance of Britain in this regard. 'You, the British, have an elective dictatorship [Lord Hailsham's graphic phrase]. We have a Supreme Court which does precisely what you ask for, namely, measures all laws, written or unwritten, against unchanging fundamental principles of democracy and justice.' The existence of a supreme constitutional court can be justified in a democratic society as a voluntary surrender by the citizens of their otherwise absolute power to make laws; it can thus be brought within the democratic rubric, as in a sense every law is a voluntary acceptance of constraints which might otherwise not operate. But . . ., but . . ., but . . . 'unchanging fundamental principles'? The history of the US Supreme Court is surely the history of changing principles, principles which change with the personnel of the Court and with the changing social climate, in response to changing social ideas. It is now unacceptable, where formerly it was acceptable, for laws in the US to discriminate between persons on grounds of race, religion or sex. The Supreme Court took time to come round to this view. There can thus be nothing fundamental about it; or alternatively, the Court showed that it could be in error when it previously failed to recognise that there was such a fundamental principle. But admit the possibility of error, admit the possibility of change of view, and our certainties melt away. One such certainty has recently become profoundly uncertain, with the decision in the *Bakke* case; it seems that the fundamental principle, if it is such, that laws should not discriminate *against* classes of persons on the ground of race also means that the laws should not discriminate *for* persons on the same ground – or did the *Bakke* case say this? No one knows for sure.

The United States thus operate with *two* law-making elites (ignoring the federal structure for the moment): the respective legislatures which make the law and the pressure-groups which influence them form one elite, *elected* in the former case, *self-elected* in the latter. Behind and beyond them is the tight little elite of the Supreme Court, nine justices who are an *appointed* elite. The American system thus adds to the number and size of the elites who determine what the law shall be; it does not increase popular participation in the making of laws.

We may end where we began this section of our study, with industrial law. Industrial relations and action illustrate anarchy at the higher level, it may be; workers, whether organised in unions or acting unofficially, often show little regard for the laws of the land. But, and this constitutes a very powerful contrast, part of the difficulty caused by strikes and industrial action generally in Britain stems from worker solidarity, the willingness to stand by one's mates, the willingness to accept union instructions to take part in industrial action, even against the convictions of those who reluctantly take part in it. Internal union *Law* is thus marked by a high degree of compliance and hence effectiveness, exactly the qualities the governmental legislator vainly seeks for *his Law*. Why should unions be as successful as African customary societies at achieving compliance with their *Law*?

The answer is twofold: on the one hand, a high degree of solidarity, which means that workers are reluctant to go against their 'mates', even when they do not like or accept what is done; on the other hand, swift and effective sanctions for non-compliance. So far as solidarity is concerned, this goes beyond the immediate work-place, and extends to striking or picketing workers from other employments. Why there should be this extension is not so clear, except that it seems to rest to a large degree on perceived reciprocity of interests — you respect *my* picket-line and I'll respect yours. Sanctions for non-compliance include unpleasantness and abuse at the time of non-compliance, disapproval of work-mates, 'blacking' or sending to Coventry of non-conforming workers, and blacking of enterprises which try to break the strike or the limits imposed by the strikers. Such sanctions are effective only because in the past they have been seen to be effective: workers have been hounded out of employment, businesses shut down which fail to recognise unions, and so on.

Social sanctions of approval and disapproval, and economic sanctions of punishment for disobeying union orders (which, it is well to remember, are backed by no law, and may sometimes be in contravention of the *Law*) go hand in hand; the result is effective 'law'. The regular *Law* is powerless or excluded by comparison, and hence cannot win in any competition. Now it is a striking fact that it is exactly the same combination of social and forcible sanctions which makes traditional African customary *Laws* so effective, and which secured such a high degree of compliance with them. The message for any author of a modern legal system is thus obvious. He must imitate the more successful systems, or resign himself to impotence and his laws to ineffectiveness. In designing a legal system, therefore, the law-maker must seek to ensure that both wings of his enforcement mechanism are fully operative; our present laws in England fail on both scores. There is no effective mechanism of social disapproval or perceived solidarity binding the citizens together; and retribution, when it occurs (which is seldom), is slow, unequal and weak. Communist countries, such as the Soviet Union, understand the position better; the western democrat might well reply that he does not want a legal system like the Soviet one, if this is the only way of securing effectiveness. Maybe so, but then he must admit that his laws, even those which purport to be mandatory or prohibitory, are at best hortatory.

The social contract in action in Africa

The contrast between a *Law* made and imposed by a tiny elite on the citizenry, and a *Law* which represents the combined will of the subjects of that *Law*, and to which they have freely assented, is sharply illuminated by the details of the traditional Somali *Law* or *Laws*. For the Somali of East Africa their *Law* was[19] *heer*, a fascinating word

---

19. The past tense is used, because (i) the present 'socialist' regime in Somalia has given a new meaning to *heer*, and (ii) the description of traditional Somali *Law* does not necessarily apply now, when the state *Law* has purportedly totally abolished it. However, as in many other African countries, it appears that the people still follow their customary *Laws*, whatever the state *Law* may say.

which contains a whole legal philosophy within it. *Heer* means 'custom'; it also means 'contract'; it also means 'law'. Originally it meant the rope used to bind or fasten down the roof of the huts of the nomadic Somali. Their huts are demountable and transportable; the *heer* or rope keeps them together.[20]

The laws which 'bind', i.e. apply to, and keep together as a unity, a particular Somali group are the result of a contract or agreement, which is made between all the adult males of the group and which specifies the rules which will govern their disputes, especially over physical injuries and compensation for them. *Heer*, in its sense of 'treaty', can determine what compensation one group will pay to another, and thus helps to form super-groups with a shared legal system resting on a basis of bilateral contract.

Decisions in a Somali group are taken in the tribal assembly or *shir*, comprising all the adult males of the group. There is no voting by a majority; the decisions of the group are the expression of a general consensus arrived at after full deliberation.

Law, and indeed their government generally, among the Somali is thus a true social contract. *Law* is not imposed by a single leader or small elite. The Somali avoid the evils of elitism and of majority rule. Consensus legislation and *not* majority decision should be seen as the mark of the true democracy. It is a goal to which we should strive too in our own more complex but not necessarily more mature political societies. In the consensus society no one can be heard to argue that the *Law* doesn't bind him because he did not participate in making it or agree with its terms. Consensus law is effective law. How one builds a consensus, and how one determines that a consensus has been arrived at, are important technical questions in the large modern state; but they should not prevent the making of a complete and radical re-assessment of current governmental practices in Britain and elsewhere. Politicians preach consensus, but do not practise it. Nor is the consensus? of the police-state or the busybody state, as with Eastern European regimes, a true consensus, since in this case the dissenters are intimidated into silence, or are never given the opportunity of putting their views.

The women's lib. movement might criticise the Somali system on the ground that it is male-dominated, so that the consensus is taken over 50 per cent of the society only; but that is still a considerable improvement on our present elite-made laws in Britain (and the elite is similarly male-dominated!).

20. I. M. Lewis is not sure that this was the *original* meaning of *heer*. He points out that *heer* also means 'binding'! (personal communication.)

4 Environmental and social limitations on law: translocation of laws

A THE LOCAL SOCIAL AND CULTURAL ENVIRONMENT

Law operates in context; it does not exist in a vacuum. In this it is like any other communications system; after all, *Language* only has meaning as and to the extent that it functions in context. Any given law functions within the context of the legal system as a whole, the *Law* of which it attempts to form part; the *Law* has its own macro-context, the social and physical environment in which it is to operate. The work of *Law* is limited by its context; sometimes what it commands may be geographically impossible. Rent of land expressed as a bucket of snow at midsummer may have been a legal requirement impossible to satisfy in warmer northern countries before the invention of the refrigerator. There are less farcical but just as striking examples at all periods; the law on juvenile crime, for instance, in modern England supposes that parents can and should control their children, even children of 15 and 16. If parents fail to control their children, or their children commit offences, the *Law* may impute responsibility to their parents, or impose penalties (e.g. to meet fines imposed on the juveniles) *as if* the parents had been responsible. Whenever we use the words 'as if', we are in the presence of an analogical fiction, of course. What the *Law* commands thus does not necessarily fit with social realities.

To say that 'society' or 'social relations' is the context of *Law* does not by itself take us much further; we have to be more specific in relation to the analysis of social relations, and in the identification of the particular features of those relations which form part of the hypothetical facts upon which the conditional norms of the *Law* are premised. These implicit facts can, as the parental example shows, be out of fit with real life, or with the particular circumstances of the actual parent and juvenile before the court. In such a case, the matching process which application of a legal norm requires cannot take place, except by resort to fictions. If the *Law* disregards social facts in this way, those who participate in the society may be tempted to disregard the *Law*. The disregard is mutual.

The modern *Law* of a country like England can be out of fit with the social context in a number of ways, or for a number of reasons. First, there is the question of *who made the law*. The presuppositions and understanding of the law-maker are largely controlled by his own formation and background. Almost by definition, as mentioned in Chapter 3 above,[1] the law-making elite is detached from the mass of society. Legislation is class legislation at all periods in the stratified society; the only question is, what is the class composed of which has legislative power at any given epoch? The royal or aristocratic elites of former times have given place to the modern elites, elites of power and influence. There is a coherence about the modern law-making elite in Britain which transcends party divisions. What binds them firstly is a *conviction of rightness*; otherwise they would not dare make laws. They know what society needs.

Secondly, there is general *agreement about means*. There is no attempt to step outside the given framework of *Law*, or to view a problem from a new angle, as is suggested in our earlier analysis. Thirdly, they are *prisoners of history*. They do not start with a clean slate or *tabula rasa*; they must make do with what is and has been passed down to them. Their new law must be fitted into the patchwork of the old. These features reinforce conservation, even among the proclaimedly radical; they also reduce or eliminate the need for serious social enquiry, or the willingness to think again about the people, their needs, role and wishes. The imperious legislator is likely to be blind.

Next there is the question of *when the law was made*. Laws have ambitions towards permanence or even immortality. Provisional and temporary laws do not appeal to the law-maker (though he may cloak them in this disguise to increase their acceptability). So laws tend to carry on from generation to generation. And yet the social context, in which we must here include popular attitudes as well as social arrangements, now alters with surprising speed. The change (or apparent change) in attitudes to laws affecting industrial relations from 1959 to 1971 has already been referred to;[2] but there has been an equally profound change in formal and informal matrimonial relationships, such that the 'common-law wife' is now an accepted figure along with her more regular sister.[3] That laws made in the Victorian era might now be out of date or out of fit with contemporary society is obvious to everyone; that a law made in 1976 which allows 'secondary picketing' and blockades in aid of a strike can be already out of fit with the society of 1979 is a much more impressive instance of rapidly changing social realities. The tempo of change is continually accelerating.

Lastly, there is the question of the persons *to whom the law applies*. It is not merely that new generations of persons take the places of the

1. See p. 94 especially.
2. See p. 82.
3. See Chapter 8, below.

old, that the 'servants' of a former generation, as the *Law* knew them in the 'master-servant' relationship, are now the 'employees' of today, with all the implications of changed attitudes and relations that the change of vocabulary hints at. The same person can change too. The subjects of the *Law* develop new attitudes, needs and ambitions.

The lack of fit between *Law* and society can be dealt with in various ways. Courts are the great adjusters of laws to social realities; they perform their work of adjustment with or without the licence of the legislator. When we come on to a discussion of informal matrimonial relationships, we shall have occasion to illustrate this process of adjustment as it touches such aspects of family law as rights of succession and residence, and such aspects of property law as rights of statutory tenants. Courts seek such adjustment for most of the time by (a) *re-definition of instrumental legal terms*. I use the term 'term' rather than 'concept', as favoured by writers like Williams and Gluckman,[4] because what we are dealing with is the actual lexical item or phrase such as 'reasonable man'. Such terms are instrumental, because they are part of the connexion mechanism between the facts as perceived and found by the judge and the legal rules he applies to those facts. The terms are redefinable (a term I prefer to 'elastic' or 'permeable', as favoured by Gluckman) because, although they may be precisely defined, i.e. their function is prescribed, for any particular case or set of cases, they are always open to re-definition by another judge or for another period or for another set of cases.

The typical representative of this class of terms is the 'reasonable man', through whom or which so much of the modern law of negligence in tort is mediated. Judges use the reasonable man to answer two questions in negligence cases: (i) Is the relationship between plaintiff and defendant, from or in connexion with which the harm complained of arises, one in relation to which the law should lay down that the defendant owes a 'duty of care' to the plaintiff? (ii) In relation to that duty of care, if found to 'exist', has the defendant behaved 'reasonably' in what he has actually done, measured against what one might expect a 'reasonable man' to do in such circumstances? The reasonable man, sometimes expressed to be 'the man on the Clapham omnibus', is not and never has been an actual individual.

The way in which the English law of tort operates the term 'reasonable man' is well illustrated in the recent case of *British Railways Board v Herrington*,[5] in which the House of Lords had to reconcile competing principles: that a trespasser on land cannot complain of harm which he suffers there, that he trespasses at his peril; and that the owner of land is under a moral duty to protect those who come on his land, whether

4. See Max Gluckman *The ideas in Barotse jurisprudence* (Manchester, 1972), pp. 22 ff.; and G. Williams 'Language and the law' (1945) 61 LQR 71, 179, 293, 384; (1946) 62 LQR 387.
5. [1972] AC 877, [1972] 1 All ER 749, HL.

lawfully or otherwise, from harm which they cannot avoid, either because he has set a trap for them, or because they are too young to appreciate the dangers. Nineteenth-century English law took a stern view of the matter, and a child trespasser could not generally recover for harm, even if the harm could be said to be due to the failure of the owner to warn trespassers or to fence off the land. Twentieth-century courts have shifted steadily to the opposite view. This shift has been mediated by changing ideas of what a reasonable owner would or should do in such circumstances. So in *Herrington* Lord Reid made the railway liable for the injury suffered by a young child who strayed onto the line and came into contact with the live rail, on the ground that public policy in the matter had changed, and that 'current conceptions of social duty do require occupiers to give reasonable attention to their responsibilities as occupiers'. Lord Morris of Borth-y-Gest in his judgment appealed even more directly to the court of public opinion to decide the matter. He said:

'If the facts which I have outlined were put to any well-disposed but fair-minded member of the public, whether a parent or not, I venture to think that the response guided by the promptings of common sense would be that having regard to the dangerous nature of the live rail and its perils for a small child, the railways board were grievously at fault in allowing a fence at the particular place in question to remain for a long time in a broken-down condition.'[6]

Judgments in the *Herrington* case repeated the classic definitions of the reasonable man, which firmly locate him as the typical man of his times, even if gifted with more commonsense and foresight than many of the public. He is the 'private individual of common sense and ordinary intelligence'; the 'reasonable man, guided upon those considerations which ordinarily regulate the conduct of human affairs'. He is 'everyone of ordinary sense'.

Lord Wilberforce, however, rejected the appeal to the reasonable man. He said:

'. . . to adopt the expedient of recoiling upon the comfortable concept of the reasonable man is hardly good enough. It evades the problem by throwing it into the lap of the judge.'

And he went on to face squarely the accusation that the court might be making new law, when this was really the function of Parliament:

'But the common law is a developing entity as the judges develop it, and so long as we follow the well tried method of moving forward in accordance with principle as fresh facts emerge and changes in society occur, we are surely doing what Parliament intends we should do.'[7]

6. At 901, 760, respectively.
7. At 919, 921 and 776–7, 778, respectively.

And Lord Diplock was convinced that it was not possible to apply to a corporation, such as the Railways Board in this case, 'the objective standard of the reasonable man, by attributing to the fictitious person, the fictitious mind and judgment of a reasonable man'. He preferred to rest his conclusion on this ground:

'It [the decision of the court in this case] takes account, as this House as the final expositor of the common law should always do, of changes in social attitudes and circumstances and gives effect to the general public sentiment of what is "reckless" conduct as it has expanded over the forty years which have elapsed since the decision [in the earlier case which went the other way].'[8]

(b) *Contextual interpretation of statutes.* Many recent cases have affirmed the general principle that, in interpreting a statute, a court should have regard to the 'context' of the Act. This has primary reference to the state of the law immediately preceding the Act, but it can also take in the historical circumstances surrounding the enactment, and, at the level of particular terms, the linguistic context. In so far as the social context, either that of the date of enactment or that of the date of decision, is admitted to qualify or affect the interpretation of a statutory provision, social conditions, practices and attitudes may be imported and help to determine the law that will be applied.

The recent decision in *Dyson Holdings Ltd v Fox*[9] takes the function of contextual interpretation a stage further, by referring the meaning of a term such as 'family' in a statute to the current social context (i.e. the current popular acceptance of the meaning of the term), which may change from time to time. The facts of the case were that a man and woman had, though unmarried, lived together as man and wife for 40 years. She took his name and was known as 'Mrs Wright'. After their spending 21 years in a house which Mr Wright, the 'husband', rented as a tenant, he died. Both had lived in the house, both went out to work and used their earnings to meet the costs of running the house. Mrs Wright remained in the house after the death of Mr Wright in 1961, and continued to pay the rent to the landlords, whose records still showed the house as being in the name of Mr Wright. In 1973 title to the house was in a property company, Dyson Holdings Ltd. Mrs Wright wrote to them to ask for a statement of the weekly rent. She signed it with her own name. This provoked the landlord company to make enquiries, from which they discovered that Mr Wright had died in 1961, and that 'Mrs Wright' was not really his widow. The property company, after further correspondence, brought proceedings in the county court to recover possession, on the ground that Mrs Wright was not protected in her occupation as the surviving widow of the protected tenant under

8. At 941 and 795–6, respectively.
9. [1976] QB 503, [1975] 3 All ER 1030, CA.

the Rent Act 1968. The Rent Acts gave and give a right to a surviving relative of the deceased tenant whose possession is protected under the Acts to continue in occupation as a 'statutory tenant'. The right is given in these words:

'... the expression "tenant" includes the widow of a tenant ... who was residing with him at the time of his death, or where a tenant ... leaves no widow or is a woman, such member of the tenant's family so residing as aforesaid as may be decided in default of agreement by the county court.'

Mrs Wright had indeed been living in the house with the tenant at his death; but was she his 'widow'? Clearly not, as she had never been married to him. Did she then come in as a 'member of the tenant's family'? No, said the county court judge; he was bound by the 1950 decision in *Gammans v Ekins*,[10] decided by the Court of Appeal. There had been in that case a similar history of a man and woman living together as husband and wife for many years in a house of which he was the tenant when he died. In that case the Court of Appeal held firmly that she was *not* a member of the tenant's 'family'. Asquith LJ said:

'To say of two people masquerading, as these two were, as husband and wife (there being no children to complicate the picture) that they were members of the same family, seems to be an abuse of the English language ...'[11].

And that should have been that so far as the right of Mrs Wright was concerned if *Gammans v Ekins* was followed. But the Court of Appeal thought differently. The first hurdle which the Court had to overcome was that the earlier decision in *Gammans v Ekins* was binding on the Court in the instant case. Lord Denning swiftly brushed this objection aside. His first reason for rejecting the earlier authority was a sweeping one:

'... this court is not absolutely bound by a previous decision when it is seen that it can no longer be supported. At any rate, it is not so bound when, owing to the lapse of time, and the change in social conditions, the previous decision is not in accord with modern thinking.'[12]

But even this was not enough; the earlier decision in *Gammans v Ekins* had been wrong in itself, even at the time. '... When a statute uses an ordinary English word in its popular meaning as distinct from its legal meaning, it is for the tribunal of fact to decide whether or no that popular meaning covers the case in hand. The tribunal of fact must use

10. [1950] 2 KB 328, [1950] 2 All ER 140, CA.
11. At 331, 142, respectively.
12. At 509, 1033, of the reports.

its own understanding of the word and apply it to the facts which have been proved. A court of appeal should not interfere with its decision unless it was unreasonable . . .'

The conclusion was 'that *Gammans v Ekins* was wrongly decided'. Lords Justices James and Bridge would not go so far as Lord Denning on this point; though they agreed with him on his second point, about which he said:

'. . . we should hold that a couple who live together as man and wife for 20 years are members of the same family, whether they have children or not.'

The other two members of the Court of Appeal put flesh on this proposition, in words which were boldly chosen and widely framed. James LJ put it this way:

'Between 1950 and 1975 [the dates of the two cases] there have been many changes in the law effected by statute and decisions of the courts. Many changes have their foundation in the changed needs and views of society. Such changes have occurred in the field of family law and equitable interests in property. The popular meaning given to the word "family" is not fixed once and for all time. I have no doubt that with the passage of years it has changed. The cases reveal that it is not restricted to blood relationships and those created by the marriage ceremony. It can include de facto as well as de jure relationships. The popular meaning of "family" in 1975 would, according to the answer of the ordinary man, include the appellant as a member of Mr Wright's family. This is not to say that every mistress should be so regarded. Relationships of a casual or intermittent character and those bearing indications of impermanence would not come within the popular concept of a family unit.'[13]

Bridge LJ saw it the same way:

'. . . the question who is a "member of the tenant's family" is to be answered according to the understanding of the ordinary man, and this test has been consistently applied in all the other cases decided on this provision. Now it is, I think, not putting it too high to say that between 1950 and 1975 there has been a complete revolution in society's attitude to unmarried partnerships of the kind under consideration. Such unions are far commoner than they used to be. The social stigma that once attached to them has almost, if not entirely, disappeared. . . .

Can we give effect to this changed social attitude and consequent change in the scope of a common English word without doing violence to the doctrine of judicial precedent and notwithstanding that in this case the defendant's status must be considered at the date of the original tenant's death in 1961? I have felt some hesitation on both these points.

13. At 511, 1035 respectively.

but in the end have concluded that it would be unduly legalistic to allow either consideration to defeat the defendant's claim. On the first point, if language can change its meaning to accord with changing social attitudes, then a decision on the meaning of a word in a statute before such a change should not continue to bind thereafter, at all events in a case where the courts have consistently affirmed that the word is to be understood in its ordinary accepted meaning. On the second point, where the modern meaning is plain, we should, I think, be prepared to apply it retrospectively to any date, unless plainly satisfied that at that date the modern meaning would have been unacceptable.'[14]

Mrs Wright accordingly got her right recognised under the Rent Act.

We ought to be clear about what the members of the Court of Appeal were purporting to do in *Dyson Holdings Ltd v Fox*. They were meant to be applying a statutory provision; the fundamental philosophy of interpretation of statutes in English law is that the task of the judges in such a case is to give effect to the will of Parliament as the legislator, such will to be ascertained by and through the words which Parliament has chosen to use. In interpreting those words, the basic rule is that their meaning is to be taken as that which prevailed at the date of enactment. Quite clearly, any other rule would lead to absurdity, if one adheres to the principle that it is the intention of Parliament which counts. Now the judges in this case were saying that their job is not just to carry out the will of Parliament, but to adjust the results of following the wish of Parliament to the changing social context. In a typically English way they have used a routine for interpreting *words* as a way of recognising a changed *reality*.

A differently constituted bench of the Court of Appeal in the very recent case of *Helby v Rafferty*[15] were not at all happy about this approach. This case too involved succession to a statutory tenancy by one partner in an informal relationship; though there were differences, upon which the Court of Appeal seized, between the facts of this case and *Dyson*. In this case the tenancy of the flat in question was vested in the female partner, who was a statutory tenant when her contractual tenancy ran out. The male partner lived with her in this flat; but they had no intention of getting married, did not hold themselves out as man and wife, and the female did not assume the male's name or describe herself as 'Mrs'. Stamp LJ would have followed *Gammans v Ekins* in holding that the male partner was not a member of his deceased partner's 'family', had not the authority of *Dyson Holdings v Fox* got in the way. 'The ordinary or natural meaning of the expression "member of a family" would not, in my judgment, apply to a person in the position of Mr Rafferty [the surviving male partner].'

14.   At 513, 1036, respectively.
15.   [1978] 3 All ER 1016, CA.

Stamp LJ was not at all happy with the procedure adopted by James and Bridge LJJ in *Dyson* for referring to the changing social interpretation of a statutory expression like 'family', by relying on changing popular meanings of the word. He said:

'I confess that, apart from authority, I would have taken the view that the language of a statute by whatever process you apply to its construction, whether you construe it in its natural and ordinary meaning or whether you construe it in a popular way or whether you construe it in what has sometimes been called a "legal way" (and I am not sure I understand what the difference is) cannot alter its meaning from time to time and that, in order to find out what Parliament intended by the statute, you must ascertain what the words of the statute meant when Parliament used those words ... it appears to me that the difficulty of determining whether a particular meaning of the words in an Act of Parliament would be given to those words by popular vote or not would be of a different kind. Do you listen to the vociferous minority or do you imagine what the silent majority might have said at a particular time?'[16]

Despite these doubts, Stamp LJ proposed to follow loyally the decision in *Dyson Holdings v Fox*,[17] (even though one could hardly say that the decision in *Dyson* had loyally followed the earlier authority of *Gammans v Ekins*![18]). Choosing the formulation of James and Bridge LJJ rather than that of Lord Denning, Stamp LJ found significant differences between the circumstances in the two cases of *Dyson* and *Helby v Rafferty*. There was not such permanence and stability as to justify the conclusion that each party in the relationship was in the instant case a member of the family of the other. Miss Taylor (the female in the partnership) had expressly kept her freedom and her own name; she could have withdrawn from the relationship at any time.

Roskill LJ was of a like mind:

'I confess I know of no authority, and none has been cited, to support the view that where you get almost identical language repeatedly used in a succession of statutes, starting in 1920 and ending in 1977, which is the date of the present Rent Act, it is possible to give the same word a different interpretation in 1977 from that which it bore in (say) 1920 or 1950.'[19]

As was Cumming Bruce LJ:

'I have the greatest difficulty in following how the meaning of that word [i.e. an "ordinary English word"] and the intention of Parliament

16. At 1018.
17. [1975] 3 All ER 1030.
18. [1950] 2 All ER 140.
19. At 1024.

in relation to the selection of that word by the draftsman changes its meaning over a period of 25 years. I still find it difficult to see how the change in social habit, to which their Lordships referred in *Dyson Holdings Ltd v Fox,* has the effect of changing the meaning of the word enacted and re-enacted in successive Acts of Parliament, the word being an ordinary word . . .'[20]

The agonies of the two sets of Lords Justices of Appeal in these two cases spring from the clash between rigid rules or canons of construction on the one hand, which cannot be abandoned without throwing the certainty of the law and the authority of judicial precedents into doubt, and the desire to give effect to major changes in social institutions and attitudes on the other. The Court in *Dyson* used 'family' instrumentally to mediate the recognition of a change in the law, in its turn reflecting a change in society. The term 'family' was not, however, an 'instrumental legal term' within our definition and use of that expression, because their Lordships specifically said, and repeated, that although 'family' had been used by the draftsmen in successive Rent Acts, yet it was not a term of art or legal term, but a mere 'ordinary' or 'popular' word. Instrumental legal terms are terms which only courts know the meaning of (whatever gestures in the direction of popular usage they may make in passing, as in *Herrington*). 'Ordinary or popular words' are terms which the judges declare they do not know the meaning of any better than the man in the street, to whom they appeal for enlightenment. The Court in *Helby v Rafferty* went the other way; what its members said in effect was that, once a term has been used by the draftsman in a given statute and has received authoritative judicial interpretation, it becomes a legal term, whatever its origin in popular usage may have been. This renders subsequent appeal to popular usage improper, however correctly judges, when first confronted by the term, refer to the ordinary or dictionary meaning of it as ascertained by investigating popular usage.

In this conflict of views, the later Court had the better of the argument, if one is to keep the canons of statutory interpretation intact; however, if part of the job of the judge is to adjust the *Law* to changing social reality, then the judges in *Dyson* had the right mind, even if their technique offended against correct and classical canons of judicial behaviour. A better solution altogether might be, and might have been, if either the legislature or the courts frankly confronted the need to recognise new practices and new institutions from time to time, rather than admitting them partially, gradually and grudgingly to legal recognition. The will of Parliament was doubtfully served by the decision in *Dyson*; but maybe justice was done to the social obligations which the parties had created by their conduct. When we come on to a detailed discussion of the 'common-law wife', we shall argue that it is

20.   At 1026.

high time that the legal system afforded a more systematic recognition of this institution; such clarification is especially needed because while the rights which the parties create *inter se* by their own contracts and understandings are largely their own affair, and can be left to the law of contract to sort out, once third parties come into it, whether as creditors, landlords, or children of the parties, then the *Law* must take a hand.

So although the courts in England constantly adjust the laws to changing social conditions, whether these laws are unenacted common law or equity or enacted statutes, yet it is generally the case that the legislator must intervene eventually if all aspects of the desirable changes are to be sufficiently covered before controversy arises.

B TRANSLOCATION OF LAWS

Twenty-five years, according to the Court of Appeal in *Dyson Holdings Ltd v Fox*, were enough to work 'a complete revolution' in society, and hence in the law applicable to matrimonial relationships. The result of such a revolution will be a major mismatch between law and society, even though the law in question was originally generated by, and was designed for, that society. No interval of time at all is required to make a *Law* which is transposed — from the society which gave it birth to a new society overseas — out of fit with the receiving society. This would be so even if the two societies, giving and receiving, were broadly comparable — as were, say, England and the Australian colonies at the time of the general reception of English law in Australia. *A fortiori* when the receiving society is in fact a collection of traditional non-European peoples ruled by customary *Law* or religious *Law* of a non-Christian kind, and imported western *Law* is imposed on them *en bloc* and immediately. And yet this was exactly the history of colonisation in the Asian and African continents; it was the standard procedure for the European powers (and here Britain was no different in its basic provision from other European colonial powers) to impose on their newly acquired territories a legal system deriving from that of the mother country. Compulsory imposition *ab extra* is thus one major mode of what we may term 'translocation of laws'. Quite literally, this means that a law, whether a complete legal system or a specific part of it, is shifted bodily from its home territory to new ground. Other writers have referred to this as 'migration of laws', or 'transplantation of laws'. The former usage has tendencies towards the pathetic fallacy, as if the laws themselves had decided to wander; whereas the truth of the matter is that the laws have been forcibly shifted by human agency. Sometimes, it is true, migrant colonists take their laws with them: this has been one of the great principles of British colonial law, and explains how the American colonies were equipped with the English common law from their beginnings. But if we analyse the legal reasons why the common law migrated in such cases, it is that the metropolitan legal system for its own purposes and reasons declared this to be the governing meta-norm. At bottom, then, these laws migrated because they were made to migrate. As for 'transplantation', the botanical or horticultural metaphor is an attractive one. Lord Denning, for one, has been much drawn to it, as in the leading case of *Nyali Ltd v Attorney-General*[1]. A provision in the East Africa Protectorate Order in Council, 1902, as amended, article 15, said that the English common law was to apply in the Protectorate 'subject to such qualifications as local circumstances render necessary'. Denning LJ said, in commenting on this provision, that:

'The next proviso provides, however, that the common law is to apply "subject to such qualifications as local circumstances render necessary". This wise provision should, I think, be liberally construed. It is a recognition that the common law cannot be applied in a foreign land without considerable qualification. Just as with an English oak, so with the English common law. You cannot transplant it to the African continent and expect it to retain the tough character which it has in England. It will flourish indeed, but it needs careful tending. So with the common law.'[2]

The metaphor of an oak is an apter one than might be imagined. Firstly, the oak has a deep tap-root, which anchors it to the soil in which it grows and draws sustenance from it. Sever this tap-root, and one risks depriving the plant of nourishment. Secondly, the oak is a typically temperate-zone tree, which is likely to be unable to resist the droughts and scorching suns of the tropics. Thirdly, the nutrients it seeks and requires are unlikely to be found in the impoverished soils of Africa. Just so with the common law. Its deep tap-root in English life and history is what it feeds on; the African and other societies to which it has been applied are not fertile soil for it; and the oak of the common law could only survive if soil is sent with the tree, and if some shelter from the burning, arid sun is provided for it. In our export of common law we have commonly neglected these requirements. The exported common law is shallow-rooting; and we have not enriched the soil in which it is set.

Official limits on the application of English law

The English common law (and here we must remark that the exported law included the English doctrines of equity, and English Acts of Parliament as in force at a certain date in England) was, by the Orders in Council or Ordinances, as the case may have been, imposed totally and at one fell swoop on the colonial territories after they had been

1. [1956] 1 QB1, [1955] 1 All ER 646, CA.
2. At 16, 653 respectively.

newly acquired. The extension and application of English law in such colonies were not without limits or qualifications, though. Firstly, there is the limitation to which Denning LJ's remarks in *Nyali Ltd v Attorney-General* have already drawn attention. That case was a fascinating exploration of byways of colonial acquisition and trans-location of laws, which can serve as a starting point and illustration of some of the limits on the application of English *Law* in the colonies. Though the case concerned the East African territory of Kenya, the action was commenced in the English High Court, and went from there on appeal to the English Court of Appeal — to the lasting enrichment of the jurisprudence of colonial law. The plaintiff was a company, Nyali Ltd, which sought a declaration as against the Crown in England that military forces of the British Government (other than military forces and vehicles of the Kenya (colonial) Government) were not exempted from paying tolls for crossing the Nyali Bridge, which connected the island of Mombasa with the mainland. This bridge, erected by the company in 1931 after an agreement with the Government of the Kenya Colony and Protectorate in 1929, was a toll-bridge, and the agreement expressly provided that 'No tolls shall be levied in respect of police or military on duty or their equipment, baggage or transport'. When war broke out in 1939, no traffic came across the bridge other than military traffic, which would have paid no tolls. By special agree-ment between the Government of Kenya and the bridge company, however, a lump sum was paid to the company in lieu of tolls, thus enabling the bridge to be maintained. At the end of the war in 1948, the army authorities refused to pay any tolls on the lapse of the agreement.

These circumstances, unusual enough, were made even more exceptional by the special status of the territory within which they occurred. Mombasa Island and the mainland opposite were part of the then Kenya Protectorate, which was a ten-mile strip of land along the East African coast which in theory was still part of the possessions of the Sultan of Zanzibar, even though, by agreement with the Sultan, it had been placed in 1890[3] under the protection of the British Crown. Mombasa had been the gateway to British East Africa, which later became Kenya Colony. The jurisdiction of the British Crown in a protectorate, albeit a colonial protectorate of this kind, was limited in British constitutional theory, and extended only to such powers as had been acquired by treaty, etc, within the terms of the Foreign Jurisdiction Act 1890. The Kenya Protectorate so constituted was administered with the Kenya Colony (when this was formed in 1920), and the law applicable in the Protectorate was as provided for the East Africa Protectorate and later for the Colony, viz.:

3. Incorrectly stated as 1895 in the *All England* report of Denning LJ's judgment.

'[Indian Acts, local colonial enactments, and] so far as the same shall not extend or apply . . . the substance of the common law, the doctrines of equity, and the statutes of general application in force in England on August 12, 1897 . . .

Provided always that the said common law, doctrines of equity, and statutes of general application shall be in force in the protectorate so far only as the circumstances of the protectorate and its inhabitants and the limits of Her Majesty's jurisdiction permit and subject to such qualifications as local circumstances render necessary.'[4]

We shall ignore entirely the limits on the reception of English *Law* into Kenya consequent on the choice of words in the 'reception formula', save to draw attention to them and refer the reader to a more extended discussion in *New Essays in African Law*.[5] These limits comprise:

(i)   the *substance* of the common law, etc;
(ii) statutes of *general* application;
(iii) the limiting date or *date of reception*, in this case August 12th, 1897.

Here we concentrate attention on the proviso. The phrase, 'the limits of Her Majesty's jurisdiction', has both a geographical and juristic connotation, the former being defined by the limits of the area subjected to the jurisdiction of the Crown, the latter by the nature of the jurisdiction acquired in that area. Far more important is the limitation of the application of the English *Law* to cases where 'the circumstances of the protectorate and its inhabitants . . . permit'. In theory this would appear to have given judges in colonial territories a free hand in rejecting any part of the received law of England which they felt was out of fit or keeping with local circumstances. The most obvious of such local circumstances must have been that the inhabitants were, as to the vast majority, not English people, or even persons from Britain or Europe, but indigenous Africans with a sprinkling, in the case of the Kenya Protectorate, of Arabs. The local population, moreover, was at the time of initial colonisation living a totally non-European way of life, and even at the date of colonial independence (1963 in the case of Kenya) was still living in part in accordance with its own customs.

One must pause for a moment to contemplate the juristic enormity of what was done by the colonial power. A legal system, which had partly evolved organically from the Middle Ages, and had partly been reshaped by Victorian reformist legislation in the interests of the newly industrialised society of 19th century England and of new social ideas about the status and treatment of women, children and working people, was transferred lock, stock and barrel to the shores of East Africa, where there was a population of simple agriculturalists living without

4. East Africa Order in Council 1902, art. 15.
5. A. N. Allott *New Essays in African Law* (1970) Chap. 2.

any chiefly rule or vestige of a state structure in grass huts and subjected to the nominal suzerainty of an Arab sultan in another island further along the coast, living in his turn in accordance with the prescriptions (somewhat watered down) of Islamic *Law* and the pattern of life prescribed by the *Shari'a*. The white men who were there to impose western rule and order, start the railway to the interior, and begin to develop commerce with the outside world, were a tiny and conspicuously different minority. Savigny and those like him who see *Law* as an organic growth within and from a people could not but have a fit in contemplating the resultant situation. The progressive sociological school of jurists would find nothing in East Africa which fitted in with their views of how *Law* works. Only the imperative school could feel happy: the sovereign commanded — that was sufficient ground of validity. If ever there was an illustration of the programmatic use of law-making, that is, the use of *Law* not to create an immediate, binding system of norms but to set a model to which the pattern of social living could evolve in the future, this was it.

The saving virtue of the proviso was in fact rarely called on by the colonial judges, whether of East Africa or elsewhere. The cases are rare in the law reports of these territories in which the proviso has been invoked, or even complied with by implication. The proviso, as will be seen, gave the judge the power, not only to disallow received laws which he thought were out of fit with local circumstances, but to rewrite those laws to make them fit: '. . . subject to such qualifications as local circumstances render necessary'. Judges were remarkably inhibited in exercising these powers; when they did, the result was often disastrous. This timorous approach contrasts oddly with the more adventurous spirit which came into Anglo-American jurisprudence in the 20th century, and of which Mr Justice Holmes in North America, and Lord Denning himself in England, were prime examples.

Another, and much more substantial, limitation on the application of the received English *Law* was the concurrent continued recognition given to indigenous customary and religious *Laws* in cases where the parties were Africans or non-Europeans. As this is a large topic, and as it is not involved in *Nyali Bridge* with which we are at the moment concerned, we can postpone discussion of it to a later section.[6] Let us then return to our case.

There are few more arcane branches of the English *Law* than that which relates to ferries, bridges, and tolls, where these are operated, constructed, or demanded (respectively) by private citizens. The law on the Crown grant of a franchise of pontage is to be found in the ancient common law of England; it was significant that the first authority cited by Denning LJ was one decided in 1602, and that he could say that 'There are no modern instances of a Crown grant of

6. See pp. 115 ff.

franchise' [sc. in England]. A Crown grant of a franchise of pontage is an exercise of the royal prerogative. Did such a prerogative run in a protectorate? Yes, said Denning LJ; but in a protectorate such a prerogative applies with 'such qualifications as local circumstances render necessary', and this proviso must be 'liberally construed'. The qualification adopted, in order to render possible the exercise in the protectorate of the prerogative power to grant franchises of tolls, was that the technicalities of granting the franchise (i.e. by formal record through a charter or letters patent) would not be needed, and a grant of a franchise to take a toll could be granted by the governor by an agreement in writing without any formalities, such as formal enrolment.

But then one comes on to the claim by the Crown to be exempted from all tolls exacted under such a franchise, and we return to technicalities of English common law with a vengeance, because, said Denning LJ, whether the Crown is exempt or not depends on whether the toll is a 'toll-thorough' or a 'toll-traverse'. The broad difference is that a toll-traverse is one demanded where a man makes a new bridge or crossing; a toll-thorough is one where the public have already been in the habit of crossing from time immemorial. The Crown is exempt from toll-thorough, but not from toll-traverse, and this, said Denning LJ, was a toll-traverse. Despite his review of this law, and indeed his willingness to find that this was a toll-traverse, Denning LJ shortened the discussion by refusing to 'go into all these subtleties. They are quite unsuited to the Kenya Protectorate. Toll-thorough and toll-traverse have as little place there as they have in modern England'.[7]

His conclusion was that the Crown was not exempt from tolls in this case unless the agreement provided to the contrary. Under the agreement one could not, he said, make a distinction between locally raised troops, e.g. the King's African Rifles, and imperial or UK troops. On the construction of the agreement, it exempted military vehicles driven by a driver on duty, and soldiers in such a vehicle; but men on leave, wives and children must pay a toll. A similar conclusion was come to by the other members of the Court of Appeal.[8]

7. At 654.
8. A certain sentimental annotation of the *Nyali* case may not be out of place, affecting both myself and Lord Denning. Having served in Kenya in the King's African Rifles in 1944–6, having been lodged at the Nyali Beach transit camp, and having consequently frequently used the Nyali Bridge and having, through my service in East Africa, been led to an interest in Africa and eventually in African law, I naturally was personally concerned with the case and its details, as well as academically assisted by the discussion, albeit in an unusual context, of fundamental problems of the application of English *Law* in Africa.

   As for Lord Denning, I suspect that this may have been the first time when he was exposed, in such completeness, to the legal systems of Africa in his judicial capacity (though he was later, during his time in the House of Lords, to gain further African experience by sitting on some very significant appeals in the Privy Council). The impatience with the minutiae of antique

The *Nyali Bridge* case touched only on the limitation to the application of English law in British African colonies imposed by the proviso to the general reception of English *Law* making it applicable only so far as local circumstances permitted; and it was by invocation of this proviso that the Court of Appeal refused to apply the technicalities of the English common law relating to franchises of pontage in the Kenya Protectorate. The case was a strange one in that the argument used by the Court bore no special reference to Africa or to the nature and culture of its inhabitants, and the decision could have been the same in any other part of the world with an underdeveloped administrative system. And yet the main limitation on the application of English and English-type *Law* in African countries has come, not from this proviso, but from a quite separate provision of the statutes which introduced English *Law* as the basis of the general colonial legal system; this limitation is enshrined in legislation of which we may take that of Uganda in 1902 as representative of the common East and Central African form (a more complex form of words was used for West Africa):

'In all cases, civil and criminal, to which natives are parties, every court . . . shall be guided by native law so far as it is applicable and is not repugnant to justice and morality or inconsistent with any Order in Council, Ordinance, or any regulation or rule made under any Order in Council or Ordinance . . .'[9]

The effect of this vaguely worded provision was to exclude the application of English *Law* almost totally in civil disputes between Africans, and also to begin with in most criminal cases too. Such cases were tried in indigenous tribal, native, or customary courts by African judges in accordance with African customary *Laws*. A sort of legal apartheid was thus constituted: English-type courts and English-type

---

learning in the common law with little relevance to the present day which has marked his judgments may be detected in this appeal. Lord Denning went on to preside over the Conference on The Future of Law in Africa, held under the auspices of the Colonial Office in London in December 1959; to preside over a committee to review professional legal education for students from Africa in the United Kingdom in 1960; and to develop wide contacts with, and deep interest in, the *Laws* and lawyers of Africa and other parts of the Commonwealth. The *Nyali Bridge* case has thus had peripheral consequences of some importance.

Lord Denning and the present author share an interest also in silviculture, which is why the arboricultural metaphor with which we began this section must have appealed to Lord Denning. This is also good reason for looking closely at the appositeness of the metaphor, and the possibilities of cultivating trees of temperate lands in the tropics; here Lord Denning's possible lack of experience in tropical forestry may have led him astray!

9. Uganda Order in Council 1902, art. 20 (now repealed and replaced).

laws for the tiny non-African population, for commercial dealings, and for the small fraction of the African population which gradually became sufficiently westernised or in contact with western civilisation to attract the law of England to them; African-style courts and African laws for the majority African population. This sharp division was broken down in time, firstly by the enactment of Penal Codes and other criminal legislation which was applied to Africans; and later by the offering to Africans otherwise subject to customary *Law* of the option to make use of English legal institutions, such as contract and marriage, real property, and testamentary dispositions.

To revert to the botanical metaphor: the English oak had been transplanted to Africa, but to begin with it grew only in a well-tended garden immediately surrounding the colonists; it did not take its chance in the forest or the wilderness outside. Its rooting system was shallow, as it soon struck the impermeable layer of lateritic soil underlying the whole of the terrain, this layer being the African cultures which were there when it arrived and which were highly resistant to western influence. Its manuring and tending were entrusted to a tiny band of lawyers trained in English, Indian, or other common-law systems. They were rather unimaginative gardeners. As time wore on, so the former impermeability of the African pan was broken down by missionary influence, education, and the development of commerce; the English oak started to root outside its former compound. Nutrients from the African soil began to work their way through these roots into the main body of the tree, causing it to shed some of its leaves and branches, and altering the coloration of the rest. Indigenous African lawyers looked after the plant in a different way from their European predecessors. Finally, in a development which would astound the botanists of Kew Gardens, the oak developed hybrid features consistent with an intergeneric graft.

Types of translocation

This general transplant by an alien political superior of a legal system to a new environment has been only one of the ways in which laws have been translocated in different continents and different centuries. It is not possible to explore them all here; but we must remember that the process is an ancient one — the spread of classical Roman *Law* to many parts of the Roman Empire being a case in point. Even in this case the triumphal progress of Roman *Law* was not uninterrupted or overwhelming; conquered Greece led her rough conqueror captive[10] to such effect that, by the time of Justinian, Roman *Law* was in some measure Greek legal institutions in Roman dress:

10. Graecia capta ferum victorem cepit: Horace, Ep. 2, 1, 156.

'It is held [by modern scholars] that an element of the greatest importance in the development of the post-classical law lies in the adoption of principles derived from the native Hellenistic law of the Eastern Provinces, which was able, in spite of the *constitutio Antoniniana*, to assert itself successfully against the Roman system. But it is also held that Hellenic influences were felt in another way, and that the law, as it appears in the Corpus Juris, has been profoundly affected by the application of Greek philosophical methods and conceptions in the schools, and the consequent development of generalisations and classifications alien from the practical spirit of the true Roman law.'[11]

What an irony! Roman *Law* spread throughout the world, not just in the first period when it was a concomitant of imperial power, but in the medieval and modern period when it was seen as the flower of intellectual achievement in the juristic sciences; and yet it was the customs and way of life and thought of slaves, provincials and non-Romans which had prevailed. It is far too early to say whether the history of English common law in African and other countries to which it has spread will be the same; after all, from Augustus to Justinian took five centuries, while those who ushered in independence in Africa are still alive.

Translocation of laws by act of government. Apart, then, from their imposition by a political superior from outside, and their spread through intellectual channels in the universities, legal institutions can be brought into new locations by act of governments and act of parties. The autonomous governments of modern states have, or have given themselves, the power to make new laws; but making a new law is a difficult task. Legislative originality is rare. The commonest way of making a law today is to imitate someone else's law; no wonder that the English Law Commission is adjured to inspect foreign systems of law before recommending changes in our own; no wonder that the draftsman in an African country commences his task by taking down from his shelf the current law of England, or of some other African or other country, which he can use as a model. Laws are still being actively translocated by this means. If we may cite recent African legislative experience, the English divorce law of 1969, introducing a radical new concept of breakdown of marriage, was rapidly imitated in Ghanaian and Nigerian legislation by legislators who claimed that they were modernising their law and making it more relevant to *their* conditions.[12]

Translocation of laws can either be piecemeal, as in the instance just given, or wholesale. One of the most celebrated examples of the latter

11. H. F. Jolowicz *Historical Introduction to the Study of Roman Law* (1932), p. 518.
12. See the English Divorce Reform Act 1969, the Nigerian Matrimonial Causes Decree 1970 (No. 18 of 1970), and the Ghana Matrimonial Causes Act 1971.

is, of course, the reception of foreign law in Turkey under Kemal Ataturk. In revolt against the Ottoman system, Ataturk sought immediate modernisation of his country through law; he thought that, to modernise a country, one must modernise its laws, and that it was simpler to do this by taking over another country's laws rather than by inventing one's own. He lighted on the Swiss civil law as appropriate for his purposes, and adopted a new law for Turkey by re-enacting the Swiss Civil Code. The social and legal problems to which this gave rise must be explored in Chapter 6, which deals with the employment of law for purposes of social transformation; here all that need be remarked is that there had been no prior cultural or legal connexion between Switzerland and Turkey, and one could hardly imagine two countries farther apart in location, size, ethnic composition, religion, political institutions, or history.[13] Similar examples can be found in Japan, and in a multiplicity of countries which have at different times adopted, for instance, the French Code Napoléon or the Soviet system of *Law*.

It would be quite wrong to think that the *gradient of translocation* always slopes one way, from the highly developed (industrially as well as legally) countries to the less developed, even though a good deal of adoption of foreign laws is attributable to colonial imposition, while another goodly portion is the result of attempts at modernisation by under-developed countries. There is quite a trade between countries at a similar level of development, though this for the most part takes place within legal families (the common-law family, the civil-law family) rather than between them. On the common-law side, the juristic influence of American laws and practice on the evolution of English *Law* is persistent and pervasive — at the official and at the unofficial level. At the official level one can cite the Bail Act 1976, which undoubtedly owes much to American influence and innovations. At the unofficial level, one may mention our friend the 'common-law wife', who is fighting her way into English *Law*, and the pressure for 'due process' in police procedures. Legislation about racial and sex equality is also heavily in debt to American precedents. The English law-maker does not hesitate to look at, and often adopt or adapt, the laws of other Commonwealth countries. In the 19th century laws made in and for British India had the greatest effect in England (cf. Sir James Stephen and the Indian Evidence Act for one example). In the early 20th century Scottish influence, especially on criminal matters, was much in evidence. Now it is countries like Australia and New Zealand which are pioneering, and which the English legislator tends to follow — 'no-fault liability' in the law of torts may be a future instance.

There are even instances where a case can be made for saying that legal influence has flowed up-hill, from less developed to more developed

13. One does not know the truth of assertions that Ataturk was influenced in his choice of Swiss law by a chance meeting with a Swiss law professor

countries. As a specialist in African customary *Laws*, I am constantly struck by the tendencies in modern English *Law* which seem to copy African traditional legal approaches and institutions. The most striking example by far of this tendency is in the law of divorce. The modern English law of divorce has retreated completely first from the position that marriage is indissoluble, and then from the position that marriage may only be dissolved at the instance of one party for a matrimonial offence committed by the other party, and that divorce is a judicial act. The modern law incorporates 'no-fault' divorce, the concept of the matrimonial offence is gone (though its ghost haunts us, it is true), and the will of the parties to end the marriage, even in concert, is the socially effective act which terminates it (even though the *Law* must rubber-stamp their decision). Write-in and quickie divorces use the machinery of the court merely as a registry; and the remnants of judicial power in dissolving marriages have no more significance than the functions of the Vehicle Licensing Centre at Swansea in recording changes of ownership of motor vehicles. Now all these features of the modern English *Law* resemble the most characteristic features of African customary divorce procedures. Is the resemblance accidental? One would be tempted to think that it was; but a closer examination of the biographies and personal experiences of some of those who have been at the centre of the agitation for the reform of the English divorce law, or who have had a hand in its drafting, will show that a significant number of them have had African experience, which, it is fair to presume, may have given them a quite different perspective on the possibilities and functioning of divorce laws.

Translocation of laws by act of parties. People do not have to wait for their rulers to make law; they can make it themselves. Such popular law-making can work in one of two ways: (i) in conformity with the existing *Law*, which gives discretionary power to its subjects to choose legal regimes or adopt their own; (ii) in contravention of existing *Law*, when parties begin to disregard the rules and requirements of the *Law* and substitute their own. Popular norm-making of the first type is *catanomic* (in accordance with or in pursuance of the law); of the second type *paranomic* (contrary to the existing provision of the law, illegal or unconstitutional). The practice of conveyancers in England is catanomic and law-making; large portions of the English law of real property represent a codification of the practices of conveyancers. Similarly with most agreements recognised by *Law*; the parties are given freedom, within the framework set by the *Law* and subject to any restrictions as to content or form which any particular statute may impose, to make their own law. The continued practice of commercial men in a particular business or trade will similarly be law-making, either because it is made eventually into statute law, as with the Sale of Goods Act 1893, and many other similar Acts, or because the courts are prepared to recognise it as commercial custom or usage, binding by deemed incorporation in contracts of particular types.

By exercise of their catanomic law-making powers subjects of the law can choose foreign models or ideas as the basis of their legal relationships. Sometimes, as with foreign commercial contracts, this choice may be total, and the contract will be regulated exclusively by a foreign law. Although in theory English traders can use foreign laws in their foreign contracts, and perhaps also in their domestic contracts,[14] the usual trend has been the other way, and English *Law* has been extensively adopted as the law of the contract in cases where neither the parties nor the subject-matter of the contract have an intrinsic connexion with England. English *Law* has thus been diffused and translocated throughout the world of commerce. The adoption of uniform commercial laws has a similar effect; in such a case, the uniform law may not exactly represent the existing law of any signatory or adherent to it. However, to the extent that the code relies on foreign features, so those features are translocated; and it is often the case in practice that the codes rely disproportionately on the dominant legal systems in international commerce, which may be American or English.

Popular law-making can also go on at the domestic level without reliance on foreign models. Thus the 'common-law wife' in England represents an English adaptation to changing social circumstances in England. At its base lies a voluntary choice by the parties to such a relationship of a particular normative pattern. It would be difficult, however, to ignore the influence which the very idea of 'common-law marriage', spread from American films and television, has had in giving shape, and eventually respectability, to the relationship, and which is gradually converting it from paranomic to catanomic status.[15]

14. See the dicta in the leading case of *Vita Food Products Inc v Unus Shipping Co Ltd* [1939] AC 277, PC and in the subsequent cases and academic writings in which the point — whether parties have complete freedom as to which legal system they choose to regulate their contract — has been discussed.

15. For a full discussion of these developments in the context of English *Law*, see Chapter 8 below.

5 Exclusion of law by other normative systems

Law is only one normative system among many which compete for the attention and the allegiance of those to whom they are addressed. Religion, morality, community *mores*, are three examples of such normative systems. To the subject, the recipient of normative messages, the difficulty is, as already pointed out in an earlier Chapter,[1] to discriminate between these normative messages of different types, and, if his concern is to detect and obey the legal message, to filter out those messages which are not legal. Two main issues arise from this competition: the problem of detection or discrimination of the legal message; and the exclusion of enfeeblement of the legal prescription by other prescriptions which the subject takes to be of prior importance or to have prior claim on his allegiance. The first is the problem of *noise*; the second is the problem of *persuasion*.

A DETECTION OF THE LEGAL MESSAGE IN COMPETITION WITH OTHER NORMATIVE MESSAGES

The theoretical problem

To the law-emitter or norm-giver the legal message is *his* message, which must get through to its intended recipient and influence his behaviour. The communications medium is saturated with other messages, some of which are or purport to be normative. Let us begin by recalling what has already been written about this situation:

'. . . not every message carrying normative instructions about behaviour is a legal message. The recipient is receiving messages from a variety of sources telling him what he "ought" to do: messages from his religion; ethical messages; messages from those he regards as authoritative in matters of conduct, such as leader-writers in newspapers, and television

1. Pp. 14 ff., above.

or radio commentators; messages from his work-mates, his neighbours, his family, his friends; messages from the past. Can the legal message override all these competing messages (where they do not reinforce each other, as they often do not)? The legal message has a special interest and importance for its recipient, because it says to him that this is what his society, or persons with authority in that society and over that society, command or suggest he should do.'[2]

The main antithesis usually employed is that between 'law' and 'morality'. The suggestion generally made by writers is that *Law* is what is made by an authority in a political society for those subject to it in order to regulate their behaviour, and that it is generally (imperative school) or often (other schools) accompanied and supported by sanctions for disobedience, such sanctions being imposed by the authority or in accordance with routines approved by that authority. Morality, on the other hand, is presented as the dictates of *right behaviour*, not generally or necessarily made by an authority in a political society. There may be overlap between the dictates of morality and the norms of *Law*, either in the sense that the same action is commanded or prohibited both by *Law* and morality, or in the sense that obedience to the *Law* may itself be a moral precept. The sanctioning of moral precepts does not attract the political authority's intervention (or this would turn it into a legal reaction). Quite often the *Law* commands what morality does not command: in such a case, either (i) what the *Law* commands is morally neutral, in that it attracts no specific moral precept for or against the commanded action, or (ii) what the *Law* commands goes against morality, in that either (a) the *Law* commands what the precepts of morality prohibit, or (b) the *Law* fails to command what morality requires. In case (ii) (b) we say that 'there is a moral obligation to so something, but no legal obligation'; in case (i) we say that 'there is a legal obligation, but no moral obligation'; and so on.

To be able to write the preceding paragraph it would seem essential to be able to discriminate, by definition or otherwise, between *Law* and morality, or the sentences of the types quoted will have no patent meaning. But all definitions are circular and return on themselves. Some attempt was made at a preliminary sorting out of the differences in Chapter 1;[3] but this attempt followed the philosophy adumbrated at pp. 2–3, viz. that use of terms is always provisional, and that one adopts a working hypothesis as to appropriate uses of given terms to see whether these assist with the clarification of reality. There is not, and never will be, a god-given definition of either 'law' or 'morality', since each term refers to what is a human construct, the content of which is ever-changing. This is the theoretical problem which must be faced by every person who purports to tell us how *Law* differs from morality. If

2. At p. 14.
3. See pp. 23–6.

one seeks for a *discriminating characteristic* — such as that (1) *Law* deals with external behaviour, morality with the inner man; or (2) *Law* is part of a political system, morality is not; or (3) *Law* (= a legal system) has secondary rules which prescribe who may make valid norms (= a legislature) and who may authoritatively decide disputes about the application of such norms (= courts), while moral systems lack such institutions — then one is asserting that there is something in the essence of *Law* which marks it out as such from morality. But *Law* and LAW have no essence; so no characteristic can be essential.

When in a difficulty of this kind it is often a good idea to refuse to play word-games. One should stop the questioner who poses awkward Socratic questions of the type, How can one tell *Law* apart from morality?, and pose him a counter-question, 'Why do you want to know?'. If his only reason for knowing is idle curiosity, to fill his book, or to tie his respondent up in verbal knots, the best answer is to withdraw from the game! All explanation of linguistic terms and usage, that is, must be *functional* and *action-orientated*.

Why then, do we want to know? We can begin with the ordinary citizen, the subject of the *Law*, and *his* problem. A variety of normative prescriptions of various types reach him from different sources; if told that 'You must do such-and-such', he might well wish to ask:

1. 'Who says that I must do it?'
2. 'What authority has he got to tell me what to do?'
3. 'What happens if I don't do it?'

We must add, if he doesn't, one or two formal and additional questions:

4. 'To whom is the prescription addressed — to an individual, or to a class of individuals?'
5. 'What is the content of the prescription?'
6. 'What is the machinery through which the reaction mentioned in Question 3 will be determined and applied?'

The answer to these questions can be crucial to the citizen. Told that he must not marry his niece,[4] he will wish to know who says so and on what authority. He will certainly wish to know what will happen to him

4. Strictly forbidden, naturally, in English law as it is today. But the Roman emperor Claudius, so Tacitus tells us in the *Annals*, was in the fortunate position of being able to introduce legislation in the Senate to change the old Roman *Law* so as to permit him to marry his niece Agrippina, even though many of the senators may have thought that, though now legal, it was still immoral and shocking. And yet other systems of *Law* recognise marriage between a man and his niece as valid (e.g. one or two sections of the Ibo of Nigeria, Jewish *Law*, and a number of other customary *Laws*). In *Cheni v Cheni* [1962] 3 All ER 873, Simon P had to consider what the English courts should do about a marriage which took place in Egypt between two Sephardic Jews in accordance with Jewish rites. The husband was the maternal uncle of the wife. In 1957 they came to England. The wife sought before the English courts a declaration that the marriage was null and void.

if he goes ahead and tries to marry his niece — will the marriage be valid? is he liable to go to prison? has he committed a mortal sin? He may wish to know, and we shall certainly want to know on his behalf, why there should be this prohibition, and whether he, the addressee, is uniquely prohibited from such marriages, or there is a general prohibition of this kind.

The ordinary citizen does not exist in the abstract: he is a member of a particular society at a particular time. The sort of society of which he is a member is crucially important in answering these questions. We

---

Expert evidence was given that Egyptian *Law*, which referred the validity of Jewish marriages to the Jewish religious law, would recognise the marriage as valid. Evidence was given by expert witnesses that 'a marriage between uncle and niece is in accordance with general Jewish law'. Sir Jocelyn Simon conveniently summarised the evolution of Jewish and Christian doctrine on the point. 'After 1064 the Western Church [sc. the Roman Catholic Church] maintained its prohibition of marriages between uncle and niece and first cousins, but the impediment was capable in special circumstances of dispensation by the Pope. The uncle-niece impediment would be dispensed with only to avoid some greater evil, generally of a political nature. This is still much the situation in the Roman Catholic Church.' (at p. 879) After the Reformation the Protestant churches generally reacted against this dispensation, and reverted to a stricter view, referring to Leviticus for indirect authority. The Anglican communion, including the Church of England, follows the Protestant Calvinist line on this point, and prohibits absolutely marriages between aunt and nephew, and uncle and niece.

Simon P found that today such marriages are 'incestuous by the general, even though not the universal, consent of Christendom'. But several Christian countries do consider a marriage between uncle and niece as valid. If the test was whether an English court should, under the rules of private international law, recognise a union which was incestuous by the general consent of Christendom, then Simon P refused to accept that this general consent was made out; if the test was whether such marriage was not merely void in England but not to be recognised on grounds of public policy, he did not find such public policy made out in the instant case. His general remarks on these points, exemplifying the moral criteria which may now be invoked by English courts, are worthy of reproduction here:—

'I do not consider that a marriage which may be the subject of papal dispensation and will then be acknowledged as valid by all Roman Catholics, which without any such qualification is acceptable to all Lutherans, can reasonably be said to be contrary to the general consent of Christendom . . . If public policy were the test, it seems to me that the arguments of the husband, founded on such inferences as one can draw from the scope of English criminal law, prevail. Moreover, they weigh with me when I come to apply what I believe to be the true test, namely, whether the marriage is so offensive to the conscience of the English court that it should refuse to recognise and give effect to the proper foreign law. In deciding that question the court will seek to exercise common sense, good manners and a reasonable tolerance. In my view, it would be altogether too queasy a judicial conscience which would recoil from a marriage acceptable to many peoples of deep religious convictions, lofty ethical standards and high civilisation.' (at p. 883)

The marriage was held valid.

have already[5] illustrated the wide difference in overlap between *Law* and morality in traditional and modern societies respectively; we have mentioned that in traditional societies there is reinforcement of the legal message because of its concentricity with the message of morality. This makes the *Law* more effective, but reduces the ability to discriminate between *Law* and morality. In the modern societies the areas of *Law* and morality are eccentric with respect to each other, and there is less common ground. There are also more distinctively legal institutions for answering questions 1, 2, 3 and 6 above. If we can use a metaphor, the citizen is pulled along (rather than 'bound', which we are trying to avoid) by a rope of command. In the traditional society the rope is many-stranded, the legal strand being buried in with the other strands of prescription and control. The rope is strengthened, its pull is less easy to resist, but the assessment of the contribution made by the legal strand to that pull is less easy to make. In the modern society the legal strand has now become in part a separate hawser, clearly identifiable as such. Its pull is sometimes in the same direction as, and sometimes contradictory to, the pulls of other hawsers which tug at the subject. The citizen in each case has the option of letting go of the rope altogether; but if he does so, then he forfeits his claim to be a member of that team. The citizen in the traditional society does not have to worry so much about whether the tug on him is coming from the legal strand in the rope; in a modern, disintegrated society the question may be all-important: to which pull should he yield when these cables exercise forces in different directions?

Analysis of normative systems

From the time of the Greek philosophers there has been discussion about the relationship of *Law* and morality. Sophocles's *Antigone* dramatised the conflict of pulls. Numerous legal philosophers have broached the question, often at length. Many of the acutest controversies in modern jurisprudence, labelled as the Hart-Devlin debate or the Hart-Fuller debate, and so on, are about this issue. It is profoundly unlikely that there is anything useful that I can add to this debate, not least because this is not the main theme of the present work. However, I feel it necessary to try to clarify my own thoughts on the relationship between these various normative systems; and this may throw up some objections to arguments advanced by earlier writers, as well as throwing the difficulties of the practical legislator into sharper relief. I shall proceed by examining, in the light of questions 1 to 6 of our theoretical citizen, the four systems of *Law*, religion, morality, and mores. I shall

5. See pp. 23 ff. above.

do this by looking at normative messages of these four kinds under the following heads:

Form.
Emitted by.
Content.
Aims.
Addressees.
Form of compliance.
Results of non-compliance.
Non-compliance monitored and rectified by.
Conflicts of the normative system with *Law* or other normative systems.

First, however, I look at the four systems.

LAW. Lex.

Law is what is made in a political society, if it is autonomous, for the regulation of behaviour of persons in that society. The Latin *lex* expressed the notion of legislated law; popular participation in its making was originally of the essence, a *lex* being valid if made by the people in their assembly.

RELIGION. Fas.

Religion is more than a system of norms. It purports to be an *account* of reality, of what it is and why it is there, as well as being a set of rituals, practices and prescriptions which the adherent must adhere to if he is to appease the supernatural powers which are presumed to lurk behind and inform the observable world. The informational side of religion has nothing to do with our present theme; but in so far as it purports to prescribe right living, to command and regulate behaviour, its overlap with *Law* is obvious. *Fas* was the Latin word which expressed the numinosity and other-worldliness of religion, suggesting powers which were not under the control of, and certainly not springing from, human activity. Whether one can have a religion without a super-natural or other-worldly element is a contested point; the example of Buddhism, which is frequently cited in this discussion, proves nothing. As soon as the purer teachers of Buddhism have tried to expel the other-worldly element, it has come back in the practices of its believers, and even in the formal ceremonies of its shrines and monasteries. The argument that Buddhism is a non-institutional religion cannot be reconciled with the evident importance of its institutions in Buddhist countries. But Buddhism is certainly other-worldly, preaching that there is another and infinitely more precious world, the world of knowledge or the spirit, than the world of the senses; and it teaches how to gain access to that world. In this it is very close to religions like

Christianity and Islam, both with their own fundamental principles of right living with a view to eternal salvation.

Religion was originally, if we may quote customary societies, not something one adopted, like a new fashion; it was part of the given of life in that sort of society. And yet religious innovations have come in, thanks to the vision of priests and prophets; and religious syncretism and selection have come in too. To that extent, in many societies in the 20th century, though not before, adherence to religion is a voluntary act.

MORALITY. *Ius.*

It is hard to define morality. Taken globally, a moral system is a set of precepts for right living, which may or may not be associated with the sort of belief in and about the supernatural implied by religion. There is debate whether the imperatives of morality are external or internal, whether they arise from commands from outside, from God or some authority, or from inside, from the springs of conscience. An internal, individually generated morality can hardly be thought of as a system, still less as a shared system; which is why some people see morality as a shared system of prescriptions generated and imposed by the community to which the subject belongs. On the other hand, a case can be made for saying that a so-called system of morality is like a natural *Language*. No two speakers of a *Language* speak exactly the same language. Each has his resources of vocabulary, the rules which he follows or does not follow; the so-called *Language* is a statistical averaging of frequent usage by individual users, a highest common factor. Is morality like that? The Latin word *ius* originally expressed that which *joined*, as well as that which *bound*.

MORES. *Mos.*

It is an odd situation that we have to use a Latin plural to refer to what is a common feature of our, and other, societies — their habitual practices, folkways, conventions, etiquette, usages. On the face of it, mores differ from the other three systems in that they are what is done, rather than what one has or ought or is told to do. But this difference does not persist, as people soon come to the conclusion that they ought to do what everyone else is doing; and everyone else starts ensuring that this is so by correcting those who do not conform. Just as religion has an informational content, though, so mores have a practical or factual as well as prescriptive content, and this we must remember.

Four systems; four three-letter Latin words, *lex, fas, ius, mos,* conveniently available to refer to them. The movements in meaning or function of those Latin words give us a warning, and illustrate the difficulties of separation. *Lex*, as being statute law, might be taken to be only one form of law. However, it, and its derivatives in Latin and*

*Text continued on p. 134.

SCHEMATIC ANALYS

Law	Religion
Form	
(We include *implementing orders* as well as *norms* and *institutions* in so far as they are embodied in normative statements.)	(Normative statements in religion may also include implementing orders, e.g. priest in confessional, excommunication.)
Not necessarily written; oral in preliterate societies. Orders may often be oral even in societies with written law. English law typically oral when norms are invoked or recited (cf. spoken judgments, putting charge to defendant orally).	There are the religions with sacred scriptures (e.g. Christian Bible, Islamic Quran, Buddhist scriptures), which are written sources of normative statements.
French and other civil-law systems distinguish *droit écrit* (written law = legislated law) and *droit coutumier* (customary law) — is this symptomatic?	Many religious statements are oral, being made by priests, prophets, agents of cults or deities.
	Religious communication may also be by *signs*: e.g. use of divination.
Emitted by	
Approved and recognised emitters. In developed societies means those having separate institutional right to emit — legislature, minister, judge; in simpler societies there may be institutional authorities such as this, or emission of norms may be recognised as function of assembled citizens, in court or elsewhere. In latter case, note that much norm-emission will be provisional, a 'proposal', until adopted, whether by express agreement or tacit compliance.	Is it possible to have a religion without an emitter or religious statements? It would seem not.
	Religious normative statements are either general instructions (cf. resolutions of Vatican Council) or particular directions (e.g. of parish priest).
	Statements in scriptures are given special authority as: word of God (Christian); word of God's prophet speaking for God (Islam); word of the enlightened one (Buddhism).
Norm-emitters, whether institutions or not, have *authority* to emit norms. This authority conferred by super-norms, which eventually trace their validity to *social approval*.	*Authority* to emit normative statements is specially recognised in these religions.
	Religions in simpler societies lack scriptures, but recognise priests and prophets, often seen as agents of deity. Authority thus derives from *deity*, or access to *truth*.

₹ NORMATIVE STATEMENTS

Morality	Mores
No settled or authorised form of normative statement. Such statements may be oral and/or written. *But* many moral codes are generated by and are integral parts of a religion; in such a case, there may be an orderly statement of moral norms.	In so far as mores are practice, what happens, they are not statements but observable facts or behaviour. *Reminders* of current practice may be made: new practice may be *agreed* by those affected (e.g. rules of game, business practice) − hence term 'convention' specially applicable to these statements. As mores generate norms, so these may be brought to attention or applied to particular cases by interested persons. Norms generated by practice may be formless, or precisely codified by one claiming authority or knowledge.
Are there recognised and institutional emitters of moral norms? Some argue that there are no moral legislators. There may be no evident, authorised emitter; or there may be. Cf. newspapers and TV 'authorities'; writers; in integrated societies, those having roles of influence in the society. Argued that no legislated change of morality possible; incorrect: cf. role of churches in church-dominated societies. Authority to emit moral norms derives from self-appointment, recognition by others, or possession of extraneous authority. The main express emitters of moral norms heretofore have been the various religions, whether traditional or higher (world, developed).	No one emits practice; they do it. Where scope for conventional norms, these are agreed by participants. Members of society emit norms derived from their personal inferences from behaviour of fellows in their community. Authority to emit normative statements, so far as relevant, may be *concessionary* from other members of community, or claimed on own authority. Authority ultimately derives from *common practice*.

Law	Religion
Content	
Cf. discussion of commands, prohibitions, permissions, etc.	A large informational content in the messages of religion.
Can relate to any aspect of life in society or personal behaviour.	Prescriptions can relate to any aspect of man's life, in society or out of it. Some religions pay special attention to interior attitudes and thoughts; other religions deal only with externals of ritual compliance.
Although most law deals with overt, exterior conduct, law can purport to regulate interior thoughts and attitudes, measuring these or ascertaining them by reference to exterior signs.	Religions can command, prohibit and permit.
Thus requirement of *mens rea* punishes a guilty mind, though using objective tests to ascertain whether the mind is guilty.	
Thus offence of insulting behaviour is handled subjectively: a person who did not wish to insult would escape liability in English law. Thus the law punishes the *wish*.	
Communist and other totalitarian systems of law constantly seek to regulate thoughts.	
Aims	
Human order in society. Justice: fairness as between man and man. Enlargement of life possibilities; making possible the better life.	Divine order. Illumination: revelation of the truth about the seen and unseen world. Individual betterment: right living.
Addressees	
All members of a political society; but may be differentially addressed to different groups or classes within that society.	All human beings and even non-human life; *or* All adherents.

Morality	**Mores**
Morality can regulate every aspect of man's behaviour. Typically thought to be especially concerned with man's interior attitudes, but in fact deals with external conduct as well as internal desires or motivations.	Deals with external behaviour only; though such behaviour may express or be taken to express an internal attitude (e.g. 'You should feel grateful for . . .' = 'You should *demonstrate* by your conduct, e.g. expressing thanks, giving return gift, that you are grateful for . . .')
If no emitter, then no aim! Moral norms transmitted externally: inducement of respondents to act *rightly* and think rightly; definition of 'right' comes from transmitter. Moral norms created internally: inducement to recipient to act *consistently* with his own perception of right (= conscience).	So far as mores are mere practice, even if common to group or community, they are not normative and have no aims. Where mores generate norms, aim is to produce *conformism*, a uniformly patterned life. Where mores generated by agreed convention, aim is *regulation* and *easy operation* of relationship covered by convention.
If no emitter, then no addressees, only recipients! Externally transmitted: within the moral community, *or* purportedly universal. Note differential addressees, e.g. re role of parent. Internally generated: self-addressed.	Where normative, all members of a group, community, or association. Different members may be addressed differentially: e.g. role of inferior; role of goalkeeper in football.

Law	Religion
Form of compliance	
Compliance is *compulsory* so far as mandatory and prohibitory norms are concerned;	Compliance is compulsory for unchallenged (e.g. in customary society) religion, or religion which claims universal mandate (as Islam).
is voluntary, so far as facultative norms are concerned.	Non-believers, backsliders, non-members avoid compliance or necessary compliance with religious norms *de facto; de jure* when religious adherence voluntary and religious practice subjected to control by legal super-norm.
There is no possibility of opting into or out of the compulsory sector, save by ceasing to be a member of the society.	
Compliance consists, according to the circumstances, of doing/not doing (as case may be) of what the law commands or prohibits; of doing what the law allows or provides for facultative norms; in other words, compliance = *conforming conduct*	Compliance consists in conformity, both in conduct *and mental attitude*, with norms of the religion, i.e. doing what the religion commands, not doing what it prohibits.
	Compliance may thus be either compulsory or optional, according to circumstances.
Results of non-compliance	
With *controlling* norms (commanding, prohibiting): imposition of undesired consequences for person or property or associates: corporal punishment, incarceration, fines, damages, etc.	May mean loss of salvation = *damnation* in next or further world; i.e. deprivation of reward or fulfilment.
With *enabling* norms (creating facilities): compliance gives *validity* to arrangements or transactions, and *protection* against invasions of these interests; non-compliance means lack of validity and lack of protection.	Non-compliance may cause immediately *disapproval* of (i) superior being or force (e.g. God); (ii) fellow-adherents; (iii) those having authority in the religion.
Non-compliance thus means the *suffering of a detriment*.	Non-compliance thus means possible detriment in another world or existence, not this one, and/or disapproval or detriment in this world.
	Non-compliance with organised religion can lead to expulsion from religious group: excommunication. Social consequences, attributable to mores, may flow from such censure or expulsion.
	Where there is a legally established or supported religion, non-compliance may attract legal sanctions; but in such a case the matter has moved over into the law domain.

Morality	**Mores**
Compliance consists, according to the circumstances, of doing/not doing (as case may be) of what morality commands or prohibits.	Compliance is *conforming conduct*.
Compliance may be *interior*, so far as morality regulates thoughts and attitudes.	Compliance is *optional*.
Compliance is *mandatory*; it does not make sense to talk of enabling or optional morality. Where morality does not command, there is no normative message.	
Compliance is thus *obedience* by rectification.	

Non-compliance, for externally imposed morality, leads to *condemnation* by others.	Non-compliance may lead to
For internally generated morality, non-compliance leads to *guilt-feelings*, and possible desire to make amends. Guilt-feeling may also be produced by external condemnation.	(i) *disapproval* of other members of group, etc.;
Non-compliance does not lead to detriment in person or property; detrimental consequences (e.g. physical aggression, expulsion) are not attributable to morality, but to sanctions of (i) law, or (ii) mores, or (iii) religion.	(ii) voluntarily accepted *penalties*;
	(iii) *repressive action*;
	(iv) *termination of membership* of group.

Law	Religion
Non-compliance monitored and rectified by	
Individual subjects of the law, affected by the non-compliance; invoking where available –	Divine beings or forces. Religious authorities: incl. shrines, priests, oracles.
The community at large; *or* a section of it (cf. community action in Kikuyu); *or*	Fellow-adherents monitoring; rectification by authorities.
Special group to which complainant belongs: e.g. family group, age group.	
Institutions in the society specially charged with monitoring and rectifying non-compliance: e.g. courts and arbitral proceedings; secret societies (e.g. 'maskers' in Nigerian tribal groups); oracles and shrines (e.g. Zande, Ibo).	

other languages, broadened out to mean *Law* in the widest sense, so that we happily oppose 'legal' to 'moral' in the discussion we have entered upon. *Ius*, the moral word, retained its moral flavour. The Latin *iustus*, as used to translate Scripture, means the God-fearing and upright man, not the equal dispenser of justice in the narrow sense. But *ius* also shifted its ground, to become a word for *Law* in the broadest of senses, as well as of rights acquired under the *Law*. Its derivatives, giving us 'justice' and 'jurist' as well as 'jurisprudence', have this broader sense. Is 'jural' broader than 'legal', as some legal anthropologists try to insist? As for *mos*, from meaning habitual behaviour it came to mean binding customs and usages on the one hand, thus taking on a legal flavour, and morality or good conduct on the other, thus taking on a moral flavour. 'Moral', it need hardly be pointed out, is its main offspring.

Differentiation of norms

What conclusions can we draw from this summary analysis? The first and most obvious is the considerable overlap. The *form* of a normative statement by itself does not identify it as relating to *Law*, religion, morality, or mores: all will be couched in the hypothetical-conditional mode. The use of writing is not significant. It is wrong to say there are no organised codes of morality: quite the contrary – there are very precise codes as appendages to many religions. Mores may not be codified; but forms of mores, e.g. rules of games, clubs, voluntary societies, may be codified and appear to have a *Law*-like form.

When we come on to the *emitters* of normative statements, there is greater separation. Many emitters are *transmitters*, not *originators*, of

Morality	Mores
For religiously generated morality, *see* Religion. Other morality: no 'moral courts'; but for externally generated morality, public opinion of moral community acts as monitor and (through moral pressures, condemnation, etc) rectifier. Internally generated morality: self-detection and rectification.	Detection of non-conformities in hands of community, group, etc, and individual members thereof. Within *conventional* associations (i.e. groups with agreed voluntary norms), often machinery for detection and rectification of breaches of norm; cf. disciplinary committees in sports like football or bridge. Within *non-conventional* associations (e.g. unstructured family), members and/or social authority monitor and rectify.

the norms they emit. Customary practices and conventions within the sphere of mores may emerge from conduct, and have no precise form until articulated; but the same is true of customary *Law*. Only legal norms emerge or are claimed to emerge from the politically organised society, or from those having roles of influence and power within them; the emitters of legal norms put forward as their *validating principle* that they *are* the community, or speak *for* the community, or are authorised to speak *by* the community. Emitters of religious norms either claim a revelation of truth which is intrinsic in the world, or claim an express transmission of truth handed down by a deity or supreme teacher. So far as religious norms are ritual, these are or may be generated by those having authority in the religion; but the validating principle claimed for them is that they are ordained by the deity or supreme teacher, or will better achieve his purposes. There are many self-appointed emitters of moral norms. Some claim authority for their statements as being the revelation of intrinsic truth about man and his life in society. Unlike religion, morality is directed solely at human behaviour.[6]

Mores are special in that practice emerges rather than is imposed to begin with; but in many spheres of operation, conventional norms may be the result of frank 'legislation'. The authority claimed for normative statements, when they are articulated, is conformity to common practice, and/or adherence to agreed convention.

There is no way to separate normative statements on the basis of their *content*. There is too much overlap; the same norm may be imposed simultaneously by *Law*, religion, morality, and common

6. Though note the trials of animals for non-conformity in the Middle Ages!

practice. A separation on the basis of internal and external behaviour does not work either; while it is true that mores relate to external conduct, and legal machinery purports to operate on the externalities of man's behaviour, while religion and morality may claim to affect and regulate a man's thoughts and attitudes, the separation is not precise in practice, as the table shows. Many statements of religion are not normative but informational. Statements about common practice (as opposed to normative usages or conventions) are factual only. *Law* is not informational but normative; though talking *about Law* (i.e. 'the *Law* provides that so and so . . .') is conveying information.

There is a clear separation of *aims* as between the different systems; though again there is a set of major overlaps. *Law* is this-worldly, and deals with order in politically organised society; but its aims of justice and enlargement of life possibilities could also be claimed by religion and morality, while its aim of order could be claimed by mores.

The addressees of all normative systems are defined by membership of the relevant group. (The sole apparent exception would be with a self-generated and imposed system of morality; but − as remarked above − the personal morality system of an individual forms part of a universe of moral discourse, as with *Language*, so that the privacy of the moral system is more apparent than real.) The *Law* group is the politically organised community; *Laws* may occasionally try to legislate for events and people outside the community (cf. laws about piracy and genocide), but when they do so they are asserting that those outside the community are for this purpose to be treated as if they were within the community. The religion group is, with universalist religions, the whole of mankind; with particularist religions, the adherents of it. Is morality community-bound or not? There is a constant dialectic between (i) those who claim that moral systems are relative and generated by, within, and for a particular community only − on this basis, killing can be moral in one society and immoral in another; and (ii) those who say that moral norms are universal − unjustified killing is wrong, wherever it occurs. It is not possible to say that a given national law is unjust (as with Nazi legislation against Jews) if there is no supranational standard of justice by which to measure the justness of a particular law. Moralists often write in one way and behave as if the contrary were the case. The ordinary person is in no doubt, whatever community he belongs to, that moral principles transcend community boundaries; though at the same time he is ready to assert that his own moral system, even if it differs from that of the neighbouring community, is wholly valid. Mores are by definition in and of a community. In so far as mores represent common practice, this must mean the common practice of a given group or community. In so far as they are conventional, the agreement defines the community affected.

When we turn to *compliance*, and the machinery by which compliance is sought, we may feel increasing hope of finding a safe way of distinguishing legal and other norms; but is this hope justified? Compliance with legal norms is *conforming conduct*; but so is compliance with religious, moral and conventional norms. Is compliance compulsory for *Law*, and not for the other systems? The advocates, emitters and monitors of religious, moral and conventional norms would not say that compliance was optional. There are loopholes which permit optional compliance: thus compliance with enabling legal norms is optional (though compliance with the protective norms which prevent others denying validity to these options is compulsory); compliance with religious norms may be optional, if, for instance, a religion offers a good and a better way of conforming conduct,[7] or if an adherent can withdraw from the religion altogether. Compliance with the dictates of morality is never optional. Compliance with social customs is mandatory for those who wish to be members of the given group or community; social disapproval or rejection follows non-compliance. If you wish to play a game, you must stick by the rules.

But is it the *means of ensuring compliance* that is the test? Some jurists would say Yes: *Law* uses *force* as a sanction for non-compliance, while other normative systems do not. 'Force' is wider than 'violence' or bodily constraint; it means the imposition of a constraint on someone against that person's will, or the deprivation of some good to which he would otherwise be entitled. Religions impose sanctions for non-compliance which do not depend for their imposition on voluntary acceptance by the person sanctioned. Damnation is not a voluntary consequence of misbehaviour. Damnation affects the body (or the whole person) just as much as a legal sanction, and in the end does so more devastatingly. The fact that the constraint or penalty is not immediately visible on the exterior does not affect the point that it is forcible. Moral norms too by their very definition apply against the will of the person governed by them. It would make no sense to say that moral norms apply only if the person affected so chooses.[8] There is no compliance machinery for moral norms in the same way as there is for non-compliance with legal or religious norms. But disapproval of those who share the moral community is a sanction, and is one which morality shares with other normative systems, e.g. mores. Detriments suffered by a person's body or property are not attributable to morality or the machinery of the enforcement of moral norms; this picks morality out from the rest of the set. Mores, though expressly contrasted with *Law*

---

7. Thus Christianity recognises a minimum good way of behaviour: loving God and one's neighbour; and a better way: 'If you wish to be perfect . . .'; Buddhism recognises a good way, the acquiring of merit and good behaviour in this life, and a better way for advanced adepts, of contemplation leading to extinction of self.

8. Even though a person internally generates a moral code, or voluntarily adopts allegiance to an external moral code, once he does so he feels that 'he must' do what the code says.

in that only *Law* involves the invocation of constituted authority within a political community, do, however, connote sanctions, of disapproval, penalties or expulsion, which resemble those of *Law*. If these penalties are compulsory, then they are part of the legal system. A 'fine' imposed by a domestic governing body, e.g. of a profession or a college, is in conformity with *Law*, and the processes of *Law* can be used to require it; so legal sanctions can protect voluntary bodies and associations. Apart from such disciplinary bodies, whose authority derives from agreement and convention, there are no disciplinary bodies which adjudicate on breaches of community mores.

Let us now, by way of conclusion, answer the six questions which our ordinary citizen posed some pages back.[9] The answers are those which will be given if the norm is legal:

Q1 Who says that I must do what the norm says?

A   If the norm is legal, then it is a person or institution in a politically organised society who emits the norm.

Q2 What authority has this person or institution to tell me what to do?

A   Where the person or institution has a distinct and separate role attributed to him or it by society to emit norms of this type, then his authority derives from this role and its attribution by the affirmation or assent or non-dissent of the society. Where the person is not an institution in the society, then his authority derives from the acceptance by the society *ex post facto* of his emitted norm. Such acceptance may be demonstrated by express act or by tacit acquiescence through conforming conduct.

Q3 What happens if I do not comply with the norm?

A   This depends on the nature of the norm. If the norm is mandatory or prohibitory, non-compliance will render you liable (though not automatically so) to reaction which will be to your detriment in this life, as by penalties or forfeitures attaching to your person or your property or affecting other rights or privileges which you currently enjoy. The imposition of these penalties or forfeitures will be expressly commanded or approved by the society, or tacitly endorsed. If the norm is facultative or enabling, failure to comply with it will be to your detriment, in that you will not acquire rights, privileges and protection which you would otherwise acquire. Compliance with the former type of norm is compulsory, in that penalties and forfeitures for non-compliance may be exacted against your will.

Q4 To whom is the prescription addressed?

9. At p. 123.

A   The normative prescription is addressed (a) in some instances to all the members of your society, (b) in some instances to a class of persons members of the society, and (c) in some instances to an individual. Whether the norm is directed to you depends on whether you are, as the case may be, (a) a member of that community, (b) a member of that class, (c) the individual addressed.

Q5   What is the content of the prescription?

A   The prescription will relate to your behaviour, and consequentially to the behaviour of other persons, who may be ordered (a) not to interfere with any rights, powers or privileges accorded by the prescription, or (b) to activate or administer machinery for ensuring compliance with the norm. The prescription will relate to your exterior conduct, and may in some instances control your interior conduct or attitude in so far as it is ascertainable from your external behaviour. The behaviour affected will be mostly, though not wholly, your behaviour towards other members of the society and vice versa; though your behaviour to animals or inanimate objects, or to other-worldly forces or beings, may also be covered by the norm.

Q6   What is the machinery through which the reaction for non-compliance with the norm will be determined and applied?

A   The activation of the machinery depends on the exercise of a human will or wills. The will concerned may be that of an individual injuriously affected by your non-compliance, or concerned to ensure the implementation of the norm, or it may be that of a person or institution with authority to monitor non-compliance, or both.

B THE LAW IN COMPETITION WITH OTHER NORMATIVE SYSTEMS: EXCLUSION OR WEAKENING OF THE LEGAL PRESCRIPTION

These various normative systems compete for the allegiance of those to whom they are addressed; their overlap is considerable, the possibilities of contradiction considerable. How and when will *Law* be reinforced, and how and when will it be weakened or excluded, by the dictates of other normative systems?

To answer these questions is to move into the realm of sociology rather than legal theory. It is typical that a *Law* claims to be pre-eminent in its right to order citizens what to do; its exponents and institutions say that *Law* must take precedence over the dictates of religion, morality or community mores. To say otherwise would be to say that *Law* is an optional or inferior system of control of behaviour in society. Occasionally a legal system allows scope for deviation from legal norms; thus in a pluralistic society religious conformity is not required, and many civilised countries admit the possibility of conscientious objection to military service. These examples do not show *Law* as being voluntarily displaced by other normative systems, as the recognition of varieties of religious beliefs is achieved either by expressly so commanding or by the *Law's* failing to legislate against religious non-conformity; while the conscientious objector's right is one given him *by* the *Law*, and not asserted by him *against* the *Law*. It may be that the social explanation for such tolerance or concessions is to be found in the weakness of the legal system or those who administer it, or in the habitual disregard by its subjects of the former prescriptions of the *Law*; but the social explanation is not the legal justification.

However, each of the other normative systems also makes claims to paramountcy. Religion normally offers itself as the supreme rule and guide for men in society; by claiming access to ultimate truth, it asserts superiority of information as well as transcendence of norms. The true believer is required to follow his belief and the dictates imposed by it, even if they conflict with other normative systems. Similarly with morality — hence the *Antigone* debate. Though the *Law* does not agree with this position, morality dictates that a person should follow his conscience, or the externally imposed and validated moral code, even if this leads into conflict with a legal system or with conventional mores. As for mores, those belonging to the relevant community, group, class or association often feel constrained to follow the prevailing mores of the community, despite the fact that these are in opposition to *Law*. The current state of industrial relations in Britain, in which a man must follow the mores of his mates in preference to the law of the land, shows the overwhelming pressures to compliance which operate in what is purportedly a non-compulsory system. The claims of *Law* to pre-eminence are thus contestable, and, in the whirlpool of social obligations, contested. That *Law*, according to its own lights, ought to win this contest is neither here nor there; if religion, morality or mores succeed in gaining the allegiance of the community in preference to *Law*, *Law* is weakened and its norms become frustrate. They do not thereby lose their validity; they merely lose their efficacy. The legal norms cease to describe possible ways of behaving in society.

I shall now look at some examples of competition between different normative systems, and the way in which the different systems interlock.

Law and religion

The relationship between a legal system and religion in general or one religious system in particular can range all the way from:

	(i)	Fused
through	(ii)	Infused
	(iii)	Co-ordinate or equipollent
	(iv)	Subordinate
	(v)	Tolerated
to	(vi)	Suppressed.

Religion and customary law. In many traditional societies the relationship was a *fused* one, by which we mean that no conflict is possible, that *Law* and religion are seen as part of the same cultural complex, that the society, in other words, has an integrated normative system. Ancient Egypt may also have been an example of such a fusion.

Islamic religion and law. It is typical of Islam that some of its greatest thinkers were jurists, that Islamic belief and Islamic practice often expressed themselves in juristic terms. At the core of Islamic religion is its canon law, derived from the holy book dictated by Allah to his Prophet, the *Quran*, and from the practice of the Prophet, the *Sunna*. To the Muslim Islamic *Law* is so intimately connected with his religion that they cannot readily be separated one from each other: the relationship is one of fusion. The sacred *Law*, the *shari'a*, is more than a law in the western sense:

'... it contains an infallible guide to ethics. It is fundamentally a DOCTRINE OF DUTIES, a code of obligations.'[10]

Religion, law and morality are all one. But the science of jurisprudence, *fiqh*, as practised by Islamic legal scholars, is narrower and more technical than the *shari'a*; not every moral obligation created by the *shari'a* forms a legal obligation too under *fiqh*.[11] The familiar dialectic between law and morality thus returns. However, the fundamentalist and fusionist approach of Islamic lawyers radically affects their treatment of every human situation; they are not willing to concede what the modern secularist lawyer or politician in the West so readily concedes, that religion should be kept out of law, and law out of religion. Much modern legislation in the Near and Middle East, and in North Africa, has apparently displaced the canonical religious law of Islam; but the legal devices by which this has been done preserve the juristic fiction that nothing that has been legislated is actually contrary to the *shari'a*, and that most, if not all, of the new legislation can find some justification somewhere in a religious text or the opinion of a Muslim jurist.

The *shari'a* or sacred law is not the sum total of *Law* in a Muslim society. Although the Muslim ruler must enforce and observe the

10. A. A. A. Fyzee *Outlines of Muhammadan Law* (1955, 2nd edn), p. 15.
11. Ibid., 21.

sacred law, he is given in Islamic legal theory a very wide discretion to make secular law — especially constitutional, criminal and administrative law — which seeks no support from religious texts. However, the pious ruler cannot legislate anything which is contrary to any of the norms of the *shari'a*. The result is the creation, in a Muslim state, of two types of law, one religious and one secular, and of two sets of courts: *shari'a* or religious courts and secular courts. We may say that the secular laws which the ruler makes must be *infused*, that is inspired, by Islamic beliefs and principles, though they do not codify them. This separation of ecclesiastical and civil courts is highly reminiscent of the similar dualism in England after the Norman Conquest; in the result sacred and secular *Laws* form co-ordinate and equipollent partners in a single macro-system. The same sort of dualism was also admitted and recognised by Britain as a colonial power in several of the possessions which she acquired — notably in East Africa and in Northern Nigeria. In British India, however, the British hastened to suppress the religious courts and judges, leaving only secular courts set up by and under British imperial rule to administer both secular and religious law.

What happens to Islamic *Law* in a state which is not Islamic, where the ruler is not Muslim, where Muslims are in a minority? British India shows one path that has been followed. There are others. There are several alternative postures that can be adopted by the non-Muslim ruler in such a situation. (a) He can give general recognition to Islamic *Law* where it is the *Law* of the community, or the *Law* of a distinct community within the whole. The basis of recognition is then as community *Law*. This is what was done in British East Africa, in the Sudan, and in Northern Nigeria. The Islamic *Law* is no longer applying in its own right, of course, but constitutes a distinct legal system or *Law* within the terms in which we defined *Law* at the beginning of this work.[12] Its status is that of a *subordinate* legal system within the ruling legal system of the state. (b) A lesser degree of recognition is given when the Islamic *Law* is recognised, not as the *Law* of a community, but as the *Law* of a person or class or persons, i.e. as a 'personal law'. In effect this is what was done in British India, though, with the recognition of customary variations of the Islamic *Law* as prevailing within particular communities, there was also a certain degree of community recognition. (c) The recognition of Islamic *Law* as determining personal matters or rights in property under the English conflict of laws is as a personal law, though the connecting factor in such a case is initially membership of a given community, viz. possession of a domicile in a country where Islamic *Law* is recognised. The second-stage connecting factor will then be a personal one, that this individual is a Muslim.

Originally English *Law* accorded no recognition to statuses and rights acquired under non-Christian legal systems. The history of

12. See p. 7.

centuries of conflict arising out of the Crusades and the attacks of the Muslim world on Europe prejudiced English courts against any such recognition. In the last 100 years the degree of recognition accorded to Islamic *Law* in English courts has steadily grown. The case of *Hyde v Hyde*[13] restated the fundamental principle of English *Law* that it would accord recognition to foreign marriages only if they fell within the definition of 'Christian marriages'. This expression meant, not that the marriage had been celebrated in accordance with Christian rites, but that it conformed to the essentials of a marriage as recognised in Christendom, and contained nothing offensive to this notion. Such a notion included obligatory monogamy; on this basis Islamic marriages, which are potentially or actually polygamous, could not satisfy the test. But first the courts,[14] and later the legislature,[15] watered down the impact of this principle, so much so that today English *Law* readily accords recognition to Muslim and other marriages which are potentially or actually polygamous for all matrimonial purposes; and the parties to a polygamous foreign marriage can now seek divorce or other matrimonial relief in English courts, a right previously denied to them.

Of all the world religions Islam poses the greatest problems from the legal point of view when its adherents form a substantial proportion of the population of a non-Muslim state. This is because of the limitless nature of the legal demands made by its adherents, who, in the name of freedom of religion, demand free and full recognition of their religious *Law* as well — a claim not made in such absolute terms by other religions in the modern world.

Christianity and law

Though Christianity from its earliest beginnings was in conflict with the secular *Law* of Rome, that conflict was not of its choosing. Submission to the ritual demands of Roman emperor-worship was used as a way of breaking allegiance to a religion which the secular government saw as subversive. Christianity has never had a legal system of its own, regulating ordinary life as well as religious affairs, to the same extent as Islam; though there was a period in the Age of Faith when it made very wide and overreaching claims. First, it claimed that secular rulers only enjoyed power by delegation from God, and that their exercise of such power was thus subject to oversight by God's vicars on earth, the Pope and his bishops. Secondly, it claimed (like Islam) that the pious ruler must in his secular laws preserve the interests and aims of the Church and legislate nothing that ran counter to the moral or disciplinary code of Christianity.

13. (1866) LR 1 P & M 130.
14 See such cases as *Srini Vasan v Srini Vasan* [1946] P 67; *Baindail v Baindail* [1946] P 122; *R v Sarwan Singh* [1962] 3 All ER 612.
15. Matrimonial Proceedings (Polygamous Marriages) Act 1972.

Thirdly, it claimed exclusive jurisdiction in various domains, both as to persons (clerics or clerks) and as to subject-matter (heresy, family affairs). For this the law of the Church borrowed extensively from that of Rome, though its rules were instinct with the religious insights and attitudes peculiar to Christianity, its treatment of marriage being a case in point. Fourthly, it claimed to bring to bear on secular affairs, such as the making of contracts and the holding of interests in land, a critique of conscience, which in England became institutionalised as the doctrines and practices of equity. Secular law, as is well known, continued to regulate commercial dealings and land holding; but the English jurisdiction of the Chancellor (before the Reformation always a cleric until the epoch-making appointment of Sir Thomas More) embroidered in the fabric of the common law the threads of conscience, natural justice and equity – three elements which were later to recur in legislation for the application of English and indigenous law overseas. Christianity's contribution to the making of modern English *Law*, then, was immense.

To review English legal history briefly, in Anglo-Saxon times there was integration of church and state to the extent that bishops advised the King along with secular magnates, and sat *ex officio* in shire courts. Much of pre-Conquest English *Law*, and especially its legislation or codifications, is heavily instinct with religious details and principles. We can say that at this time English *Law* was *infused* with Christian principles. There were no separate church courts.

After the Norman Conquest in 1066, Christianity's legal role changed. Separate ecclesiastical courts were set up as part of the settlement between Church and state; these ecclesiastical courts had a very extensive jurisdiction, not just in church matters strictly so called, but in regulating the law of personal relations, and especially marriage and testamentary succession, which were outside the jurisdiction of the common-law courts, these latter being happy to follow the Church courts in their rulings. The law of ecclesiastical organisation was part of the exclusive jurisdiction of the Church. As for the rest of the *Law*, the Christian influence and the dogmatic principles by which the Christian ruler was required to act and which have been mentioned above continued, though to a less pronounced degree than in Anglo-Saxon times. The partial separation of Church and state, and the diminution in the political and legal role of bishops, contributed to this. At this stage we can say that Church and state law and courts represented two parallel, *co-ordinate* and equipollent systems. The basic norm which allowed for these two systems could be said, from the point of view of the secular ruler, to be a legal one: it was his wish and arrangement. From the point of view of the Church authorities the ruler's power to make such arrangements came from God as represented by the Church; so that the super-norm was religious. The conflict of view led to the disagreement between Henry II and his martyred bishop, Thomas à Becket, which ended after the latter's death with the apparent submission of the King. But the struggle was taken up by another Henry, Henry VIII, and resolved in a different sense.

After the Reformation, the position was radically altered. There was no doubt, according to the *Law* of England, as to which system was dominant. It was the secular one, and the religious system became strictly *subordinate* to it. The Church of England and its courts were subordinated, and their law in effect became part of the *Law* of England. Some aspects of that *Law* were triable by the King's courts or majesty; the law itself was made by the authority of Parliament. The infusion of Christian principles into English *Law* was still strong, though less so than formerly. Only the 19th century marked a growing secularisation of the *Law* (even *Hyde v Hyde*,[16] with its willingness to recognise various forms of non-Christian marriage as 'Christian', was part of this process of secularisation), which has led to an almost complete break in the 20th century, such that it can no longer be said, as it once was said with confidence, that the Christian religion is part of the *Law* of England. Today much Christian doctrine has remained as convention though it has vanished as law. A divorced person can remarry in the secular fashion, while he or she may be unable to do so in a Church of England church; what restrains such re-marriage is no longer law but convention. The recognition, or more precisely *toleration*, of other Christian sects, such as the Catholic and non-conformist, also operates at the conventional level. This tolerance now extends to non-Christian religions and even to atheism; but the restricted recognition given to Jewish and Islamic divorces, for instance, is only through the operation of private international law, and not as part of the legally approved mechanisms of English domestic *Law*.

The new super-norm defining the position of religion as regards the *Law* thus recognises Church law, but only for the Church of England, and then in a strictly subordinate capacity; has transformed and removed personal law from the jurisdiction of ecclesiastical to that of secular courts (since 1857); and has retained surviving remnants of laws infused with Christian ideals. Of these survivals the law against *blasphemy* is a current controversial example. *R v Lemon*[17] was a striking instance. The details of this case, heard only in 1978 by the Court of Appeal, need not detain us, save to say that it concerned a prosecution for blasphemous libel against the editors and publishers of a magazine called *Gay News*. Roskill LJ, delivering the judgment of the Court of Appeal, summarised the historical connexion with Christianity in these words:

'It is clear that the offence was originally in Christian times ecclesiastical. ... The state only became interested in the offence if the actions of the alleged offender affected the safety of the state. An attack on Christianity in general or a total denial of the Deity was punished by the state on

16. (1866) LR 1 P & M 130.
17. [1978] 3 All ER 175, CA; [1979] 1 All ER 898, HL.

the assumption that the foundation of the state and of the society on which the state was founded was thereby endangered . . .'.[18]

There were many prosecutions for blasphemy in the 19th century; but by the middle of the century these diminished as the courts became more tolerant of publications which attacked Christian belief in a moderate and pacific manner; by 1883 the offence had been cut down to 'indecent and offensive attacks on Christianity or the Scriptures, or sacred persons or objects, calculated to outrage the feelings of the general body of the community. . .'[19].

Is the offence obsolete in modern England? Can there be any justification for special protection now being accorded to the beliefs of one religion, albeit that followed by more adherents than any other? The Court of Appeal did not pursue the question of obsolescence. Counsel for the accused/appellants abandoned this line of argument, even though there had been no prosecution for the offence for half a century, and some authorities had thought that the offence was now obsolete. Nor was the specialness of the protection still accorded to believers in Christianity canvassed by the Court. It saw its function as merely applying the law of the land, and not criticising it, repealing it, or making suggestions for its amendment. The thrust of judicial dicta since the Victorian cases has been to switch emphasis from the protection of the state against subversion or disorder to the protection of believers against statements which will annoy or insult them, in a word, which will 'outrage the feelings of the general body of the community' (Lord Coleridge CJ). Neither the state nor the Christian religion as such now enjoys a special protection under the law against blasphemy. But if it is a question of outraged feelings, the feelings of, say, Muslims in Britain will be at least as outraged by slurs on the character, behaviour or sayings of Muhammad as will those of Christians by similar slurs on the character or behaviour of Christ. There is strong argument for extending the law of blasphemy to cover outrage to any religious sentiment.[20] Much, doubtless, can be dealt with by way of prosecution for offences under the Public Order Act,[1] as tending to insult or threaten and provoke a breach of the peace; much can be done with prosecutions for offences against the race relations laws;[2] but these last specifically do not cover language or conduct which attacks believers of a given faith, rather than persons identified by nationality or colour.

18. At 182.
19. Per Lord Coleridge CJ in his charge to the jury in *R v Ramsay and Foote* (1883) 15 Cox CC 231 at 232.
20. And this approach found favour with Lord Scarman in the House of Lords: [1979] 1 All ER 898 at 921.
 1. 1936, as amended by the Race Relations Acts 1965 and 1976; see especially s. 5.
 2. Now incorporated in the Public Order Act, by s. 5A.

When we look at modern countries outside Britain, we find that Christianity enjoys a position ranging all the way from that of established or state religion (as previously in Spain and Malta, for instance), to privileged religion, to a tolerated religion along with others, and finally to that of forbidden or discriminated-against religion (as in practice, whatever Soviet constitutional theory may say, in the USSR). The United States, though a liberal democratic country, is somewhat paradoxical in its treatment of religion. Held tight by the constitutional requirement that Congress shall not make any law for the establishment of religion, it has hardly come to terms with sectarian schools or with acts of religious worship in schools.

One rarely finds anything equal to Moslem intransigence when one looks at agitation by Christians for Christian legislation in a secular state. The Moslem community in Kenya, at the time when commissions were sitting to review the reform of the laws of marriage and succession there, was clamorous in its demands for the undiluted recognition of Islamic *Law* within the state system.[3] Muslim chauvinism went so far in Ghana (a country where Muslims are in a small minority) that an Accra barrister, who was a Muslim, could demand that the state's personal law should codify Islamic *Law* for everyone because, he said, Islamic *Law* was the command of God and so the state could not find any better system! Why is there no comparable Christian intransigence? Christianity was to begin with an equally demanding religion. But, although it forbade the worship of Roman emperors, it did not command a code of legal or quasi-legal norms. And today Christian apologists (who are fewer in number and less assertive than they were) in England do not demand special laws for Christians, as Muslims would; all they ask is the non-enactment of certain laws, e.g. about abortion, and even then not on the ground that abortion law would offend the Christian conscience but that it is unjustifiable on non-sectarian, general moral grounds. There have been martyrs galore at all periods, Christians who refused to compromise their beliefs when required to do so by the state, whether by doing what was forbidden (holding religious services, proselytising) or not doing what was mandatory (abjuring Christian beliefs, taking part in ceremonies held to be heretical). This persecution continues to the present time, as events in countries as far afield as China, Mexico and the USSR amply show. Malawi in Africa has persecuted adherents of one deviant and quasi-Christian sect, the Jehovah's Witnesses, who have also fallen foul of the law in many other countries by reason of their refusal to compromise and to accept earthly authority which they think contradicts the truths of their religion.

While benign or contemptuous neglect of Christian beliefs and values has now replaced, in post-Christian countries, the former insistence on

3. See the *Report of the Commission on the Law of Marriage and Divorce*, Nairobi, 1968, pp. 5–6, 'The Muslim Case'.

them or repression of them, as the case may have been, it would be too optimistic to hope that the era of conflict, frank or covert, between law and Christianity is at an end. New areas of disagreement are constantly being opened up: the 'right to die' and the 'right to kill' are just two of them.

Law and morality

Much morality, as already noted, is an essential element of religion. This does not exhaust the topic, far from it. For a start, we have a general confrontation between law and morals in every society where the legal system itself is not concentric with moral beliefs and practices. Eccentric systems, and those where new moralities have obtruded into formerly monolithic societies, provoke the question of the relation between the two types of norm. There is a tremendous area of debate and analysis open to us here. Let us mention a few of the more significant topics within the field:

1. *Law* and justice. Legalism and the critique of 'justice'.
2. Natural law: theories and practice.
3. The right to disobey laws.
4. Legislation which expresses or rejects a moral attitude.
5. The fundamental rights debate.

These topics overlap with each other, but each is the signpost to a major controversy. A few words on each will serve to show how the sphere of *Law* may be cut down, or its effectiveness reduced, by competition from moral principles and values. These moral principles work by weakening the allegiance of the subjects of the *Law*, by proclaiming that there are other norms which, if they differ from the legal norms, have priority. Their effect, then, is persuasive; but as we have seen the effect of legal norms also as persuasive and have rejected the notion of 'compelling' or 'binding' norms, the struggle reduces to a decision as to which set of norms will prove to be more persuasive in the given case.

1. Law and justice. Is the definition of *Law* (not LAW, which we cannot define) to include a reference to 'justice'? In other words, is a given set of norms in a given political society to be called '*Law*' only if it tends, and its purpose is seen to be, to promote justice? And, if this is correct, what are we to understand by 'justice' here? The first words of Justinian's *Institutes* seem to confuse the two notions:

'Iustitia est constans et perpetua voluntas ius suum cuique tribuens. Iuris prudentia est divinarum atque humanarum rerum notitia, iusti atque iniusti scientia.'[4]

4. Bk I, 1. 'Justice is the constant and unceasing will to give everyone his right or due. Jurisprudence is the knowledge of divine and human affairs, the science of what is just and unjust'.

The student of Roman *Law* thus started firmly on the wrong foot, justifying Moyle's criticism:

'The words are those of a moralist, not a lawyer; and the failure to distinguish sufficiently between jurisprudence and the other sciences, notably ethics, resulted in logical faults, especially of definition, which mar in no small degree the excellences by which the Roman law is on other grounds distinguished.'[5]

A definition of a legal system, a *Law*, in the terms so far proposed in this study contains no overt reference to justice or morality; a legal norm is defined by the nature of the society in which it operates, the authority which emits it, and the nature of the processes invoked for its transmission or enforcement. None of these is a just or moral end or means. If we say boldly that *Lex iniusta non est lex* — a law which is unjust is no law, we assert that the justness of a law (= legislated or man-made law) is an essential part of its definition or validity. But we must then be prepared to answer some awkward questions:

(i) What is 'just' and 'unjust'?
(ii) Who judges whether any given law is just or unjust?

We can readily appeal to higher authority — God, divine revelation, interior conscientious conviction — to help us with the defining of 'justice' for this purpose; but we may have a hard time of it persuading the persons operating a given legal system, or even those who with us are members of the community governed by the *Law*, that this understanding or definition of justice is the correct and only one, sufficiently sharply delineated to be instantly applicable to a critique of man-made laws. This is not to say that we should not make such an appeal, or seek to persuade others of the rightness of our conclusions; if our fellow-members or our rulers are easily persuaded, or declare that they already accept our view, then the need for persuasion disappears — but so does the problem, because the shared community definition of 'justice' becomes by this fact part of the community mores, part of the social language which rulers and subjects are already using, part, indeed, of their laws. The antithesis between law and justice evaporates.

Two principles compete: the first is that of *legalism*, that a law is a law is a law, and it is not competent for anyone to challenge a law or its authority on any non-legal criterion. It is open to such a person to seek to change the law by the usual processes of legislation; but until this is done, it is valid law, and he should comply. The second principle is that of *legality*, that everyone has the right in every kind of society to have legal rules fairly made and fairly applied to him; a differentially punitive, unfair or arbitrary law will then offend against the principle of legality. Legalist principles made it the sovereign duty of judges in Nazi Germany

5. J. B. Moyle *Inperatoris Iustiniani Institutiones* (1912, 5th edn), p. 62.

to apply Nazi laws, however unjust or immoral, provided that they were in due form and made by the competent authority. The legislation of South Africa does not offend against this principle of legalism. Legality says that one cannot act like that, to punish Jews or differentiate against black people; if one does so, the laws are formally valid, but their claim to allegiance is destroyed. All states everywhere tend to talk and operate in terms of legalism. Legality limits the authority of laws, legalism confirms it.

2. Natural law. Natural law theories have, from the earliest attempts of Greek philosophers, tried to define those principles of justice which create duties and give rights independent of those assigned by any contingent legal system in the here-and-now. Are there bodies of norms, deriving not from direct divine precept or human command, which have intrinsic validity because they correspond to, and spring from, fundamental characteristics and necessities of the human being and his life in human society? If there are, how are they to be ascertained? And how to explain that human societies everywhere tend to overlook many of the norms of this natural law, or even legislate in contradiction of it? Is it that their rulers have been denied a revelation of their existence and content; or is it that they have constantly rejected it?

The history of natural law theories is like that of the phoenix. Many times the mythical bird has flown from Arabia and roosted at the top of its palm-tree in Egypt, its plumage admired, its unique value accepted. Many times the rationalists have immolated it, leaving no more than ashes behind. Many times it has sprung up again, at 500-year intervals, from those same ashes, perhaps in slightly different plumage, to resume its temporary reign. Austin and his followers must have thought that natural law was dead, its life forever extinguished by the shrewd blows and scepticism of rationalists like Bentham (and later on by Mill). Very few reputable jurists, in England at any rate, would have admitted to a belief in natural law, any more than they would have admitted to a belief in fairies, unless from a strong sense of religious commitment. But the belief (and perhaps the fairies?) struggled on, maintained in continental schools especially. The conclusion of the war against Germany and the Nuremberg trials which followed demanded a rational justification for retributive action against the Nazi leaders. If this could not be found in the municipal law of Germany, it must be sought elsewhere; the victors found it in a new *ius gentium*, a supranational moral law whose principles the Nazis had transgressed. The United Nations, restructuring relations in and between states on a more moral and pacific basis, were inspired by the same vision, which expressed itself in the Universal Declaration of Human Rights in 1948.

It is ironical that the same rationalistic jusists, who might raise the loudest voices in denying any role to common perceptions of morality in the framing of municipal legislation, have been at the same time some of the most ardent advocates of a higher justice or legal morality, which they could use to attack institutions of the positive law which they disliked, such as racial or sex discrimination. Morality, in the sense of legislating a common moral code, has no place in the making of law, they would say; only a utilitarian aim is valid. But this sort of front corresponds at no point to the way laws are actually made, or the inspiration behind them. Every legislative system seeks to incorporate the value system of those who make it or control it. 'Equality', say, is a value, to be realised by progressive taxation and levelling through law. If this value, why not others? Natural law, on this view, is merely one source of values given separate identity through treating it as if it too were a legal system.

Whatever we *say*, then, we all *behave* as if values were part of a super-system, one on which we can call to inspire or criticise human laws. What is the content of this super-system? Hart, as usual, has helped to clarify our ideas; one should refer to his treatment of 'the minimum content of natural law'.[6] Through this term he seeks to explain the natural imperatives (using that term in a different sense from legal imperatives) which make the having of a legal system, and the particular features of a legal system which are desirable, necessary for man's survival in society. These he discusses under the heads of human vulnerability, approximate equality, limited altruism, limited resources, and limited understanding and strength of will. These *limits* of human beings require provisions and protections which are provided through law. The natural limits, while limiting the function of law in some directions, extend it in others.

3. The right to disobey laws. To say that ideas of justice and morality have no function in defining the existence and validity of legal norms *within* a legal system, to reject the notion that law is valid only and so far as it tends towards justice, is not to buy *in toto* the purely positivist thesis. The corrections to positivism must, however, be introduced at a different level into the discussion. A law (that is, a specific norm of a specific *Law* or legal system) is formally imperative or instructive, telling us what we must do or may do; it is a valid norm if made in accordance with the meta-norm requirements of that system. 'But', the counter-argument may go, 'how can you say that such a norm is binding if it is flagrantly immoral or unjust? Do you not open the door to Hitlerism, the dictatorship of the proletariat, or moral anarchy?' What about the striking words of St Augustine? — 'Without justice states are nothing but organised robber bands'.[7]

Yes, of course; but the difficulty comes through injecting material and tests from the higher level into the system at the lower level; that

6. In *Concept of Law*, pp. 189 ff.
7. *De civ. Dei*, IV, 5.

is, a legal norm, taken at its own level in its own system, is valid; but that does not mean (indeed, must not mean) that we do not test that norm as measured against standards at a higher level in a different system. The effect of such testing is not to make a binding, valid legal norm into a non-binding or invalid norm; the norm remains valid, but it was never binding. All our difficulties come because of the obsession with the idea that norms are 'binding'. Norms do not bind, they can only *persuade*. A norm, couched in an imperative mode or mandatory form, seeks to persuade its recipients to a certain course of action. Whether the recipient is persuaded or not, whether he 'obeys' or 'complies with' or 'disregards' the norm, depends on a variety of factors and their interplay.

Within a legal system, then, everyone must 'obey' the *Law*; but the *Law's* demands are not the end of the story; and the norms of the *Law* must attract the compliance, persuade the allegiance, of its subjects. Its subjects in their turn cannot and must not stay within the legal system in deciding whether to comply or not; there are other systems — religious and moral, in particular — which, if they owe allegiance to them, must be examined to see if compliance with the legal norm would not offend norms of those other systems. If such an offence would occur, the subject must refuse to obey the legal norm. In the competition for allegiance, the legal norms have lost. But the word 'allegiance' draws attention to the fact that whether a given subject recognises a superior moral or religious normative system, and what the content of that system will be, and how he will apply that system to his current problem, are all matters within the discretion of the subject. He has given his allegiance to such a non-legal system; his allegiance may be forced (by birth into a family or community in which it prevails) or unthinking (few bother to challenge current values or dicta); but allegiance it remains. Just as a medieval knight could switch his allegiance to another lord, so can the subject of a moral or legal system.

It would be wrong to say that a person has the 'right' to disobey a law which he judges to be immoral or unjust. The right obviously does not come from the *Law* itself, or his purported disobedience would actually be obedience to the legal norms! Nor do rights come from outside, from the moral or religious system, because talk of rights can only work when all the parties in a dispute are sharers in the same system, and have accorded each other reciprocal claims and privileges. If a law-giver denies the subject's 'right' to disobey the given law, he denies that he belongs to the same moral system as the subject. It would be more exact to say that a subject always has an *option* to comply or not to comply with a law; he may exercise that option because of his moral or religious convictions. The only question which remains is to see what such convictions may entail.

A purely moral code differs from one which is divinely inspired or given in that the contents of a divine code theoretically cannot be modified except by its maker. Humans cannot set the limits of the code or vary its provisions. But codes need interpretation, and humans must perform this task. Even a divine code (as the history of Islamic *Law* amply shows) can be very variously and casuistically interpreted. A moral code not of divine origin can, as remarked earlier, be framed or enunciated by some external authority; or it may be internally generated (though this is often a shared and social act). In each instance, though, the code has value only so far as it claims and receives the allegiance of its adherents. In this way it matters little whether the code is externally or internally generated, because in the competition with legal norms it is the strength of the allegiance to each system which counts.

We cannot seek illumination from particular legal systems as to when a subject has the 'right' to disobey; where do we go to look? I can only give my own moral system, so far as it is worked out, without claiming for it any universal value. First, it is a moral value to live in society, and to abide by its laws. Compliance should therefore be the norm. Without general compliance, the laws will become useless, and the society will disintegrate or become more unjust. This basic principle is only a *prima facie* action routine, however; it does not license obedience to laws which are, to one's own moral sense, flagrantly unjust; because it might be a moral good if those laws were rendered useless, and that society disintegrated.

A further general principle is that compliance with legal norms does not exhaust one's moral duties. A person who only did what he might be forced to do by *Law* would almost certainly be acting immorally. He would not be 'loving his neighbour', 'giving every man his due', cherishing the weak, sick, poor and unfortunate.

At the opposite extreme life in society would be impossible if no one wholeheartedly complied with any legal norm, and was always refusing to obey a norm on the ground that it did not correspond exactly with his own moral perception. It can thus be put forward as a moral principle that, while not requiring anyone to act against his conscience in major matters, a person's conscience should not be so pernickety as to lead him to question every trifling failure of a legal norm to match up to his own perceptions. *De minimis* is a sensible policy, not only *for* the *Law*, but *about* the *Law*.

Where a legal norm is in breach of a person's moral value system, what action should he take if the matter is not a minor one? Violence, and the subversion of the whole system by force, may be unjustifiable. Self-defence is legitimate, of course. If police, in execution of a law which is grossly immoral, come to remove you, you can resist with force; otherwise every Jew arrested by the Gestapo would have had to go like a lamb to the slaughter. (The fact that most Jews in Germany *did* go like lambs to concentration camp and death was not an expression of their moral view, but a hopelessness or a failure to realise the awfulness of their fate.) We cannot investigate the morality of revolution, or of an attempt to overthrow the legal order by force, here; it may well be that there are situations when such an attempt would be morally justified; but mere dislike of the capitalist system (or even of the communist system, to reverse the argument) would probably not be a sufficient ground. Edmund Burke put it thus [Letter to Fox, 8 October 1777]:

'People crushed by law have no hopes but from power. If laws are their enemies, they will be enemies to laws; and those, who have much to hope and nothing to lose, will always be dangerous, more or less.'

Writing and reading in safety in our comfortable liberal democratic societies of the West, we probably think that the unjust robber-state is the sort of thing they have in Africa, South America or South East Asia, not with us. But it is not only concentration camps and bloody dictatorship which make a robber-state. Let us look at a more mundane example nearer home. A state, even with a democratic constitution, has the right, and certainly has the power, to impose a taxation system in order to raise revenue. The right to impose taxes may be granted by the people who will pay them, or more frequently it will be self-granted by the ruling elite who purport to speak in the name of the people and who claim a mandate, carefully expressed as a mandate of representatives and not of delegates, to raise taxes to pay for government. Should people pay such taxes?

On the face of it, Yes. If the laws providing for the tax system are validly enacted according to the norms of the *Law*, the *prima facie* rule comes in that citizens should comply, unless there is major injustice. Major injustice could arise if either the tax laws are imposed by force and not by voluntary act, or the dispositions of those laws are themselves unjust, i.e. unfair. Injustice arises in the former instance because taxing someone is to take their property against their will; the fact that the property taken is money and not goods, or even that it is intercepted before it gets into the hands of its nominal owner, does not destroy the point that taxation is a taking of property, and the concomitant principle that taking of another's property is on the face of it unlawful and immoral. Taking of property is not moral merely because the state does the taking. It must positively justify its actions. The state cannot justify its taking by saying that the taking is necessary for its purposes; otherwise every poor man could turn to banditry with complete moral justification. The state must add two requirements to the one that it needs the money: viz., that there is assent to the taking, and that the taking is fairly arranged. Assent is demonstrated in a pseudo-democratic society by the vote of the elected Parliament, or maybe by direct referendum (as in California). We have had occasion earlier on to point out the deceptive nature of the claim to democracy in countries such as Britain; what we have got in this country is an undemocratic and largely unfettered law-making elite. The faithful Commons who demonstrated their unfaithfulness to kingly rule in the time of Charles I and the revolt over ship-money at least had the argument on their side that they were more representative of the taxable class than is a modern Parliament. Assent to taxation by referendum seems more democratic and not open to the same objections; but the defeated minority in such a referendum (which might comprise all those, say, who were going to have to pay a new property tax) could say that *their* assent had never been given. At most, what assent they had given would be generally to government by referendum, rather than particularly to this specific proposition of law. By these means we return to the fiction of the Social Contract — 'if you don't like life in such a society, you can always leave!'[8] Democracy sanctioned by secession. Strangely enough, when we move to black Africa in traditional times, this was exactly the most powerful sanction against unjust rule, as anthropologists like Gluckman have amply demonstrated.[9] But individual departure from a society is often not feasible, legally or financially or emotionally, in our modern world of passports and exchange control and exit visas; while mass secession can only be organised if one forms a distinct ethnic minority, like the Welsh, Scots, Irish or Québecois.

If in a 'democratic' society there is taxation without consent of the taxed (and this may be true even in a direct democracy governed by referendum), how can one possibly justify taxation at whatever level in the absolute polity? The only recourse of the taxing governments in every type of society is to deny the major premise, that taking of property without consent is immoral. They substitute a rider, that such taking is moral if ordered by a government. But why select governments for this amoral privilege? Why not the Mafia, the local church, the trade union branch, the highway robber? To say that life in a modern state would be impossible if the state could not take the money it wanted for its own purposes is perhaps to say that the modern state is a fundamentally immoral institution. The general assent of the governed to the state and its operations is a fiction; even if it were not a fiction, it cannot be taken to include assent to unjust taking of property.

There remains the argument from reciprocity: you cannot deny your obligations[10] to a society, which might and probably will include the

8. For a true social contract society in Africa, see the Somali democracy based on agreement, mentioned above at pp. 96 ff.
9. See M. Gluckman *Order and rebellion in tribal Africa* (1963), 'Introduction'; and I. Schapera *A handbook of Tswana law and custom* (2nd edn, 1955), p. 85, etc.
10. 'Obligation' is used in this and succeeding sentences, not because the objective existence of obligations is accepted nor because use of the term modifies the analysis, but solely as a short-hand way of saying that there are things which the *Law* (in the case of 'legal obligations') or morality (in the case of 'moral obligations') requires you (= purports to direct or persuade you) to do. 'An obligation to contribute generally . . .' thus = 'You must contribute generally' = 'Legal norms say that you should contribute generally, or else . . .'.

obligation to contribute to its maintenance, if you receive benefits flowing from the fact that the other members of society recognise a similar and reciprocal obligation. There are two 'Buts . . .' to append to this argument:

But (1) — An obligation to contribute generally cannot be construed to equal or cover an obligation to contribute whatever is demanded, just or unjust. Society cannot force us to write it a blank cheque, which can be filled in with any amount that society chooses.

But (2) — If the obligation to pay is a social or moral consequence of the right to receive, then should not the extent of the obligation be conditioned by the amount received? In other words, if I, being one such member of that society, benefit in nothing except, say, common defence by the armed forces and police and use of roads and main services, and choose to spend my time in my Welsh mountain retreat self-sufficiently looking after all my other needs, why should my obligation to pay not be restricted to that benefit which I derive; and why should I pay for, say, health service, schools, aid to industry, or a thousand and one other things on which the government chooses to spend 'its' (= our) money? What is more, if the obligation derives from the benefit, why I should pay differentially more just because I have more resources in income, or have saved more of my earnings? If life in society is like joining a West End club, we should very much resent being charged a double membership fee if all we got for it was the same as other members paying a single fee. If that is not the correct principle, where is the additional principle of 'qualified reciprocity' to come from? Any why should I assent to it, or be taken against my will to assent to it?

So much for the question whether the tax laws have been unjustly made or imposed. Now let us look at their content, to see whether they are just in their demands and distribution. Most modern 'progressive' (a warning word in itself) opinion accepts that progressive taxation, taking more from the rich, is morally justified. Let us concede that point (though a complete shift to expenditure taxes would reverse the argument). How 'progressive' may taxation justifiably be? Suppose A pays 1% of his income, and B 99% (or even 100%); is that morally justifiable? It may be argued that if one accepts the principle of progressive taxation (which one has done only for the sake of the present discussion), then the levels of taxation cannot be censured morally, since they only represent variations of quantity and not of principle. But a sufficient variation in a quantity may constitute a variation in the quality of an act or a principle — beating a child is an ordinary example. Levels of progressive taxation can be so oppressive as to represent a new principle of taxation, not of proportionate contribution but of differential confiscation. Where this level is to be set is open to serious contention — in Gladstone's day, perhaps, more than 1s. in the £1 might have been taken to be confiscatory. All this proves, however, is not the failure of Victorian government to appreciate its entitlement, but an ever-increasing rapacity coupled with a resigned acquiescence on the part of those who pay. Taxation can be used as an instrument of class-warfare, to grind down the faces of the poor or to despoil the rich. Confiscation does not cease to be such merely because it is called taxation. It remains robbery. A government, say, of an ultra-socialist persuasion seizing power after a revolution might confiscate all the property of its class enemies; to say that such confiscation is not merely legal (following the path of legalism) but moral (following the path of legality) would be less than self-evident.

In other words, many modern 'democratic' governments have become robber governments in Augustine's eyes, because they deny one or other form of justice; and they deserve the same respect as one would accord to any other band of robbers. Hart for one (and many others have made the same point)[11] has sought to distinguish the orders of a gunman: 'Hand over that money!' from the orders of a state transmitted by its legal system: its laws. The one is temporary and particular, the other is general, and is supported by a general and not a temporary habit of obedience. Suppose, though, that a government confiscates the wealth of one man (not unusual in revolutionary situations, as ex-rulers like the Shah of Persia know well); there is no general pattern of obedience to such an order. Suppose further that the gunman and his gang instal themselves in the capital, and habitually demand money from the inhabitants: many coups in African and other countries have been carried out by such gunmen. The fact that the gunmen bear guns because they were in a formerly legitimate army changes the matter not one whit. The 'law' of the gunman-government is still gun-law. Its justice comes out of the barrel of its gun.

4. Legislation which expresses or rejects a moral attitude. Conflict between a law and a citizen's perception of morality, leading perhaps to a 'right' or 'duty' to disobey that law, can arise in a variety of ways. There are laws, to begin with, which expressly set out — according to the declarations of their makers — to express a moral attitude: race relations laws are one such example. There are laws which purport to be neutral, but by their very neutrality take up a moral position. For these laws, though not for the first category, it is said that the law should not pick and choose between alternative moral views, which it leaves to the decision of the individual subject. Such are the present laws on homosexuality in Britain, which on the face of it neither affirm nor condemn homosexual practices. But on this kind of assertion one has sympathy with the marxist approach to *political* attitudes and decisions; to take a political decision is obviously political, but to refuse to take a political decision is also a political decision. So with moral decisions. The moral

11. See *Concept of Law*, pp. 20 ff.

decision which the state takes in enacting a non-committal law about homosexuality is that (a) it sees nothing sufficiently wrong in homosexuality to justify it, the state, legislating against it; (b) it positively affirms a moral stance where such decisions are left to the individual. This latter is an internally generated and validated type of morality, as opposed to a community-generated and imposed morality, of which race relations laws are representative. The two kinds of legislation are thus in contradiction with each other.

A moral commitment in legislation can be tacit and implied, rather than express; for many centuries England purported to legislate in accordance with Christian morality; Muslim states still do so in accordance with Muslim morality (and communist countries legislate in accordance with their own communist morality). It is part of the revolution of the secular and pluralist society in the West, though not in the communist world or in many countries of the Third World as yet, that they should break away from this prior and general moral commitment, in favour of a secularising and individualising approach. Lawmaking in traditional communities, whether governed by a religious or a customary type of *Law*, habitually expressed an inbuilt moral commitment, as we have observed several times in this study.

What are the consequences of each type of situation? The consequences are most significant for the subjects of the *Law*. Their moral attitude to matters governed by the morally committed type of legislation is prescribed for them. If they do not like the attitude, their only remedies are disobedience or departure. They can seek to change the legislation, of course; but such a step is only possible in pluralist societies, and meets all the obstacles which the law-making and controlling elite places in the way of popular law-making. It says much for the strength of popular power to make and unmake laws that so much has in fact been achieved by popular resistance to laws which offend the people's notions of morality.

The result of an imposition of a law which contradicts popular moral ideas is to weaken and make more difficult the enforcement of the law. This aspect is considered at greater length in the discussion which follows in Chapter 6 about social transformation through law.

5. The fundamental rights debate. Lastly, in our rapid survey of some major issues in the law and morality relationship we come to fundamental rights. Advocacy of fundamental rights need not be allied to or derive from a frank natural law position, though it necessarily implies that the advocate subscribes to the view that there are prior or anterior 'rights' which persons possess inalienably and which every human legal system should respect, a position coterminous with the natural-law approach.

It is impossible to accommodate fundamental rights and the absolute sovereignty of the legislator in a single theory. Fundamental rights doctrine says that there are limits on a legislator's power to make laws, limits which he cannot transgress. If he transgresses those limits, there are no sanctions within the legal system; and, in the absence of some supranational enforcement system with teeth, no sanctions from outside the legal system. The consequence of making a law contrary to some fundamental right is to forfeit the claim to allegiance of the contravening law. If the absolute legislator voluntarily adopts a code of fundamental rights, builds them into his own system, he must give up his absolute sovereignty. If the United Kingdom Parliament, to take an example, legislates a code of fundamental rights which cannot be derogated from and which will invalidate non-conforming future legislation, then Parliament must be taken to have abandoned its dogma that one Parliament cannot bind its successor.

Law and mores

Law prescribes what people ought to do; mores reports what they habitually do — how can these two both be normative systems, and how can they be in conflict? Only too easily, is the answer. Even at the non-normative level, if people habitually do what the *Law* says they should not, or do not do what the *Law* says they should, a tension is created, and a strain is placed on the legal norms whose degree of compliance has dropped or vanished. Failure to conform weakens the effectiveness of the *Law*; diminishing effectiveness is expressed as decreasing claim to allegiance. In theory popular disregard does not, in England, repeal laws; in practice it does so, by making their enforcement improbable or impossible.[12] We have already discussed examples of such disregard leading to the unmaking of laws.[13] Sir C.K. Allen[14] mentions the fact that, according to the Roman jurists, 'the same foundation of popular consent was assumed, constitutionally and legally, to lie at the base of all legislation'; and he mentions Julian's dictum: 'ipsae leges nulla alia ex causa nos teneant, quam quod judicio populi receptae sunt' (statutes themselves will bind us only for the reason that they have been accepted in or by the judgment of the people) — though Allen characterises this as no better than a fiction by the time of the absolute imperial monarchy.

But mores are more important in helping to make *Law* than to unmake it. In a customary-*Law* society, this after all is the major source of new principles, and the reinforcement of old ones. It is not, however, always appreciated how important mores are as a material source of *Law* in societies with a non-customary legal system. The play of social forces is endlessly moulding the existing principles of the *Law* and leading to the formation of new ones. One of the best and still current

12. And see also the discussion of 'Law and behaviour' in Chapter 7 at pp. 251 ff.
13. See pp. 82 ff.
14. *Law in the Making* (3rd edn, 1939), p. 77.

examples of this process at work is the gradual emergence of the institution of the 'house-mate' or common-law wife' in English *Law*.[15] Conflicts arise during the process of emergence of such an institution, because of the tension between the formal letter of the existing law and the aspirant law which is seeking to emerge.

To summarise, the conflicts and competition between *Law* and other normative systems arise because *Law* is persuasion. Submission to *Law* is conditional, limited and not absolute. We submit or conform, sometimes because we believe that we should — 'obligation'; sometimes because we believe that we have no alternative — 'power'; and sometimes because we believe that it is to our advantage to do so — 'interest'. But these words add no new or extra truth, and do not alter the effect of *Law* in the long run, that it is persuasive.

15. See Chapter 8.

6 Limits on the utility of law for social transformation

Codification: types and limits

If *Law* is persuasion, to be used by a law-making authority to persuade its subjects to a certain course of action, how far and fast can the legislator go in seeking to change current modes of behaviour and the structures of society? It is time to address this question, not at the theoretical but at the empirical level, by examining what legislators have tried to do at different periods of the world's history, in various countries, and for various purposes. Although our present concern is especially with the developing world, it would be an error to think that the use of law as a tool for rapid social transformation, for the promotion of development, whether in its restricted economic sense or not, is confined to 'developing countries' so-called. There is no one kind or category of country in which alone the legislator, once he ceases to be a passive follower of trends in social behaviour and becomes an initiator of them, uses *Law* in this transforming way. Both the nature of the vision of the law-maker, and the kind of legal means he adopts, vary quite widely.

(a) In one kind of country he can be a religious leader, transforming his society into a new kind of polity built on the tenets of a powerful religion. Such, for example, has been the case in societies where Muslim rulers took power over what was previously a non-Muslim society. Islamic *Law* and religion, as we have already observed, are totalitarian in their ambit, and the separation between sacred and secular is not made in the same terms as in modern secularising states. Islam would thus yield many examples of our theme.

Similarly with Christianity. The major colonisers of the pre-industrial world were European powers who happened to be Christian (if we exclude previous empires like those of the Romans, the Mongols, the Chinese, and the Turks). Their being Christian was to begin with part of their credentials to rule less fortunate folk; and the bringing of Christian institutions to barbarian and pagan peoples was seen as part of their colonising and 'civilising' task. As a consequence of such conquests, then, new systems of *Law* were introduced (of which we have made

161

mention, in the African context, in Chapter 4), which were inspired by, or at least not contrary to, Christian moral and other notions. The British in Africa offered their *Law* to the native African populations by way of a *model* alternative to the existing model under indigenous *Laws*. This model the population were left to adopt or not at their choice; it was optional. We discuss examples of such models below.

(b) The makers of new and transforming laws could have, and today generally have, secular ambitions. One of the first wholehearted transformers was Napoleon (or rather the body of *savants* who acted in his name and at his direction to produce a new code of civil law for France).[1] The transformation was firstly in the political structure of the state, from a decentralised country, almost federal in its recognition of local legal systems, to a highly centralised bureaucratic and unified structure which contained no room for the local and customary (though partially codified) *Laws* of the *ancien régime*. But the ambitions of the Napoleonic reformers in the period from 1800 to 1811 when they were actively at work went further than a mere re-distribution of emphasis in political arrangements; the basic presupposition of the new civil law was strongly secularist in character, and the element of social restructuring in the provisions of the law, especially that which related to marriage and the family, was quite marked. The *Code civil*, which was published in 1804 and which has since had an astonishing influence on codification around the world, was a new law which, however, embodied elements of the old: of the old *droit écrit* of southern France, of the customary laws of the rest of the country, especially 'the custom of Paris', which had some pretensions to become the *droit commun* of France, and of the revolutionary laws which had already destroyed feudalism, secularised marriage, introduced divorce, and changed the law of succession.

It is not our intention to review all the great codifications of western Europe, and more recently of other regions of the world; but there is one element in many of these legal transformations which is worthy of remark. The declared aim of the codifier has often been to bring order into what had previously been legal disorder, by reason of the existence and recognition of diverse statutory or non-statutory sources of the law, especially a multiplicity of local and customary *Laws*, some of which had not even been reduced to a standard written text. He substitutes order, precision, authority and uniformity for what had previously been confusion, imprecision, doubtful authority and diversity.[2] His

1. Though not the first in point of time of the modern European codes, jurists agree that it was original in its approach, and seminal in its significance.
2. The Code of Hammurabi of c. 1750 BC seems to have been of this clarifying character, though it is almost certainly not a code in the usual sense of the term, but rather a collection of royal decisions or decrees. Certainly the main aim of the codes of Draco (621 BC) and Solon (?593 BC) was to reduce the arbitrary element in judging and imposition of penalties, and to make for greater certainty and uniformity in adjudication.

ambitions thus stated are those of a legal mechanic, trying to improve
the mechanisms of the *Law*, without necessarily being committed to
any particular world-view, or to producing a social revolution or transformation through his codes. The German codification of the
Bürgerliches Gesetzbuch or Civil Code (promulgated 1896, introduced
in 1900) is a pre-eminent example of *technical transformation of laws*.
Such an aim is shared by many of the modern law reformers; and the
work of the Law Commissions in England and Scotland is primarily
directed to this end. The codifiers of the received English *Law* in
19th-century British India, starting off with Lord Macaulay's draft Indian
Penal Code of 1837, at once the most ambitious and the most original
of the Indian codes, were primarily concerned with making the non-
indigenous *Law* of British India technically better and easier to
administer. A second aim was to improve the law, and to rectify or
remove some of the weaknesses of the old system of law and equity
borrowed from England. A third aim was to ensure that it was better
adapted to the needs and social circumstances of the native Indian
population, to indigenise the *Law* in some degree (though not to go
overboard for a wholesale adoption within the codes of Hindu and
Muslim principles of law, the sort of aim which some 20th-century
codifiers in the Third (non-European) World now avow).[3] What was
missing was a fourth aim, to impose a new way of life on the people
through the making and forcible application of a new *Law* to them:

'It is time that the magistrate should know what law he is to administer
— that the subject should know under what law he it to live. We do
not mean that all the people of India should live under the same law:
far from it ... We know how desirable that object is; but we also
know that it is unattainable. We know that respect must be paid to
feelings generated by differences of religion, of nation, and of caste.
Much, I am persuaded, may be done to assimilate the different systems
of law without wounding those feelings. But, whether we assimilate
those systems or not, let us ascertain them; let us digest them. We
propose no rash innovation; we wish to give no shock to the prejudices
of any part of our subjects. Our principle is simply this; uniformity
where you can have it; diversity where you must have it; but in all cases
certainty.' (From the speech of Lord Macaulay in the East India
Company debate of 10 July 1833.)

When we come to the codifications of modern India, we shall notice a
startling change in governmental objectives. Certainty and uniformity
remain as paramount objectives; but an equally vital one is the changing
of the society as a whole through *Law*.[4]

3.   Macaulay also entertained at one time the idea of codifying the applicable
     rules of Hindu and Muhammedan civil law; but nothing came of the proposal.
     Had it been completed, it would have been the earliest restatement of either
     law in a form which Bentham might have approved of.
4.   See pp. 181–2, below.

Technical improvement, then; simplification; greater certainty; even uniformity — these have been the aims of much codifying legislation. The legislation has to be in code form, that is, a systematic and purportedly exhaustive set of legislative provisions dealing with a whole area of human life or a separate division of the *Law*, because it is only in that way that the aims can be achieved. However, it is my contention now that technical improvement, and especially innovating codification, tends to have an inescapable side-effect which may not be intended by the legislator: that is, to change the legal regime under which people live, and thus indirectly to change the way of life which the *Law* permits or encourages them to pursue. This consequential effect is often masked by the codifying law-makers, not least for reasons of policy. It is easier to sell a new law to its subjects if it is represented that it will merely make the existing law simpler and clearer and not disturb existing established social patterns. Sometimes the codifier may not appreciate what the side-effects of his code may be. A good illustration of such side-effects is given by laws enacted in the last decade or two in African countries to 'improve' the land laws there, of which the Kenya land legislation of 1959 to 1968 is a sovereign example.[5] The draftsman puts forward as his claim that existing rights in land will not be disturbed, and will either figure on the register or be protected as overriding interests. At the same time, out of the other corner of his mouth, the legislator is claiming that the new land law will lead to complete transformation of the economic exploitation of land. To suppress customary clan and family rights in land or to keep them off the register must inevitably devalue them or destroy them, or lead to massive non-compliance with the law if the people refuse or fail to change their land tenure practices and to record their entitlements on the land register. This is what has happened in Kenya; there is a parallel system of rights in land which survives or has been created alongside the formal system of registered titles; the unrecorded titles may be invalid in legal theory; but, if the register does not record transfers and sub-alienations of recorded rights, it ceases to be an accurate guide to who is entitled to what interests (or rather, who in practice asserts his title to what interests). It is politically unthinkable that a government in such a case should stand firmly on the letter of the law, as expressed in the register; it must permit and give effect to the theoretically non-legal tenure. The same has occurred in a country like Turkey with its law of marriage; the actual position and the theoretical legal position defining who is validly married to whom are completely at variance.

A further frequently declared aim of codification has been *popularisation* of the law. Popularisation has a dual meaning: (i) allegedly to make the law more democratic, i.e. influenced by and corresponding to popular wishes; and (ii) allegedly to make the law more accessible to

5. See pp. 191 ff. below.

its subjects by making it simpler and easier to understand. Both aims relate directly to the effectiveness of law: if the people are more involved and committed in the making of the law, their readiness to conform will be increased; and if the people know what the law is, they are likelier to follow it. Both the framers of the French *Code civil*, and Lord Macaulay in his Minutes on his Penal Code, emphasise the latter point, that law should be of and for the people, and thus necessarily it must be intelligible to them. Whereas the revolutionary forces in France might have satisfied the requirement of democratic participation by direct democracy, in British-ruled India, without democratic political institutions, the democracy – if that is what it was – was of an indirect and presumed kind. The law-makers did what they thought the people would know and accept paternalistic but benevolent elitism of a pattern very familiar in modern non-colonial states.

If either or both of these aims were realised, it could not, on our analysis, help modifying the acceptability and efficacy of the resultant law; but do the achievements of the codifiers live up to their prospectus? We are put on our guard immediately, in the case of the Indian Penal Code, by Macaulay's claim in his celebrated Minutes on the subject that the Code was an original work which did not rely on any previous model and which did not codify, even at one remove, the existing penal law, whether of England, the British administration in India, or the indigenous Islamic criminal law. Subsequent critics have refused to accept this self-assessment, and see the Code, though in many respects original in both form and content, as deriving ultimately from the criminal law of England. Did that codified law correspond to popular wishes? We only have Lord Macaulay's word for it; sure it is that the law it replaced was in part of a quite different character. Since the people did not participate in its making, we cannot be sure; and by the time it was finally enacted in revised form into law in 1860, the opportunity for popular consultation and amendment was past. It was the views of the professional men, the commissioners and the judges, which counted.

As for the *Code civil*, I do not know enough of French history to be sure how far the text was the result of popular debate and accepted only after popular consultation; certainly its preparation was a task for expert jurists, drawing on a long pre-revolutionary tradition of treatise-writing. But the machinery of consultation, even in revolutionary France, would not satisfy the strict requirements of total democracy.[6]

How about the other stated objective, in these and similar instances: to make the codified law intelligible to the people subject to it, by using language which they could read and understand? One has merely

6. I am assured by my friend and colleague Professor L. Neville Brown, for whose comments I am most grateful, that, although the drafts were circulated to the various cours d'appel for comments, there was no consultation of popular opinion in any real sense.

to mention this requirement to see its absurdity when applied to Victorian India, in which only a minute fraction of the population could read English, and even fewer could understand abstract legal ideas. We are told that several of the provisions of the French Civil Code have entered popular consciousness; what this means and how effective this is in making the law intelligible and acceptable to the population at large one does not know. But, even if it is true, one must remember that the Code by itself is not the law; the law comprises the Code together with the writings of jurists commenting on and explaining it, *doctrine*, and the decisions of the courts, *jurisprudence*. It would be as unsafe in France to take the letter of the Code as a sufficient statement of the applicable law as it would be in England with an English statute.

These reservations continue to the present day and to modern codifications. In countries such as those of Africa where the official language is not the language of the home, the texts of laws can have little meaning, however carefully phrased, for the majority who cannot read the language; this was a major issue at the time of the enactment of the Northern Nigerian Penal Code in 1959, and led to the official and immediate translation of the Code into Hausa, the predominant language of the North, with a view to making it accessible to all. The Hausa into which it was translated, though a work of art in itself, was also difficult for the ordinary man to comprehend. But − and one cannot emphasise this point too often − the language of any law, code or not, is a foreign language to the ordinary citizen. This is especially so in England, where the language of statutes has never been the language of ordinary converse; but it is true to a lesser extent everywhere. The reason for this is that statute laws are necessarily statements of an abstract and theoretical nature, and ordinary people do not communicate in such statements. So code language is a foreign language.

This is not to say that there cannot be more obscure and less obscure statements of the law, that language cannot be simplified or even made more popular; but look at the disasters in England when popular language is used in a 'clear' statutory provision! Nothing could be more homely than the use of the word 'family' to define the class of persons who are entitled to take over the benefit of a statutory tenancy under the Rent Act; and yet *Dyson Holdings Ltd v Fox*[7] and the many other cases which discuss the term 'family' in this context show the doubts and difficulties into which even professionally trained judges can get. Nothing could be more straightforward than section 1 of the Rent Act 1977:

'Subject to this Part of this Act, a tenancy under which a dwelling-house (which may be a house or part of a house) is let as a separate dwelling is a protected tenancy for the purposes of this Act . . .'.

7. [1976] QB 503, [1975] 3 All ER 1030, CA; see above at pp. 103 ff., and below at pp. 264 ff.

and yet every word, even every form-word, has attracted endless judicial discussion and disagreement. The meaning of a provision like this is not to be sought in the codifying statute itself but in the law-reports. No citizen could gain access to the latter; and hence he could not gain access to the meaning of the former. The aim of making the law intelligible to all through codification is thus either a deception or an illusion.

Lastly, we may call attention to the *speed* at which many of the most revolutionary laws have been drafted. This is not to say that their implementation has been similarly rapid; but it shows that it need not take a decade or even half a century to get a radical reform under way. Napoleon as First Consul in 1800 gave the order for the constitution of a commission to reform the law; in 1804 its Civil Code was published. True that they built on previous attempts at codification; but the speed is remarkable. Especially astonishing is the rapidity with which Macaulay and his Commissioners produced their draft Penal Code. In 1833 Macaulay moved the British House of Commons to codify Indian criminal law; the Indian Law Commission was then constituted with Macaulay as President; by 1837 the Code was drafted and circulated to the judges. Two years apparently sufficed for the actual drafting of the Twelve Tables in the Rome of c. 450 BC (if we exclude a mission to Athens to study Solon's code). As for Solon, he would appear (though information is wanting) to have pushed through his code in the single year of his archontate. These were all original works; today even a derivative code takes longer, and is usually heavily reliant on other existing models.

One issue which there is little need to revive here is the possibility or impossibility for the codifier of making his code comprehensive and effective (effective in the sense that it is *his* will, as law-giver, that prevails and not that of the courts or other administering agency). There has been endless discussion about styles in codes, gaps, and similar fundamental problems. Should the codifier lay down a general principle, leaving the courts and administrators of the code to fill in the casuistic details? Or should he try to cover every case? There is no clear answer. If we are to judge by results rather than by declared objectives, it does not seem to matter much which strategy the codifier adopts, in the long run. An 'open' code of general principles demands much more in the way of ongoing interpretation from the courts. They, with their decisions, will fill in, amplify and extend its provisions. But at the same time there is more chance that the fundamental principles will be left intact, and will be resorted to by the courts at a later period. With a detailed code so much casuistical material will be supplied to interpretative judges and jurists that they will be able to manufacture new law almost at will by balancing one text against another — the treatment of Islamic *Law* and its detailed rules (though not legislated) is a case in point. The judicial handling of the English Statute of Frauds can be set beside that of the American Constitution and its leading amendments.

A LAW AS MODEL

1. Law is a model. In a most important sense, all law is a model. This is inescapably part of the structure of normative statements, which consist of an If- part which describes a hypothetical or model situation, and follow this up by prescribing legal consequences which shall flow if the actual fact-situation matches the model of the norm. In so far as the consequent of the norm persuades a subject to adopt or conform to the pattern of behaviour specified in the model, to that extent one can say that the norm-giver is persuading the subjects of the law to a particular pattern of behaviour.

But a law can go further or more deviously than this. It can seek to *command* a particular type of behaviour, by imposing stringent sanctions for non-conformity; or it can neutrally *allow* for particular types of behaviour, where the norm consists of a permission. By providing facilities the legislator may or may not hope to induce a particular pattern of behaviour. Most of the examples which we shall be citing in this section represent instances of *strong permissions* where the legislator has hesitated to command behaviour of a given type, but has nevertheless nourished an objective of persuading the subjects of the *Law* to that type of behaviour. This objective defines the model-giving laws as designed to be socially transforming.

2. Model status relationships. The pre-eminent case of this category is provided by the legally recognised, defined and protected status of marriage. Customary *Laws* (just as much as modern western *Laws*) recognised and recognise special statuses of marriage, and the legal provision for them is strongly reinforced by the almost universally shared social imperative making marriage the normal and desired state for physically suitable persons. This social imperative, without commanding matrimony, looks with disfavour on the unmarried, who would be exposed to ridicule and censure if they remain voluntarily unmarried. The customary *Laws* often went further by providing institutions, such as widow inheritance and levirate marriage, by which a particular relationship could be prolonged beyond the lifetime of one or both of the partners. These institutions helped to ensure that no one was left in a single state unnecessarily.

Marriage, then, is a status relationship, the incidents of which are in part regulated by legal norms. However, adherence to the relationship (except for some instances of forced marriages in the old days) was voluntary; and even where a particular young person had to comply with the wishes of his or her parent or family-head, the voluntary character of the relationship was preserved by reason of the fact that it was the will of those *giving* in marriage that constituted the marriage.

Marriage is a facultative institution connoting a status relationship. It is, however, *entered into* by way of contract; and the details of the relationship are *filled in* by contract (or by the will of one party coupled with the acquiescence of the other). The combination of *status + contract* is typical of the sorts of models that we shall be looking at. The combination incidentally gives the lie to, or renders difficult the application of, the dichotomy between status and contract and the progression from one to the other which we owe to Maine. Where a relationship is not obligatory, it typically consists of a status modified and added to by contract; and these status + contract relationships are well represented in the modern laws, both of developed countries like Britain and of the developing countries of the Third World whose *Laws* are in transition.

The 'framework laws' at which we look below in section 3 provide for models which are forms of association; while in section 4 we look particularly at 'transforming models', as I call them, where the legislator's aim is not merely to facilitate and define the limits of a relationship or institution within the existing legal system and its assumptions, but to use the relationship as part of a general shift from one kind of legal system (and one kind of life implied by and inspiring it) to another.

3. Framework laws. The French, with their 'loi-cadre' or outline law, have the advantage over us in terminology. I use the English 'framework law' as an inexact equivalent — inexact, because we are not discussing here legislation which allows subordinate legislatures to make decrees or regulations. We are discussing laws which allow persons to act as subordinate law-makers in a private capacity; such subordinate norm-making and ordering will, in our terms, be *catanomic* or law-conforming.

Laws providing for the establishment and regulation of various forms of association are outline laws. The history of English *Law* in the last two centuries has been the history of the multiplication of various forms of legally approved associations — partnerships; corporations formed by character; friendly societies; companies formed under statute; co-operatives; and so on. New categories of association and corporation constantly manifest themselves; public corporations are a new category, and even this category in English *Law* is developing new variants.

These associations and corporations are instrumental to some end. It is instructive to ask what end is served by the recognition of any particular kind of association; and thereafter to ask what end is served by any particular example of that kind of association. Trading companies represent a way of mobilising capital, of giving a structure to a complicated enterprise, of encouraging initiative, of assuring the supply of goods or services. All these are values which the society accepts as important or even vital; and an examination of the sorts of goods or services so supplied tells us much about the goals of that society. Building societies have comparable, though different, objectives, the mobilisation and enterprise are there, the encouragement of initiative by reward is less pronounced.

Joint-stock companies, building societies, and the like were not found in traditional African societies (or elsewhere in comparable societies). If they are found today in modern African countries, it is because they were introduced as a policy decision by the then rulers. Of course customary societies placed a high value on association and co-operation, and they had several alternative principles of association around which such association and co-operation were built – blood ties (family and lineage systems); common residence (households, village communities, local districts); cults of deities; military organisation ('companies', age regiments); age or generation (age-groups and grades); economic activity (fishermen's and cattle-herders' associations). All these customary associations and forms of co-operation have been weakened, and in some instances destroyed, by the bruising impact of western institutions.

When the British colonial power, for instance, enacted a Companies Ordinance for the Gold Coast Colony[8] at an early period of the history of colonisation, there were no limited companies of the type now provided for already in existence. The model selected was a purely English one, so much so that the text of the laws was often a carbon copy of the current English statute. Adaptation to local circumstances was not thought about, and did not enter into the drafting. Since there were no companies, the contradictions between law and society did not matter. But clearly the *offer* of such a legal framework was made in the expectation, and even the hope, that it would eventually be required. Certainly the expectation was that it would be foreign, expatriate enterprises which would need this form, and the idea that the native population might also make use of it probably did not enter into the legislator's calculations. Even a foreign company would have an impact on economic activity in the colonial territory; the participation of the indigenous people in this quite strange form of enterprise would have an even more profound one.

It was only in the course of decades that many indigenous people took up some of the opportunities offered by these framework-laws, and even then only after extensive propaganda campaigns and the investment of time and personnel to promote them, especially co-operatives. By the time of independence in Ghana (1956), for instance, there were practically no indigenous companies. The picture 20 years on is quite different in Nigeria; but this is due to a remarkable expansion

8. No. 14 of 1906.

of commercial and manufacturing activity coupled with a deliberate government policy of forcing the indigenisation of corporate enterprises.

4. Transforming models. By far the most interesting forms of models are those I label 'transforming'. These models were introduced legislatively through the enactment of statutes which, in the case of British colonial territories, offered the native populations (i) the option of entering a monogamous marriage (through the terms of Marriage Ordinances which provided for religious or civil 'Christian' marriages); (ii) the option in some territories only of disposing of their disposable property by written will; (iii) the option of dealing with interests in land, acquired and held in accordance with customary *Law*, by means appropriate to English *Law*, i.e. through written conveyances and documents; and (iv) the option of holding land through individualised and western systems rather than through the community-based tenures which are a feature of customary *Laws*. Voluntary schemes of land reform for 'improved' or pioneer farmers were set up in several territories for this last end. Most broadly and generally, (v) the dual system of law in force in the colonial territories, with the ever-present possibility of making agreements under English *Law*, meant that there was an unbounded set of other relationships which parties could construct for themselves, and which would take them out of the stereo-typed institutions of their own *Laws*. Contract as a catalyst of social change would be a theme for a book in itself.

Many of these possibilities, and the legal issues which arise from them, I have discussed elsewhere.[9] They led to major problems in, for instance, internal conflict of laws: how free was a person subject to customary *Law* to employ these alien devices and institutions and free himself from the restrictions and burdens of his own legal system? Once one accepts, as the legislation in the colonial territories generally recognised, the right of persons to make their own law and liberate themselves from the personal and community *Law* into which they had been born, the possibilities are endless; and one is struck by the solvent power of contract (the expression of the individual will) in destroying the consensus and common practice of the aboriginal *Law*. The contractual genie was out of the bottle, and would never be got back in again.

It is important to emphasise that these were not forced changes, that possibilities and not commands were put in front of the subjects of the *Law*. But there was undoubtedly a hope in the ruling circles of the colonial system that there would be a progressive move away from tradition and in the direction of 'modern' law; and various carrots were provided to assist movement in this direction. Thus marriage under the Marriage Ordinance in monogamous form and with monogamous

9. See, for instance, *New Essays in African Law* (1970).

requirements often led to a new and individualised property regime being applied to the estate of the spouses at their death. Written conveyances of land led to the weakening of community controls over land; the written will, which was generally unknown and even abhorrent to customary *Law*, made the will of the testator and not of his family group decisive as to what happened to his assets at his death. Contract, the assertion of individual will, is in its essence a partial denial of community solidarity. All, then, conspired to strengthen the scope for individual action, to weaken responsibility to the group, be it kinship or territorial, to weaken the power of the group to determine how people were to live. Weakening of the legal powers of the family and community weakened too their social powers, and weakened the reinforcements in morality and religion which went with them. The integrated society was on the way to its destruction. Laws, then, produced greater social transformation through such models than through direct commands.

Transforming models in English *Law*

So far I have talked mostly about the situation in the former colonial possessions of Britain (a similar account could be given of other colonial territories). The reason for this concentration is that the transforming effect of models is more visible and more profound in such societies. It mirrors a similarly visible transformation in clothes (trousers rather than skins or cloth), architecture (mud huts with grass roofs give way to poured concrete and corrugated iron), transport (the foot or horse gives way to the car and lorry), education (social instruction at puberty or continually through association with grown-ups giving way to 'teachers' in 'classrooms'), religion, political organisation, music, art — the list is endless. We, living in Britain, say, find it much more difficult to detect similar transformations at work in our own country. That they are at work is evident. The evidence can be seen in industrial relations — totally transformed from the autocratic hire-and-fire structure of the factory before 1914; in family relations; in marriage (*and* divorce); in property relations; in consumer activity. If it is true that the provision of *models* by a law-giver can lead to social transformation of the most radical kind, even if adoption of the model is voluntary, then we must look for such models in English society over the last half-century. An excellent example is to be found in divorce. Ever since divorce was secularised in England (from 1857), there has been a progressive liberalisation of, which means freer access to, the machinery and grounds for dissolution. The latest Divorce Reform Act of 1969 has led to a positive rush to divorce. We are told that the original framers and promoters of the 1969 reforms thought that, once ancient unhappinesses had been dealt with (as where someone had sought her freedom from an unhappy marriage for many years, but had been denied it because the husband had refused to take action), the figure of divorces would settle down at a reasonable figure. All the experience since 1969 has totally falsified this projection: the number of divorces has continued to grow, and is far higher than in pre-1969 times. We are rapidly approaching the American situation of unstable marriage and repeated unsuccessful marriages.

What is the conclusion to be drawn from this? The first response is to provoke a profound suspicion of the motives and the perspicacity of those who originally pushed this legislation. Either they knew what would happen, did not care, and concealed it — the knave option; or they did not know and could not foresee — the fool option. Gross disturbances in social relations are produced by the introduction of new models into the legal system: this must be our second conclusion. It is no answer for the advocates of the new law to say that they did not wish this end; those who introduced liquor to the American Indian population may not have wished their psychological and social destruction, but they are responsible for it nonetheless. It is no answer to say that it is not the legislator who breaks up marriages but the spouses themselves, if the legislator hands the dissatisfied spouse a wrecking bar. The availability of a possibility which was previously un-thinkable or not thought about transforms the psychology of the subjects, as well as the legal possibilities. Their expectations and tolerances alter.

Options are about the human will — the individual can decide to take the option or not. But his decision is a 'dirty' one, not a clean one, as he is impelled and attracted by forces which we might, as a society, disapprove of, such as selfishness and greed. The choice is a self-regarding one in many cases, even though in many other cases the voluntary act can be liberating and beneficent for others (I decide to give my wealth to the poor, say). Those who provide new and potentially transforming legal models must think carefully of the consequences, and must be taken to have willed the consequences which actually flow until the contrary is demonstrated.

The main limit on the use of models for transforming society is therefore the incalculability of the consequences which may be provoked. Models may be *too* effective. Given the interconnectedness of the structure of a society, consequences can ramify far from their original source. Who is to say that the crisis in authority in British society today is not to be partly attributed to changing domestic relations? Man, though claimed as a rational animal, might, in his modern version, be also termed the 'irresponsible animal'. He lightly launches into the atmosphere substances which may accumulate and destroy our environ-ment (like ozone or radio-active materials); he as lightly launches into the atmosphere of society substances (legal models, in this case) which may have a similarly destructive tendency.

To summarise:

All laws provide models. Model status relationships are not designed to be transforming but confirming of the existing social order and its aims. They do, however, leave room internally for catanomic law-making. This links them to framework laws, which are intended both to favour individual law-creating initiative and to realise new goals. These in their turn shade into transforming models, which are part of the legislator's planned reconstruction of society. There is thus continuity between the four categories of models which we have described.

B LAW AS PROGRAMME

Social transformation using law as a model exploits the voluntary mode of procuring the end result. Now we turn to the use of law as programme, where the legislator, eager to reconstruct society to his image, is no longer willing to wait, to leave transformation to occur as the piecemeal and eventual result of countless individual decisions. The social engineer, for that is what he is, is too impatient or unconfident to wait. The social engineer, once he has gained access to the springs of power (and, since he cannot rely on persuasion alone, that is the necessary pre-condition of his getting to work), builds his Utopia according to a programme which is imposed on the people subject to him. What the 'Utopian engineer' (Popper's phrase) is seeking to do is to create or make over an entire society in its social and economic relations in accordance with a preconceived overall plan, image, idea or goal. The plan or programme is preconceived; it is not, like much legislation introduced from time to time even by dictatorial governments, merely a reaction to the problems of the moment. The plan is an overall one, though the immediate trans-formation of the whole of society in all its aspects is not a necessary part of such legislative engineering. As Popper again points out, social engineering can be total or piecemeal. Much of the law-making we shall look at has tackled only one aspect of a society; an example would be the reform of land law in Kenya initiated under the British, and continued by the independent government (in the 1950s and after). But if one asks what inspired such a piecemeal reform, one would discover that behind it lies an 'informing principle' of complete generality which could be, and probably will eventually be, applied to the whole of society when the time comes – in the Kenya case, the aim was liberalising and mobilising of the country's economic resources, and represented a world-view in which such mobilising should be set in motion by the state, but continued by the individual citizen motivated by the search for profit.

The characteristics of the individuals or the small elite group who introduce legislative programmes of this nature are thus typically:

(i) that they are *impatient*, with a sense that there is no time to waste, and that leaving matters to the natural evolution of events will not serve;

(ii) that they are *arrogant*; being informed by their private vision, they are convinced of their own rightness and feel that they possess ordained authority to carry their vision into effect. If asked who has given them this authority, they are likely to appeal either to forces of social evolution or ultimate political convictions, or even to a popular mandate which has rarely had an opportunity to express itself in any concrete form — such people are the modern *Illuminati* who now rule us from their mountain;

(iii) that the changes they seek are not only *fundamental*, but *irreversible*; and that

(iv) what they seek cannot be achieved through persuasion or conversion or the offering of options, but solely through *command*.

(It may be prudent to re-assert and explain that, when we speak of laws as 'commands' and contrast what legislators seek to achieve through using persuasion, we are by no means abandoning our analysis of laws as persuasion. Laws *function* as persuasion, whether or not they have the *form* of commands. The distinction we are trying to make is between two types of aim on the part of the legislator: one being where he seeks through law merely to *persuade* by presenting the subject with an option, and the other where he seeks to *command* by apparently presenting the subject with no option.)

I propose to explore the programmatic use of law for purposes of social transformation within the following classifications:

1. Types of informing principle.
2. Examples of social transformation through law which illustrate these informing principles at work.
3. Resistances to transformation.
4. Techniques.
5. Success or failure.

In making these analyses, we may remind ourselves that legal transformations may be secured (i) through codes or other comprehensive legislation, (ii) through displacement of the previous foundation norm, e.g. by revolution or a fundamental change of constitution. It may be that change of the fundamental norm precedes a legal transformation; but this is not a necessary preliminary.

1. Types of informing principle

Behind every purposive attempt at social transformation through law there lurks, patent or latent, an 'informing principle', the basic idea which the law-giver hopes eventually to realise. Often a transformation may be inspired concurrently by more than one such principle. The main types are:

(a) Unifying. It is a paramount objective in many new states, and even in some old ones which are beset by ethnic or religious pluralism, to make or consolidate the unity of the society, the very political existence of the state. In so far as modern states are organised around the nation-principle, this objective may be described, and is often so described by politicians in developing countries, as 'building the nation'.

Building the nation has a positive and a negative aspect. On the positive side, it means providing a state structure which conduces to unity, a central parliament, a centralised executive, and so on. The providing of a national *Law* (an objective which the heirs of the French Revolution sought to realise in France) is an important support for such a policy.

What should the national *Law* be? In the successor states which have emancipated themselves from colonial rule, the new governments find themselves already equipped with a national *Law*; but it is a peculiar national *Law* in many instances in that it does not apply nationally and generally, still less uniquely and exclusively. The main reason for the limited application of such an inherited national *Law* is the co-existence of local and particular customary and religious *Laws*, which are the other wing of the dual system of laws that is so characteristic of colonial rule. If the new government suppresses the local *Laws*, and leaves only the inherited territorial *Law*, what will it have? The answer is, a legal system of almost totally alien character. Such an answer is hardly acceptable to ardent nationalists, who wish to have a *Law* uniquely expressive of their own nation's history and culture, let alone its political and social objectives.

However repugnant one might think such a policy might be, retention of the old colonial-type *Law* as the new national *Law* is the policy which has found favour with a number of new states. Indian legislation since independence generally trends in the europeanising direction; but African states of the francophone tradition such as Ivory Coast and Burundi went much further than that − they adopted civil codes which were close copies of the codified laws of the metropolis. (That this adoption was almost totally ineffective in practice does not immediately concern us!) The policy of the pre-independence Uganda administration was equally hostile to non-European laws, and as committed to the building of a national legal system based on modified English *Law*. The independent governments of Uganda have not made up their mind on how far they wish to carry forward this process. If we look at examples, we shall see how often the bare policy of one national undiluted alien *Law* has in practice been qualified by residual recognition of other laws or nonconforming practices, or by the adaptation of the received *Law* to local philosophies and traditions.

Some successor states have opted for a new national *Law* which should be as unlike the old colonial *Law* as possible. Where there has been a 'socialist' revolution, for instance, the government may choose to construct a 'socialist' legal system (equally borrowed from outside) with which to unite (as well as to mobilise) the nation. There are also the backward-glancing states, those who seek to reconstruct tradition. Their national law will then be built on old materials from the customary or religious past.

The negative side of the objective of unification will be the suppression of all that weakens or dilutes that unity. Policies of non-recognition of personal laws or of local customary *Laws* will thus be a corollary of the institution of a monopolistic national *Law*.

(b) Modernising. Most governments do not rest content with the mere objective of unifying the laws. Their advisers see this as a sovereign opportunity to modernise the laws at the same time. But the two objectives are distinct: it is possible to have a single *Law* which is out of date; it is possible to modernise some components of a plural legal system without suppressing others.

The very word 'modernising' begs every question, and reveals latent attitudes to cultural phenomena. Again, the attitudes may be positive or negative. The negative attitude is that of rejection of the inherited, the old, the traditional; the positive attitude is that of the embracing of what is seen as a new way of life, new structures, new patterns of social relations. It is a peculiar fact that to many law reformers in the Third World modernisation of laws means europeanisation (and it does not matter whether it is Europe of the West or the East which serves as model). 'Droit moderne' more or less equals French *Law* in the mouths of many francophone African jurists. The irony of this latent prejudice is that the indigenous customary *Laws* are often more up-to-date, more adapted to the needs of the present (through the process of continuous revision by usage to which they are subject) than the 'modern' *Laws* of France or England. English *Law* as it was in Victorian times was exported to British Africa; it is now grossly out of date. The unreformed Napoleonic Code can hardly be taken to be the expression of the most modern attitudes and institutions in France.

(c) Secularising. We live in a secular age. The predominant and received opinion in developed western countries is profoundly secularising. It is the business of a modern government, it is felt, to concern itself solely with this age, this world, the secular in its etymological sense; and laws should neither touch nor express interests and activities inspired by other worlds than those of the senses. Any law which expresses the

contrary philosophy is a candidate for early suppression. Sunday observance laws are just one instance.

Some countries have gone further than neglecting or omitting to regulate or express the other-worldly. They have boldly and frankly legislated against the non-secular, seeking to destroy other-worldly influences, beliefs and structures. The Soviet system is a prime example, where atheism and antitheism are state policy.

(d) Regressive. And yet not every state, and not every thinker, accepts the secular philosophy. To secularise the legal institutions of a Third World state means to weaken or destroy its traditional religions, whether these are world religions like Islam or local cults. We can see in a number of the successor states attempts to restore, through law, the old traditional ways and values. This type of regressive policy can be sub-divided into (i) the non-religious, and (ii) the religious.

(i)   Non-religious regressive legislative policy means the restoration or maintenance of old traditional, generally customary, *Laws*. In Africa, Malawi and Zaire (the latter with its overt traditionalism reinforced by the rejection of European names, all in the name of *authenticité*) have both opted for a customary-*Law* base for their legal systems (though in neither case has the regression been comprehensive).[10]

(ii)   Religious regression is much in the news at the moment, as Islam makes a reverse takeover bid in one Muslim country after another. It is not – and this point must be underlined – a question of not adopting modern western laws in countries like Pakistan or Iran; it is a question of positively *rejecting* modern laws which have been introduced there, and of regressing to an earlier Islamic past through the re-introduction of undiluted Islamic criminal and family law.

(e) Liberalising. A fifth objective, not identical with the modernising one, is that of liberalisation (one can modernise without liberalising). The typical objectives here are to make the activity of the individual freer; to liberate individuals from oppressive order; to give equal rights and protection to all, of whatever sex, race, or religion. In short, the liberalising legislator is seeking to liberate the individual, to expand his opportunities, to reduce his inhibitions or restrictions. Such a liberalising policy cuts across the conventional and often misleading polarity between Left and Right. It is of the Right tendency to free the individual in his economic activity (private enterprise, even laisser faire); it is of the Left tendency (in western countries) to oppose censorship, to argue

10.   For one point of view on the historical background to the regression in Malawi, see Martin Chanock 'Neo-traditionalism and the customary law in Malawi' (1978) 16 African Law Studies 80, and references therein.

for women's lib. or racial equality. Nor is there consistency in governments which follow liberalising policies in some matters; they may be
highly illiberal in others. To free some individuals from the burdens
imposed by sex or race, by legislating against sex or race discrimination,
is to tie up other individuals who must be prevented from discriminating.
That is the liberal paradox. No authority must control what is said on
the stage, radio, TV or the press – no censorship; and yet such an
attitude can go with the censorship of racialist utterances. The left-
leaning liberator of social mores – advocating, say, freer divorce, abortion
or euthanasia – may well oppose the liberalising of economic mores
represented by private venture capital.

(f) Mobilising. The liberalising tendency sees the state and its laws at the
service of the individual, by extending the scope of permitted action;
the mobilising tendency sees the individual at the service of the state,
by requiring him to contribute to national development and national
objectives. The liberalising tendency is for the plural society; the
mobilising tendency is for the monolithic. Fascist and socialist states
are the typical examples of mobilising states; though every country in
time of war may take on the same character.

The mobilising state is the social engineering state par excellence.
Each individual is a cog in the state machine. Many, but not all, of the
modern states which have adopted this aim and posture are marxist or
marxising in inspiration. In seeking social engineering through *Law* such
states are false to their founding spirit and first prophet. Marx was
resolutely opposed to Utopianism and to social engineering. As Popper
puts it.[11]

'He [Marx] denounces the faith in a rational planning of social
institutions as altogether unrealistic, since society must grow according
to the laws of history and not according to our rational plans. All we
can do, he asserts, is to lessen the birthpangs of the historical processes.
In other words, he adopts a radically historicist attitude, opposed to all
social engineering.'

2. Examples of social transformation through law

Of the *unifying* states, many if not most post-colonial states are good
examples. Their problems are those of weak states, weak governments,
and weak sense of nationhood. The pluralism implicit in the artificial
manufacture of new states out of fragments of old and disparate
societies is their most evident enemy. Such states are exactly at the
opposite pole from the nation-states of the 19th and early 20th centuries,
which came into existence in pursuit of a national idea – Italy, Poland,
Germany, the successor-states of the Austro-Hungarian Empire, even

11. *The Open Society and its Enemies*, (London, 1945) I, p. 164.

modern China. The nations who sought to express their nationhood in statehood had a common language (or set of related dialects), a common religion (though not everywhere: cf. Bismarck's Germany), a common culture. Today new states want to express their statehood in nationhood; but it must be an artificial construction.

Legislation to achieve such unity is not only directed at the suppression of variant *Laws* (though this has been an important part of the programme); it is directed too at the encouragement of the common social features which were lacking, and at the suppression of the dividing factors which existed at independence. Nationality can be created at a stroke of the legislative pen; nationhood cannot. A common language is the first task. The colonial rulers left an official language or languages behind them, often one which was alien to the country which they ruled. The official language can become the national language; but some states, Tanzania prominent among them, have tried to create a national language in parallel with the previous official language, and which will eventually take over from it. Thus Swahili becomes the officially encouraged and prescribed medium for more and more government business and private transactions in Tanzania; and a variety of laws and administrative practices are designed to secure this predominant place for it. The study of language laws is a fascinating branch of the study of national unification through law; and it is one of the most significant, because the tongue that we pick up from our mothers in infancy is ours in a very personal sense. Either a dual personality is created — with one language spoken at home (in Tanzania usually one of the many local Bantu dialects) and another at work, in school or in public life (in Tanzania Swahili and to a less extent English) — or one, and the more entrenched, personality must be eradicated in favour of that which is officially required (as happened with Welsh during the period of English rule). The social engineer using law to achieve his goals cannot expect a higher obstacle than in the language field to the achievement of his goals — a state may make decrees as much as it likes, but it will find it difficult to change people's linguistic habits. The French, with their centralised tradition and imperious attitude in matters of language, have not only not succeeded in destroying Breton (though it is indeed on the wane), but have had to admit defeat in their attempt to legislate *franglais* out of existence.

Language legislation is interesting, because it is a paradigm of the difficulties experienced by social legislation generally. A law to suppress variants in the laws of marriage, for instance, is seeking to eradicate similarly entrenched habits and attitudes, and will meet with equally impeding obstacles.

The problems caused by lack of a common religion are nearly as serious. There are new states which have a common religion, Christian or Muslim, say; and these have no difficulty — if they so choose — in legislating that religion into law, in adopting it as the state religion in other words. But by doing so they are not adding any new factor of unity to the old; on the contrary, they are sowing the seeds of future disunity and conflict, because by this act such states effectively declare that non-conformers and foreigners have no place in such a society. The closed society is the weak society. Many of the new states, though, have no shared religion. Where there are two or three major religions present in roughly equal proportions, the task of the new government is daunting. Tanzania again provides an example, with Christianity (in more than one variety) and Islam both strongly represented. Is such a state to opt for the secularist approach, giving no formal recognition to religion (in which case it neglects a potent force in directing the behaviour of men in society); go even further, by adopting an anti-religious posture (as some of the new marxist states have done); or make the invidious choice of one religion over another as the officially approved one? Each choice has its dangers; each type of legislation will have its resistances.

India

Of the many areas in which states seek to promote unity through law, it is naturally in the legislation *about* law that the jurist will see the most interesting examples. Laws are made by lawyers; it is natural that a lawyer turns first to the formal structures of the *Law* in considering what to do about unity. There is hardly a country in the developing world which has not adopted a unifying approach to law. India has steadily legislated against local customary *Laws*, and has gradually reduced the significance of religious differences as factors indicating a different legal system — and this in a country where before independence the most relevant legal fact was adherence to a religion, which served to determine what personal law every person should be subject to. However, the Indian legislator has gone very cautiously, especially in his handling of minority religions. Islamic *Law* in particular has been tenderly treated. This tenderness is partially a consequence of the size of the Muslim minority, which, in any country less populous than India, would be a massive one measured in sheer numbers, and it is partially a consequence of the special sensitivities of Muslims, who see any encroachment on their personal law as an attack on their religion. The Indian governments have been hesitant to stir this sleeping dog into hostile action, despite the commitment represented by Article 44 of the Constitution of 1950:

'The State shall endeavour to secure for the citizens a uniform civil code throughout the territory of India.'

This aim, which reflects the secularising and unifying tendency of Nehru's thinking, has certainly had profound effects on the Hindu religious *Law* and on customary *Laws*; but with this achievement it has come to a complete halt. The 'Directive Principle of State Policy' represented by Article 44 has no legislative effect, but it articulates the inarticulate major premise which inspires, or should inspire, the legislator. What is interesting is that Article 44 was not intended to affect the continuing application of religious personal laws; and a person's religion therefore continues as a connecting factor in determining what personal law to apply to a given subject.

African states

Pre-independence. There are many examples among the African states of the unifying policy as applied to the legal system. It would be wrong to see this trend towards unification of laws, and the radical changes in social arrangements which it entails, as a product of the attainment of independence. The policy long antedates independence, both in the civil law and the common law areas of Africa. It was only to be expected that the civil-law powers, notably France, should be in the lead in promoting unification of laws; the Napoleonic tradition of suppressing customary *Laws* and of institutional centralisation would see to that. The official French colonial policy was one of progressive assimilation; assimilated Africans would eventually gain full citizenship and adopt the French way of life. But, after an initial period of theoretical assimilation, the history of the French African colonies was one of very slow movement towards this goal; and in practice large parts of the African customary *Laws* and Islamic *Law* were retained for the benefit of the African populations. What emerged, therefore, and continued until independence, was a dual system of *Laws* not too dissimilar from that which the British, starting from entirely different premises, had installed in *their* colonies.

France moved more slowly in the direction of unified *Law* than one might have expected from the prevailing juristic climate in the metropolis; Britain moved more quickly than might have been inferred from a policy labelled 'Indirect Rule' — formalised by Lord Lugard but not originated by him — which adopted the principle that the native populations were best administered through and under their own institutions. Their own institutions included pre-eminently their systems of government, *Law* and courts; most of the British African territories thus acquired a system of 'native administration', with native authorities, native courts and native laws in parallel with the system of territorial administration and laws. The movement towards unification of laws in the British territories had, after the first period of colonisation, followed the path of voluntary persuasion through the offering of transforming models (to which we have already referred) of marriage, the family and property. But there was also compulsory unification in the field of penal law, a unification which closely corresponded to the

French colonial policy which led in 1946 to the suppression in the French territories of all penal law other than that which was to be found in the Penal Code and other legislation.

In the era after the Second World War, there was a perceptible shift in British colonial policy. The old assumptions about indirect administration and slowly developing self-government in the more advanced territories were displaced by abandoning traditional institutions and establishing new ones, these latter being close copies of the British metropolitan ones. Central government now moved towards the Westminster model and eventual independence; local government took over the forms and ambitions of English local government; the courts and the laws were similarly developed in the English direction. 'Integration' of courts and laws was now the watchword. The gradual professionalisation and anglicisation of customary courts and procedure were the first step, synchronised by two Judicial Advisers' Conferences in 1953 and 1956. In a typically English concentration on adjectival rather than substantive law, it was clearly assumed that anglicising the courts would lead eventually to anglicisation of the laws. Integration of the laws was the second phase of the operation — a much more sensitive step, where the way ahead was less clearly charted and where the governments moved much more cautiously. They started with the criminal law, adopting the constitutional principle, which was beginning to be written into the new self-governing constitutions, that no one should be tried or punished except for an offence whose terms and the punishment for which were laid down in a written law. Uncodified laws, such as those of traditional society or Islam, must necessarily be discarded when this principle was adopted.

The first steps were now taken to unify the civil laws. Land law was an early candidate for reform. Here the path of development was seen to lie through reducing all land titles to entries in official land registers, constructing a uniform system of land rights and land control for what had previously been completely different forms of tenure, customary and 'English'. The most thorough and the earliest example of this reform was to be found in Kenya, where the accidents of a civil war (Mau Mau), a strong civilian administration, a weak commitment to customary law, and ample cash for reconstruction led to the 'land consolidation' procedures by which customary rights in land were ascertained in the African areas, converted to a registrable equivalent, and recorded on a register, which entirely displaced customary clan and family interests. A start was made in 1953 with the Kikuyu country, which had been the heart of the Mau Mau movement, in advance of any legislative sanction. In 1959 the laws which formalised the process were enacted.[12]

12. Native Lands (Registration) Ordinance 1959 and Land Control (Native Lands) Ordinance 1959.

The Kenya model of land reform and unification, applied piecemeal from district to district but total in its effects when applied, derived much of its inspiration from legislation in the Anglo-Egyptian Sudan. It thereafter constituted a model for similar land registration programmes in other African countries (e.g. Malawi, Lagos) and even outside Africa. Despite claims that the land registers preserved customary land rights in a new form, the real effect of the legislation was to destroy the customary system entirely, and to substitute for it a sophisticated registered land system, interests under which were analogous to those of English *Law*. Clan and family rights and powers had originally no place in such a system, except for the preservation of customary laws of succession. (We look elsewhere[13] at the success of these reforms; here we may note that law and reality diverged through the obstinate resistance of the people to these implications of the new law.)

Not many African territories had begun, let alone completed, such ambitious integrating measures before independence; but the trend was clear. A similar trend revealed itself in another branch of the customary *Laws*, that which related to the family, and notably that which related to marriage and succession. Here again steps were taken to study the possibilities of developing the dual systems of marriage and succession law, always with the goal of an integrated system in view; but again not much had been achieved by independence. (After independence it was a different story.)

A unification measure of a different and intermediate kind was launched in some countries and affected customary *Laws* only. A progressive official resistance to variations in customary *Laws* made itself felt; judges declared themselves impatient when confronted with local variations whose justification was not rational but accidental; administrators and legislators found themselves embarrassed by having to take into account local variations in customary *Law* when framing legislation. A movement towards unification of customary *Laws* attracted favour in some of the territories. A step towards this goal was the recording in writing in a common form of all the customary *Laws* in a given territory. This process was aided by restatement techniques developed by the Restatement of African Law Project of the University of London. After independence there were further moves in this direction in such countries as Kenya, Malawi and Botswana. Reduction of individual customary *Laws* to a common form and the wearing away of tribal differences had a double consequence: on the one hand, it would make easier the eventual integration of customary and non-customary *Law*, both of which would now be accessible in written and comparable form; on the other hand, such measures served to detach the customary *Laws* from the social and cultural background in which they were embedded. *Laws* were treated as detachable sets of formal rules rather

13. See pp. 209 ff. below.

than as sociolegal systems. As such, the possibilities of popular resistance to them, or even of popular lack of comprehension of them, were greatly increased.

After independence. The most striking of all the unifications of laws was in *Ethiopia*, where the Civil Code of 1960 purported to destroy and replace utterly the then existing customary and religious *Laws*. Drafted on the advice of a leading French comparatist, Professor René David, it suppressed customary, Coptic, and Islamic *Laws*, substituting for them all a uniform set of provisions modelled in most cases on the revised provisions of the Napoleonic Code. Of all the codifying legislation of the independence era in Africa, the Ethiopian Civil Code was the most frankly programmatic: its purposes, as was officially emphasized on its introduction, were to build national unity and to procure the modernisation of Ethiopian institutions. It thus combined three aims — unifying, modernising and secularising. So ambitious a law could not possibly hope to be made effective overnight; but its draftsman declared himself content if it was eventually adopted within a century or two.

A law like this is not like laws enacted by the British Parliament, which make an instant demand for compliance; the Civil Code was a goal or target, at which it was hoped that the people would eventually aim.

That this philosophy is not restricted to Ethiopia is shown by legislation in the *Ivory Coast* and *Burundi*, to which I have already referred.[14] In the Ivory Coast, legislation in 1964 suppressed the customary family and marriage systems in favour of a uniform code deriving closely from French *Law*. Payment of the marriage-consideration or *dot*, formerly a necessary feature of customary marriage, was now not only unnecessary but a criminal offence. Can one destroy a customary social system overnight? The answer is given below, at pp. 197 ff. *Tanzania* has also been active in unification of *Laws*. It set up its Unification of Customary Law Project in 1961, with the aim of reducing all the variant customary *Laws* of mainland Tanzania to a single form. To begin with, the scheme was meant to declare the rules of each customary *Law* in written form (in Swahili), thus making them more accessible; but two other objectives were added to this change of form — the first was to make the *Laws* more modern, by which was intended to make them more in line with current needs and future aspirations; the second was to make them more uniform. Strong pressures were applied to local authorities to cause them to agree to this remodelling of their *Laws*. It is surprising that these authorities agreed to such radical transformations, theoretically voluntary but actually

14. And see, for the laws, Mark Dumetz *Le droit de mariage en Côte d'Ivoire* (Paris, 1975) with critical review by Robert J. Mundt at (1978) 16 African Law Studies 176.

compulsory, without demur, as in some cases the change required was as important as a switch from matrilineal to patrilineal succession. The changes were compulsory, not only because of the governmental pressures applied and the way in which the task of securing a declaration of the new customary *Law* was achieved, but because the local authority, and *not* the ordinary people subject to the *Law*, was the body which made the new *Law*. What purported to be a declaration by the users of the *Law* was thus effectively legislation by the elite which controlled the users. Resistances to this remodelling, and to the transformation of customary land tenures through the imposition of the *Ujamaa* policy, have been considerable, and have even led to bloodshed.[15]

To summarise, practically every African country has now adopted the unification of laws policy. The way in which they go about it, and the speed at which they move, may vary; but the effects are the same. The eventual shape of the resultant uniform legal system can vary widely, according as the governments adopt a liberalising, secularising or mobilising policy concomitant with the initial purpose of unification.

Turkey provides the prime example of the *secularising* approach, combined in its case with the aim of modernisation. At one go the Ottoman *Law* of Turkey, which had not only been partly based on religious precepts but which had contained within it recognition of other religious personal laws, was swept away. On the civil side, its place was taken by the adoption of the Swiss Civil Code and Code of Obligations, in 1926. Startling though this change was, and however radical its effects, the legislation of 1926 under Kemal Ataturk was in one sense the culmination of a process which had been going on for a century in the Ottoman Empire. First, the principle of codification had established itself from 1839 AD, the date of the initiation of the *Tanzimat* or period of reform. The main objective of the government was clear, to enable the Ottoman Empire to move fully into the world of international relations, and especially into the world of commerce which had been opened up by European powers and traders. To do this, it was felt, the commercial law must be codified; not only that, but the penal law, the judicial law and the land law should be put on a more modern footing, both as regards form and content. Secondly, the reception of European law, mediated by trading concessions and capitulations, was extended to the domestic Ottoman *Law*.

The most striking achievement of the Ottoman jurists was the celebrated *Majalla*, or Ottoman Civil Code. This was finally promulgated between the years 1870 and 1877, but had been in preparation for a considerable time before then. It was unique in that it was a codification of Islamic law of the Hanafi School as modified by Ottoman legislation. The religious basis of the civil law was thus conserved. Other parts of the *Law* had, however, been radically altered in a European direction

15. See p. 302 below.

(with the influence of French *Law* being predominant): a Commercial Code was introduced in 1850, a Maritime Code in 1863, and a Penal Code (also based on French *Law*) enacted in 1858. There was a parallel adoption of French civil and criminal procedure.

The innovation of Ataturk was to break clear of the religious past; his jurists had been discussing the possibility of a new civil code based on updated Muslim law; Ataturk boldly turned in a new direction, that of Switzerland. His aim was to give a jolt to the modernisation, not just of the state, but of social relations within it, which was symbolised in other respects by the adoption of western dress and romanisation of the alphabet — both potent symbols.

India's secularisation of its private law has already been mentioned. With the retention of Islamic family law this secularisation has not gone as far as the reformers might have wished; though in the field of Hindu *Law* the religious basis of the rules has been largely dismantled, a basis which had been diminished substantially and progressively under the British *Raj*. With the enactment of the amending Act of 1976, the Marriage Laws (Amendment) Act, the leading western expert on Hindu *Law*, J. D. M. Derrett, could read the funeral oration over Hindu *Law* in India:

'Many informed readers of reports of the debates and the passing of the Act will have known that, for practical purposes, Hindu law died on the 27 May 1976.'[16]

So he could express his reaction to this latest development in the onward march of secularism in India. But the Indian legislator has not yet achieved the final goal set by the Constitution of 1950, Article 44:

'The State shall endeavour to secure for the citizens a uniform civil code throughout the territory of India.'

Ethiopia too, with its imperial reforms, was secularising as well as unifying and modernising. Although the text of the Civil Code of 1960 was influenced in some respects by the traditional *Law*, the *Fetha Negast*, the Code assumed the almost total separation of church and state, and its provisions would not be out of place in a modern European country. This was a stark reversal of the previous position, when religion had been one of the most important factors both as a source and as a control of *Law*. Islamic *Law* was in theory totally displaced by the Civil Code. The fact that these reforms, now overtaken in some measure by the Revolution, were changes on paper rather than in practice (a matter which is discussed at pp. 207 ff. below), does not affect the analysis of the aim lying behind the reforms, which, put crudely, was the total transformation of the country through law. This was an enormous weight to put on a fragile code and a fragile system of administration.

16. In his *The Death of a Marriage Law* (New Delhi, 1978), p. vii.

Many of the law reforms in the Arabic-speaking *Middle East* in the last 100 years can be described as both *modernising* and *secularising*. Modernising in that the law-giver was seeking to adopt new laws which would give recognition to new values and new institutions, such as the status of women and the demands of commerce; secularising in that he would be impeded in this object by the forms and terms of the religious law of the *Shari'a* – and he could only achieve his aims by circumventing this law in some way. The content of such reforms has been amply discussed by J. N. D. Anderson in a number of works, of which the latest is his *Law Reform in the Muslim World*.[17]

A hundred years and more of exposure of the Middle East countries to the influence of French law in particular have left their mark. A new wave of codifications has taken place in the Middle East countries, led by Egypt through its Civil Code of 1948; so that some brief discussion of its style and content may help to illustrate the secularising trend which has now established itself. The Egyptian Code was the product of a Committee set up by the Senate, masterminded by the famous law-reformer, 'Abd al-Razzāq al-Sanhūrī, but it was not an original piece of work. The reformers had 70 years of experience with codification, mostly with codes based on French law, to draw on, as well as the decisions of Egyptian courts and previous Egyptian legislation. The new Code accordingly proclaims its close kinship with the French *Code civil*. This is not to say that it was not adapted to the circumstances of modern Egypt, and did not mirror the transformations in social life which had already occurred there; but it does raise the question of how far the Code, in a predominantly Muslim country, could be said to be a Muslim code or reflect Muslim ideas and principles.

The answer is that it is largely secular in tone. There were concessions to the *Shari'a*; but in sum these were not so important as the divergencies, and many of them give the impression of being window-dressing rather than the practical application of Islamic rules. Thus Article 1 of the Code firmly provides that, where there is a gap in the Code, due to absence of provision,

'the Judge shall decide according to custom and in the absence of this, in accordance with the principles of the *Shari'a*. In the absence of any of these, the Judge will apply the principles of natural justice and the dictates of equity'.

The problem of gaps, the residual source of rules in a codified law, is one of the main issues which affects any code and any codifier. We all know how important in practice the residual provisions in a code may be; after all, the residual principle in British India and in the Sudan that, in default of any express rule, the judge should decide in accordance with 'justice, equity and good conscience' had the effect of

17. London, 1976.

importing practically all the English *Law*, which then constituted a general law within the dual system of laws. But we are assured by jurists, notably by Anderson,[18] that the provision of Article 1 has little practical effect in the Egyptian Code. Again, when the Egyptian jurists had to choose a foreign model for any of their provisions, they were influenced in their choice by their decision as to which model represented a closer accord with Islam. This was a similar basis of choice to that which the draftsmen of the Penal Code in Northern Nigeria in 1959 later adopted. The result is still the application of a foreign law, but one which, on that point, appears not to be in conflict with Islam. There are also special institutions and rules which have been drawn from the *Shari'a* and which are not incorporated, or re-incorporated, in the Code. All this, though, does not add up to a Code which is Islamic. The predominant tinge and trend of the Egyptian Civil Code are strikingly secularist; and the list of Islamic legal institutions which are put on one side by the Code is a long one.

Not only was the Egyptian Civil Code imitated in other Middle East countries, such as Iraq and Syria, but there were independent movements towards reform and codification in most of the other countries of North Africa and the Middle East. Practically all represented a diminution, in some instances a dramatic diminution, in the scope of application of Islamic *Law*; and this diminution was particularly important when reform of Islamic family law was in question, as this is seen as the heart of Islamic *Law* proper. Abolition of polygamy, the judicial regulation of divorce, enhancement of the legal status of women, were just three of the most significant kinds of change.

The resistances to this movement to secularism in Muslim countries have been strong; in some places, the pendulum has begun to swing back the other way – but all this must wait until we examine resistances to social transformation through programmatic laws in a later section.[19] What can be said is that the assumption made by most expert observers that the inevitable movement of the *Laws* in Middle East and other Muslim countries was towards a secular and modernised system is now being shown to be a hasty and ungrounded one, and that the clock *can* be put back. If, one may ask, the clock can be put back in Muslim countries, why not also in Christian ones, where a similar secularising tendency has been at work for even longer? The arrival of large Muslim minorities in countries such as England may well lead to a partial reversal of the trend to secularisation. Who would have guessed, a few years back, that road traffic laws would be affected by religious considerations? (Cf. Sikhs and crash helmets.) The *regressive* tendency in law-making is stronger than many would have supposed. It is not only in the religious context that such regression can be observed at

18. Op. cit., pp. 89–90.
19. See pp. 198 ff.

work; customary legal institutions which most observers thought were
dead and gone in countries like those of black Africa not only have
refused to die, but have in some instances been given artificial respiration
by governments. Pakistan, Libya, Iran are examples of regressive
religious states. The return of customary courts to Nigeria, which has
been adopted as federal government policy there and which has led to
the enactment of new laws in 1978 for the restoration of customary
courts, is equally striking. The trend was previously firmly towards the
total suppression of customary courts. Integration of courts and the
professionalisation of the magistracy were the pillars of judicial policy
in practically all the black African states. It was the resistances to the
implementation and underlying assumptions of such a policy which
have led to a change of mind by some states. Customary courts were
now considered to be cheaper, more effective, more in tune with local
habits of mind and behaviour. Customary courts did not institutionalise
the judiciary in opposition to the executive (farewell to Montesquieu!);
customary courts did not demand the services of lawyers, who were
seen as typically expensive, troublesome and opponents of government.
It has been popular opinion and practice too which have led to the up-
holding of customary courts and modes of dispute settlement. Even
where courts were suppressed, the people in many areas continued to
resort to traditional authorities and tribunals for the settlement of their
differences, rather than go to government courts staffed by magistrates,
which were seen as alien, ill-informed, arbitrary or absent. *Malawi* has
been an example of governmental hostility to non-traditional courts,
as represented by the High Court particularly. The objections of the
government, and especially of its head, Dr Hastings Banda, have been
to what appeared to be pettifogging and unmeritorious rules of law and
procedure which helped the guilty to avoid conviction. On the civil
side, the High Court would not claim to be expert in local customary
laws, which still retain their force.

Malawi has therefore given extensive criminal jurisdiction to its
'Traditional Courts', with the enactment in 1969 of the Local Courts
(Amendment) Act.[20] This step was completed by the passing of the
Traditional Courts Act 1971.[1] Though Traditional Courts are expected
to apply the Penal Code (broadly a codification of English law) and not
customary criminal law, they are instructed by statute to guide themselves by native law in doing so. It appears that the main effect is to
import customary ideas and assessments into the rules of the Penal
Code. The rules remain, but their effect changes.

Popular resistance to unification of courts has been observed in
countries as diverse as Ghana, Tanzania and Zambia, where in each
instance the government courts which have supplanted the traditional

---

20. No. 31 of 1969. See P. Brietske 'Murder and manslaughter in Malawi's
    Traditional Courts' [1974] JAL 37.
 1. Cap. 3: 03.

customary courts have been ignored by the local population to some extent.

Our *liberalising* examples will be drawn from developed as well as undeveloped countries. This is because much of the impetus towards liberalisation, however it is defined, has come from the industrially and politically developed world. Europe was the seedbed of liberalism, in the sense of individualism and the 'rights of man', a phrase which served as a banner leading the forces of social emancipation from the tyranny of hierarchy and status allocated, not on the basis of individual merit, but on the grounds of ethnic origin, sex, class or function. The 'rights of woman' are now at least as important as the rights of man as the catchword of the moment, and at least as devastating social changes have been proposed under it as were the fruits of the French and American revolutions. The 19th-century development of laisser faire economics, which we have seen as one of the products of individualism, told against the old community-based economic order, just as the struggle for political rights for all told against the old political order. Both forms of emancipation, the economic and the political, were among the principal exports of the colonising countries to their colonial territories. Liberal economics allowed in foreign enterprises, with drastic effects on the indigenous economies; later on, they led to the installation of indigenous entrepreneurs, operating especially in the agricultural sector. Enterprise does not have to be big and factory-based to be individualising. The small-scale peasant farmers of tropical Africa who took up the cultivation of cash crops were led on by the pull of economic opportunities provided by the market; but the tremendous growth of export agriculture could never have taken place had not the legal means been provided for it. Many of these means were in the nature of facilities or models; new land-holding models were provided or recognised by the colonial legal systems, and the law of contract in particular provided models of entrepreneurial organisation and activity.

With the passage of time colonial governments were eager to accelerate this process of economic change; individual decisions and models individually adopted would not do the trick fast enough, so, in a process on which we have already remarked, specific programmes had to be instituted to produce these effects immediately and extensively. The thinking of the East African Royal Commission, 1953–5, and of the agricultural legislation in Kenya which followed it, represents the apogee of this policy. The Commission favoured a

'policy concerning the tenure and disposition of land [which] should aim at the individualisation of land ownership, and at a degree of mobility which, without ignoring existing property rights, will enable access to land for its economic use.'[2]

2. *East Africa Royal Commission 1953–1955 Report*, Cmd. 9475, chap. 23, para. 1.

The Commission was particularly anxious to dismantle tribal and racial barriers to land ownership, a policy which the Kenya Government of the time, bearing in mind the vested interests of the White Highlands, did not wholly espouse. The aim was to get land into the free market, and to leave it to market forces to stimulate economic activity. However, this liberalisation policy marched with a protective policy towards the fledgling African entrepreneur, a policy which, in the Kenya case, was expressed by land control facilities which effectively meant that the market would be a managed one.

Thought had already been moving along similar lines in *Kenya*, as represented by the 'Swynnerton Plan', a policy put forward by the government agriculturalist R. J. M. Swynnerton in his *A Plan to Intensify the Development of African Agriculture in Kenya*,[3] and which had been adopted by the colonial government of Kenya as its official line. The Plan envisaged consolidated holdings held on a system of tenure which would provide the farmer with 'such security of tenure through an indefeasible title as will encourage him to invest his labour and profits into the development of his farm . . .', with larger acreages and fewer but more efficient farmers, cultivating cash crops like coffee for the market as well as subsistence crops for the maintenance of their own families; in other words, a policy of small-scale rural capitalism. Despite the parallels sometimes quoted with the enclosure movement in England, and the liberalising effect that this had had on agricultural enterprise there, the two situations were by no means the same. Enclosure in England had especially favoured the large landowner with the resources both to ensure the initial enclosure of formerly common, open or waste lands and to exploit them efficiently when he had appropriated them;[4] enclosure in Kenya meant the elimination of community rights and powers over land and the squeezing out of many small and inefficient farmers, but what were left were still small farmers on holdings that were often of sub-economic size.

Land consolidation, as we have seen, started as an administrative response to the disturbed conditions of the Kikuyu reserve, and only later became a generalised territory-wide policy with an official legal framework. This legal framework was based on the concept of land registration rather than on customary and unrecorded titles, and on a compulsory and general, rather than sporadic and voluntary, change-over from the one system to the other. Before the appropriate laws had been enacted, the process was already fully under way; though official legislative backing was lacking, consolidation was *de facto* a

---

3. 1953.
4. See the (British) *Royal Commission on Common Land 1955–1958* Report, Cmnd. 462 (London, 1958); and also J. D. Chambers and G. E. Mingay, *The agricultural revolution 1750–1880* (London, 1966), esp. chap. 4, which gives a rather different picture from that conventionally given.

compulsory rather than an optional procedure, as no customary right-holder in a district where consolidation was in process could afford to be left out. Sorrenson's comments on this situation, given special authority as coming from one of the leading students of the administrative machinery by which land consolidation was achieved in Kenya, are of particular interest to us here because they show the inter-relation between policy and implementive laws, and the extent to which an economic change can be brought about by persuasion or administrative action rather than by formal decree:[5]

'One striking feature of the Kikuyu land reform was that full scale consolidation operations started before there was any legislative backing whatsoever. Consolidation involved a final determination of ownership; it needed to be followed by the registration of titles. But, as has been shown, government long hesitated before providing effective legislation to validate the consolidation process and to provide for registration of titles and control of transactions in registered land ... Baring [then Governor of Kenya] considered it unnecessary to follow up with substantive legislation for two or three years.'

This comment might lead one to conclude that programmatic transformation of social and economic life does not necessarily have to be achieved by using law as a tool, and that administrative fiat and political pressure may be sufficient to achieve such a transformation. While this is true enough, it is not the whole story. First, legal means *were* devised by the Kenya administration before 1959 to cloak and control the process of land consolidation; and secondly, it was highly significant that resort was eventually had to comprehensive legislation to achieve these goals. This was not merely so as to legitimate what had been done before, though the concept of legalism played an important part in the thinking of those who had responsibility at the centre for these changes; but it was because a comprehensive law seemed the more potent tool for completing the process of transformation throughout the country and for securing the end of a single, unified law.

If Kenya is the example of the use of programmatic laws to transform the economic life of a country in the liberal direction, the United Kingdom provides many recent examples of the use of laws to transform social life in the same way and sense. Britain, with its recent legislation on race, sex and other forms of discrimination, has not been the pioneer: the credit for that goes to the United States, where the race cleavage was much sharper, and the legal implications of racial discrimination clearer because of the Constitution and the dicta of the US Supreme Court, and where agitation by women who felt themselves

5. M. P. K. Sorrenson *Land Reform in the Kikuyu Country* (Nairobi, 1967), p. 183.

disfranchised or discriminated against was much more radical. (Though in an earlier age, with the struggle of the suffragettes to win political rights for women in England, that country had led the world.)

The laws *against* racial and sex discrimination in England, or *for* individual equality irrespective of ethnic origin or sex (if one wants to take the positive view), are programmatic in our sense, in that what is sought by the legislator is a transformation of society, radical in its effects and compulsory in its nature. The slow processes of social evolution, though they may explain *why* the legislator acts, are not for him sufficient. These laws may be viewed as liberalising, because they seek to emancipate the individual from historic restrictions.

In so far as these laws try to bring about an immediate and major change in human interrelationships by force of law, they are bound to run up against strong resistances, which we study below. The way people live; the social arrangements which they have in their homes; the attitudes and practices of employers at work; the prejudices of the people, are all powerful and deeply entrenched. The legislator seeks to override them, and to use law to do so. Can he succeed; or is this a case, as with industrial relations laws, where he seems almost bound to fail? Since the programme is mandatory and the resistances are strong, the legislator must use criminal or penal sanctions to achieve his purpose. We are in the presence no longer of a possibly advantageous economic reform, as with Kenya land tenure, but of a destruction of privileges which their former bearers will bitterly resent. The legislator cannot change the inner man by legislation; he must, as with penal law generally, direct his action at the external behaviour which manifests the inner attitude. But repression of an undesired action by penal law does not necessarily change the inner attitude which inspired the offence and which may inspire its later repetition — otherwise the prisons would miraculously empty, and there would be no recidivists. Sometimes repression leads to still stronger feelings; Freud might be called in aid here, as could every national revolt of an oppressed minority.

In the result, a panoply of laws and bureaucracies has to be brought into existence to shield the transforming change. It is notable that in England earlier attempts at non-punitive and advisory methods of dealing with racial discrimination have now given way to a more punitive approach, with new sanctions and a readier recourse to them as against non-conformers. The problems for the effectiveness of law which all these circumstances pose must be explored below.

Meanwhile, we move on to the sixth type of informing principle, that of *mobilising* people for the nation, which is to be contrasted with the liberalising approach in the way that we have already indicated, in that the mobilising state is the command state: it orders, and its subjects obey. But is the contrast as sharp as these words imply? We note a paradox and an irony. The liberalising state is forced to seek the aid of ever stronger weapons of compulsion to secure its liberalising end; the gap between the penal sanctions imposed on those guilty of racial discrimination or racially insulting remarks under the laws of England, and the penal sanctions for those guilty of 'economic crimes' in a socialist state, is hard to discern. In each case, the programmatic law-giver has a programme; in each case he punishes behaviour which infringes the realisation of his programme; in each case, he has convinced himself that the programme is for the benefit of those he rules; in each case, he seeks an interior change of heart through exterior sanctions. We might add that in each case obedience or compliance will be partial, and will be no more in the command state than in the allegedly democratic and persuasive one.

Mobilisation as a policy has a special appeal for developing countries. Their governments may even resort to the rhetoric of war to justify their actions and give point to their commands. The Atlantic powers in the last war may be considered to be at fault with their talk of the 'war' against poverty, hunger, disease and ignorance, which was to be set side by side with the war against an external aggressor: at fault because, however praiseworthy the objectives of abolishing poverty, hunger, disease and ignorance in the world, the use of the war metaphor could easily suggest to the suggestible that the same means of total war were necessary to combat them as had had to be used against the Germans and the Japanese. Total war in the civilian context means total mobilisation of all resources, human and material, and a temporary shutdown on considerations of conscience and individual rights in favour of the larger and higher goal.

Such talk was bound to feed the power obsessions of new, and fundamentally weak, rulers of new nations. That they seemed to be in absolute control of the destinies of their new states, often elected by an overwhelming majority of their people, given a *carte blanche* in their policies, was part of the *great illusion*, the powerlessness of power. Elites in pseudo-democratic states have proved themselves evil enough in their readiness to impose policies on their subjects, even behind the cloak of democracy; how much likelier will the absolutism of power become if the cloak is removed, and its removal applauded by those in other countries who should know better!

Socialist states generally are the prime examples of the mobilising tendency in the modern world, and none more so than the Soviet Union. Pashukanis, the early Soviet jurist, though discredited in other respects, is not discredited when he describes Soviet legal policy as being to leave 'no scope for autonomous private legal relations', that all must be subjected to the paramount requirements of the general economic plan. African and other Third-World states which claim to be socialist have taken over the second part of this philosophy, even if they compromise on the first. The Tanzanian political philosophy articulated and enforced by President Nyerere, as embodied in the Arusha Declaration of 1967 and other documents, is one of mobilisation.

Private rights go out of the window in such a state; individual political rights must not stand in the way of national objectives, so that detention without trial becomes an accepted instrument of government. Rights in private property are not sacrosanct, and their holders can be expropriated if the state so desires. Resources are 'national resources'.[6] These last few remarks serve to remind us that the mobilising tendency can also be found much closer home, and is much in evidence in contemporary Britain. Petroleum and other energy sources are 'national'; even our children are a national resource and must be manipulated as such. Bureaucracies of states find their salvation and satisfaction in mobilising policies; hence the tendency of government departments and public corporations to involve themselves in daily economic management for which they are ill fitted.

3. Resistances to transformation

The law-giver proposes, man disposes. There is practically no example of a programmatic law which has been entirely successful, if by successful we mean succeeding in its aim of securing a radical transformation of society, the way people live and behave. Although, as we have seen, governments often try to achieve two or three aims simultaneously, it may be more helpful analytically to examine the resistances to each type of policy separately, because the immunities to change are specific to the change, just as antibodies are specific to the organisms they fight against. One reason for the specificity of resistance is that it is a characteristic of social transformation through law that it contains the seed of its own resistances. The social transformer has no *time*, he is unwilling to resort to *persuasion*, he displays no *responsiveness* to people's feelings and desires, he is not prepared to make any *accommodation*: while all the qualities underlined are essential ingredients of a successful attempt to cause people to change voluntarily and effectively.

Resistance to unification

Why should anyone resist unification of laws? They may be provoked into resistance both by what they get and by what they lose. We can ignore for the moment the vested professional interests in multiplicity of laws — the lawyers who resisted the fusion of law and equity in England, say; or the judges of customary courts who see their careers destroyed; and look instead at the popular resistances.

What do people give up when their law is unified? Not just a legal system, though they may be very wedded to that, but a way of life and

6. 'Because the land belongs to the nation, the Government has to see to it that it is used for the benefit of the whole nation and not for the benefit of one individual or just a few people'. (*Arusha Declaration*)

even a vocabulary in which it is expressed as well. Customary, particular
or religious *Laws* have all grown out of the social background or been
modified by it over centuries — suddenly they are discarded. Only
insensitive theoretical lawyers who fail to appreciate the symphytic and
interactive relationship of law and society could imagine that they
could change the law without hurt or harm to the society.[7] In the
unification case, if social transformation is the aim, the insensitivity is
conscious, as the aim *is* to damage the society through affecting its law.
But changing the law is more than changing the letters on a piece of
paper; it is not a question of old orders written on new paper with a
new heading. Since the law-giving elite have presumably already moved
in the direction in which they now wish the people at large to move,
they, the elite, perhaps cannot appreciate what they are asking the
people to do.

This resistance is labelled 'conservatism', 'particularism', or even
'separatism' — each, in our modern received vocabulary, being a
damaging allegation. And yet the same advocates of unified law may
well have asserted the inalienable right of subject peoples to throw off
colonial rule and colonial law and the colonialists' way of life — an
assertion of just such particularism as they now attack! These resistances
have been consistently under-estimated by legislators in developing
countries, who, with their centralist and 'capitalist'[= working in or
affected by the values of the capital city] values, cannot make the
imaginative effort to project themselves into the minds of those at the
periphery who will be affected by these changes. The attitudes of those
at the periphery are demonstrated by their behaviour rather than their
assertions — they carry on as if the new law had not been passed.
Examples of this general passive resistance are too numerous to
mention: a few instances only can be cited. (i) *Ethiopia*; a general
refusal to give up customary and Islamic personal *Laws*, despite the
Civil Code of 1960. (ii) *Ivory Coast*: total refusal to abandon customary
family and marriage law. (iii) *Kenya*: old customary tenures and practices
maintained despite their having in theory been destroyed by land
consolidation and registration.

The insensitivity of the unifying legislator is matched by his
impotence. He lacks the machinery of judges and inspectors to check
that old ways have been abandoned. It is no use his legislating that
people who follow the old laws will be punished, or that their 'rights'
and transactions under the old laws will be deemed invalid. One need
only compare the situation in, say, *Kenya*, where the volume of transactions *not* in accordance with the new land registration law is so vast
that no government could ignore it without provoking a revolt. What

7. Ironies in our subject are many. Quite a few of those who advocate, rightly,
   a 'law in society' or a 'law in context' approach to legal institutions in
   writing about law are in the forefront of drafting legislation which shows the
   sort of insensitivity mentioned in the text.

the government decides to do is, Nothing. The blind eye is turned; two parallel systems of living and law are thus established, the official and the actual.

It is not just loss of the old laws that may rankle or cause difficulty. It is the form of the new law which may excite resistance. Take the matter of language by way of illustration. The old laws were vernacular in every sense; they were expressed in, and operated through, local vernacular languages. All could understand them; all could discuss them or argue with and about them. The new unifying law has none of these attributes or advantages. Only a highly paid lawyer may now be able to interpret the law, or assure people their rights under it. If it is central legislation, as it must be, it must be framed in the official language. Even where knowledge of the official language is now widespread through education, it is unlikely to have the same intelligibility or impact as the home language. Quite often, the official language may lack appropriate terms, which have to be invented and which thus lack meaning for everyone, experts included. This has happened with official Swahili in *Tanzania*.

It is not only backward countries which experience the difficulties of unification of laws. *Britain* itself is now caught in a multiple web of unification or harmonisation of laws. There are the voluntary inter-national efforts under the auspices of UN agencies or other international bodies, seeking to harmonise the laws of trade or transport or the treatment of diplomats, and there is the harmonisation of laws within the EEC, where British people for the first time for many centuries are learning what it is like to have faraway bureaucrats, as they are seen to be, imposing uniform laws which are 'foreign' to our country. A head of steam is now being built up by politically active people, quick to spot a trend or a chance, against legislation from Brussels, and appeals are being made to atavistic instincts.

Resistance to modernisation

How could anyone in his right mind resist 'modernisation', the 'modern' legislator might ask, so sold is he on the advantages of modernisation for its own sake. And yet there are profound resistances to modernisation. The resistance to modernisation in countries like Turkey or the Arab countries of the Middle East, or now in Pakistan or Iran, cannot all be put down to religious conservatism, though this has been revealed as a most important element. Much of the resistance must be taken to be opposition to change as such. Such resistance is not necessarily imprudent. We have already lived with the consequences of one generation, or one century, of divinely inspired and infallible technocrats, who have transformed the material appurtenances of our world, the technology, the houses we live in, the social arrangements within them and outside them; and it is not only ignorant peasants who have come to doubt whether all these changes have been for the better. Some changes have been decidedly for the worse — the destruction of forests and soils through modern land-exploiting or cultivating methods; damage to the atmosphere through the injudicious and uncontrolled activities of modern technology; the pollution of the oceans, the depletion of our wild-life; the soul-destroying characteristics of too many modern cities. With this record, a wise man might well be dubious if told that a change was for the better *because* it was modernising. Ignorant peasants have even more reason than concerned ecologists to doubt whether changes will prove beneficial in the long run. There are two reasons for this:

(i) They can less afford to make mistakes which may destroy their livelihood, and it is no comfort to them that they were advised to do so by experts.

(ii) The scene is now littered with too many failed schemes, where the little learning of the 'experts' could not encompass all the factors, including 'bad luck'. The job of planning is to take the bad luck out of life; so bad luck, like Sahelian droughts, is not an excuse. The cattle-keepers in an African country who changed their ancient transhumant practices and settled around new irrigation wells on the edge of the desert, wells which could not fail according to the experts who provided them, learnt a lesson an extremely hard way when the wells failed in the drought years. Were the experts back in their offices in Rome, Washington or Geneva, one wonders, when the wells failed? The peasants had no such option.

An exploration of all the resistances to modernisation in the modern world would take too much of our available space, and would involve a searching investigation of the inner psychological attitudes and drives which impel people or hold them back. These psychological attitudes and drives are law-creating and law-sustaining. Firstly, people like routine. They like their behaviour, and that of those with whom they deal, to fall into a pattern, a pattern of predictability. If every time that we had any dealing with another person the outcome of that dealing was quite unpredictable, the psychological strain on us would be enormous, and few of us could face the endless bargaining and uncertain conclusion that would be entailed. Buying a ticket on the bus would be an enterprise like securing a Middle East peace treaty. We expect and demand the quiet life. Behaviour which starts as an accident, a chance, quickly becomes a routine, and finally becomes a demand. If norms, whether of law or social behaviour generally, thus come into existence through people's search for pattern in life, equally strong forces sustain the· patterns in being once they are established. This resistance to disturbance of accepted patterns is annoying for the reformer and innovator; it is the salvation of the bureaucrat, because he too depends on predictable patterns for his operations and his success.

It is in the nature of elites, especially intellectual elites rather than those of wealth and power, to innovate; it is in the nature of subjects to resist innovation.

Resistance to secularisation

Such resistances come in too when a secularising policy is adopted. Religious resistances are of enormous power. Here it is not only established patterns of behaviour that cause resistance to change, but the fact that religion is another sanctioning system with sanctions which are immune from control by the innovating secular power. The durability of religious belief and practice in countries like the Soviet Union, which has waged war for 60 years on every manifestation of religion, is amazing. Poland provides an even more striking instance. The Middle East countries show the staying power of Islamic ideas, and still more of Islamic practices. The recrudescence of Islamic fundamentalism is becoming a live issue in Turkey, which, for so many years after the trauma of Kemal's rule, seemed to have moved firmly into the secularising camp.

Resistance to regression

These resistances may eventually express themselves in a regressive policy, as one elite takes over from another. Resistances to regressive legal transformation evoke the old enemies who now find themselves displaced: lawyers, for instance, in a society where the lawyers are excluded from the courts, and hence from power; the previously modernising elite, when their work is undone.

Resistance to liberalisation

It is the bureaucrats again who are most resistant to liberalisation. Bureaucrats depend on a bureaucratic system for their *raison d'être*. A bureaucratic system is one in which controls are imposed on people's behaviour in accordance with patterns devised and operated, not by the people themselves (as in customary *Law* systems), but by bureaucrats and for the attainment of goals set by bureaucrats. The emancipation of an individual is his liberation from control. Some of this control may be imposed by his fellow-citizens, directly or indirectly; but much of it is imposed by a bureaucracy, in which we include the legal bureaucracy. If ordinary people dislike losing their patterns of behaviour, their routines, bureaucrats, whose diet is routine — sauced with the exercise of power — are even unhappier. Few welcome the involuntary loss of power. The planned economy is the bureaucratically controlled and determined economy; liberalisation of economic activity is anathema to the bureaucrats who control and determine. The story of economic life in Britain in the last decade or two is the installation, in more and more areas of the economy, of controls — over labour, over capital, over marketing, over design; and these controls are by laws, directions, discretions, supports. There is now a vested interest in bureaucratic control; to reduce or dismantle it would throw many thousands out of a job or reduce their power. There are indeed parasitical hierarchies of bureaucratic control: create a Gas Board to control the supply of gas nationally, and a Gas Consumers' Council must be created to control it by criticism. The bureaucracy thus forms a 'New Class', which runs the risk of being dispossessed if new men get into power. Like any class, it is tenacious of its power.

Resistances of a different kind manifest themselves to some forms of liberalisation. In each case it is a group or class with something to lose. Males resist women's equality; those with strong ethical convictions about the sanctity of life, even unborn life, resist liberalised abortion; trade unions resist liberalisation away from the tyrannies of the closed shop. One must not underestimate the force of these resistances, as they can wreck any law which goes contrary to them. To concede the whole programme of the more militant women's libbers requires males to dismantle their own pyschology as well as their domestic role — a mighty demand. To impose racial equality and non-discrimination requires people to abandon their deepest-seated prejudices, against the person who is 'not like them'. To dissolve the closed shop is to ask trade unions to relinquish the monopoly power which, like the landowners of 18th and 19th century England, they have accumulated.

Resistance to mobilisation

Lastly, mobilisation and its resistances. It is not just that many people may find themselves losing their possessions and their freedom of disposal over them — and it is not only the property-owning classes in the marxist stereotype who may lose in this way, but small peasants and workers with pathetic life savings — but that people will lose something still more precious, their right of self-disposal. Even in a state or society which is not declaredly mobilising, the individual's power of self-disposal is small. It is a truism about traditional life in customary society that the society is all and the individual little or nothing (though this is often a gross misrepresentation of the way in which individuals gain a hearing and are accorded their rights by the community); in the complex modern state (even one which claims to be liberal in economics and politics) the individual feels weak, powerless and flattened by the powerful forces which control his life. The big corporations control his economic life; big governments control his social life as well.

Now imagine the process taken further, much further. It is no longer accidental that a man's economic life is controlled by the big corporations (which may be state-owned) and by government, but it is official government policy, from which there is no escape without change of government — and in many such states with one-party dictatorships there is no chance of changing the government without committing treason, while to change the official policy is to attack the constitution. Previously it was accidental for the state to use the individual, his private relations or his talents in the service of the state, because that was what the individual had chosen; now the state does the choosing for him. He is mobilised, called up, conscripted in the service of the state. That there should be massive internal resistances to such an overwhelming of the individual's freedom of thought and action should surprise no one; one of the prime examples of the mobilising state, China, has just begun to reveal the resistances which have existed all along to mobilisation of the rural peasantry and of intellectuals.

4. Techniques of programmatic transformation

How does the legislator go about the business of producing a major social transformation through law? Since such transformations are purposive, there are two stages in the process. In the first phase, the law-giver must determine what social goals he wishes to attain; in the second phase, he must consider what legal and administrative means he can use to attain these goals. A third stage then supervenes, that of the introduction of the legal and administrative programme. A fourth stage ought to follow, but rarely does, viz. to monitor performance and to rectify failures in effectiveness.

What has been noteworthy has been that stage 1, the formation of policy goals, and stage 2, the devising of legal instruments, have often been kept separate, and that lawyers and legal advice have only been resorted to when the goals are already so clearly cut that there is no effective dialogue between means and ends. Lawyers have rarely been found as members of the primary policy teams. There are exceptions, notably when the leader or a prominent member of the policy formation group is himself a lawyer; but even then the thinking tends to be at a highly conceptual and not at a practical level, law being seen as akin to mechanics rather than to basic design. Africa however shows several instances where policy formation has been undertaken by lawyers; and in a number of post-colonial countries, whether influenced by the Left or the Right, these lawyers have been foreigners — what I have referred to elsewhere not as *eminences grises* but as legal *eminences blanches*. Particulars could be given; but, in view of the difficulty of publicly demonstrating the efficacy and form of behind-the-scenes influence without transgressing the law of defamation, one must content oneself with general assertion.

Without reviewing the whole political history of the post-war world, it would not be possible to set out at adequate length the sorts of economic and social policy-making which have helped to set goals in one country after another. Rarely, if ever, have the springs of these policies been autochthonous. One great stream of influence has been through liberal-democratic ideas taken from the west, and especially from Britain and France. Constitutional changes show this influence (formally, at any rate) at its clearest. A second stream represents varieties of orthodox economic, and especially welfare economic and development economic, strategies; here again the contributions of the west, and especially of the United States, have been most visible. In the last decade or so these economics have taken on a more leftish and radical tinge, as the old stratum of western economists has yielded, in the universities of the west, to the new. Thirdly, there has been the influence of 'socialist' countries and thinking, especially from the Soviet Union itself and China. Economists and political strategists of whatever persuasion would rarely seek the advice or co-operation of lawyers at any phase of this preliminary work.

This work of policy formation — which in practice often means a process of conversion of the 'ignorant' power-holders rather than of dialogue — usually proceeds without any attempt at popular consultation. Devising economic and social strategies for new countries, and even old ones, is the job of the elites (or so they would see it). One personal experience in an African country which at that time had an extreme left-wing government, brought home to me the force of this elitism, and the estrangement of the policy-formers from their nominal constituents. A major programme of legal change, involving radical reform or abolition both of customary laws and of the imported law, was under consideration. I naively asked the European expert who was responsible for thinking up, devising and implementing this programme what ordinary people thought about the changes to be introduced, as I expected that there would be serious incomprehension or even sustained resistance to such changes in their accepted way of life. He told me scornfully that they would not think of consulting the people first about such changes, that their opinion on the matter was not relevant. In this given instance nothing ever came of the proposals; first the adviser fell out of favour and was sent home; then the proposals were abandoned; then the government itself fell, and a new regime was substituted by force. But, if the programme had gone ahead, it would have encountered all the resistances we have already mentioned; and it would have experienced no more success than the many other programmatic reforms which have failed in other parts of Africa.

The role of foreign experts, foreign ideas which they bring with them, foreign models of laws, foreign technocrats, and foreign education when the ideas men are indigenously born but educated overseas, has thus been pre-eminent. The same charge which could be brought against old-style colonialism, — that it meant the introduction and wholesale application of forms of law and administration which were totally foreign to their subjects — can be brought against this new-style intellectual colonialism, what I have christened 'neo-paternalism' or 'Daddy knows best'. There are few original indigenous devisers of societies or laws. Regressive legislation is by definition unoriginal; whenever there has been an attempt to revert to an earlier society or its *Law*, it will usually be found that the new system is a watered down travesty of the old, often based on lack of understanding of the characteristics, aims and techniques of the old *Law* which it is sought to recreate; or it may even be a perversion of the old *Law*, using the old labels but now stuck on new bottles. Thus African traditional legal ideas about the punitive treatment of crime, for instance, may be revived (even though much wrongdoing was in traditional society dealt with as private injuries between two groups or lineages); alleged traditional community control of land will be used, not to re-establish traditional forms of land control, but to provide a cover for the installation of nationalisation or socialised land tenure along completely foreign lines; and so on.

There have been praiseworthy attempts at popular consultation at the vital opinion-forming stage. Thus the reforms in the laws of marriage and succession which were mooted in the 1960s in Kenya were the result of an elaborate process of popular consultation by commissions which were specially set up to be representative of the various interests (such as women, adherents of Christianity or Islam, the legal profession) involved. Despite the fact that the two commissions issued well-thought-out reports with carefully drafted bills to implement their recommendations, these proposals languished unenacted for many years. Tanzania quickly took up the spadework which the Kenya commissions had undertaken and made it the basis of its own proposals, which saw the light of day as the Law of Marriage Act 1971. Consultation of popular opinion in Tanzania proceeded at a different pace and by a different method; it obviously did not facilitate the ascertainment of public opinion that no Swahili text of the draft Bill was available to the public until three weeks before the President gave his assent to the Act.

There are also instances in other parts of Africa where pressure for a new law has built up from private bodies such as national associations of women; or where the government has been careful to float its ideas before a wide range of public bodies and interested persons before putting them into legal form. A recent example has been with the government suggestions for radical reform of succession law in Ghana, which were sent round to church bodies, traditional councils of chiefs and individuals — in the result, a large volume of very valuable comments was received back, which would undoubtedly prove invaluable to government in deciding what sorts of changes would meet with popular assent and hence would probably attract general acceptance and compliance.

Some governments have relied on consultation of parliaments or local assemblies as their way of determining what public opinion is. There may well be cases when this is a highly efficient method of taking a broad conspectus (broad geographically as well as by attitude and background) of public opinion; but there are many reasons why this sounding of public opinion can be fallacious. First, there are the tame talking-shops, where there is a single dominant party and where the main concern of members is not to get on the wrong side of government ministers. Where the philosophy of the vanguard party is followed, with the unique party setting the tone and the agenda of discussion in every kind of body at all levels, then discussion means hearing what the party functionaries say and assenting to it rather than independently express-ing a reaction.

Then there is the problem that 'representative assemblies' are usually unrepresentative. The lack of a faithful mirroring by Parliament of the public at large is sufficiently conspicuous in a country like Britain, whose population (unlike parliamentarians) does not consist entirely of trade union officials, lecturers in higher education, social workers, journalists, small businessmen, merchant bankers and lawyers; but at least all but 10% of the general population can read, and can read some of the same periodicals. In African or many other Third-World Countries the demand that assemblymen be literate immediately erects an enormous barrier of incomprehension between 'representatives' and constituents; but the culture-gap is just as bad in many other ways, from religion to family life to economic activity to house styles to eventual ambitions. A Masai herdsman is not adequately represented by a city lawyer.

Sounding of public opinion in a country like Britain frequently demonstrates a complete divorce between opinion in the 'representative' Parliament and in the population at large about such topics as immigration, harsher prison sentences, dealing with strikers, hanging, cutting of taxes, or whatever. And yet Parliament is quite happy to treat examination of its own opinion as satisfying the need to consult public opinion generally. It is probably with respect to the most sensitive subjects that public opinion is least conscientiously consulted, and that recourse is had to the parliamentary sounding-board instead. Two examples may be seen with the introduction in Britain of race relations legislation in 1965, and the abolition of the death penalty in 1967.

First, then, the devising of policy (stage 1). Next the devising of the law itself (stage 2). Typically the drafting of a comprehensive law, such as a general code transforming the whole or a substantial part of the legal system, is given to a commission (or occasionally to a single drafts-man). Commissions cannot make laws, any more than committees can design horses (they come up with camels instead); so whichever solution is adopted, it is usually the case that the work of making a draft is given to a single dominating mind, which draft may then be commented on and torn apart by others, but which will remain a whole intellectual production of a single mind. It was thus that Professor R. David, despite the aid of a Codification Commission, came to draft the Ethiopian Civil Code 1960. It was thus, though on a much less ambitious scale, that Professor L. C. B. Gower came to draft the Ghana Companies Code 1963. Each had a clear idea of what he wanted to achieve; each could ensure a clear structure to the work as a whole; each could ensure consistency of language and juristic view. Study of codes is thus largely a study of their unique draftsmen; and yet it is not yet an accepted part of legal-historical study to investigate the intellectual biography of legal codifiers in the same way as one studies the careers of 18th-century statesmen.[8]

A draftsman, even the greatest, is hard put to it to be original. Mostly he will turn to a model, at least to reject it if not to incorporate or transform it. The model which many of the foreign draftsmen in the Third World have turned to has been the lecture-notes which they have prepared for their teaching of the parent law which they will now use as a model. Many Third World codes are thus codified lecture-notes, incorporating all the improvements which the eminent draftsman would like to see in the parent law but which he is in no position to introduce there.

What happens to the draft law varies according to the extent to which governments wish to ensure the success of their code by previous consultation. The careful governments will put the text to a variety of interested bodies and parties, and will even take their comments into account in framing a revised version of the code. The impatient or high-handed governments will not have time for such a step, for fear that the pure milk of their reforming law will be watered down in the process. The first group of governments is more likely to enjoy success than the second.

Then comes the phase of implementation. The law is introduced. It may be accompanied by an official propaganda campaign, not to find out what people think but so that the people may find out what the government demands. Radio, newspapers, word of mouth may all be used in this campaign. Translation of the text into appropriate vernacular languages may be part of the procedure. One means of implementation is the gradualist one, expecting the population and the courts and administrative authorities to respond slowly and to begin with half-heartedly to the new law. Thus the new criminal procedure in Northern Nigeria in 1959 was at first introduced as 'guidance' only; thus the Ethiopian Civil Code was given 100 years to establish itself. Or there

---

8. One excepts Lord Macaulay from this criticism; while Bentham, the great theoretical codifier, is now receiving 'super-star' treatment.

may be a rush job: everyone is expected to switch over immediately and without delay to the new law. So it was when in the Sudan in 1971 there was a sudden switch from English *Law* to a Civil Code derived from that of Egypt. The new Civil Code was seen as part of a unifying and Islamising programme. It was enacted, and was immediately and theoretically in force everywhere. (In practice, it was not observed.) Impatience tends to be self-defeating – it is difficult to sustain the original momentum in the years ahead. Gradualism, on the other hand, runs the risk of being so gradual as to be imperceptible.

5. Success or failure

The best way of seeing how these techniques of implementation have worked, and the nature of the resistances which they have encountered, is to take some factual examples. I propose to take the following instances, widely spread in space as well as varying in technique and aim, to illustrate our analysis:

(a) The Civil Code in Ethiopia.
(b) Kenya land consolidation.
(c) India and the uniform civil code.
(d) Turkey.
(e) Race relations and equal opportunities laws in Britain.

(a) The Ethiopian Civil Code 1960

This may be described as the comparatists' joy. A country with many different kinds and sources of law – religious (both Christian and Islamic); traditional (both Amharic and pagan); western (affected by common law and civil law alike) – to be reduced to a single uniform legal system. Eclecticism the officially approved order of the day, so that the English 'reasonable man' can easily figure (translated) in a civil-law code, and common-law procedure can fit with civil-law substantive law. A country with an absolute ruler, so that what the ruler ordains shall have the force of law. A free hand, save only that the draftsman's colleagues must be persuaded, and the new law must respond to the ambitions of modernisation, unification and secularisation.

As an intellectual achievement the Ethiopian Civil Code ranks high. As a practical exercise it was a dismal failure. The law was programmatic in the most distant sense, in that it set a programme to which the nation and its disparate parts might eventually work and which might eventually succeed. It seems unfair, given this perspective of centuries, to measure its success in a couple of decades; but that we must do. The best way of summarising the success of the Code is to borrow the assessment of a leading scholar of Ethiopian *Law*, J. Vanderlinden.[9] The comparatists' joy is the practitioner's nightmare: it is too much to expect the fledgling or even the established Ethiopian legal practitioner to be able to handle material from so many different sources — he would prefer an affiliation to a single major legal system. The judges of the courts which should be applying the Code have not resorted to it. Worst of all, the population at large has been unaffected by the Code: why?

(i) 'The illiteracy of the population in Ethiopia (about 95%) does not at present allow most of the inhabitants to be aware of the prescriptions of the new law.'

(ii) 'The Code is in effect, for most of the population, an entirely or largely new law. In these conditions, it is not surprising that resistances to the application of the Civil Code have manifested themselves, especially in the countryside. The obstacles which have thus arisen seem to fall into two categories (putting on one side the inherent difficulty for persons who are not trained in law to understand legal language): firstly, linguistic problems, and secondly, absence of publicity for the new Code. The linguistic difficulties come as a result of the fact that Ethiopia has a national language which is spoken by less than half of the population. It is not surprising that the provisions of the new law should have little impact in the country. Because of illiteracy, only a tiny minority can read the Code. As a result, it is necessary to have recourse to other ways of publicising the Code than by use of the printing press if one wishes to ensure the effective familiarisation of everyone with the new prescriptions introduced by the Code. For this a major imaginative effort is essential, and this the Ethiopian government seems unaware of up till now. Now, if such an effort is not made, it is self-deceptive to hope that new institutions can have such an impact on traditional society. Considerations like these do not apply only to the civil law, but effectively to everything that one may call the law of development, that is, the law which has as its purpose to transform society rather than to be the fruit of such a transformation. These considerations are especially important in the field of private law, because it is in this area that the resistances offered by tradition risk being the most serious in view of the tight involvement of such institutions with society itself.'

One could not hope to summarise more clearly the obstacles which the Civil Code has met, or the reasons for its almost total failure (even though it provided at last something for the nascent law faculty in Addis Ababa to teach as national law). Ethiopia is merely a special and extreme case of a general problem. How the problem is compounded

9. In his *Introduction au Droit de l'Ethiopie moderne* (Paris, 1971).
   (Translations from the French are by myself — ANA). See especially pp. 212 ff.

by politics is attested by the vicissitudes of the country since the fall of the Emperor in 1974, and the seizure of power by a revolutionary socialist regime. The *Grundnorm* of the old *Law* has now gone as well. Will the new socialist government be any more successful than its imperial predecessor in remaking Ethiopian society, in all its variety and with all its resistances, to its own image? One takes leave to doubt it.[10]

(b) Kenya land consolidation

The reasons for success or failure with the Kenya land consolidation programme, or the total transformation of land law and tenure implied by it, seem as different as they could be from those which obtained in Ethiopia. Religious and ethnic variations as between different African communities have not been the problem in the land field (though they can be, and are, important in the field of family law). There has long been an effective administration. There has been a long experience with land registration before this was used as the main plank in the reforming platform. There was popular involvement through the use of local committees in each area as it became ripe for consolidation, these committees helping to sort out who was entitled to what sorts of interests. Publicity for the changes was thus at a high level; awareness and even acceptance were high. There were clear-cut economic rewards for those who participated in and gained from the process.

At the formal level, then, all seemed plain sailing; and, if one measures success by markings on the map which show areas now covered by land consolidation and the Registered Land Act, then success seems complete and convincing. But there are nagging doubts.

There are three main weaknesses in the scheme as it actually operates. The first is that the law recognises the possibility of co-ownership, though it limits the number of persons who may be concurrently registered as co-proprietors of the same parcel to five; the second is that the customary *Laws* continue to operate so far as the laws of succession to registered interests are concerned; the third is that the effect of equity on the beneficial enjoyment of registered land has not been excluded. Two further weaknesses, which are not weaknesses of the scheme but of its practical application and subsequent effects, have been the difficulty of policing the proper and immediate registration of transactions affecting registered land, and the pressure to recognise clan and group rights in land, which led to a modification of the basic law in 1968 with the enactment of the Land (Group Representatives) Act. This was a concession to the 'tribal' framework of the customary

10. See Heinrich Scholler and Paul Brietzske *Ethiopia: revolution, law and politics*, (Munich, 1976), esp. at pp. 80 ff.: 'To the extent that the Proclamation [for revolutionary reform of land tenure in 1975] remains unimplemented, unenforced or unenforceable, traditional tenures will, of course, continue to influence events in rural Ethiopia'.

land laws which had not been in the contemplation of the original framers of the legislation, who hoped – vainly – to wipe the slate clean of customary interests.

The limitation on the number of co-proprietors was imposed for fear of the re-introduction of fragmentation of holdings, which had been one of the principal evils of the previous land tenure position, and which had been 'cured' by consolidation. It was feared that if the customary laws of succession were allowed to continue (and this was conceded, because of the shock that would otherwise be inflicted on the African social system), this would inevitably lead to a division of the land among numerous heirs, the customary succession systems being for the most part what I call 'divisory', where partition of the estate, rather than its conservation as a single working unit, was the norm. The answer to this was felt to be a restriction on the number of co-owners, so that sub-division could not go too far; and a restriction on the minimum size of parcels, so that divisory succession would not lead to smaller and smaller separate fragments.

These precautions have proved to be totally useless. The response of the African landowners to these paper restrictions has been to ignore them, mainly through (i) failing to register devolutions on death, with the result that the successors by inheritance enjoy their 'rights' and land *de facto*, but the register continues to show the deceased proprietor as the land-holder; and (ii) permission by the registered proprietors to others to occupy the land on whatever claim or title – permissive occupation, which is not prohibited by the law. A mountain of unrecorded transactions and transmissions has thus accumulated, which makes the register an increasingly inaccurate guide to the actual title position or the actual occupation position. Estimates vary as to the factual accuracy of the register as compared with the de facto situation on the ground. Apart from failures to register devolutions on death, and permissive occupation under subordinate 'title' granted outside the framework of the Registered Land Act, there are the *inter vivos* dealings which have not been reported or registered as they should have been. Simon Coldham, who has made a special study of the practical working of the land registration system in Kenya, reports in an article published in 1978[11] that:

'The present writer encountered many instances where dealings in registered land had occurred without any attempt being made to have them registered or approved by the land control board. This undermines the basis of the statutory system of registration and control and indeed prompts doubts about the wisdom of introducing the system in the first place. The fact that the dealings in question are void will not prevent there arising in the not too distant future a large number of

11.   'Land control in Kenya' [1978] JAL 63 at p. 74.

disputes, disputes of the type and complexity that existed in many areas before land adjudication and that land adjudication was designed to stop.'

In a further article[12] Coldham draws attention to the other way in which customary rights and interests are making a come-back despite their theoretical extinction and replacement by registered titles; and this is through the law of trusts. The courts in Kenya, though reluctant, because of the finality of first registration under the Registered Land Act,[13] to rectify the register if it does not record the previous title position under customary law, and reluctant to recognise customary rights of *occupation* which could and should have been registered, have shown themselves very willing to hold that a registered proprietor must be deemed to hold his title in trust for some other person or persons. Many of these trusts are what we may call 'customary trusts', i.e. where the beneficial rights arise under customary *Law*, either on succession or because the first registration did not correspond with the true entitlement of the proprietor (if, say, he procured his registration through fraud).

It is curious that this divergence between the state of the register and the actual position of occupation on the ground bedevilled, at an earlier stage, the registration of titles at the Kenya Coast, under the Land Titles Ordinance 1908. Large numbers of claims were never adjudicated; many of the paper titles were never collected by those entitled to them; devolutions of such titles remained outside the official system.

It is noteworthy too that the weakness of control over transmission by succession had already made itself felt by 1963, when F. O. Homan reported that he had calculated that 'after four years of registration in Kiambu alone over 3,000 titles were registered in the names of deceased persons'.[14] Experience since then has been confirmatory of this early trend.

This has provoked Sorrenson to ask if 'the intractable problems of succession' can be solved. The holders of the smallest units, which cannot be further sub-divided as they would be less than the minimum acreage, are in the worst case:

'In such circumstances the Kikuyu are taking the only way out by not notifying the death of landowners and unofficially sub-dividing the land between all heirs who wish to cultivate it . . . [Land control boards are not standing in the way of sub-economic sub-divisions.] Government has now got the worst of both worlds: the control machinery has broken down and anyone who bothers to apply for a sub-division is

12. 'The effect of registration of title upon customary land rights in Kenya' [1978] JAL 91 esp. at pp. 102 ff.
13. Registered Land Act, s. 143.
14. See Sorrenson, op. cit. 215, quoting Homan 'Succession to registered land in the African areas of Kenya' (1963) J. Local Admin. Overseas, II, 1, at pp. 49 to 52.

granted permission . . . . All holdings which support more than one family (or a polygamous family) are in effect divided up so that, in the traditional manner, each woman can have a distinct area for her crops.'[15]

What has gone wrong? The Kenya land consolidation and registration programme may justly be claimed as the showpiece of programmatic economic legislation in the land tenure field. It was carefully studied as it went along; detailed investigations of the field situation were made; there was ample examination of the legal, economic, agricultural and social requirements and problems; there *was* monitoring of the success or failure of the scheme after the event, represented by the 'Lawrance Mission', which reported in 1966[16] after a most thorough and enlightened survey on the ground of the present working and future possibilities of the programme. If expert advice and sensible planning were what was needed to achieve such a radical transformation of African farming, it was there in plenty. Not merely that, but there was intensive and extensive governmental propaganda for the introduction and spread of the new programme and widespread public demand for the benefits of it.

Let us isolate some of the main difficulties. The first one is a simple one of administration. Land registration means paper titles; customary land titles depend on people's memories. It is often assumed by the educated western reformer that paper memory is more accurate and durable than personal recollection. This is so, provided (i) the right information has been impressed on the written memory in the first place – the problem of efficient and comprehensive inputs; and (ii) the right steps have been taken to conserve and update the information in the second place – the problem of maintenance of records. Neither condition has been fully satisfied in Kenya. The administrative framework, which is necessarily a complicated one both for the initial compilation of a register (after consolidation and/or adjudication) and for its subsequent maintenance, has proved to be too elaborate for the resources of manpower and insufficiently open to satisfactory inspection and control. *The most wonderful law will not work if the administrative machinery for its implementation is not there and operative* – that is the first lesson.

Secondly, the machinery provides too many opportunities for distortion, evasion or fraud. *The machinery has to be rigorous and effective in its reach* – that is the second lesson.

Thirdly, what the legislator proposed was a revolution. As the *Lawrance Report* wisely said:

'. . . individualisation strikes at the very root of tribal society.'[17]

15. Sorrenson, op. cit., pp. 216–7.
16. *Report of the Mission on Land Consolidation and Registration in Kenya, 1965–1966* (Nairobi, 1966).
17. Id., p. 6.

Exactly! The main purpose of the programme was to transform land tenure; the side-effect, not willed but inevitably implied, was to transform traditional African society. Resistance to the side-effect (which is not a subsidiary or minor point to those who belong to such a society) provokes resistance to the main purpose; and the possibilities of evasion and so on — the perversion of the machinery — allow this resistance to take effect. It was really incredibly naive of those who believed that ingrained social attitudes and established social patterns of behaviour would be readily and immediately abandoned, displaced and suppressed by the opportunity to make more money out of the land. African traditionalism has won. So the third lesson is: *the inbuilt resistances of tradition and habitual patterns of thought and action are always far stronger than the reformers allow.*

What about the machinery for selling the programme, and its acceptance by the public? Here the *Lawrance Report* is very helpful in clearing the air, and revealing to us the real processes at work. The Report mentions:

'continuous and dedicated urging and propaganda by officials and leaders of public opinion'.[18]

But the propaganda seems to have been partially self-deluding on the part of the elite who put it out, and ephemeral in its effects on the people aimed at. A demand for land registration and consolidation was generated among some people in some areas; but the factors which explain this demand were, firstly, greed — the hope to profit from the programme by gaining a much larger and assured income from a consolidated and registered holding; and secondly fear — anxiety that otherwise the individual holder would lose his rights. But as the realised gains turned out to be less than anticipated, so the enthusiasm waned. The profit motive led many farmers to expect that they would easily raise credit on the security of their new registered holdings from banks and other lending agencies — this had been part of the propaganda of land consolidation. But the readiness of such agencies to grant credit turned out to be less than expected; and many of the borrowers obtained loans which they immediately misapplied, not to the generation of more capital but to its dissipation on social purposes or for ostentatious acquisition. The percentage of the agricultural loans made by the Agricultural Development Corporation which were actually repaid as agreed is pathetically small.[19] In the result, the Lawrance Mission described public attitudes to land consolidation as 'generally far from enthusiastic'. The public support which was believed to be there was shallow-rooted and scattered.

There is a fourth lesson, perhaps the most important of the lot, to be learnt from this — that *massive disobedience of or non-compliance with*

18. At p. 23.
19. See C. A. Hayanga 'Loans to agriculture in Kenya' [1975] JAL 105.

a law will triumph in the long run. It is the sheer weight of illegal and non-conforming transactions and of 'rights' acquired thereby which means that no Kenya government will dare to rely on the letter of its law, and to declare all such 'rights' invalid. This has been a common history of land registration and reform schemes in many parts of the world — the land tenure position in parts of the Caribbean, where there is in theory no customary law, shows this to be so. Non-compliance with the law, as we have already seen, wrecked laws in Britain; it wrecks laws in Third World countries too.

(c) India and the Uniform Civil Code

There is no need to dwell at such length on the successes and failures of the post-independence governments in this field, because such successes as they have had are now coming to an end, and policy seems to be at a standstill. One must remind oneself that the Indian Constitution contains express legislative provisions on the one hand, and 'Directive Principles of State Policy' on the other. The latter do not have legislative effect, and function at the level of aspiration rather than of law. However, the founding fathers must have had a reason for incorporating a novel feature of this kind (which resembles the Preambles with which other constitutions habitually begin and which recite their devotion to the Rights of Man or whatever it may be), though it is fair to recall that this is an imitation of a similar feature in the Irish Constitution. The reason for the directive principles is to give a goal for the legislator, and a prod to the judges who may lean to one side or another when interpreting the Constitution. The directive principles are in addition to the Fundamental Rights provisions of the Constitution, which are already sufficiently general in character, one would have thought.

The social and political thought which lay behind Article 44 is quite clear: it is that of a modern westernising elite. Division between different races, religions and social classes and local particularisms was particularly strong in India at independence — the bloody confrontations between Hindu and Muslim had been a sufficient token of that, not to mention language rights, local customs, the tension between north and south, and many other such factors. Gledhill points out the nature of these tensions.[20] Religious differences, he says, were more important than social differences (one might be tempted to reverse the order of priorities in India today); 'India has wisely chosen to be a secular State; there is no established religion or church and freedom of religion is a fundamental right'.

Dismantling of variations in civil rights and duties had both an internal and an external aspect, if we may speak from the point of view of religious personal laws. Internally there were the cleavages within Hinduism, and most flagrantly the divisions in social status as between

20. A. Gledhill *The Republic of India* (1974, 2nd edn), p. 75.

castes. The status of untouchability particularly called out for treatment. The remedy was to legislate the abolition of untouchability, and to try to provide, by various laws and devices, for the redressing of disabilities which might afflict the lowest castes. Positive discrimination as well as proscription of negative discrimination were called in aid. The conduct caught by the law abolishing untouchability, the Untouchability (Offences) Act 1955,[21] was public discrimination in the provision of facilities, e.g. access to shops, restaurants, water supplies. The law did not seek to control social conduct not amounting to denial of facilities, e.g. boycotts. So social disapproval and conduct cannot as such be legislated out of existence by law; and it is notorious that in modern India social disabilities, rather than legal disabilities, persist.

One of the technical problems is that the Constitution preserves the right of freedom of association; and to the extent that a caste can be seen as a voluntary association, so it can be upheld under the fundamental rights provisions. As Marc Galanter, the leading student of Indian social legislation, has put it:

'Within the Hindu law itself, the constitutional ban on caste discrimination has not been read as abolishing differences in personal law between Hindus of different castes ... The Hindu Code Acts of 1955–56 have largely abandoned the shastraic basis of Hindu law and established a more or less uniform law for Hindus of all regions and castes ... the new legal view of caste furnishes recognition and protection for the new social forms through which caste concerns may be expressed ... We may anticipate that the new legal view of caste will not only sanction but stimulate and encourage new forms of organization ...

We can visualize the judiciary as mediating between the Constitution's commitment to a great social transformation and the actualities of Indian society. The courts must combine and rationalize the various components of the constitutional commitment – voluntarism and respect for group integrity on the one hand, and equality and non-recognition of rank ordering among groups on the other. They must do this in the process of applying these constitutional principles to claims and conflicts which arise within the existing structure of Indian society. In working out the application of these principles, the judiciary have produced a picture of caste which no one proposed and no one anticipated.'[1]

---

21. Now renamed 'Protection of Civil Rights Act'; as amended 1976, it now punishes a person who 'directly or indirectly preaches "untouchability"', and provides for imposition of a collective fine on the inhabitants of an area who fail to help in bringing offenders against the Act to justice.

1. In his 'Changing legal conceptions of caste', [in] *Structure and change in Indian Society* (ed. M. Singer and B. S. Cohen, Chicago, 1968), at pp. 311, 332.

The external aspect of the uniform law programme was to provide a single civil code for all citizens. This now seems no more than a distant mirage. As already remarked, the governments have gone as far as they can in the secularising and generalising of Hindu *Law* so-called, so that a reconciliation between Hindu personal law and other forms of personal law (excluding the Muslim) seems possible; but there is no visible way ahead in the reduction or removal of the cleavage between Muslim and non-Muslim personal law, and the Muslim *Law* persists, and will persist, subject only to such minor modifications as may correspond to the reforming programmes of Muslim countries of the Near and Middle East. Now, with the re-awakening of Muslim puritanism, even on the Indian sub-continent, it is doubtful whether even this minor gain will be made. The *aims* of the Constitution are clearly set out by Galanter:[2]

'The Constitution sets forth a general program for the reconstruction of Indian society . . . it clearly sets out to secure to individuals equality of status and opportunity, to abolish invidious distinctions among groups . . . to give free play to . . . generally the widest personal freedom consonant with the public good.'

'The Constitution contains a commitment to replace the system of separate personal laws with a "uniform civil code". In spite of its strictness against discrimination on the ground of religion, the Constitution has been interpreted to permit the continuing application of their respective personal laws to Hindus and Muslims. The continuing validity of disparate rules of personal law and the power of the state to create new rules applicable to particular communities has been upheld. [See, e.g., *State of Bombay v Narasu Appa Mali* 1952 Bom. 84].'

The primary aim of unification of laws has not been achieved, though there has been some removal of nonconformities of customary *Law* and Hindu *Law*; the secondary aim, the ultimate aim — a single, integrated society — is now far from the grasp of the legislator.

What went wrong? India, with its history of thousands of years of caste and racial discrimination, and with many hundreds of years of religious separatism, could not be expected to abandon all this overnight. The social foundations for a legal revolution were not there. The resistances, which there is no need to spell out here, were too great.[3] Nor is there more hope of achieving the same aim by opposite means, that is, by changing the personal laws in the direction of uniformity so as to

2. Op. cit., pp. 310, 311.
3. The laws against the giving of dowry by the parents of a bride upon marriage have apparently proved equally impossible to enforce, despite the fact that penalties have been increased when the earlier legislation proved a failure. It is reported that parents of brides are reluctant to report to the authorities that dowry has been demanded (illegally), because this would prejudice the chances of their daughters getting married. Non-payment of adequate dowry is sanctioned by illegal means, even crimes, such as burning the new daughter-in-law to death.

promote uniformity of social behaviour and attitude. What Lord Macaulay and his colleagues wisely perceived more than a century ago – that the entrenched forces of resistance of social custom were too strong to allow the imposition of a uniform code – has now been borne out in the conditions of modern India. Despite the fact that the first Indian governments had overwhelming electoral support, that there was now a large modern and modernising element in society which shared a common culture gained through the universities, the press and other shared institutions, that the state machinery was now a hundred times more powerful and interventionist than it had been in Macaulay's day, that it was operated by the indigenous people themselves and not by alien imperialists, that the apparatus of the modern technological state was now fully in place – despite all this, and the history of the past century, the Indian government cannot go faster in the direction of a uniform, secular society than it has in fact done. If it tries to go still faster, as Mrs Gandhi's government did, it risks overwhelming public rejection and disorder.

Changing the legal forms, as with untouchability, did not disturb the underlying social patterns and attitudes. These continue. The long history of codification in India has not, in this instance, been of much avail either. Certainly the lawyers are prepared to accept codified law – it is their daily fare; but the masses who will be forcibly manoeuvred and reshaped by such codes are not touched by this historical precedent. Religious feeling, resistance to all change, ingrained prejudices, have won the day.

(d) Turkey

The changes that were hoped for in India after 1950 were of the same kind as those which were successfully made in Turkey after the commencement of Kemal Ataturk's transformation of the country in the 1920s. Why should Ataturk succeed where the Indian governments have clearly failed? After all, the last vestiges of Ottoman *Law* and of religious control of family law have been swept away. If the Swiss Code could apply in Turkey, the Turkish Code could apply in Switzerland: what crisper example of a new and totally transforming law could one find?[4]

4. The apparent novelty of the legal revolution in Turkey and the general adoption of foreign laws (not only Swiss) in place of the previous religious and Ottoman laws have attracted considerable attention from comparative lawyers, led institutionally by the International Association of Legal Science, which inspired the convening of a Conference on the Reception of Foreign Law in Turkey in Istanbul in 1955. This was attended and contributed to by numerous Turkish lawyers, as well as foreign comparatists. Its papers were published in vol. 9 of the International Social Science Bulletin for 1957, as well as in the Annales de Faculté de Droit d'Istanbul for 1956 and 1957. (See also article by C. J. Hamson in (1956) 5 ICLQ 26). See also June Starr and Jonathan Pool 'The impact of a legal revolution in rural Turkey' (1974) 8 Law and Society Review 53.

The problem with lawyers is that they tend to ask legal questions; and the sort of questions which comparatists have asked about the Swiss Civil Code and its adoption in Turkey have been mostly directed at the technical and textual aspects of the reception of a foreign *Law* — how was it effected? what differences of interpretation have there been between Turkey and Switzerland? what adaptations have there been in the Code to make it suitable for local conditions? — while the questions which we wish to pose are those which library lawyers are quite unable to answer, such as: how effective has the Code been in changing the behaviour of people on the ground? how has the behaviour of the people changed the interpretation and functioning of the Code? Such questions can only be answered empirically.

Such empirical studies are much thinner on the ground. Only two of the papers at the Istanbul Conference tried to assess the effectiveness of the Code in Turkish conditions, those by Stirling and Timur. As June Starr, the American legal anthropologist who has made a special study of the subject, says in her important new work, *Dispute and Settlement in Rural Turkey: an ethnography of law*:[5]

'Although over five decades have passed since western criminal and civil codes were introduced in Turkey, there has yet to be a comprehensive assessment of how such far-reaching changes in both substantive and procedural law have affected the lives of Turkish people.'[6]

Legal anthropologists, who are likely in this connection to make a more useful contribution than ethno-jurists (though the work of each should be complementary and mutually corrective), have yet to work in any numbers in such societies, preferring studies of peasant communities in the more fashionable areas of Africa (and now New Guinea). I cannot hope in this work to be better informed than our sources; what I can do is to point out some of the main factors and questions, the first being unidentified and the second unanswered, and leave the issue to the patient field-research of other scholars. The questions which concern me are the following:

(i)   What are the factors which would assist, or make more difficult, the sort of legal/social transformation which Ataturk envisaged?

(ii) What are the measurements of effectiveness that one can use, and how is one to go about making them?

(iii) What conclusions, necessarily preliminary, would one come to about the success of the Turkish experiment?

(i) The factors. The past history, experiences, and institutions of Ottoman and revolutionary Turkey are the first set of factors. Here the very first question to resolve is whether the introduction of the Swiss

5. Leiden, 1978.
6. At p. 6.

Civil Code in 1926, and the other western codes, was as revolutionary and literally shocking as it is often made out to be. Granted that there was and is little congruence of languages, culture, religion, political structures, technology, geographical location and ambitions between Switzerland and Turkey, there would seem to be an enormous gap between the societal context of the Code in the two countries. Does this matter? If a Code, and its detailed prescriptions, is a mere mechanism or vehicle, then it may be used to transmit a variety of cryptic messages for quite different purposes. The same vehicle can take one person to church, and another to an assignation. Words are what the context says they are: the context gives them meaning. Change the context, but leave the words, and one might argue that one has a new message. Thus East and West can happily subscribe to the same declaration of respect for human rights at Helsinki, though the politico/social systems in the western liberal, and the eastern socialist, countries give it quite different meanings. But if the Code is more than words on paper, and is an integrated structure of spoken and unspoken rules, procedures, institutions and expectations, then its translocation without effective change of function and with lively hope of success is more problematical. (The same point was clearly brought out in the *Adegbenro* case in Nigeria in 1964:[7] can one translate the constitutional conventions of Westminster into an African political setting; and if one does, what is the result?)

In one sense, then, the translocation of the Swiss Code, and other codes, to modern Turkey was a major shock to the body politic there. But the gap between pre- and post-Code was not as great as is often made out. As has already been briefly mentioned,[8] there was a century of code-making, law reform, and the introduction of western laws and behaviour into Ottoman Turkey before Ataturk's revolutionary gesture of 1926. Codes, especially codes on the western model, were nothing new. There were jurists capable of handling them, in and out of court (unlike, say, Ethiopia).

The greatest shock was undoubtedly the suppression of the *Shari'a* or sacred Islamic law. But — if the experience of other Islamic countries in different parts of the world is anything to go by — one is willing to bet that the actual law of marriage, the family and succession followed (theoretically in accordance with Islamic precepts) was in reality a multi-tier sandwich of Muslim *Law* and local customs. Abolish the official *Law*, and you do nothing to touch the existing customs; those customs are likely to continue to affect and co-exist with the new official *Law*, however different it may be from the old *Law* (and this

---

7. See *Adegbenro v Akintola* [1963] 3 All ER 544, PC which affirms that one must abide solely by the express terms of a written constitution, and not qualify them by reference to British implicit conventions.
8. See pp. 186 ff.

seems to be one of the messages of Starr's study). This in itself will be both an element of continuity and a resistance to change.

The political position at the time of Ataturk's assumption of power, and the sort of power that he wielded, are important components in the situation. Few leaders find themselves in a more powerful and dominating position. Nor was the situation complicated by the sorts of religious rivalry and conflict, or separatist tendencies, which have made the task of assuring a new, unifying and modernising *Law* so difficult in all the other countries we have studied (and which, to our surprise, we may find bedevil the success of transforming legislation in contemporary Britain). This is not to say that there were not divisive factors (e.g. the position of the Kurds) or geographical divisions. The first stratification was between the elite, the leaders in political and social evolution, and the masses. The second stratification, important in a predominantly rural country like Turkey, was between town and country. The two stratifications reinforced each other. Starr draws attention[9] to the problem of enforcing the law in a country with a smallish population widely scattered through numerous villages. On her figures, 70 per cent of the population live in c. 40,000 villages; and she comments that in such circumstances 'in rural communities . . . the writ of law may be extremely difficult to carry out'. (One would add that a modern largely urbanised country like England is divided into numerous communities – though not 'villages' – in its different cities and towns, and the policing of law-compliance in a country like England is just as difficult as it is in rural Turkey: probably more so, as in a village at least the authorities have a clearer idea of what is going on than they would have in a suburb of London or Birmingham.) The new Turkish law was urban law; its failures were to be expected in the countryside. It is also in the countryside that old customs die hardest.

(ii) Measurements of effectiveness. Has the introduction of the Swiss Civil Code been a success? How do we measure that success? If we answer that question by asking how effective the Code is, what do we mean by 'effective'?

'Effectiveness', according to my view of the matter, means compliance by the indicated subjects of the law. So far as mandatory or prohibitory provisions of the law are concerned, do people observe the positive precepts and avoid the prohibited activities? So far as permissive or facultative aspects of the law are concerned, do they make use of these facilities sufficiently to justify the expectation of the legislator, in those cases where we may presume him to have given a strong permission? To decide whether there has been compliance with mandatory or prohibitory norms, we would have to show in what ways the new legal regime differed significantly from the old; otherwise we should be facing, not

9. At p. 6.

deliberate conformism or compliance, but the perpetuation of old habits. One of the main areas where the new Code differed substantially from the old Islamic law was in the area of family law: the procedures for getting married, the capacity to marry, the status of marriage and the rights and duties flowing from it, the enforcement of those rights and duties, and the means of dissolving the marriage were all new. Similarly the new law of succession was fundamentally different from the old Islamic and mathematical system of succession. Islamic law is biased towards males in giving a double share to a male heir when compared with a female heir of the same degree. It provides a complicated calculus of interests or shares, which relates to succession to the non-disposable two-thirds of the estate. Islamic succession is in my terms a 'divisory' system, rather than a solidary one. The exact shares taken by each class vary according to the class and also according to the variable assembly of different spouses and relatives left by deceased. The Turkish Civil Code gives the widow if any a fixed share (like the Scottish legitim) in the estate, while the children inherit the residue in equal shares irrespective of sex (a system very like that of modern English law). How far do relatives comply with these requirements in making distribution of the estate?

The anthropologist Paul Stirling, who worked in two Turkish villages in the period 1949–1952, provides valuable evidence of provisional answers to some of these questions, at least so far as one may assume that, as he affirms in his text, what he found is typical of the Turkish countryside generally at that period. However, though his study[10] was published in 1965, one cannot tell how far matters may have changed since he did his field-work there. Stirling states that his villagers treat the Civil Code as largely irrelevant in the field of family and marriage law: 'the effect of those parts of the Civil Code that govern marriage and the family have at present [= the period of field-work] almost no bearing on the village' (p. 271); and he spells this conclusion out in greater detail in his book. So far as marriage is concerned, villagers ignore the Civil Code, claim to conform to Islamic law, but in fact do not; what they conform to is semi-islamicised custom (p. 209). Divorce is rare, and does not take place either under the Code or under the now-superseded Islamic law (p. 210). A large percentage (over 50 per cent) of village marriages are not registered, as the Code requires for their validity (p. 274). The stability of marriage is totally unaffected by State laws (p. 220).

So far as succession to property ('inheritance') is concerned, villagers acknowledge three sources of rules, the Civil Code, Islamic *Law*, and custom; but whereas only the Civil Code has theoretical legal validity, the influence of these three sources on the actual distribution of estates is in inverse relationship to their formal legal authority – custom

10. *Turkish Village* (London, 1965).

dominates; there is a limited reference to Islamic *Law*; and none to the Code provisions.

On this basis, then, one would measure the Turkish reforms as ineffective; but this is not the official story, as the next section, which discusses the success of the reforms, shows. Our difficulty is that we have quite inadequate general data to judge of the success of the reforms, and in making such a judgment we must have regard both to place and to period.

(iii) Success of the Turkish reforms. On the face of it, the Turkish reforms successfully displaced the previous religious and Ottoman *Law*, at least in the towns; but there are suggestions in the literature that there have been failures of effectiveness (a) in regard to the new law of marriage, (b) in regard to the rural areas, (c) in regard to procedures rather than to substantive law. As for marriage, the Turkish governments have been obliged to enact recurrent acts legitimating the marriages and their offspring of people who have chosen not to marry within the forms prescribed by the Civil Code. Such acts were passed in 1932, 1934, 1945, 1950, and 1955. By itself this information has merely formal significance, as one does not know, without sociological enquiry, *why* the parties chose to unite themselves outside the Code provisions. Research has been done into the statistics of such paranomic marriages, and Starr quotes Timur, a social scientist, as estimating in 1955 that 'close to half the couples in Turkey who considered themselves married, and who were having children, had not registered their marriage with the state'.[11] I have no more recent or accurate information on current trends; but this situation, 30 years after the introduction of the Code, suggests a massive disregard of the formal law of marriage. However, Starr's own evidence from the village she investigated, and which she pseudonymously named Mandalinci, does not correlate with this picture of massive disregard. She says:[12]

'Although Stirling . . ., Timur . . ., and others have suggested that villagers are lax in obtaining state marriage licenses and court-decided divorces, I found little evidence in Mandalinci to suggest this to be the case. Villagers seemed to accept the procedures which the state requires to legitimate or terminate a marriage.'

There are several possible explanations for this discrepancy. First, the earlier researchers may have been wrong, or their samples may have been untypical. Secondly, Mandalinci may be exceptional for rural villages.[13] Thirdly, there may have been a substantial change in

11.   Starr, op. cit. p. 69, citing H. Timur 'Civil marriage in Turkey: difficulties, causes and remedies' (1957) 9 International Social Science Bulletin 34–36.
12.   At p. 276.
13.   Starr would strongly deny this.

compliance with the law in the 10–20 years since these figures were compiled. Such a change in compliance might, in its turn, be due to several different factors. For example, the younger generation may be much more affected by 'modern' (= western European) ideas through the cultural influence of westernised media, or through direct contact with western European cultures through working in Germany or other places; or there may have been, which is not necessarily the same, a weakening of attachment to old religious and customary ideas. What was a shock to the first generation which met the revolution in their adulthood – the impact of western laws – is now part of the accepted scene for the new generation. A parallel with Soviet Russia suggests itself. The arrangements and presuppositions of the communist structure are now part of the given background for the young Soviet citizen in a way that they were not for his parents or grandparents. What this would mean is that the new laws are now part of the cultural, that is customary, scene, and win acceptance for this reason. (One could illustrate from many societies this theme of what was rejected in the first generation being taken for granted in the second – the switch between Indian and English *Law* in Kenya is one good example, where the older legal practitioners were generally opposed in the thirties to the adoption of English rather than British Indian codes.)

Another apparent source of failure pointed to by Starr is the unwillingness of villagers to resort to the agencies officially set up by the Turkish state for the settling of intra-village disputes, the village council and the village *muhtar*[14]. They use other informal means of settling disagreements. However, when the disagreements become too sharp, or one of the parties is litigiously inclined, then there is ready resort to the official courts. Starr summarizes the position as follows:

'These cases [the ones she has just been outlining] also reveal that villagers are not opposed to asking Turkish authorities to intervene when they feel that their self-interest is served by so doing. Village attitudes are not uniformly closed against Turkish law enforcement and bureaucratic agents; any individual who invokes them will not necessarily be censored [sic], ridiculed, or ostracized. Remote and isolated as Mandalinci villagers seem to be in some respects, they use law enforcement agencies of the state when it suits their purposes. This means that Mandalinci villagers have been drawn into the national Turkish administrative system and thus have become receptive to the value system inherent in and promoted by the Turkish legal codes.'[15]

A most important consideration helping to strengthen resort to the official formalities for registering marriages is the necessity, in modern bureaucratic procedures, for a married person to demonstrate officially

14. At p. 182.
15. At p. 200.

that he is married if he is seeking any of the benefits provided, say, by the welfare or tax system to the married. Wives could not get marriage allowances in respect of their husbands in the Army unless they could show that their marriage was registered and thus official.

On the face of it, then, the Turkish reforms seem a permanent success, as the new generation becomes habituated to them and accepts them into their consciousness and the patterns of their daily behaviour. But before we jump to this conclusion, it is as well to pause. External conformity may mask an internal rejection. There is now an even chance that the gales of Islamic regression which are sweeping the Middle East and Asia generally will not leave Turkey untouched. In the next five years one can foresee the possibility of the Ataturk reforms being discarded, in the legal as in other spheres, and of a possible reversion to Islamic legal practices officially recognised by a restoration of its *Law*. This would spring from a disillusion with western notions, the re-assertion of traditional values, and the pull of a dominating religion. Such a regression would expose the acceptance of the secular and western codes as being superficial only. From this we can learn a further general lesson: *a general acceptance of a new law may be superficial only, and easy to reverse, if there is no internalisation of it or incorporation of it into customary patterns of thought and behaviour*: and this despite the lapse of half a century or more since the reforms were imposed.

(e) Race relations and equal opportunities laws in Britain

The laws in Britain which proscribe racial and sex discrimination are very recent. The history of the evolution of such laws, and the gradual struggle for sex equality (since the Married Women's Property Act of 1882) and for racial equality (since the second world war), is a complicated one, which I cannot possibly trace in detail here. The present laws are themselves complicated, and raise many issues of jurisprudence and policy which again I cannot deal with: so much is this so that agitation, concern or action about race relations in Britain has now been dignified with the description of an 'industry', by which is meant a complex of pressure groups, official bureaucracies and institutions which have a vested interest in the field. As for sex discrimination, we are just at the beginning of a new social revolution of as yet unchartable dimensions. My own concern here is with one minor aspect of this whole, the effectiveness of the laws which now provide for the prevention of discrimination. What we must ask is: (i) What is the role of law in the prevention of discrimination? (ii) By what means were these laws introduced, and how far were they and are they acceptable to those subjected to them? (iii) What are the prospects of success of these laws; and, if they prove to be relatively ineffective, what are the reasons for this ineffectiveness?

There is no doubt that these laws represent a change of attitude and a change of policy on the part of the law-making authorities. While the abolition of slavery, and the earlier and historic judgment of Lord Mansfield in *Sommersett's Case*,[16] established or re-affirmed the principle that all human beings were carriers of rights under the common law, this was by no means the same as saying that persons subject to the law had the same status, and hence the same pattern of rights and duties attaching to them. The common law (like the customary *Laws*) was a system of differential statuses: some classes of persons were differentiated against on grounds of weakness, e.g. infants; some on grounds of social status, e.g. as voters to Parliament; some on grounds of sex, i.e. women; some on grounds of origin, e.g. non-citizens, some on grounds of religion, e.g. Catholics. The reduction and virtual elimination of these differential statuses have been a very slow business. Women achieved gradual economic emancipation from what was previously almost total servitude to their husbands, beginning with the Married Women's Property Act 1870 — a process which only now is reaching completion; but their differential political status was not cured until the 20th century. Religious discrimination has now been almost totally removed (with the exception of the discrimination against Catholics in regard to the Throne and royal family). Discrimination on grounds of weakness has been retained; we may term this protective discrimination; indeed, new categories of protected persons, such as consumers, have been discovered. Discrimination on grounds of origin, at the unofficial level, has been reduced through the legislation we shall be looking at in a moment (though discrimination at the official level, e.g. in regard to immigration and rights of citizenship, remains).

This movement towards treating all as equal before the *Law* seemed to have reached a resting point in the immediate post-war period. The answer to allegations of discriminatory treatment by individuals of other individuals was that all were equal in the eyes of the *Law*, and all were equally entitled to the protection of the *Law*. Colour-blindness and sex-blindness were the official policy. In itself this was a praiseworthy stance, if one accepts such an objective as desirable; but the critics of the *Law* said that it did not go far enough, because it ignored (a) economic and social realities, such as the virtual monopoly in family property enjoyed by the husband in marital households, and (b) discretionary discrimination not caught by existing laws in such fields as the engagement of labour or the letting of houses and flats. The agitation for changes in the *Law*, (a) to change the balance of social realities by introducing new vested rights for those currently deprived of them, and (b) to bring new areas of discrimination within the reach of the *Law*, mounted in the post-war years, undoubtedly fed by the parallel movement, first to racial equality and then to sex equality, in the United States.

16.   (1772) 20 State Tr 1.

The attitude and policy of the official authorities, the governments of the day and those who guided them, changed in response to these pressures from pressure-groups. The change in attitude was official in the one case (at the governmental level) and sectional in the other (in that membership of these pressure-groups was tiny and unrepresentative of the nation at large). This left popular attitudes in an unconsulted limbo, and created the tensions between laws and people which we must now explore. In this exploration, it is most important to emphasize, I am not making a judgment as to the desirability of the liberal objectives which these laws express. One might well say that they are in essence admirable. But this is not to deal with the question whether laws are the right instruments for achieving these objectives, and whether the laws actually enacted have proved successful – these are matters of political judgment on the one hand, and of sociological observation on the other. To criticise the laws is not to criticise the objectives; I under-line this point because one is now confronted with the predictable reaction to any criticism of these laws that one is thereby demonstrating or favouring discrimination. Quite the contrary: an ineffective law which tries to eliminate discrimination may itself favour discrimination by convincing people that the objective is itself undesirable.

I deal first with racial discrimination.

Racial discrimination

(i)   The role of law. The original role of *Law* (as already noted) was seen to be neutral – to abstain from discrimination. The weapons and the rights of *Law* were seen as available to all its subjects equally. Now the position is quite different. There is first the public order aspect. The Public Order Act 1936 had originally been passed to strengthen the law for the maintenance of public peace and order in face of the threat posed by the provocative actions of the then Fascists and the conflicts between them and their communist opponents. The Fascists played the race card, or the anti-Jewish card; but the Act struck mainly at the formal means by which this sort of policy was pushed forward – the wearing of uniforms, the marches – and not at the policies and attitudes themselves – the anti-semitism, the racialism. The Race Relations Act 1965 was the first breakthrough for those who had long advocated the use of law to enforce better race relations; its section 6 created a new offence of incitement to racial hatred. What was caught was public behaviour with public consequences; this behaviour included publishing or distributing threatening, abusive or insulting written matter, and the use of words at a public meeting or in a public place, with the intention of stirring up racial hatred. This criminal weapon against the expression of racialist views was hedged about with safeguards, notably the requirement that there must be an intention – very difficult to prove –

to stir up racial hatred; and secondly, the need to obtain the consent of the Attorney-General to a prosecution. The section was little used, and speeches of prominent politicians which their opponents felt stirred up racial feelings were not proceeded against, presumably because of the difficulties in proving a deliberate intention.

There were two ways of dealing with this evident failure of the law. The first was to repeal it; the second was to strengthen it. The latter course was followed in the new, and current, Race Relations Act 1976 by section 70. This did two important things: it transferred the provision to the Public Order Act 1936, in which it now figures as section 5A; and it removed the need to prove intention. Now the offence of publishing, etc, material is established solely by evidence that it is

'a case where, having regard to all the circumstances, hatred is likely to be stirred up against any racial group in Great Britain by the matter or words in question'.

In other words, persons are fixed with legal responsibility for the natural and probable consequences of their acts, and there is no need to prove a specific intent. However, in accordance with the general requirements of *mens rea*, a general intent to commit the acts which will bring the offender within the provision must still be proved. The recent trial of Robert Relf has shown this law in operation. The criminal side of disturbing race relations is thus segregated from the civil side.

On the civil side, there has been a history of rapid evolution of the law. This has been always in the direction of creating new and more powerful enforcement bodies for pursuing infringements of the law, and in creating more stringent requirements designed to prevent racial discrimination, and which penetrate further and further into the ordinary private civil relations between citizen and citizen. The first and landmark Act, that of 1965, dealt only with discrimination in places of public resort. There was reluctance to extend the law to other areas, such as housing and employment, this reluctance being inspired by doubts as to whether the law could work in such areas. These doubts were assuaged by the *Street Report* on Anti-Discrimination Legislation published in October 1967. The consequence was the enactment of the Race Relations Act 1968; this struck at discrimination in the provision of goods, services and facilities, and now extended for the first time to education and employment. A Race Relations Board was established to police the Act; but the main chosen means of proceeding was by way of conciliation (i.e. persuasion) rather than litigation or compulsion.

This law in its turn was judged ineffective. It was judged ineffective on at least two counts. The first was the absence of sufficiently sharp teeth. The second was the inability to affect and transform structural discrimination in housing and unemployment especially. The current Race Relations Act 1976 was designed to deal with both these weaknesses. It substantially extends the definition of discrimination, and now covers both 'direct discrimination' and 'indirect discrimination'. Direct discrimination by section 1 (1) (a) covers cases where a person 'on racial grounds . . . treats [another person] less favourably than he treats or would treat other persons'. 'Indirect discrimination' is covered by section 1 (1) (b), whose terms are so complex that they are best reproduced verbatim:

'[A person discriminates against another in any circumstances relevant for the purposes of any provision of this Act if −]

   (b) he applies to that other a requirement or condition which he applies or would apply equally to persons not of the same racial group as that other but −

      (i)   which is such that the proportion of persons of the same racial group as that other who can comply with it is considerably smaller than the proportion of persons not of that racial group who can comply with it; and

      (ii) which he cannot show to be justifiable irrespective of the colour, race, nationality or ethnic or national origins of the person to whom it is applied; and

      (iii) which is to the detriment of that other because he cannot comply with it.'

Direct discrimination involves a perception of consequences by the discriminator; he applies his mind to the situation of the victim, and this is what influences his discriminating behaviour. Indirect discrimination may be quite unconscious, however; not in the sense that the discriminator did not intend his actions, but that the discriminatory consequences of his actions (as defined by the Act) may have been entirely outside his perception and unwilled by him. To that extent the Act catches involuntary non-conforming behaviour. Language tests for steel-workers are just one example: do they discriminate against Asian employees?

The main thrust of the 1976 Act is directed at employment. A much more active policy is now followed; and the new Commission for Racial Equality has been given power to investigate company employment policies for evidence of discrimination. Those who apply for jobs, those in them who seek promotion or to enjoy other benefits or privileges, those who are dismissed, can all claim the right not to be discriminated against on grounds of race, colour, etc.

Another important area of enforcement is in property transactions, including those between private citizens. The 1976 Act repeats and strengthens the provisions of the 1968 Act in this area. A vendor or lessor of property, for instance, must not discriminate against prospective purchasers or tenants on racial grounds.

On the enforcement side, there are now two main channels of enforcement. The first is provided by the newly established Commission for Racial Equality. This can conduct formal investigations of organisations or individuals; it can subpoena witnesses and documents for such investigations. It can issue non-discrimination notices to ban contravening practices, and can apply for injunctions to restrain breaches of such notices. Individuals too have a remedy under the Act. They can seek the aid of the Commission, or pursue their remedy on their own account. If the matter is an employment one, then the correct tribunal is an industrial tribunal.If the matter does not concern employment, the correct forum is the County Court in England and the Sheriff Court in Scotland. In race discrimination cases the judge or sheriff does not sit alone, but sits with two lay assessors advisory to him, and drawn from a panel.[17]

The courts are to treat complaints of racial discrimination as if they were claims in tort; the measure of damages in such cases includes not only the usual heads of damage, but compensation for injury to feelings. What the law has done, then, is to create a new family of torts. Where an industrial tribunal is asked to deal with an employment case, other powers come into play. It can order compensation up to a maximum of £5,200; it can make an order which declares the rights of the parties; it can recommend remedial action to be taken by the discriminator.

How successful all these provisions have been is a question which we postpone to our discussion under (iii).[18] We can summarise the position by saying that the proponents of racial non-discrimination see law and more law as the most effective, though not the sole, means of bringing it about.

(ii) The introduction of these laws. To put the matter quite straightforwardly, the race relations laws were not the result of popular demand or pressure. They were advocated, and eventually realised, by a small and concerned minority, or set of minorities, organised as pressure groups and wielding power and influence, direct or indirect, on the making of law. The first Act of 1965 was the result of repeated attempts to get a private member's bill through Parliament (on nine separate occasions). The pressure-groups included, at an early stage, the British Caribbean Association, church bodies, and other race relations organisations. By 1964 the introduction of a Race Relations Bill had become Labour Party policy; and when it came into power in 1964 it set about redeeming this promise. The Labour Party commitment had been worked out by the Society of Labour Lawyers (itself a pressure-group), which had been given the task of revising the Bill put forward by Fenner Brockway from time to time as a private venture. The Bill was further revised after consultation with the Opposition, and managed to pass into law in 1965, though shorn of its criminal sanctions and with its operation limited to public places. The newly formed Campaign

17. The influence of African experience (where trial with assessors is common) on this provision may be suspected.
18. See pp. 233 ff, below.

Against Racial Discrimination had a hand in the discussion, as did Maurice Foley, the new and specially appointed minister charged with responsibility for this area.

If we ask what role the public and public opinion had in the formation and drafting of this first Bill, the answer must be almost nil. The Bill was smuggled through Parliament, in a curious way which has been described by one writer as 'a haphazard, secret and inefficient process'.[19] If the people were not consulted (and it is not possible to build a theory of general popular acceptance on the mere fact that Labour had included a proposal for legislation in its campaign manifesto), what was their presumed reaction to the new law? The study by Rose,[20] published in 1969 and carefully documented, essays to discover this reaction. Dr Mark Abrams describes the results in Part VII under the heading of 'Attitudes of the British Public'. A five-borough intensive survey was made in 1966–67, and a less intensive national survey in March and April 1967. The boroughs were selected as places where there was a substantial immigrant population. The survey identified only 10 per cent of the respondents from the adult white population in the five boroughs as being 'highly prejudiced'. This prejudice was spread over all classes and components of society. The survey team advised that, in attempts to improve race relations, one must expect the prejudiced 10 per cent to retain their 'irrational' prejudices whatever was done. 55 per cent of the population made specific and limited criticisms, which the survey attributes partly to error or misunderstanding. Later research in 1967 and 1968 specifically sought to ascertain popular attitudes to race relations legislation.[1] We may quote from the table (at p. 597) which sets out the results of the answer to the specific question, 'Do you approve of legislation against discrimination?' (or, after April 1968, 'Do you approve of the Race Relations Bill?'):

	ORC, 1967	Gallup, early '68	ORC 1968	Gallup, late April '68	NOP, May '68
Yes	58	42	53	30	44
No	31	29	36	46	44
Don't know	10	29	11	24	12

It will be seen that three polls showed more Yeses than Noes; one poll showed more Noes than Yeses; and one showed exactly the same figure. The significant shift in opinion apparently shown in the last two polls suggests both the volatility of the responding public and the effect of the bringing of the matter into public consciousness by the

19. As quoted by E. J. B. Rose et al., in *Colour and Citizenship: a Report on British Race Relations* (London, 1969), p. 226.
20. Op. cit.
1. See op. cit., pp. 596 ff.

introduction of a Bill in Parliament and a widely reported speech by
Enoch Powell MP.

Nothing like a consensus in favour of legislation is shown by this
evidence. It is even doubtful whether, at the time, there was a majority
of the general public in favour of legislation. Whether this matters or
not depends on whether one attaches importance to popular acceptance
as either a necessary condition for the effectiveness of law, or as a
moral requirement in a democratic society. The elitist approach to
legislation would deny the latter; the dictatorial, compulsive approach
would deny the former. The best that can be said is that there was not
overwhelming popular rejection of the elite-sponsored legislation (as
there was, and has been, with legislation abolishing the death penalty).

However, there are two other and related aspects which must be
mentioned. There is first the aspect of *superficial conformism*. In a
society in which a person feels that it is no longer respectable or
permitted to entertain an opinion which he considers is contradictory
of the official and general line of thought reaching him from the media,
from government, and otherwise, he will keep his opinion to himself
and conform in his outward response to what he thinks is the permitted
line. We can easily trace such a response in many societies and situations:
citizens in modern eastern European communist states soon learn to
conform to the formal verbal requirements of marxism, and their
internal rejection of this conformism is only demonstrated when a
revolution occurs, as with the Prague Spring of 1968, which showed
that 90 per cent of the Czech population did not subscribe to the
communist thesis. Citizens in religiously-dominated societies also learn
a similar conformism of word and behaviour. What is said in reply to an
opinion pollster, and what is said and thought in the privacy of one's
own home or work-place, may thus be quite different: the respondent
gives the pollster what he thinks is the socially acceptable or demanded
answer. The second aspect is a corollary of the first: it is good policy
to disregard what people *say*, and examine what people *do*, if you want
to find out their true and genuine attitudes. Christ put it that way 2000
years ago: 'By their deeds ye shall know them.' Does popular behaviour
correspond to the thesis that prejudice is limited to the 10% prejudiced
sample which these surveys purport to throw up? I would say, No; if it
had done so, there would have been no need to enact the Race Relations
Act 1976.

This leads us on to a paradox. If public opinion is generally in favour
of non-discriminatory practice, at home, in the office or factory or elsewhere, why is it necessary to pass a special and complex law to enact
such practice? Why could not one deal with the occasional eccentricities
of the highly prejudiced either by other means (e.g. under the disturbance
of the peace or sedition provisions) or by ignoring them altogether, as
one disregards the misdemeanours of the pathologically insane with
whom this 10 per cent is sometimes compared? If public opinion is not

generally in favour of anti-discrimination legislation, where is the mandate for such legislation?

Sex equality

(i)   The role of law. The use of law to procure greater equality between the sexes long antedates, as already remarked, the passing of the Sex Discrimination Act in 1975. The Married Women's Property Act 1882 emancipated married women from the harsh common-law rule under which practically all their property upon and after marriage vested in or fell under the control of their husbands. It consolidated the work of equity and of chancery lawyers, who, in the interests of justice, had already secured this benefit for wealthy wives. The legislation was in pursuit of a social objective of equality, philosophically underpinned by the belief, as expressed by John Stuart Mill and other liberal reformers, that equality in property rights led to equality in social and political treatment. The divorce laws also unfairly favoured husbands and disadvantaged wives, and in due course these laws too were ameliorated so as to provide for equality of treatment between the spouses.

In the employment field the Equal Pay Act of 1970 was the first step; the Sex Discrimination Act 1975 introduced a broad spectrum of provisions for the greater securing of equal treatment between the sexes. The Act was notable, not only for this, but for two other points: first, although designed to eliminate all discrimination in favour of either sex, it was drafted in the feminine and not the masculine habitually employed in other statutes; 'female' embraced 'male' and not the other way round. Secondly, its terms formed the precedent upon which the Race Relations Act 1976 was drafted, with the specific purpose of trying to keep all anti-discrimination legislation in the same terms and so avoid disparities of judicial interpretation. The foundation section is section 1 (1), which says that:

'A person discriminates against a woman in any circumstances relevant for the purposes of any provision of this Act if —
   (a)   on the ground of her sex he treats her less favourably than he treats or would treat a man . . .'

The main attack of the Act is in the employment field. There is not the broad spectrum of activities caught by the Act such as one finds with the Race Relations Act. An Equal Opportunities Commission is set up to police the Act, just as the Commission for Racial Equality does with the race relations laws.

(ii)   Introduction of these laws. There is no need to dwell on the exact processes by which these various laws have come into existence, except

to say that one will not be surprised to find that once again they were not enacted in response to enormous popular demand but were rather the result of lobbying and pressure by sectional bodies and elites.

(iii) Prospects of success for the anti-discrimination laws. I propose to treat the race and sex laws together because (a) there has been convergence both of their wording and the instrumentalities through which they are enforced; (b) they are inspired by the same informing principle; (c) they meet the same kinds of resistance and problems of enforcement.

The first thing we note is the continuing failure of the race relations laws to meet the purposes set for them by their sponsors. Each in turn has been adjudged ineffective. The first Act (1965) was quickly criticised as a toothless wonder which did not get down to dealing with the real social problems. The *Street Report*, 1967, drawing on American experience and precedents, argued that it was possible to extend the ambit of the law, and to deal with discrimination in housing and employment by legal means. So the 1968 Act was passed. It was concluded that it too was unsatisfactory, because of the restriction of enforcement action to the Race Relations Board and the complexities of the conciliation machinery by which compliance was sought. More teeth were called for, and new enforcement procedures. The penal provisions of the 1965 Act were found to be inadequate, because they could be evaded by the need to prove strictly an intention to incite racial hatred.

So the current 1976 Act was passed. It amended the criminal law to remove the need to prove a special intention. It amended the civil law, as we have seen, by providing, inter alia, much more extensive policing and enforcement powers, and machinery of individual recourse to tribunals and the courts. The sponsors of this law should surely be happy by now? Not a bit of it! Ian Macdonald, an author highly sympathetic to the objectives of the legislation, in his book on the subject published in 1977,[2] declares himself not at all content with it. The civil side looks unsatisfactory, he says:

'. . . it is assumed that the enforcement of the new Act will be effective. For reasons developed more fully in later chapters, it is doubtful whether many individual victims of discrimination will be able to prove their cases either in the courts or tribunals. Secondly, most of the discrimination which occurs is hidden and indirect, and it is very doubtful if individuals will have the time, energy or resources to collect the sort of evidence which will be necessary to prove the kinds of indirectly discriminatory practices referred to in s. 1 (1) (*b*) of the Act.'[3]

2. *Race relations: the new law* (London).
3. At p. 8.

Nor is he any happier with the penal provisions in section 5A of the Public Order Act:

'What is not at all clear is whether the changes in the law are going to make the slightest difference. Proof that an offence has been committed will be easier. But it can as easily be used against the black community as it can against the inflammatory propaganda of racists and fascists. The stated aim of the provision is to reduce racial tension, but all it is likely to do is to change the style of racialist propaganda, make it less blatantly bigoted, and therefore more respectable.'[4]

There have been opposite reactions to the lack of effectiveness of these laws. The new provision (now in the Public Order Act, section 5A) making incitement to racial hatred a criminal offence was specifically criticised by Rose et al. writing in 1969 about its predecessor, section 6 of the Race Relations Act 1965.[5] They said:

'In our view, this provision suffers from serious disadvantages. First, by penalizing not only speech or writing which is likely to result in violence but also speech or writing which incites racial hatred, Section 6 comes close to encroaching upon freedom of speech. Secondly, in view of the existing law relating to public order, sedition, and criminal and obscene libel, it is doubtful whether Section 6 was a necessary or desirable extension of the criminal law.'

Other reasons for its rejection were that it might arouse public sympathy for those who were prosecuted, or give publicity to the views expressed, and that it would only catch the cruder expressions of racial prejudice. Lastly, it might give the impression that the law against racial discrimination was also a curtailment of freedom of expression. For all these reasons, they recommended repeal of the section. This they were not granted; and their alternative suggestion, to incorporate it in another statute such as the Public Order Act, was followed instead.

An anti-discrimination law may fail to be effective, (a) because it meets with too great a degree of internal public resistance, both in custom and in attitude; or (b) because the machinery for enforcement has to be more complicated and expensive than the state can find resources for. The anti-discrimination legislation may be seen as programmatic law in its acutest form: it seeks a fundamental transformation of vital sectors of public behaviour through law. Can the programme succeed? Our first difficulty is that we are probably not much better informed about its success than we are about the success of the Turkish Civil Code. There is probably a hidden dark mass of actions and activities which theoretically contravene the laws and of which we – that is, the official machinery – learn nothing. The very small number of prosecutions for racial offences suggests difficulty of application as

4. At p. 139.
5. Op. cit., p. 687.

much as a high standard of conformity. The machinery of the civil law becomes ever more ponderous. Can one expect a transforming law which has to overcome deep-rooted prejudices to be likely to succeed if its terms are so complicated as to defy simple explanation? The arcane wording of the provisions on indirect discrimination illustrates this point: not one citizen in a thousand could hope to be aware of the effect of such provisions, or indeed to allow them to affect his behaviour. Keeping law simple seems a sound policy. The multiplication of provisions, crimes, procedures, agencies is not the assertion of strength but of weakness. In the continual tightening up of the legislation to overcome previous ineffectiveness one is reminded of the vain attempts of the Kenya government to repress robbery with violence by ever more punitive sanctions. In the Kenya case increasing the penalty, then providing for minimum sentences of imprisonment for the offence, then making it capital, have gone hand in hand with an ever-increasing crime rate. Deterrence did not work. Is there more hope in the equality field in Britain? One doubts it. Rather is it likely that citizens will become disillusioned and hence less ready to accept the law, whether applying for them or against them, and will be led finally to disregard it. I have already mentioned the resistances to transforming laws of this kind – to accept that governments cannot achieve everything, including making people good, by legislation is not a counsel of despair but a counsel of prudence.[6]

It is answered to this last point that the legislation touches on exterior behaviour only; and at this level it can be effective – people will conform out of fear even if their hearts are not changed. To this there is a double response: first, that the law will be much more difficult to enforce if this is the only type of conformity which can be achieved; and secondly, that in any event it is the aim of the law to change people's hearts as well as their behaviour. Superficial conformism to the law will be shed as soon as it is safe to do so; some future political or economic calamity could easily provoke this kind of reaction, and the watering down of the law. Rose et al.[7] argue strongly against the view that laws cannot change attitudes. Drawing on American experience, they say that:

'. . . individuals predisposed towards hostility to Negroes for personality reasons (authoritarianism) express that hostility when the social situation permits it, but suppress it in situations where it is unacceptable. In this

6. The point was put sharply by the American James Coolidge Carter, writing in 1900 in his book *Law: its origin, growth and function* (New York), at p. 22:

   'Nothing is more attractive to the benevolent vanity of men than the notion that they can effect great improvement in society by the simple process of forbidding all wrong conduct or conduct which they think is wrong, by law, and enjoining all good conduct by the same means'.
7. Op cit., p. 592.

sense, the old saying is quite untrue: men's hearts *can* be changed by passing laws. Evidence over time from opinion polls shows that in the Deep South attitudes towards Negroes have become consistently more favourable as Civil Rights legislation has broken down discriminatory barriers between the races.'

Yes, there *can* be a change over time, if the provisions of the new laws are internalised and reflected in new custom; but I would suggest that in such cases it is not the law which changes attitudes so much as the accompanying education and persuasion. There is a great risk of attributing to the law the transforming effect which belongs to the education. But at the same time the effect of the forcible suppression of habitual practices and attitudes may be to build up a head of resentment which will eventually explode with much more dramatic and deleterious effects than prevailed before the law came into force. It can thus be a race between two forces pulling in opposite directions.

Think back for a moment to the Indian situation. Legislation against discrimination on caste grounds seems to have had minimal effect on social practices or attitudes. It is ironical that some of those who may now complain about discrimination in Britain on racial grounds may be perpetuating *within* their communities the same discriminations that are objectionable outside them. My personal view is that the elaborate structure of anti-discrimination legislation is misconceived and self-defeating. *Much simpler and less ambitious laws would in the long run stand a greater chance of success.* This must be our last lesson from these examples.

7 The no-law state: power, dictate and discretion

'We called this chapter "The Law Today". It should rightly be called "There Is No Law".

The same treacherous secrecy, the same fog of injustice, still hangs in our air, worse than the smoke of city chimneys.

For half a century and more the enormous state has towered over us, girded with hoops of steel. The hoops are still there. There is no law.'

(A. Solzhenitsyn *The Gulag Archipelago* (vol. 3, trans. H. T. Willetts, London, 1978), p. 525.)

These, the final words from Solzhenitsyn's last chapter in the third and final volume of his great work, are an epitaph and an epitome of Soviet power in the Soviet state. The USSR, as Solzhenitsyn presents it in his powerful diagnosis, has no predictable system of *Law*; it has an arbitrary system of sanctions meted out by courts which act according to the secret discretions and instructions of party officials, from which there is no appeal, and to whom there is no possibility of effective argument. He concludes:

'The Law in our country, in its might and its flexibility, is unlike anything called "law" elsewhere on earth.'

Law, we have said, implies regularity; it consists largely of 'rules'.[1] Although we do not have to go as far as Austin in demanding that legal imperatives should be general or universal in character, we habitually oppose 'law', the general rule, and 'discretion', the possibility of acting without prior commitment to any particular rule. The American realists and others have discussed 'law' in terms of predictability, borrowing some elements from those of natural laws. The prediction of what the courts will decide is one possible definition of the *Law* in action. But imagine prediction without information; the jurist who knows none of the 'rules' or laws, and who cannot detect any regularities in the behaviour of the courts he is observing, will be as lost in making his

---

1. See Chapter 1, pp. 18 ff.

predictions as the punter who has to bet on horses without knowing any of their previous form, and without access to the guidance of experts in the newspapers. Prediction becomes a farce; the decisions of courts and other tribunals become literally unpredictable. The matter is as serious when it comes to criticisms of the *Law* as in its ascertainment; we habitually contrast the 'Rule of Law' (which I refer to under the head of 'legality'), where people are only liable to be punished or disadvantaged by the legal system in accordance with fair, known, and equally applied rules, with the arbitrary state, the discretionary state.

Is the Soviet Union a 'no-law state'? Indeed, is it unique in being so, if it is? Because, if it is such a state, our analysis will be left in confusion, and the assumptions, not only of previous Chapters of this work but of many jurists, will be falsified. We have assumed that *Law* is a product of a 'political society'; this term was defined broadly, so as to bring in societies at different stages of cultural evolution. The attack on smaller and simpler ('primitive') societies and their *Laws* was beaten off: the accusation that their norms were not legal, not part of a *Law*, was rejected, and — on the analysis adopted — refuted. Have we succeeded in bringing the systems of norms operating in the smallest and least powerful societies within the ambit of *Law* only to let the normative systems of the largest and most powerful states escape from that ambit? Kelsen believed that law and the state were effectively aspects of the same phenomenon differently presented; on a Kelsenite analysis, should one conclude that the Soviet Union has no *Law*? Or, an even more difficult conclusion, accept that it is therefore not a state?

We should not be deceived by appearances. The Soviet Union has a constitution, as do each of its constituent republics. There are several all-union codes of law, and each union republic has at least a dozen such codes for various branches of law. There is a whole apparatus of legal institutions — courts, judges, lawyers, law faculties. But, if we accept the argument of Solzhenitsyn and of the others, lawyers and non-lawyers, who have described the Soviet system in similar terms, there is scant correspondence between the letter of the *Law* and the behaviour and experience of these institutions. The Soviet constitution, as is well known, contains many articles which declare or protect fundamental rights, such as the freedom of association, of worship, of free speech. The same critics allege that they are not observed in practice. But non-observance goes deeper, according to Solzhenitsyn; in the practical day-to-day administration of the penal 'law' courts do not do what rational courts do in other parts of the world, investigate the facts, try to discover the truth, determine which are the relevant articles or principles of the laws, and apply them justly and fairly to the case before them. No, says Solzhenitsyn: the facts, the evidence, the arguments of the accused, have no effect on the decision of the court or its sentence. These are determined by political instructions to the court on the telephone from above, and are calculated solely in accordance with the political interests and perceptions of the ruling power-structure or bureaucracy.[2]

It would be premature at this stage of our enquiry to decide whether Solzhenitsyn's account is an accurate picture of the Soviet legal system, or an exaggeration (based, maybe, on characteristic features of the present or former system of penal justice) which forms the basis of a polemic against the type of ruling structures found in the Soviet Union. Many competent students of the Soviet *Law* in action would claim that there are serious exaggerations and misconceptions in his account; as for human rights and their observance in the USSR, apart from actual instances of departures from the generally proclaimed (though not necessarily generally observed) standards accepted internationally, some of the difficulty for a western observer may lie in the quite different conceptions of rights and of human rights which apparently prevail in the Soviet system. But, for our general analysis of *Law* and its limits, the Solzhenitsyn thesis remains an important challenge, even if factually unjustified in this case. The challenge is to the analyses of western jurists, who earnestly discuss the role of the judge, judicial logic, and even the 'leeway' open to a judge through creative interpretation or the matching of facts to norms.

Without rules and rational application of them (and however far one goes in accepting the realist hypothesis which sees judges as being influenced by non-rational and emotional factors), these analyses (based on western *Laws*) would, if Solzhenitzyn is right, have as little application to the realities of the Soviet power apparatus as the writings of medieval theologians about the personalities and characteristics of angels and devils had to real people living in real societies.

It would not be fair to say that western jurists have entirely ignored communist legal theory. Several writers[3] have written studies of marxist legal theory, of which one notable example is the book by Hans Kelsen on *The Communist Theory of Law*.[4] But many of these studies stay expressly at the level of theory, devoting much attention to the scattered indications in Marx and Engels and later legal philosophising by such as Vyshinsky. Marxist legal theory, in Marx himself, was rudimentary; and the later developments of it, which fall into violently contrasting

2. A most amusing, and at the same time horrifying, example of this practice is given by Solzhenitsyn. A group of alleged Estonian war criminals went on trial in Tartu in 1961–2. The official journal of the Public Prosecutor's office, in its issue of 27 December 1961, reported the questioning of the witnesses in the trial, their cross-examination, the reactions of the public, the public prosecutor's speech, and the fact that sentences of death were passed. Unfortunately for the journalist, all these facts, though correct, did not happen until *after* the journal had been published, as the trial had been postponed, without the journalist's knowledge, until 16 January 1962.
3. E.g., John Hazard, R. Schlesinger, H. J. Berman, and more recently I. Lapenna.
4. London, 1955; reprint edition New York, 1976.

schools, are marked by their divergence from the practice of the Soviet (and later other communist) state. Such marxist analysis of law can best be equated with speculative theology rather than with sociological description, and marxist theories of LAW and actual communist *Laws* have little in common except the rhetoric.

Among examples of this speculative and other-worldly character of marxist legal thought, the most celebrated is the Marx-Engels line on the withering away of *Law* and the state when the communist society arrives. Most competent non-marxist jurists see this withering away theory as neither warranted by the past history of political institutions (the basis on which marxism claims to analyse and predict social development) nor at all the probable outcome of the present line of evolution in 'socialist' countries. In other words, the withering away theory, to which disproportionate attention has been devoted by marxists and non-marxists alike, is no more than romantic Utopianism, and has more in common with the offer of Paradise, in another and better world than this one, to believing Muslims or Christians than with serious analysis of legal development. Even marxist jurists in the Soviet Union and elsewhere devote little importance to this topic in their analysis of actual legal relations.

The Marx-Engels conjecture about the withering away of the state and *Law* might, if realised in the Soviet Union as it moves towards communism, have gone far to prove the assertion that the USSR is a no-law state, though for different reasons from those put forward by Solzhenitsyn. Indeed, the original theory would have seen the true communist society as a 'no-law/no-state' one. Later Soviet jurists have been careful to explain that the Soviet state is, in some way inaccessible to western jurists or careful analysis, not a 'state' in the western sense, and Soviet *Law* is not a system like bourgeois law. Despite this, Soviet jurists and legislators have tried increasingly to give a western appearance to Soviet legal institutions and the discussion of them, and have used terms and categories familiar to western jurists to describe and prescribe them.

One may search the writings of western jurists largely in vain for a discussion of the theoretical problems which the allegedly arbitrary Soviet-type legal system poses for a description of *Law*. Hart, as usual, is one worthy exception to this conclusion; in his *Concept of Law* he discussed at length a hypothetical game of 'scorer's discretion'. As we shall see when we examine this example more closely, Hart concludes that such a game would be fundamentally different in character from the sort of game where there are rules, and the scorer can be appealed to to say how they should apply in the particular situation to which a game has come at any stage.[5] Hart does not in terms refer to the Soviet-type system. In fact, discussions of *Law* and non-*Law* have been directed

5. See op. cit. at pp. 138–142; and the discussion of *discretion* generally below at pp. 244, 252 ff.

at the precisely contrary case, such as was posed by Nazi Germany. The problem with the Nazi system was not that there were no laws, but that judges too faithfully adhered to them, even though an outside observer would have rated these laws as unjust. Is an unjust law a valid law? This is the converse of the Soviet case, and involves a discussion of legalism. There was no discussion whether Nazi laws lacked any of the other attributed elements of a law, like regularity and predictability.

Kelsen is a good case in point in discussing the limits on the analysis so far made of the Soviet system. If one is to write a proper and acceptable description of western legal systems today, one must deal with the actualities of the *Law*, the *Law* in action; and a purely formal analysis such as Austin attempted would no longer be enough. Even Kelsen with his pure theory of LAW was forced, as we have seen, to descend into the empirical arena. In his study of communist LAW (already cited) he is very careful to preface his work with the following disclaimer:

'Finally, the author wishes to make it as clear as possible that he is not dealing with communist law but with the general theory of law advanced by writers applying, or pretending to apply, the principles of communism; and he is dealing with the policy of the communist government of the Soviet Union only in so far as this policy influences the communist theory of law.'[6]

In other words, his book is not a guide to the actual practice and experience of Soviet *Law*.

These strictures do not apply to the work of H. J. Berman, whose *Justice in the USSR*[7] is one of the most stimulating examinations, not only of modern Soviet *Law* and its development, but of its philosophical and national origins. Berman is concerned to see modern Soviet *Law* as a new type of *Law*, partly Russian, partly socialist, and partly original. His starting point is a distinction between 'official law' and 'unofficial law', which echoes many of the analyses and points identified by myself in the present work. He says (at p. 279):

'To understand a legal system it is necessary to distinguish between the official law proclaimed by the state and the unofficial law which exists in the minds of men and in the various groups to which they belong. Each of us has his own conception of rights, duties, privileges, powers, immunities — his own law-consciousness. And within each of the communities in which we live — the family, school, church, factory, commercial enterprise, profession, neighborhood, city, region, nation — there is likewise an unofficial and largely unwritten pattern of obligations and sanctions. The official law of the state, with its authoritative technical language and its professional practitioners, cannot do violence to the unofficial law-consciousness of the people

6. At p. viii.
7. Revised ed., Camb., Mass., 1963.

without creating serious tensions in society. At the same time, official law is more than a reflection of popular law-consciousness; it also shapes it, directly or indirectly.'

Berman argues that Marx/Engels envisaged a society with no official law, so that in a classless society control will rest in the mores of the good society, its habits and standards. The task of the Soviet law-givers is seen by them to be to shape this eventual unofficial law-consciousness as it will emerge, through the present legal system (the official *Law*). He discusses at length the educational role of *Law* in the Soviet Union, which he sees (and the rulers see) as all-important. Soviet *Law* has broad ambitions, and invades spheres of private life out of which *Law* normally stays in western society. Soviet *Law* is 'parental law', he says, and treats the whole nation like one enormous family. It guides, preserves and fosters relationships between the parties, and between parties and the state, by giving legal sanctions to moral obligations.

George C. Guins, in his *Soviet law and Soviet society*,[8] raised the question whether there is really any law in the Soviet Union, the issue with which our present chapter is concerned. Guins argues in the negative: 'Soviet law is an expression of might rather than of right'. Berman discusses this issue at pp. 371 ff. of his own study, rejects what he calls the 'exaggerated assertions of Soviet lawlessness', and says that Soviet *Law* and justice are central to the society. Though Soviet *Law* appears a unique departure, Berman, following Karl Llewellyn, holds that 'parental law' is the type of law which is taking over in other countries too (the law which I have christened that of the 'Nanny state').

Despite Berman's rejection of Guins's point (which echoes that of Solzhenitsyn), we must persist with our enquiry, not just into Soviet *Law* but into other legal systems in which discretion plays an important or overwhelming part. We must still ask the basic question: do western jurists follow the same sceptical approach when looking at communist legal systems as when describing western *Laws*? While recognising the considerable amount of factual study of the Soviet system which has been made in the last two or three decades, I think it would be fair to say that there is still an observable tendency to deal with the surface rather than the reality of Soviet *Law*. The same criticism, it will be remembered, could have been made about western juristic writing on 'primitive law' a few decades ago. Such writing was library work, generated from the top of the jurist's head or the seat of his pants rather than from accurate observation and careful reflection. Diamond's books on primitive law are examples of this library approach at its best; their validity vanishes as soon as empirical studies are made of simpler societies and their results are analysed by a master, such as the late Max

8. The Hague, 1954, p. 362.

Gluckman, just as theories about the surface of the moon were invalidated overnight when the first astronauts landed on it. And, it is important to recall, the same criticism can still be made of many accounts of western *Laws*, despite all the opportunities for realist sociolegal enquiry which now present themselves in the West.

In other words, to an outside observer western jurists have not yet got round to the task of making studies of Soviet *Law* in action to the same extent and in the same way as the studies of legal sociologists and ethnojurists in the underdeveloped world. The political, financial and physical obstacles in the way of their so doing are patent and need not be detailed (even researchers into *Law* in Britain are not unfamiliar with the obstacles erected by bureaucratic secrecy and structures!). But this partial lack of information means that jurists have to draw on materials which writers and subjects within the system – such as Solzhenitsyn and others – can provide, just as earlier anthropologists went to the wise ones of the tribe to seek information about their customary *Laws*. Such materials are not enough, but they are a start, and they are a corrective. At the same time one must underline the limitations of such materials. Experienced researchers into customary *Laws* are familiar with the dangers of taking what the elders say about their own *Law* as unchallengeable gospel; often they describe an idealised picture of a *Law* which never was, or only existed in the remote past. A similar distortion, though in a negative sense, is possible from those who have suffered under a Soviet-type system.

However, one must confront the fact that the relative absence or neglect of practical studies of Soviet and similar systems in action limits and impoverishes the world-wide reach of juristic analysis, and can throw open the dicta of jurists to as yet unpredictable qualifications as the result of further study, so that their entire theories of LAW or *Law* may be thrown into doubt or completely controverted in the future. I cannot pretend to have made such studies myself; I too am limited by the material which is available; but I can at least raise the doubts which already occur. It is important to note that these doubts remain important and valid even if it turns out that the account of Solzhenitsyn and others is erroneous, and that things do not happen, or do not always happen, the way they say they do. We must sfill meet the challenge of the 'no-law state'. We must still explain how a legal system can exist which is based on discretion and not on rule. We must still answer the question whether a state can exist without a legal system based on rules.

Once, however, our curiosity is aroused by this summary picture of Soviet *Law*, we may look around us and see that the Soviet Union is not unique in its juristic problems. It is not only other communist and socialist countries that may exemplify the same characteristics (and China's *Law* still remains largely a thing unknown); but many other countries of various kinds present some or all of the same features. The

Uganda of Idi Amin had claims to be a 'no-law state', except that there one found no centralised and all-powerful bureaucracy, but rather the uncertain will of one all-powerful man. The courts still functioned in Uganda; there was still a Chief Justice; the Law Faculty at the University of Makerere still studied something which it called 'the law of Uganda' — in other words, the contradictions were present there too. Wherever military men have seized power in a coup, as in so many countries of Asia, Africa and Latin America, it is the gun which rules, it is the discretion of the military hierarchy which determines what is lawful and lawless at any one time. Under military rule in Nigeria, which preserved some of the federal elements of the constitution though asserting the supreme power of the Federal Military Government to make laws throughout the country, a former military governor of the North was accustomed to make laws ('Edicts' in the official terminology) which a citizen could only know about by listening to the radio. The radio one evening would tell the citizen, if he had a set and listened to it, that a new and maybe draconian law had just been made by the military governor; if he did not hear such a broadcast, he might retrospectively find to his peril that something which he believed to be legal had suddenly become illegal. This was the problem of 'off-the-cuff', immediate, secret, arbitrary law-making.

It is not, though, only in communist countries that officials have discretionary power to decide the rights, privileges, and penalties of citizens. Administrative discretion runs largely unchecked through the western bureaucracies. Of course these discretions are exercised within the *Law*, in terms of enabling powers given by some specific enactment; so that the discretionary powers are in our terms 'catanomic' and not 'paranomic', whereas in the Soviet Union the discretions appear to be paranomic. But the extent of the operation of such discretions is essentially limitless, and the results of such operation not precisely predictable. Are we then to say that in western countries too we find a no-law situation? Or perhaps a state with a 'half-*Law*' rather than with a *Law*?

Furthermore, it was one of the complaints against *Law* in customary societies that it contained so large an element of discretion that it could not be said that there were fixed rules of law. This complaint was dealt with by showing that discretion is a universal feature of legal systems.

A whole series of questions is provoked by the alleged situation in the USSR:

(i)   What are the relations between law and power?
(ii) How far is dictate a source of law, or the negation of law?
(iii) Is it what the legal norm says, or what people do, that constitutes the valid legal norm?
(iv) What is the role of discretion in legal systems generally?
(v)   Is the no-law state a fact or a phantom?

Law and power

Law is about power and its exercise; on this most of the jurists agree. *Law* and power are connected firstly by the function of power as the *basis* of *Law*. Secondly, laws prescribe who may *exercise* powers. Olivecrona's thesis was simple: law (? = LAW or *Law*) is to be seen as 'rules about force'. *Law* regulates the use of force (= physical force) in society. To Kelsen laws lay down the sanctions which are to apply or be applied if a particular norm is transgressed. Laws are about sanctions, and sanctions are about the application of physical force. Let us separate these two conceptions, of (i) force as the basis of *Law*, and (ii) *Law* as the allocation of power.

The basis of a *Law* or legal system must be that one set of persons is issuing normative statements to another set of persons telling them what they must or may do or may not do. The form of these normative statements has been analysed already.[9] Anyone can issue normative statements to anyone else about anything; what makes legal normative statements special are the character and the claims of those who make the statements, and the consequences which may follow non-compliance. Those who issue legal norms are those with roles of power and influence in the society, to whom society attributes 'authority', whether that authority is gained by respect and competence in the sense of skilfulness, or is wrested by force and demonstrated power. Power may be conceded or taken, then. In the latter case it creates its own competence, in the sense of the right to issue imperatives of a legal kind.

The situation is not different where the persons issuing (emitting) legal norms are, or are drawn from, those to whom norms are directed. This situation prevails in many customary societies, where members of the society construct and help to shape and emit the norms; but it prevails too in democratic societies where the law-makers are drawn from the subjects of the *Law* and are not set in opposition to them. Power is power even if it is voluntarily granted.

A norm-emitter loses his competence to emit valid norms if he is deprived of this power by means already provided for within the normative system (as with a change of government after an election), or if forcibly removed (as by a revolt), or if he abdicates his power, or if he finds that no one listens to and complies with the norms he emits. This last case causes the greatest theoretical problems. Non-compliance thus not only limits the effectiveness of particular norms, which will be valid but frustrate, but may call in question and eventually delete the power to issue norms of any kind, by refusing the authority previously conceded to the norm-emitter. A government or ruler in exile may continue to make 'laws'; but they will cease to be valid norms within the system. The system has been changed.

9. See Chapter 1, above, at pp. 19 ff.

Who or what gives the norm-emitter power to make norms? In the case of societies where the constitution is democratic, as in many customary societies and in modern western states, the power is apparently conceded by those who will be affected by its exercise. But this concession is generally of a non-particular nature; there is not a new commitment of competence to an incoming ruler, be he king or cabinet, each time he takes office. There is rather a stepping into the well-worn shoes of the predecessor. The shoes are still there when the previous owner of them dies or is removed; they do not have to be manufactured afresh. This demonstrates what we may call the *continuity* or more aptly the *momentum* of a legal system. At any point in time what carries the *Law* on is largely the inertia of those who are subject to it and who operate it. The inertia is a tacit acceptance of the *Law*, both as a general conception and in its specific provisions, demonstrated by people's willingness to regulate their behaviour by its norms without too close an enquiry into the ultimate validating principle. This inertia is even enough to carry a society through and past a period of civil turmoil, perhaps a violent revolution, where for a time there is no clear authority, no legitimated emitter of legal norms. In such a case it is the continued conformity of the subjects of the *Law* to its provisions which constitutes its authority.

Kelsen for one, and many after him, have investigated this 'ultimate validating principle' of a legal system or legal order. Call it a *Grundnorm*, basic norm, apex norm, or what you will, it is the case that, in regressing from one norm to another norm in the search for validation, one may eventually come to a stop, to a discontinuity. The pyramidal image which 'basic norms' or 'apex norms' use is hardly an adequate one, since the *Law* is a system, and (as we have explained earlier)[10] the different parts of the system interlock and feed back information on each other in such a way as to make it difficult in all cases to say which norm is superior and which inferior. In any event, we can see the legal system as a discrete whole, interlocking whether hierarchically or circularly, and thus validating its own elements within its own structure. But what validates the system itself, the structure? It cannot be anything within the system. We move out of the system and into a different world. The system *is*. *Why* it is is a question of history or sociology and not of LAW.

Kelsenite theorising about the *Grundnorm* seemed of purely theoretical interest (as perhaps he would have wished!) until a rash of coups and unconstitutional changes of government by force made the matter one of practical politics and law-making. Violent changes of territorial boundaries by conquest and secession also raised the same issues, and were similarly frequent in the post-war world. How English and common-law judges approach these problems has been interestingly demonstrated in a trilogy of cases from the Commonwealth. The first

10. See p. 23.

was from Pakistan, *The State v Dosso* [1958] 2 PSCR 180; the second from Uganda, *Uganda v Commissioner of Prisons, ex parte Matovu* [1966] EA 514; and the third in the Privy Council, though relating to Rhodesia: *Madzimbamuto v Lardner-Burke & another* [1968] 3 All ER 561, PC.

What these cases show is that laws depend on the existence of a legal system or legal order which validates them. A legal system or *Law* is the combined product of the wills of those who have power or influence in the society where the *Law* is presumed to hold sway. Either, on the one hand, there must be some norm-generating authority which is recognised by the test of the foundation norm as having such authority to emit laws for the citizens of the society (frank legislation; court manufacture of laws), or to make constitutive acts establishing institutions in the *Law* and regulating their processes, or to make implementing orders which carry out the purposes of such laws, institutions and processes; or, on the other hand, there must be some norm-authenticating mechanism to which reference can be made when a norm appears to be a latent one, and the question of its existence and content comes in issue, as with societies governed by customary *Law*. Both types of authority are validated by their exercise; their exercise is limited by the willingness of subjects to comply. Lack of such acceptance destroys the authority. Norms purportedly issued by such an unaccepted authority? will be phantom norms, by definition invalid in that society, however much they bear the apparent marks of validity upon them.

We call it a 'foundation norm'; unlike other norms it is self-validating. To that extent it is quite unlike any other norm within the system. Indeed, in an important sense it is outside the system, and not capable of being tested by the norms of the system. In the cases just mentioned, the courts had to face a contradiction between (i) the answer offered by the norms of the system itself, which would say that the new norm-emitting authority and its norms were invalid as being in breach of the 'constitution': no constitution can authorise its own breach; and (ii) the answer given by the reality of power, that the person or body indicated by the constitution/foundation norm as having authority could not exercise it, as one fundamental condition for its exercise, viz. the securing of compliance with it, had been effectively destroyed.

The effect of the destruction of the previous foundation norm is to destroy the *Law*; the effect of the installation of a new foundation norm is to create a new *Law*. The features of the new *Law* may, except for the definition of who has norm-creating authority, be identical with the old; but it is not the old system varied, but a new system. New legal systems are not created merely by their replacing old ones; a new *Law* must emerge whenever there is a new society which demands it. The division of one old society into two or more new ones, by civil war or secession, is one example of such a process; the coming together of many different societies to form a new nation is another.

Might, then, *is* right; having power to issue norms gives one the 'right', or more precisely the 'authority', to do so. This is not to say that the exercise of this might may not be limited by the acceptance or non-acceptance by the intended recipients of its normative messages; if they do not accept these norms, then of course the power of the authority is by that fact limited. So we need not worry too much about the positivist flavour of the saying; and still less because the moral system justifies the recipients in deciding whether to offer their allegiance to the norms so emitted.

Moving now to the internal aspects of the legal system, the norms generated by the norm-emitting authority are mostly about the *allocation of power*. Some such allocations are implementive of the overall purposes of the system, as where courts are established with power to decide cases and make orders, or ministerial officers are installed as roles in the system to execute its purposes. But power can be and is allocated to ordinary citizens too, to do a variety of things which either they could not otherwise do, or could only do in a non-institutionalised form. It does not matter in a way whether one sees these enabling norms as being *concessive* — granting powers that persons would otherwise not possess, or *regulative* — controlling the exercise of powers that persons inherently have from their nature and their situation in society; because the results of such enabling norms are the same, and the limitations on them are the same, *within* the legal system, whichever philosophy we adopt. Outside the system, of course, the situation is quite different; those who argue for natural rights naturally take the point that the powers of the citizen to do any of the million things that they are able to do, from walking along the road to marrying each other, are prior to any regulation of them by any human legal system.

Exercise of subordinate powers of this kind within a *Law* is *catanomic*, or law-conforming, as we have already remarked. By using his catanomic powers, the individual (or the group) can create his own subordinate system of norms valid for himself and those affected by his action. For two persons to marry each other can thus be seen as a partial exercising by the couple of their legislative powers, as they create a normative system for themselves, which the *Law* furthers by according it recognition and protection.

Dictate as a source of law, or a negation of law

In discussing *Law* and morality[11] I had occasion to point out that many modern 'democratic' governments might be considered to be robber governments; I went further in pointing out that there seemed no distinction in principle between such governments and those which were frankly based on brute force — gunman-governments such as one

11. See pp. 151 ff. above.

finds in military regimes. I wish to argue that the *Law* of the 'democratic' but unjust state, and the *Law* of the gunman-state, are both *Law* if they satisfy our criteria. (For the removal of doubts, I repeat the point that to say that a *Law* is valid *Law* says nothing about whether the citizen should feel himself morally obliged to comply with it.) It is now time to justify this approach.

Ulpian's famous dictum,

'Quod principi placuit legis habet vigorem . . .'[12],

that whatever the ruler resolves has the force of a legislated law, may be aptly termed the 'absolutist's charter', even if it bore a more restricted meaning in imperial Rome at the time. But not everything which an absolute ruler is moved to decide can be called a 'law', if we wish to restrict the function of that term to rules which establish general principles, and by analogy to other specific rulings which are made in the same form as laws. A monarch may hear individual petitions, as with the Roman Emperor, the medieval English King, or the late Emperor of Ethiopia; his responses to such petitions are not laws, though they take effect within the legal system. A monarch may establish institutions, he may make a variety of orders, and these acts are within the legal order, i.e. they are validated by *Law*. Whether his general edicts, his specific decisions of disputes, his constitutive acts or his administrative orders are rationally motivated or proceed from caprice, whether their effects are just or unjust, matters not a whit while we remain within the legal system. A tyrannised population is still subject to the *Law*, then, even if it is gun-law.

Our problem thus transmutes from an enquiry whether the dictates of an absolute ruler are *Law* into a parallel enquiry whether such dictates are laws; and how is the citizen to know whether the ruler's dictate on a given occasion constitutes a general precept for the future as well? All that one can say is that the problem, and the test to be applied, are similar in some respects to the problem with customary normative statements. A citizen observes habitual practice around him to which people seem to conform, and wonders whether this constitutes a legal norm for him and his behaviour; is this a latent legal norm, or is it a norm of some other, non-legal, system, or no norm at all? On prudential grounds he would be well advised to conform his own behaviour to the presumed norm in the case of customary practice; and the same is true of his dealings with the dictates of the absolute ruler. The citizen may often get it wrong; though he is much more likely to be deceived with the capricious ruler in a dictatorial society than with his practice-following peers in a customary society.

A system of rule by dictate therefore poses problems for the ruled. In so far as *Law*, and laws, demand predictability, there is a risk of being unable to identify those precepts which the ruler wishes to make a

12. D 1.4.1. pr.

general norm, except retrospectively and too late after a breach has occurred. But this we have seen to be a danger also in a legal system such as that of England, through the multiplication of laws and the depth of popular ignorance about them. In the latter case English *Law* has given itself the protective principle that 'Ignorance of the law is no excuse', a principle which any dictator would be happy to adopt. We would say that the situation was not that there was no *Law*, but that its working was unsatisfactory for its subjects. *Law* does not have to be the result of democratic consultation, though such consultation and accept-ance strengthen the effectiveness of the *Law*. Law-making is (a) an exercise of the will, valid when effected; it is (b) criticised by an act of reason, which may say that it is unjust or unsatisfactory. The irrationality of the exercise of the will does not affect (a) the validity, though it may affect the assessment under (b). Dictate is thus a source of *Law*, though in its capricious and unpredictable effects it may be the negation of law.

Power commands; *Law* compels — or does it? The answer is that it does not. *Law* persuades; the persuasion may be very strong when a gun is held to your head; but everyone has the option of refusal. Popular participation in the making of laws strengthens the probability of eventual compliance with them; it is a great comfort to appreciate that a law made without popular consultation and acceptance is still subject to censorship and even rejection by its subjects, and that experience suggests that the more compulsive and arbitrary the law tries to be, the likelier it is that it will not be complied with. It is not only officials who may be remiss in enforcing it; its subjects will be tempted to dis-regard it, to bypass it. Think for a moment of the laws which proscribe or limit the right to private property in communist regimes, or which make every professional an employee of the state. They are evaded constantly, so that a complete parallel private-enterprise economy, based on barter or under-the-counter transactions, develops. The state-employed plumber comes to mend your dripping tap, *out* of the state's time and in his own, and for his own reward. Goods pass from hand to hand outside the official markets. Corruption is rife, acting as a relief from the intolerable weight of bureaucratic control. Corruption, let us remember, is not only the corrupt acceptance of money or material possessions; it is every misuse, induced by a quid pro quo or a special relation, of an official power. Those who oblige their relatives or class-mates and help them to rights or privileges which the state system does not necessarily give them are corrupt, just as the petty official who allocates a scarce resource or refrains from pursuing a minor infringe-ment of the *Law* in return for money or drink is corrupt.

Indeed, one might almost treat corruption as an index, first of the excessive weight of laws, then of their unacceptability. The growing corruption (as broadly defined) in England, non-financial as well as financial, strongly indicates an excessive weight of bureaucratic, un-acceptable laws.

So one has the choice, it seems: limited laws which are the fruit of popular participation and attract high acceptance and compliance; or excessive laws of an absolutist and arbitrary character, which attract low acceptance and compliance, and high deviance. In a word, less *Law*, or more *Law* tempered by disregard and corruption.

Law and behaviour

Uncertainty about the legal message (and whether there is one) is a difficulty at one end of the communications network; uncertainty may also be created at the other, the receiving, end where there is a discrepancy between the apparent precept of the norm and the way in which it is actually observed or administered. In other words, is a norm what is *said*, or what is actually *done*? From the point of view of the recipient, he will detect the *Law* as it is, and not as it is theoretically presented. Normative statements may thus not 'tell the truth', in that they do not describe what actually happens. If the normative statement says that 'If X, then Y', and X occurs, but Z follows and not Y, what is the norm?

An occasional deviance from the norm is not sufficient to cast the content, or even the existence, of a norm into doubt, otherwise every norm would be automatically repealed each time it was disregarded. But repeated deviance may suggest that the purported normative statement does not correspond with the habitual behaviour of its addressees. Who are these addressees? Normative statements may be addressed to subjects, or groups of subjects, of the *Law*; other types of norm may be addressed to agents of the *Law*, whose task it is to carry out some of the purposes of the *Law*. Among these agents we have identified courts and officials. The answer to the question about the status of the purported norms varies according to the character of the addressees. Non-conforming behaviour on the part of the subjects of the *Law* to any particular norm represents diminished compliance; lack of compliance by itself does not destroy or invalidate the norm. The norm may thus be valid but frustrate. This will have two effects: it will justify a prediction that the behaviour of subjects will not be norm-conforming; and it *may* justify a parallel prediction that the agents of administration of the *Law* will not bother to enforce the frustrate norm. If it is the case in a given legal system that non-conforming behaviour can repeal a law, that custom outweighs the written text of the law,[13] then, of course, non-conforming behaviour and custom are law-generating. There is nothing contradictory in such a position, and the

13. Cf., for Roman *Law*, the rule that *desuetudo* (the negative side of *consuetudo* or custom) can, by lapse of time, invalidate a statute; and for Hindu *Law* the principle that an ounce of practice can outweigh a hundred texts; and, in the recognition under modern African legal systems of custom as a source of law, the fact that proof of disuse of a rule of customary *Law* effectively repeals that law.

wider purposes of the *Law* are fulfilled even if one of its laws is disregarded.

Deviation by the agents of the *Law* poses quite another problem. Their task, as assigned by the norms of the legal system and acts and orders under them, is to implement laws as directed. Such implementation can rarely, if ever, be total. No police force, for example, can ever detect or prosecute every deviation from the criminal law. Implementation requires the exercise of discretions in many cases; the exercise of such discretions is not totally controllable, or else they are not discretions. A judge when trying a case is continually exercising discretions of various kinds, as to what evidence he admits, what weight he gives to it, and finally as to how he matches the fact-situation presented to him with the hypothetical fact-situation of the relevant legal norm or norms.

Agents of the *Law* are there to carry out the purposes of the law-giver. If they fail to do so, their failure may or may not be monitored by or known to the law-giver. Is there feedback, in other words? If there is no feedback, this may be because the law-giver is not in a position to ensure it: there may be communications difficulties, for instance. We can easily imagine the case where a remote or petty court fails to implement norms in the way that it should, but its failure is never scrutinised by any government inspector or controller. The appeals system in a country like England is a rudimentary attempt at policing the work of inferior courts; but for every appeal that goes forward, there are a hundred instances where the lower court's procedure, handling of its discretions, or application of its norms could be impugned. If in England, how much more so in remotest Africa?

Failure to monitor, or failure to initiate remedial action after monitoring discloses non-compliance by agents with the norms of the *Law*, may be construed as failure to care, or even as willingness to accept an alternative pattern of behaviour to that prescribed by the norm. That is, the law-giver may be taken in some instances to have tacitly commanded a new, latent, norm which approves the non-conforming behaviour to his earlier norm. If we apply this analysis to the Soviet case, it is unthinkable that the Soviet authorities are unaware of how their courts proceed; it must therefore be the case that they approve of the way in which the *Law* is actually administered. In other words, behind the purported published norms there is a set of *crypto-norms*, those which actually prescribe and control the behaviour of the agents of the *Law*. The published norms are therefore phantom norms, giving only the appearance of demanding compliance; the crypto-norms are the truly valid norms.

Discretion in the law

Discretion is not a rare or exceptional feature of a legal system. It is intrinsic to every *Law*. To recapitulate:

(i) All legal norms require discretion in their application to cases, because the matching process can never be exact, and the fit is to be judged by the person applying the norm.

(ii) Apart from the question of fitting the norm to the case, a person *invoking* a norm has a discretion whether to do so. Whether police prosecute or not is a discretionary decision, even where the law says that they must.[14] A person who has private rights can choose or not whether to pursue or protect them by action – a discretion.

(iii) The making of laws is a discretionary act. The making of derivative or secondary norms, whether officially, as by making regulations, or privately, as by making contracts, is a discretionary power.

(iv) The making of implementing orders under norms is a discretionary act.

There is no level of discretion at which we can say that a *Law*, a legal order, ceases to exist, except where in effect there is no order at all. Of course, discretions exercised without the backing or authorisation of law are paranomic.

The no-law state: fact or phantom?

To tackle this issue, we must first discuss the relationship between *Law* and state. *Law*, as I see it, is the *structure* of a political society. Any kind of grouping or society without structure ceases to be a group or society, and is instead a mere agglomeration. The structure is the formative and operative principle of the society. The structure consists of norms which establish the subordinate elements and function of such a society. Where the society is 'political', its structure is legal. A political society without *Law* cannot therefore exist as such.

We may see *Law* as the skeleton or articulation of the society. To describe the legal system is not to give a sufficient description of the society in its actual functioning; but it is not possible to give such a description without mentioning the norms and institutions of its *Law*.

Confusion arises because of the demands of the term *state*. If a jurist or political scientist restricts his application of 'state' to some kinds of

14. In English law both the public and the private prosecuting agencies have a discretion whether to prosecute or not – note, for instance, the reluctance of the Attorney-General to prosecute in regard to matters where his *fiat* is required (e.g. race relations cases; industrial relations cases). The decision of the private prosecutor to prosecute can in England be overtaken by the Director of Public Prosecutions, who can take over the case and then enter a *nolle prosequi*. French, Italian and Dutch penal laws share the English approach to discretion in prosecuting; in Germany, however, there is no discretion whether to prosecute or not – the public prosecutor, under the *Legalitätsprinzip*, is obliged to prosecute when a serious offence has been made out (cf. the German Code of Criminal Procedure, section 152 (2)).

political society only, and if he at the same time asserts that *Law* can only exist as a function of a state, he automatically concludes that some societies which he refuses to call 'states' must lack *Law*. But the conclusion, like in the classical syllogism, is embedded in the premises; and like with the syllogism, it is important to challenge the premises, especially as what we are talking about is not the world of reality so much as how we use and apply the term *state*.

My own view is that 'political society' is and should be used more widely than 'state'. We can happily confine use of the term 'state' to more advanced political societies with a more complex structure, but there is nothing in the typology of different kinds and complexities of political societies which justifies us in making a cut at any level in the hierarchy and declaring that above the line the groups are states, while below it they are not. There is continuity of structure and function at all levels — the simpler societies are simpler, but so we would expect! United Nations practice shows how a priori classifications must yield to political facts, since ever smaller new 'mini-states' are admitted to the magic circle of states between whom the norms of international law are deemed to operate. Kelsen's view that *Law* and state are essentially one, though helpful in one way, is unhelpful in another. It is helpful in that it is true that *Law* and state are two ways of looking at the same political reality; but the two ways are not the same, and what is disclosed to the view is not the same, any more than the snapshot and the X-ray disclose the same view of the human body. The X-ray exposes the hard parts of the body, the skeleton; take away the skeleton and the body cannot function and indeed loses its identity. But few of us would agree to take the skeleton for the body, or the skull for the brain. Hamlet in the churchyard scene picked up a skull, which he took for that of a lawyer, one may remember:

'There's another: why may not that be the skull of a lawyer? Where be his quiddits now, his quillets, his cases, his tenures, and his tricks? why does he suffer this rude knave now to knock him about the sconce with a dirty shovel, and will not tell him of his action of battery? Hum! This fellow might be in's time a great buyer of land, with his statutes, his recognizances, his fines, his double vouchers, his recoveries; is this the fine of his fines, and the recovery of his recoveries, to have his fine pate full of fine dirt? will his vouchers vouch him no more of his purchases, and double ones too, than the length and the breadth of a pair of indentures? The very conveyances of his lands will hardly lie in this box; and must the inheritor himself have no more, ha?'[15]

The state entails *Law*, then; and *Law* entails the state, or some other political society.

The Soviet Union as described is a highly discretionary state, ruled by power, dictate and discretion. Let us consider how a court justifies,

15. *Hamlet*, Act V, I.

say, a decision to send a prisoner to Siberia, if the system is as Solzhenitsyn describes it. One must interrogate the judges: by what authority do you do this? They would undoubtedly reply by quoting the constitution and the laws, that is, by giving a *formal answer*. At the formal level one might find, on a review of their handling of the requirements of the laws, that courts were ordered to decide in accordance with the evidence and the norms of the laws. A decision otherwise would thus be formally paranomic. This would not mean, if the courts generally disregarded the formal norms, that the Soviet Union was a no-law state, but it would be a state with a very low level of compliance by its official agents with its *Law*.

But, and here we recall the earlier analysis, the *analyst's answer* would be different. He, when analysing what occurs in terms of power and behaviour, would point out that the asserted formal norms are not the norms actually observed. There is a set of secret norms with which the courts comply, of which the paramount norm appears to be: 'Whatever the letter of the *Law*, decide according to your own discretion or as instructed by a superior'.

Even if all orders made by agents of the *Law* are discretionary, provided only that at least *one validating super-norm* of the type just mentioned is recognised, then the orders and acts of the agents of the *Law* are law-abiding and 'legal'. In other words, a legal system can be a *Law* with a minimum of one norm!

The conclusion is that, even if Solzhenitsyn's account is correct, the Soviet Union has a *Law*, and it is not a 'no-law state', but that *Law* is either *minimal* or *concealed*. Hart,[16] in his discussion of finality and infallibility of judicial decision-making, uses his favourite analogue of games to construct a hypothetical game which he calls 'scorer's discretion'. This is a game where the sole operative rule for decision of the result or score of a game is not the substantive rules of the game, which no longer 'bind' the scorer, but his own unfettered discretion as to what the score is, which the players are forced to accept without possibility of challenge. A game with unlimited and unpredictable scorer's discretion would be a different game from that which the players thought they were playing under the rules as they believed them to be. It would be impossible to falsify a scorer's ruling on the ground that it offended some rule of the game.

Hart is dealing with the rule-scepticism of some jurists, who have asserted (or noted) that in, say, the United State constitution what the Supreme Court says is the law *is* the law, without possibility of further challenge. But if a Supreme Court gives a ruling which does not appear to accord with the set norms of the system, participants in that system can point out the inconsistency. Furthermore, in a constitution with a legislative assembly, there is the opportunity through the processes

16. *Concept of Law*, pp. 138 ff.

of legislation of correcting the view, whether in accordance with the norms or not, taken by the final court. No such chance of challenge can be taken in the Soviet Union. If the true crypto-norm is one of bureaucratically controlled discretion, then the subjects of the *Law* can appeal to the formal norms as ground for challenging the exercises of that discretion; but the result is likely to be that they too will find themselves in Siberia, rather than that the deviation is corrected by legislation or the appellate process.

Alice, in her Wonderland world described by Lewis Carroll, had difficulty participating in the Queen's croquet game, when, it may be remembered, the rules if any of the game varied from minute to minute. As Alice said:

'I don't think they play at all fairly . . . and they all quarrel so dreadfully one can't hear oneself speak — and they don't seem to have any rules in particular; at least, if there are, nobody attends to them . . .'.

The absence of rules did not prevent three of the players being sentenced to execution for missing their turns (though all played whenever they wanted to); it was the Queen who decided that a rule had been broken, and who ordered the executions. A perfect example of 'scorer's discretion'! There was only one norm, that the Queen decided unchallengeably what the rules were and who had broken them and what penalty should be imposed. It was still a game, though a very unsatisfactory one, and one which it was hard for the outsider to predict the result of.

If the Soviet Union's legal system is no more predictable, public and fair than the Queen's croquet game, it may be riposted that surely it is a terrible thing to admit such a state system as valid? Is it not arrant positivism to recognise such a travesty of *Law* as a valid legal system?

The answer is No. The Soviet system is *Law* at the legal level; but this says nothing about its justice or acceptability at a higher level. From the moral point of view it is a duty to criticise every *Law*. Judged at the level of justice the Soviet Union is not a 'no-law state' but, if Solzhenitsyn were correct, a 'no-legality state'. The reason for this conclusion is in the alternative, either that (i) the alleged laws are not observed or are arbitrarily applied; or (ii) there are no laws other than norms of discretion, and an acceptable system of *Law* requires regularity and predictability as well as justice. Our conclusion saves not only our own analysis, but that of other jurists as well.

This conclusion both indicates some comparisons with other systems, and contradicts the analyses which Soviet jurists have made at different times of their own system. First, as to the similarities with other systems. The first reason mentioned above for holding that the Soviet Union is a 'no-legality' state, that the alleged laws are not observed, reminds us of the situation in several African countries, in which there is a formal *Law* which does not describe either the decisions of the courts or the behaviour of the subjects of the *Law*. This lack of correspondence has often arisen out of attempts to legislate away customary or religious *Laws*. The legislature enacts a law which abolishes customary *Laws* completely, and substitutes a codified and non-customary system. The courts do not apply the new law, the people do not follow it but conform to their old ways. Good examples of this state of affairs may be found in Burundi, where a Civil Code purportedly eliminated customary law completely; in Ivory Coast, where the customary laws of marriage and the family were suppressed in favour of French-type family law; and in Ethiopia in the imperial epoch, when the Civil Code eliminated customary and Islamic *Laws*. What is striking is not just the total lack of observance of these new laws by the people, but the readiness of the government courts, even the highest, to admit that they, the courts, do not apply the new law and do not seek to do so!

A realistic account of the resultant situation would say that the official norms promulgated by the new law are merely phantoms, and that the crypto-norms which courts and people actually follow are the true *Law*. This would make such states not 'no-law states', but states with illusory legal systems.

As for Soviet jurists, the early writers argued that there was no 'state' in the Soviet Union, and no 'law'. They indignantly rejected the notion that a legal system was a system of norms, thus falling out of accord with Kelsen and the pure theory. Later theorists reverted to a normative view of *Law*; but this view, still the current one, would have difficulty in explaining what are the true norms of Soviet *Law*, and how far they are actually observed.

It is not fair or accurate, though, to describe the Soviet Union as a no-law state. The Solzhenitsyn attack, while it may be valid so far as penal law is concerned, seems to neglect the vast areas of *Law* which are not penal, and where there may be a reasonable correspondence between the official norms as promulgated by the state and the actual norms enforced by the organs of the state. Marriages continue, property is acquired; agreements are made: all in accordance with *Law*. If the USSR could be called a no-law state, then, it would be more accurate to describe it as a no-penal-law state.

What is frightening is that the USSR is *not* exceptional, and that one can discern similar tendencies in other states where discretion and administrative freedom of action replace the predictability and regularity of laws. The wise words of Roscoe Pound in 1941, commenting on the Report of the United States Attorney General's Committee on Administrative Procedure,[17] criticised the views of the majority in that Report, and tolled like a bell the warning that *Law* can too easily shift to no-law:

17. Washington, DC, 1941. Commented on by Pound in 'For the "Minority Report"', *Amer. Bar Association Journal*, XXVII (1941) 664, at p. 678.

'Even if quite unintended, the majority are moving in the line of administrative absolutism which is a phase of the rising absolutism throughout the world. Ideas of the disappearance of law, of a society in which there will be no law, or only one law, namely, that there are no laws but only administrative orders; doctrines that there are no such things as rights and that laws are only threats of exercise of state force, rules and principles being nothing but superstition or pious wish; . . . and finally a theory that law is whatever is done officially and so whatever is done officially is law and beyond criticism by lawyers — such is the setting in which the proposals of the majority must be seen.'

In my analysis such an absolutist administrative state is not a no-law state; what the state purports to command is 'law' at the lower level of analysis. But — and this is very important — such 'law' is not 'beyond criticism by lawyers', in Pound's words; there is a system which supplies a critique from outside the *Law*, and it is the duty of lawyers, as of others, to make this critique. What is more, as the millennium comes and all men live as brothers, the result will not be the withering away of law in Engels's phrase, but the full ripening of law. The society which will emerge will be one where everything is regulated by or at least not contrary to norms, norms which obtain universal affirmation and acceptance. Traditional customary societies point the way; if social relations in modern states can be transformed, their *Laws* will converge along this road of lawfulness or legality.

8 The 'house-mate' or common-law wife

An example of the competing contributions of state, courts and people in the making and unmaking of law

It is not often that one can be a witness at the birth of a new legal institution, and one which is not brought into being by a single and immediate act of a legislature, but is gradually emerging as the resultant of a series of diverse impulses and actions from a variety of persons and bodies. In other words, what one sees is not the 'Big Bang' which brought the universe into being, but rather the gradual condensation of a new star from the cloud of gas in a galaxy. This process is by no means complete; but each year brings new decisions from the courts, and new regulations from the legislature or the administrative authorities in England, which tend to confirm, define and establish the new institution.

The measure of the novelty of the institution in English *Law* is that no competent practising or academic lawyer 20 or 30 years ago would have been prepared to admit for a minute that the *Law* gave any recognition to the status of 'mistress', even an established one. Any agreement between a man and his mistress would have been liable to be declared illegal and against public policy as arising out of an immoral situation to which the *Law* would accord no recognition: *ex turpi causa non oritur actio*. The first glimmerings of recognition of the facts of the situation (and it is the facts which have caused the law to emerge) seem to have been in the last world war, when the armed forces were willing to recognise, for the payment of married men's allowances, what they termed an 'unmarried wife' as well as a lawfully married one. This recognition was motivated by humane concern for the position of a woman who had been living in a stable relationship with a man not her husband, and who would be left in penury if he was called up and no remittance was sent to her for her maintenance.

One should not be deceived by the appellation 'common-law wife', which figures so frequently now in the newspapers, and even in the mouths of advocates in the courts, into thinking that this is an ancient institution which has been temporarily lurking in the background and has now been revived or brought to light again. This would give a completely false picture of the history and status of the institution;

there is no exact historical precedent, as I shall show in a moment;[1] and the term 'common-law wife' is misleading if it suggests that there are two forms of marriage recognised in England: statutory marriage and common-law marriage.

Although my discussion of the evolution of the law in this area is restricted largely to England (the position in Scotland may well be different), one cannot avoid referring to very recent developments in other countries, such as the United States (and especially California) and Sweden. This is a universal problem with the decay of the old institutions and formalities of matrimony and the readiness of persons today, in many countries, to associate together in a marriage-like relationship. Thus the decay of customary marriage, with all its formalities, the requirements of family consents, and so on, has led to similar problems in Africa; and one of the commonest problems upon which one is called to advise is whether the modern evolved customary *Law* in a country like Nigeria is now prepared to accord the status of marriage to a union of a man and a woman who have not followed the traditional formalities, have not obtained the consents of the parents where required, and have merely commenced to live together as man and wife, calling themselves such, without formal ceremony either under the customary or the statute law. Much of the impetus for the development, and the emergence into popular consciousness as well as into judicial and parliamentary awareness, of this institution in England has come from American influence and controversies. None of these illustrates the influence better than the recent 'Marvin' case in California; it only takes a film-star and millions of dollars at stake to produce a story which echoes through the world's newspapers; but in fact obscure and humble people in many countries have found themselves in the same position and relationship, and it is they, and not the film-stars, who develop the custom, even if it is the stars and their conflicts who make the headlines and the law.

Why this development is so important and illuminating for my theme is that it exposes the falsity of the '*Law*/No-*Law*' dichotomy, which does not exhaust the universe of societal regulation. Beneath both of these there is a substrate of mores and customary usages, which limits the operation of the first and supplies some of the material of the second. A major limit on *Law* is thus the existence of social practice; while it is equally false to see the formal enactment of a law as one of the defining characteristics of 'law'. A law can come into existence through popular practice, then. Contrary to what some jurists may assume, popular practice is generative of laws in societies with written and legislated laws as well as in those with unwritten customary laws. One purpose of this inquiry will thus be to see the law-creating work of popular custom in action in modern England.

1. See pp. 261 ff. below.

To begin with the terminology and the history. In English *Law* there is no such animal as the 'common-law wife'. The name is a misnomer. Common law does not now recognise, and never recognised, a woman who is merely living with a man as his 'wife' in any sense. Before 1753, when the definition of marriage and the administration of the marriage law in England were almost entirely in the hands of the ecclesiastical courts, a marriage did not have to be before a beneficed clergyman of the Church of England, and might even be made clandestinely by words exchanged between the spouses taking each other as husband and wife, followed by sexual intercourse. Lord Hardwicke's Act in 1753 forbade clandestine marriage, and required a valid marriage in future to be solemnised by an Anglican clergyman in the presence of witnesses. But the law of marriage before 1753, including that relating to marriages *per verba de praesenti* or *de futuro*, was ecclesiastical law and *not* the common law; nor was mere sexual congress or a sexual relationship, however prolonged, a marriage in any sense unless a declaration had been made by the husband and wife that they took each other as such. What we are now tending to call a 'common-law marriage' would have been called and esteemed concubinage. The modern 'common-law' 'husband' and 'wife' specifically do *not* give evidence that they formally took each other, even in private, as husband and wife; they stress the informal nature of the relationship; in many instances a formal declaration that they take each other as man and wife would be impossible because one or both of them is or are married (by the *Law* of the land) to someone else at the time.

Only one form of marriage, whether celebrated in a licensed church or before a registrar, is now recognised by the *Law* of England (saving always the recognition of foreign marriages under the rules of private international law). The law did not recognise in any way other matrimonial relationships of the kind we are now considering. From the point of view of the wife, this was probably no great loss. Until the passing of the Married Women's Property Act 1882, married women were at a great disadvantage so far as their property relations with their husbands were concerned. Under common law the wife's property became in effect that of her husband, or at least under his control. If she was only a concubine, the woman would keep her property separate from that of her man, and thus retain some of her economic independence. But social concern for the lot of the wife grew during the last 100 years. The wife who divorced her husband could get maintenance from her ex-husband by court order, the neglected wife could seek the assistance of the court in getting maintenance for herself and her children. In 1938 a radical change was made in another department of the *Law*, the law of succession. Under the English law of wills, a husband could make a will leaving every penny of his property to someone other than his widow and children, perhaps to his mistress; and she (the wife) had no vested right to get anything from his estate. By the Inheritance (Family Provision) Act 1938 a widow or child of the deceased testator could ask the court for an order in such circumstances, granting them reasonable maintenance from the estate.

Another scandal was that often the husband, being the breadwinner, would buy the house in which he and his wife lived, but buy it in his name alone. She might spend her life looking after the home, the husband, and their children, and have no income or savings that she could call her own. If the husband tired of her, he might leave home, and sell the house over her head. The new purchaser could then dispossess the wife, who would find herself without husband, home or means. The courts tried to develop an equitable doctrine to protect the wife in such circumstances; the attempt did not succeed; so Parliament took over, enacting the Matrimonial Homes Act 1967, which gave the wife a right in her husband's home, if she registered it, sufficient to prevent such an eviction.

Again, under the current divorce law of England, the court has very wide powers to make such 'property adjustments' between husband and wife as it sees fit, whatever the legal title to any of the property may be. And, in the law of rent restriction and tenancies protected under the Rent Act 1977, the surviving wife or other relative of a statutory or protected tenant succeeds to the tenant's rights of occupation and protection: a valuable property right created by statute.

The irony of the situation is this, that the more the statute law tries to protect the wife, the greater the difference that it makes to a woman living with a man whether she is married, as the law sees it, to that man or not. There was a period in the evolution of English *Law*, from 1870 and the first Married Women's Property Act to 1938, when the policy of the *Law* was to treat a married woman as a *feme sole* as far as possible; in other words, to say that the fact of marriage did not make any difference to the property and contract sides of the relationship between the parties (though the status aspects, and the formal recognition for other purposes, such as taxation, were not affected by this principle). This policy favoured the unmarried 'wife' to the extent that marriage as such made no difference to the woman's property rights. Today the situation is quite different. The policy of the *Law* is protective of the wife, and tends to override property and other rights which stand in the way of such protection. This leaves the unmarried 'wife' at a major disadvantage. It is true that the mistress, concubine or long-term partner has her freedoms: she can leave at a moment's notice. without order of any divorce court; she owes no duty to maintain or assist her 'husband' financially such as is now cast on the married wife by social security legislation. But if she walks out, she leaves with that which is her property alone; if she was living in her partner's house, then she has no title to it or any claim to alternative accommodation. She did not benefit under the Inheritance (Family Provision) Act if her partner died and failed to leave her anything in his will.

Two factors are combining to change this statement of the legal position. The first is an alteration in popular practice, or at least (apparently) in the frequency with which couples now live together without benefit of matrimony. The second is an accommodation by the *Law*, both in the courts and through legislation, to the social facts and social problems created by this factual situation. As to the facts, it is important to stress that there have been previous periods in English history when it could have been asserted that matrimony didn't matter. Thus it was credibly reported from social investigations in 19th century London that the majority of the poor lived together without having been formally married to each other — but of course in those days such couples had little or no property over which to contend. It was as much as they could manage to find their daily bread; and the state provided no benefits or special privileges which the lawfully married might hope to share. Now, with the disappearance or diminution of grinding poverty, the distribution of assets among the less advantaged as well as the richer, and the many facilities and benefits which the modern welfare state affords, it has become a matter of some moment whether a woman in such a relationship (be it matrimonial or only quasi-matrimonial) can hope to share in the assets and the benefits and if so on what terms.

As already mentioned, the British armed forces took a liberal view of matrimony in granting wife's allowance to the dependants of serving soldiers. The law on family allowances as it used to be and child benefit as it now is was similarly tailored to give extra money each week to the mother of children, and not to a dependent wife as such, so that the unmarried as well as the married mother would benefit. Changes in the law relating to illegitimacy minimised the effect that the status of the mother would have on the status of her children. But the legal changes have now gone much further than this. The first such change has now been observable (by the present writer for 10 years or so while serving as a magistrate sitting in London courts) in the way in which the courts deal with the matrimonial circumstances of persons before them, and the legal importance that they attach to the exact form that these circumstances take. It is hard to put a date on the change of social practice, or the mentioning of the existing social practice in the courts (to be more exact) — from my own recollection it seems to have been within the last five years or so that persons appearing as parties in the courts, and advocates, social workers, police and probation officers, have made reference to someone or other having or being a 'common-law wife'.[2] The dropping of any previous hesitation in mentioning this

2. Thus Bridge LJ in *Dyson Holdings Ltd v Fox* [1975] 3 All ER 1030 at 1036, after referring to the modern acceptance of 'unmarried' partnerships, went on to say:

   'The inaccurate but expressive phrases "common law wife" and "common law husband" have come into general use to describe them.'

sort of fact appears to be associated with the new availability of a label with which to describe such a person – that label is 'common-law wife'. This expression, an Americanism current in the United States because of the survival in some of the States of the old law of England, is incorrectly applied in the States as well as in England if it is used to refer to non-matrimonial relationships, to those which I term 'quasi-matrimonial' – incorrectly because the man and woman have not formally, though privately, taken each other as husband and wife. But the use of the phrase in English courts has come after, and not before, the practice of the courts to take account of a man's actual marital situation in calculating what he can afford to pay, whether as fine to the court in respect of some offence or as maintenance to a wife or ex-wife. And the marital situation comprehended the fact that the man was living with, and maintaining, or even being maintained by, another woman, who might or might not (it mattered not) be lawfully married to him.

Thus the fact that a man has a woman living with him as his wife (whether she is in law his wife or not) is taken into account to reduce or increase payments out of his income, according as the woman is a net spender or contributor to his income. Obligations to a 'common-law wife', or mistress as she would generally have been called heretofore, and to the children that a man may have had by her, will be treated in a similar way to those which he owes to a wife whom he may have legally married; after the dissolution of his first marriage, what a man may have to pay by way of maintenance to his ex-wife can thus be affected by what he now has to pay to his current mistress. Put starkly, then, wife and mistress thus compete on level legal terms for the man's income – facts triumph over law.

So much for what has been going on at the lowest level of the judicial hierarchy. At a higher level, in the High Court and still more in the Court of Appeal, a much more fundamental series of legal steps have been taken to change the status of the mistress in English law. The decision in *Dyson Holdings Ltd v Fox* in the Court of Appeal in 1975,[3] to which I have already referred in discussing the work of the courts in feeding popular ideas and attitudes into the law through the contextual re-interpretation of statutes, marks one line of development in the law of rent restriction; a series of cases dealing with licensees and the equitable rights or interests of those who occupy homes on various terms, constitutes another line of development of the law. The legal techniques employed in each line of development are quite different: in the former case the courts say that the meaning of a provision in a statute has been changed, and changed in effect by popular usage, which in its turn reflects a change in popular attitudes; the courts thus use their powers to make law through interpretation of statutes in order

3. [1976] QB 503, [1975] 3 All ER 1030, CA; see pp. 103 ff., above.

to procure a change in the effect of statutory provisions. In the latter case, that of equity, the courts construct a new equitable right, or decide that an old equity applies to a new type of situation; their decision purports to be one to enforce vested and existing rights, though the fact that such rights exist and are so vested has only recently been revealed to their Lordships. The reality of the matter is that the courts are using the undefined powers and reach of equity to bring new fact-situations within their grasp. Equity is thus still a fertile and potential mother of new legal institutions; and the impregnating act is the penetration into judicial consciousness of the social demands made by social changes. We shall look at each line of development in turn, recognising that they support each other and interact.

Dyson and the mistress in the Rent Act

There is no need to repeat here the facts of the *Dyson* case, which I set out above. It will be enough to remember that the background to this case was a parallel case in 1950, *Gammans v Ekins*,[4] where the then Court of Appeal had firmly ruled that 'two people masquerading . . . as husband and wife' were not 'members of the same family' for the purpose of the then provision of the Rent Acts, under which the right of a statutory tenant could pass to a 'member of the tenant's family'; and that to hold otherwise would be an 'abuse of the English language'. In *Dyson*, however, the three members of the Court of Appeal refused to bind themselves by this previous decision, and held that a woman who had lived with a man in his rented house for 21 years before his death, and who had taken his name and was known as 'Mrs Wright', was a member of his family for this purpose. The justification for this decision, which arose out of a problem of interpreting a statutory provision including the word 'family', was that the meaning of the word 'family' had to be ascertained by reference to the popular meaning of the word; that such meaning could change from time to time; and that the law must change (per James LJ) to meet the changed needs and views of society. There had been, said Bridge LJ, 'a complete revolution in society's attitude to unmarried partnerships of the kind under consideration. Such unions are far commoner than they used to be. The social stigma that once attached to them has almost, if not entirely, disappeared [between 1950 and 1975]'. The Court then held that 'a couple who live together as man and wife for 20 years are members of the same family, whether they have children or not' (per Lord Denning).

It will be noted that the Court did not say (and, one is tempted to remark, did not dare to say) that the unmarried 'wife' of the deceased tenant was his 'widow' for the purposes of the Rent Acts; that would have been to equate the two statuses and give her a separately defined

4. [1950] 2 KB 328, [1950] 2 All ER 140, CA.

entitlement to remain. However, as we shall see in a moment, this inhibition has not restrained the legislature in a recent Act.[5] Not every member of the Court of Appeal is happy with the sweep of the decision in *Dyson*, though there is no prospect now of its being reversed. In *Helby v Rafferty*[6] a differently constituted Court of Appeal expressed its disquiet at the manner of the *Dyson* decision, and the injury that it seemed to do to accepted principles of statutory interpretation. Without totally dissenting from the social analysis and social purpose of the *Dyson* decision, the Court in *Helby v Rafferty* added a rider to the operation of the decision, by holding that in the instant case there was not such permanence or stability in the relationship of the parties as to justify the assumption that they were members of one family, and that there were other factors, such as that the woman retained her own name and did not describe herself as 'Mrs', which leant in the same direction. *Dyson* is thus not a Mistresses' Charter for every kind of mistress, including the temporary visitor; the courts will look for a stable, actually long-lasting relationship before they will confidently hold that the parties are members of the same family and thus entitled to the very substantial property rights granted them under the Rent Act.

There are two aspects of this new legal doctrine which must give immediate cause for concern. The first is that the rights of third parties, notably the landlord in a landlord and tenant case, are affected by the court's treatment of the relationship between the man and woman. It is not a question of its being their own private business or merely of the sharing out of their assets between them. The landlord is deprived of his property for a further, and possibly very substantial, period by the fact that the tenant formed a long-lasting relationship with a woman before he died. This makes the case quite different from the 'Marvin' kind of case, where the cast-off or departing mistress seeks a share in her lover's property, on the basis either of an agreement, express or implied, between them or of some equitable right generated by the circumstances. The second cause for concern is that the courts will undoubtedly be faced with a situation where the parties have lived together, apparently as man and wife, but for a short and not a long period. The legally married widow of one day's marriage has a right to succeed under the Rent Act; if the male lover of the mistress dies the day after she moves in, the situation is presumably quite different. But marriage, like quasi-matrimony, is often a purportedly rather than an actually permanent relationship; so the courts will doubtless be asked to hold that the mistress should not be disadvantaged merely because their stable relationship with elements of permanence about it actually came to a brief conclusion because of the death of her partner. James LJ had adverted indirectly to such a case in *Dyson*; he said:

5. See the Domestic Violence and Matrimonial Proceedings Act 1976, s. 1, and pp. 279 ff. below.
6. [1978] 3 All ER 1016, [1979] 1 WLR 13, CA.

'This is not to say that every mistress should be so regarded [as a member of the tenant's family]. Relationships of a casual or intermittent character and those bearing indications of impermanence would not come within the popular concept of a family unit.'[7]

The mistress, equity, and new rights of property

We must start off, not with the mistress, but with the lawful wife, because the evolution of the property rights of the wife in the last three decades has led to the development of new equitable doctrines, to new legislation, and to a tendency for the courts to mimic the effects of this law in considering the position of mistresses. Mistresses sail, in other words, in the slipstream of wives, and their rights imitate those of wives at a delay of five to ten years. The starting point for wives was the regime laid down by the Married Women's Property Act 1882, which effectively put the wife in the position of an unmarried woman with no special claim on the world or her husband, other than a personal right as against him to bed and board, i.e. to maintenance. The wife had no vested right or interest in the matrimonial home if it was owned by the husband, in default of special agreement or a sharing in the title to the home (as where husband and wife held as joint tenants). For the husband to deprive his wife of accommodation in 'his' home was a matrimonial wrong; but neither the deserted, the deserting, nor the expelled wife had an enforceable legal interest in the home. A pioneering decision of the Court of Appeal in *Bendall v McWhirter*[8] in 1952 established a new doctrine, that the wife's rights as against the husband could bind the trustee in bankruptcy of her husband, i.e. a third party to the marriage. In later cases, the dissenting opinion of Lord Denning in that case that the deserted wife had an equity which bound the trustee or a purchaser for value of the matrimonial home from the husband was followed by the lower courts. These decisions proceeded on the basis that the wife was some sort of licensee from the husband, a licence coupled with an equity; and that equity sprang from the court's conception of what was just in the circumstances. Equity, in other words, was a flexible instrument to achieve the result that the court had on other grounds decided was just. In accordance with normal principles the equity would bind subsequent purchasers of the legal estate, except a bona fide purchaser for value without notice.

No, said the House of Lords in *National Provincial Bank Ltd v Ainsworth,*[9] the deserted wife is not a contractual or equitable licensee of the husband, and has no such right. Even if she were, it is not clear

7. At 511 and 1035, respectively.
8. [1952] 2 QB 466, [1952] 1 All ER 1307, CA.
9. [1965] AC 1175, [1965] 2 All ER 472, HL.

that wives should be treated like other (contractual) licensees, or indeed what the rights of such licensees are as against purchasers.

The House of Lords had spoken; it utters the final word on any legal doctrine, on what the law is, and in this case it uprooted and cast aside the deserted wife's equity, not in its bud but when it was in full flower. But Parliament has a word even more final than that of the House of Lords *de lege ferenda*; and it swiftly enacted the Matrimonial Homes Act 1967, which gave the spouse in occupation a right not to be evicted except by court order, during the currency of the marriage. We need not concern ourselves here with the mechanics of this Act, except to mention that it protects 'rights of occupation' and gives no new title or interest in the property itself.

The next legislative development was the enactment of the Matrimonial Proceedings and Property Act 1970 (now re-enacted as the Matrimonial Causes Act 1973) which gave the courts an extensive power, in ordering financial provision for the parties and the dependants of their family upon breakdown of their marriage, to make 'property adjustment orders', by which capital and income provision could be made out of the joint and several assets of each spouse so as to produce a just result in conformity with the broad criteria laid down in the Act. Title to each portion of property ceased to matter; all went into the melting-pot and was shared out again, in a sort of community property system of a floating and indeterminate kind. In determining the financial needs, obligations and responsibilities of each party to the marriage or former marriage, the court will have regard to the man's responsibility, for instance, to maintain a woman with whom he is now living, or a second wife whom he has now married. Whether the woman with whom he now lives is married to him or not does not affect the principles applied or the determination of the court.

Mistresses, including long-term companions, had thus moved farther and farther away from wives so far as their vested or potential property entitlement was concerned (though, when competing with the ex-wife for maintenance from the man they share, a mistress is on an equality); what were the courts going to do about it? What they have done is to take the doctrines which they had elaborated to protect the deserted wife before 1965 and apply them to the deserted or rejected mistress, to spell out licences, equities, and agreements under which she gets some right to live in a house held by her 'husband' or to seek some financial compensation from him. Mistresses thus move into the pre-1965 position of wives in this respect (though not in others). The courts are not inhibited, as they were with wives, by the argument that, since a wife had already a personal right against her husband, she could not also be treated as a notional licensee of him — because the mistress has no such personal right. We must now look at some of the cases in which this new law has been defined and developed. We may select three as representative, always bearing in mind that there has been a rapid evolution in judicial recognition of the vested rights of licensees generally, of which mistresses are now among the beneficiaries. The three cases, all in the Court of Appeal, are *Tanner v Tanner*,[10] decided in April 1975; *Horrocks v Forray*,[11] decided in November 1975; and *Chandler v Kerley*,[12] decided in March 1978. The recentness of the new law is patent.

Licences

Tanner v Tanner[13] was the Case of the Amorous Milkman. In 1968 the plaintiff Tanner, a milkman and croupier who was already a married man, was going out with three other women, of whom one was a Miss MacDermott. She had a flat in which she lived; he visited her there, and eventually she became pregnant by him. In November 1969 she gave birth to twin daughters. Mr Tanner and Miss MacDermott decided that they should get a house for her and the twins. He found one at 4 Theobalds Avenue, North Finchley. By way of misrepresenting his true matrimonial position he obtained a mortgage from the local authority. Miss MacDermott (now known as Mrs Tanner) moved in with the twins. She took a hand in furnishing it and in managing the letting of the first floor. Meanwhile, Mr Tanner was also associating with another woman, a Mrs Metcalfe, who was already married to someone else. Miss MacDermott came to hear of it, and in 1971 began to suggest to Mr Tanner that the house in North Finchley should be sold, so that he could let her and the twins have the cash (he was not making any separate payment to her for maintenance, and she had been drawing social security for herself and the children). Mr Tanner did not act on this suggestion at this time. He got a divorce from his first wife, and then married Mrs Metcalfe. She also became pregnant. He, on a milkman's pay, now found himself in financial difficulty. His response was to determine to get Miss MacDermott out of the house in North Finchley and move in there himself, with his new wife (formerly Mrs Metcalfe). In July, 1973, his solicitors wrote to Miss MacDermott, reciting that she and her two daughters occupied the house under licence from Mr Tanner, and informing her that 'Mr Tanner revokes the licence forthwith', and asking her to vacate the premises. She did not; he applied to the county court to evict her. She argued in the county court that she had an interest in the house, and so should not be turned out. The submission of her counsel that Mr Tanner was estopped from turning her out was not accepted by the county court judge. An order for possession was made.

In the Court of Appeal Lord Denning MR rejected the argument that

10. [1975] 3 All ER 776, [1975] 1 WLR, CA.
11. [1976] 1 All ER 737, CA.
12. [1978] 2 All ER 942, CA.
13. [1975] 3 All ER 776.

she was a bare licensee and so could be turned out at will. She had
moved into occupation on the faith of being allowed to stay there in
lieu of staying in her flat, where she was protected by the Rent Acts.
Lord Denning observed, in regard to the argument that Mr Tanner was
entitled in law to turn her out on a moment's notice:

'I cannot believe that this is the law. This man had a moral duty to
provide for the babies of whom he was the father. I would go further. I
think he had a legal duty towards them. Not only towards the babies.
But also towards their mother. She was looking after them and bringing
them up. In order to fulfil his duty towards the babies, he was under a
duty to provide for the mother too.'[14]

Lord Denning was prepared to hold that, while there was no express
contract, the court should imply a contract by Tanner or impose a
contract on him [in other words, the 'contract' was a legal fiction] to
let them have accommodation in the house as their home until the girls
had finished their schooling. This was a licence, and a contractual
licence at that; Mr Tanner would therefore not be able to turn them out
at will, nor to sell the house over their heads, following *Binions v Evans.*[15]
As possession had been granted, and the local authority had rehoused
Miss MacDermott, there was no point in restoring the situation to what
it was before; but the plaintiff had obtained an unjust benefit and must
pay compensation of £2000 to Miss MacDermott for it.

Several important points emerge from this decision. The first is that
all three judges agreed that the defendant, Miss MacDermott, had no
proprietary interest in the house. The second was that the existence of
the children was the ground of the decision of the court that Mr Tanner
had a duty to provide for their mother as well and that he was estopped
from turning them out. The third was that a sort of consideration for
the imputed contractual licence was found in the detriment suffered by
Miss MacDermott. The fourth point was that the duration of the
contractual licence proved a difficulty to the judges, who felt some
doubt as to what term it should be accorded. Lord Denning asserted —
without citing authority for the view — that Mr Tanner had a legal duty
to maintain not only his children (which we can accept in the existing
state of the law) but also their mother, which is more dubious, whatever
his moral obligations may have been. We shall have to see in the
subsequent cases if any of the points already underlined recur, or
whether the judges feel free to decide in favour of the mistress when
one or other of the factors mentioned is not present.

The next case for consideration is *Horrocks v Forray.*[16] As we shall
find in other comparable cases where the law is in the making, the
personnel of the Court becomes relevant; and the three judges who sat

14. At 779.
15. [1972] Ch 359, [1972] 2 All ER 70; see below at p. 272.
16. [1976] 1 All ER 737, CA.

on this appeal in the Court of Appeal had none of them sat on *Tanner*. In this case Mr Sanford was a wealthy man, who was married. He died aged 68, killed in a motor accident in 1974. While married he had kept a mistress, the defendant Mrs Maxine Forray, who had been his mistress for 17 years. The executors of Mr Sanford claimed possession of a house in Kensington, which Mrs Forray occupied with two children, one of whom was the child of Mr Sanford, and the other the child of another man to whom she had been briefly married while still being and remaining the mistress of Mr Sanford. Mr Sanford had bought the house in his own name in 1973, but had allowed the defendant and her children to live there. Could the executors, who had only found out about the existence of the house and of Mrs Forray by going through Mr Sanford's papers after his sudden death, turn her out? Her counsel naturally relied on *Tanner*; this decision was explained by Megaw LJ as resting on the court having found the existence of a contract between a man and his mistress 'by which the man had agreed, for consideration, that the house which was being bought by him for the occupation of the woman and her children should remain available to her, with a continuing licence for her to occupy it so long, at any rate, as the children were of school age, or unless some other circumstances arose meanwhile which would make it reasonable for the possession to cease'. There was no express contract in *Tanner*; but the 'court was entitled to infer the existence of a contract'.

In the present case, said Megaw LJ, the usual conditions for the making of a contract must be present, including a meeting of minds and a definition of the terms of the contract, as well as consideration. All these had been found to exist in *Tanner*; but here there was quite insufficient evidence to support the inference of a binding contractual licence. One could not infer a binding promise or agreement from the alleged fact that the defendant had, at the instance of Mr Sanford, 'subordinated her mode of life, or her "life-style", and her choice of residence to the directions of the late Mr Sanford'. Scarman LJ fully agreed with Megaw LJ. One was not entitled to infer a contract just because of the continuing natural love and affection between the two parties. It was quite different if the parties were consciously trying to provide for an illegitimate child of which they were the joint parents; but there was no evidence that this was the case here. It would be unreasonable to infer a contract, especially as the late Mr Sanford had treated Mrs Forray so generously, beyond the call of his legally binding obligation to contribute to the support of his child.

The facts in the third of our cases, *Chandler v Kerley*,[17] were even more unusual. The court was presided over by Lord Scarman, sitting again with Megaw LJ, and with Roskill LJ (who had not been sitting in *Horrocks v Forray*). This case represents a meeting of the two streams

17. [1978] 2 All ER 942, CA.

of authority, the one which relates to contractual licences between man
and mistress, and the other which relates to the role of equity and the
constructive trust in licences generally. The contractual licence and the
constructive trust may be seen either as two ways of giving a licensee a
right to remain beyond the will of the licensor, or as constituting the
respective and complementary roles of law and equity in the doing of
justice. The mistress cases were represented by *Tanner* (the qualifications
of *Tanner* by *Horrocks v Forray* were apparently not adverted to); the
general licence cases, not involving mistresses but involving in some
instances the notion of the constructive trust, were represented by
such well-known authorities as *Bannister v Bannister,*[18] *Errington v
Errington and Woods*[19] and *Binions v Evans,*[20] as well as such old
favourites as *Hurst v Picture Theatres Ltd*[1] and *Winter Garden Theatre
(London) Ltd v Millenium Productions Ltd.*[2] It will be remembered
that several of these licence cases were concerned with the question
whether a licensee acquires a property right in the property which he
occupies by licence, and what the nature of this right or interest is.
Lord Scarman in *Chandler v Kersey*, the instant case, took *Bannister v
Bannister* to show, not that there was a right to occupation for life,
even if there was not evidence to support an implied contractual right,
but that, where the plaintiff in *Bannister* had given an oral undertaking
that the defendant would be allowed to live in the cottage rent-free for
as long as she desired, then the 'defendant could not show a legal right;
but she did establish the existence of an understanding or arrangement
with the plaintiff which, though giving rise to no legal right, brought
into existence an equity which the court thought it just to satisfy by
declaring the defendant had an equitable life interest in the cottage
with the plaintiff as her trustee'.[3]

In other words, the court imputed a constructive trust as a remedial
device to give effect to an 'equity' arising out of the implied obligations,
none of them of a legal character, undertaken by the parties. The use of
the constructive trust, especially in licence cases, is fascinating because
there are two quite distinct views as to its character and use. The one,
the stricter, is that a constructive trust must imply a proprietary
relationship which the court can spell out of all the circumstances; the
other, the less strict, that 'constructive trust' is a mere label or device
for forcing the party to do what the court thinks it right and just that
he should do, without carrying any property implications. *Binions v
Evans* shows both these attitudes at work on the part of different
members of the Court of Appeal. In *Binions v Evans* the landlord estate

18. [1948] 2 All ER 133, CA.
19. [1952] 1 KB 290, [1952] 1 All ER 149, CA.
20. [1972] Ch 359, [1972] 2 All ER 70, CA.
 1. [1915] 1 KB 1, CA.
 2. [1948] AC 173, [1947] 2 All ER 331, HL.
 3. [1978] 2 All ER 942 at 946.

had allowed Mr and Mrs Evans to live in a cottage on the estate, Mr Evans being a worker on the estate. He paid no rent or rates. He died; the widow stayed in the cottage with the agreement of the trustees of the estate, permitting her by written agreement to stay in the cottage as tenant at will free of rent for the rest of her life. The estate sold the cottage to a Mr and Mrs Binions, and gave them notice of the existence of the tenancy of Mrs Evans. Mr and Mrs Binions, after the conveyance was completed, sought to evict Mrs Evans on the ground that she was a tenant at will, whose occupation could be determined at any time. Lord Denning MR held that this was no true tenancy at will, nor was it a tenancy for life nor any other kind of tenancy; therefore Mrs Evans had no legal estate or interest in the cottage. She had a contractual right to stay for the rest of her life. This meant she had a licence and not a tenancy. Such a licence, arising from contract, would give the licensee an equitable interest in the land; a landlord would not be permitted by a court of equity to turn out the licensee in such circumstances. On the conveyance to a purchaser, whether or not she had an equitable right before, she obtained one now, because the purchaser took with notice:

'In these circumstances, this court will impose on the plaintiffs a constructive trust for her benefit: for the simple reason that it would be utterly inequitable for the plaintiffs to turn the defendant out contrary to the stipulation subject to which they took the premises. [And the Master of the Rolls cited *Bannister* in support.] '[4]

Megaw LJ by way of contrast found that either there was a tenancy for life, as in *Bannister*, or an irrevocable licence based on a continuing contractual obligation; and he would have spelt out such a contract from the agreement between Mrs Evans and the trustees, and the rights under such a contract would be protected as against a purchaser. Stephenson LJ gladly opted out of the choice between these alternatives by finding for the former view, that there was a life interest under the Settled Land Act 1925 created by the original agreement.

So much, then, for the streams of authority. Now for the facts in *Chandler v Kerley*. The case concerned a house at Totton in Hampshire. It was owned by the plaintiff, Mr Chandler, and occupied by the defendant, Mrs Kerley, with her two children. The plaintiff said that Mrs Kerley was no better than a licensee, and purported to terminate her licence. She claimed that she was a tenant for life (as in *Bannister*) or the beneficiary of a trust (bringing in the constructive trust approach). As Lord Scarman rightly observed, the facts were distinctly unusual. Mr and Mrs Kerley were married to each other and had jointly bought the house. They had two children. In 1974 the marriage broke down, and Mr Kerley left home. Soon thereafter Mrs Kerley met the plaintiff, Mr Chandler, and eventually became his mistress. She so continued

4. At 368 and 76 respectively.

until the relationship ceased in January 1976. Even though Mr Kerley had left home, he continued for a while to meet the building society payments on the mortgage; but he stopped doing so early in 1975, because he said he could not afford it. He and his wife put the house on the market, but failed to make a sale. Finally it was agreed between Mr and Mrs Kerley on the one hand, and Mr Chandler on the other, that the house should be sold to Mr Chandler at a reduced price. The house was duly sold to him in December 1975. It was found as a fact at first instance that the plaintiff agreed to buy the house, and that the price was as reduced substantially from that originally asked, 'on the understanding that the defendant would continue to live in it indefinitely until he [Mr Chandler] moved in'. But the original plan of Mrs Kerley and Mr Chandler to live in the house as man and wife did not come off, and within 6 weeks of the purchase the plaintiff had brought the relationship to an end. By a solicitor's letter dated 29 April 1976, Mr Chandler required the defendant to quit by 28 May. The county court judge found as a fact that the plaintiff had granted the defendant an express licence and that the notice was not effectual to terminate it. Accordingly the claim for possession failed. These findings were not challenged on the appeal. However, on a counter-claim two issues were raised: (i) what the terms of the licence were; and (ii) whether the defendant had an equitable interest arising out of a constructive trust. Both issues are vital for one's appreciation of the development of the law relating to the rights of mistresses in their lovers' houses.

Lord Scarman in the Court of Appeal was not prepared to grant the mistress an equity to remain in possession for life. He put the matter starkly (and, with respect, accurately). Either on the one hand there was an agreement valid in law for a licence for life, in which case the court should give effect to the legal interest, and there was 'neither room nor need for an equitable interest'; or on the other hand there was no binding agreement between the parties, so that 'there is nothing to give rise to an equity to that effect'. Lord Scarman summarised the true position as he saw it in the following words:[5]

'In a case such as the present, the role of equity is supportive and supplementary. Where the parties have contracted for a licence, equity will today provide an equitable remedy, to protect the legal right, for example by injunction . . . . If, however, the legal relationship between the parties is such that the true arrangement envisaged by the parties will be frustrated if the parties are left to their rights and duties at law, an equity will arise which the courts can satisfy by appropriate equitable relief.'

The argument that *Bannister* implied that the defendant must have a tenancy for life was rejected by Lord Scarman, who held that *Bannister*

5. [1978] 2 All ER 942 at 945.

on the contrary merely demonstrated the supportive and supplementary role of equity. None of the licence cases, such as *Binions v Evans*, told in the reverse sense, thought Lord Scarman. What about the 'mistress' cases, such as *Tanner v Tanner*? He found this to be 'yet another case of a contractual licence supported by equity so far, and only so far, as is necessary to give effect to the expectations of the parties when making their arrangement'.

So it was necessary to examine the facts of the instant case to determine what the terms of the arrangement, express and implied, between the parties were. There was no evidence to support a licence for the defendant to occupy the house for her life. Although the plaintiff was aware that the defendant wanted a home for her children as well as for herself, it

'would be wrong, however, to infer, in the absence of an express promise, that the plaintiff was assuming the burden of housing another man's wife and children indefinitely, and long after his relationship with them had ended. The balance of these factors leads me to the conclusion that the defendant's contractual licence was terminable on reasonable notice, and that the notice must be such as to give the defendant ample opportunity to rehouse herself and her children without disruption. In my judgment 12 calendar months' notice is reasonable in the circumstances. For these reasons I do not think this is a case in which it is necessary to invoke the support of any equitable doctrine.'[6]

Megaw and Roskill LJJ concurred without further discussion in this analysis.

This, with respect, is a most useful decision. It imposes some limits on the ramifications of the constructive trust doctrine as applied to mistresses; it minimises the chance that the ex-lover will find his ex-mistress permanently ensconced in a house in which at one time he allowed her to live. It reaffirms the importance of first of all investigating the legal position (i.e. at law rather than in equity). The first question is, did the parties come to any express or implied agreement about the terms upon which the mistress should come into occupation? If there is no evidence of such a contract, or no evidence that there was an intent to enter into a legal relationship, then there is nothing upon which the law can bite. If there is such a contract, express or implied, then the law can recognise a contractual licence as having been granted, and content itself with defining its terms and giving such supplementary relief as is necessary to give it efficacy. *Tanner* was one case where there was such a contract; *Chandler v Kerley* another; *Horrocks v Forray* was on the opposite side — there was no legal contract to be found in the relationship of the parties. The 'constructive trust' is merely supportive of the legal intentions of the parties.

6. At 947.

Trusts

A different legal situation arises where the claim is, not that the mistress is the occupant by licence of her lover's home, but a co-owner of that home, either at law or in equity; i.e. where she has a vested proprietary right in it. This situation has been the subject of a number of important decisions, mimicking the similar position of the lawfully married wife making a claim in the same sort of circumstances. The first such case was *Diwell v Farnes*.[7] The man and the woman had lived as man and wife, though not married to each other (the man in fact being at all material times lawfully married to another woman), and occupied a house of which the decreased man was the tenant. Both the man and the woman had earned money in employment at the relevant times, the woman making a financial contribution to the home by making some of the mortgage payments. There was a child of the union. This house was then sold, and the house next door bought by the man out of the proceeds. The County Court had held that, when the man died, the lawful widow, as administratrix of his estate held the house in question (their 'matrimonial home') on trust for herself and the mistress in equal shares. Hodson LJ summarised the legal relationship between the deceased and his mistress in these terms:

'The legal position between the defendant [the mistress] and the deceased is that there was an enforceable legal liability on the latter to contribute towards the keep of the child, but no contract or joint enterprise between them can be spelled out of their relationship as man and mistress, and their financial arrangements cannot be looked at as if, while they were living together, their relationship was that of man and wife.'

'Husband and wife cases [the judge went on] are in a class by themselves . . .'.

and he mentioned *Rimmer v Rimmer*[8] as authority for the view that, in matrimonial disputes about property under section 17 of the Married Women's Property Act 1882, the court can do what it thinks fit or just, rather than try to work out the exact shares of husband and wife in property to which they had both contributed. The general maxim that 'equality is equity' comes in at this stage to give the husband and wife a half-share each in property to the costs of which they have contributed, in default of exact enquiry.

To Hodson LJ this was *not* a husband and wife case; *Rimmer* did not apply, and the court should treat it as a dispute between two strangers. What exact share the mistress should get in the home must therefore be precisely ascertained by further enquiry. Ormrod LJ concurred. Willmer LJ dissented. The parties were 'engaging in a joint enterprise similar to that of a legally married husband and wife', and the same

7. [1959] 2 All ER 379, CA, at 381, 382.
8. [1952] 2 All ER 863, [1953] 1 QB 63.

principles should be followed. By the date of *Cooke v Head*[9] in 1972 (doubtless as a result of all the other mistress cases) Willmer LJ's view had become the orthodox view; and the constructive or resulting trust which the courts infer or impose in the case of a husband and wife, where the husband is the legal owner of the matrimonial home but the wife has made substantial contributions to it, in favour of husband and wife equally, should be applied by analogy to the situation of the man and mistress in the same circumstances. Miss Cooke, the mistress of Mr Head, who was already a married man, agreed with him to acquire land on which to build a bungalow for them to live in together. Mr Head raised the money, and took the conveyance in his name alone. However, Miss Cooke, though not contributing money to building the bungalow, contributed a good deal of work to it, notably by using a sledgehammer to demolish old buildings, and wheeling a wheelbarrow full of hard-core on the site. She did painting and so forth too. The couple separated before the bungalow was completed. Mr Head decided to sell the bungalow; Miss Cooke asked for her share of the price realised for it.

Lord Denning MR admitted that, under the old law as it affected husbands and wives, even a wife in these circumstances would have been adjudged no share in the absence of monetary contribution; but the courts' wide interpretation of section 17 of the Married Women's Property Act 1882 had made use of the notion of the constructive trust to give the wife an equitable interest in such cases. 'It is now held that, whenever two parties by their joint efforts acquire property to be used for their joint benefit, the courts may impose or impute a constructive or resulting trust. The legal owner is bound to hold the property on trust for them both. . . . It applies to husband and wife, to engaged couples, and to man and mistress, and may be to other relationships too.'[10]

As for wives, the main authorities are *Pettitt v Pettitt*[11] and *Gissing v Gissing*.[12] *Gissing* had carried the matter as far as it could be carried so far as husband and wife are concerned, by holding that even if nothing specific was said or agreed between the spouses about financing the purchase of the matrimonial home and even if the wife only made an indirect contribution to the purchase, as where she pays the household bills, then the wife is entitled in equity to a share in the matrimonial home. In default of an express or implied agreement about contribution, the court can 'deem' or 'impute' an agreement, provided only the court can find a constructive or resulting trust arising out of the conduct and intentions of the parties. The House of Lords did not find any such intention proved in *Gissing* (the situation was rectified by the enactment of the Matrimonial Proceedings and Property Act 1970, which gave the courts power to impose its own 'equitable' solution to any

9. [1972] 2 All ER 38, CA.
10. At 41.
11. [1969] 2 All ER 385.
12. [1970] 2 All ER 780.

dispute between husband and wife over property, whatever their intentions and without reference to any constructive trust). The dicta in *Gissing* relating to wives were openly and flagrantly applied by the Court of Appeal in *Cooke v Head* to mistresses, who thus indirectly benefited from the liberal interpretation given to section 17 of the Married Women's Property Act 1882! Mistresses followed wives in enjoying the favour of the courts and the presumption of a constructive trust to give them an interest in the 'matrimonial' home; but of course they do not yet get the benefit of the statutory power of the courts to make a 'property adjustment order' under the Matrimonial Causes Act 1973. How long will it be before this right too is extended to them?

The process of extension of a mistress's property rights continues. *Eves v Eves*[13] took it a stage further. Again the case was in the Court of Appeal, and again it was in front of Lord Denning MR. The case was not unlike *Cooke v Head* in that the parties, living together as man and wife though each married to another, decided to set up home together in a house bought for this purpose. At the time of purchase the man, who paid for the house, took conveyance of it in his own name, telling the girl that this had to be so, because she was under 21 and so the house could not be in their joint names. The woman did a lot of work in the house, stripping wallpaper and so on. Although their divorces from their legal partners came through, they never married each other. Later the man met another woman, told his mistress that he was going to marry the other woman and that he would sell the house. The man married the second woman, and left the house in the occupation of his former mistress.

In the High Court the mistress's claim to a share in the house was rejected. The Court of Appeal decided otherwise. The critical factors were that, although the mistress made no direct financial contribution to the acquisition of the house, 'this property was acquired and maintained by both by their joint efforts with the intention that it should be used for their joint benefit until they were married and thereafter as long as the marriage continued'.[14] By his conduct the man had tacitly admitted that the mistress was entitled to a share. She trusted him. Had she been a wife, she would have had a good claim to a share on divorce. The law must impute or impose a constructive trust by which the man was to hold the property in trust for them both. But not on a one-half share; that would be too much. A quarter-share was considered more equitable in the circumstances. Brightman J attached importance to the representation of the man that the woman would have some interest in the property, and that there was a sort of bargain by which the plaintiff would contribute her labour to the repair of the house; these were enough to ground the finding of a constructive trust.

It is only rarely that the courts can spell out the declaration of an

13. [1975] 3 All ER 768, CA.
14. At 771–2.

express trust by a man in favour of his mistress from all the surrounding circumstances. Ordinary people (as said Scarman LJ in the case we shall now look at) do not say to their mistresses: 'I am now disposing of my interest in this fund so that you [the mistress] now have a beneficial interest in it'! In *Paul v Constance*,[15] Mr Constance lived with Mrs Paul in the same house as man and wife until his death – the house belonged to Mrs Paul. Mr Constance was awarded damages for an industrial injury. He put the money in a deposit account at the bank, in his name only, and this was the main source of the balance in it. After Mr Constance's death, his lawful wife, Mrs Constance, as administratrix of his estate, claimed the deposit account as part of the estate. Mrs Paul, the plaintiff in this action, began an action to claim that she, Mrs Paul, had a half-share in the deposit account. She based her claim on the assertion that Mr Constance had declared a trust over the account, beneficially entitling her to share equally in it. No specific formal declaration of trust could be proved; but evidence was given of numerous informal remarks and indications, such as 'The money is as much yours as mine', which it was argued in effect constituted a declaration of trust. Two important factors influenced Scarman LJ and the other two members of the Court of Appeal to hold that these and similar words on other occasions (it could not be said exactly when) had been equivalent to an express declaration of trust: they were 'the unsophisticated character of Mr Constance and his relationship with the plaintiff during the last few years of his life'. In the result, an express trust was held to have come into existence, and the plaintiff was entitled to a half-share in the balance in the account.

Any argument that there was an *implied* or *constructive* trust was specifically abandoned in this case – this marks it out from all the constructive trust cases where the trust is as much remedial as proprietary. Secondly, it will be noted that the 'relationship' was an important determining factor in persuading the Court to hold that there was a trust – the social facts generated a conclusion of law.

The statute law and the mistress

So much for the work of the courts, which have attributed new property rights to mistresses in their lovers' homes, and new claims by way of licences for themselves and their children. Parliament has followed on, but more slowly, in the same direction. Space does not permit an extended treatment of these novelties; but the most striking innovation by far is in the Domestic Violence and Matrimonial Proceedings Act 1976. This Act was designed to protect the partner in a marriage (usually a 'battered wife') from being driven from the matrimonial home by the violence of her husband. The mechanism given by the Act to enable this object to be attained was to make a non-molestation

15. [1977] 1 All ER 195, CA.

order against the husband and to order him to quit the matrimonial home. The power to make these orders is given by section 1 (1) of the Act; the sting is in subsection (2) of the section, which says:

'Subsection (1) above shall apply to a man and a woman who are living with each other in the same household as husband and wife as it applies to the parties to a marriage and any reference to the matrimonial home shall be construed accordingly.'

Davis v Johnson[16] involved a construction of this subsection. The man and the woman were joint tenants of a council flat, in which they lived as man and wife though not married to each other. He was violent. She fled with her child. She asked for an injunction to restrain him from molesting her or their child if she returned to the flat, and ordering him to vacate the flat and not return to it. There had been an earlier decision of the Court of Appeal, *B v B*,[17] in which it had been held that the court could not exclude a man in such a situation from his own property, in which the mistress had no legal right. In *Davis v Johnson* the different factor was that the man and woman were joint tenants of the flat, so that she had an independent property right.

Lord Kilbrandon remarked in *Davis v Johnson* that the Act was not concerned with protecting battered mistresses at large:

'the English language is poor in this context. "Mistress", having lost its respectable if not reverential significance, came to mean a woman installed, in a clandestine way, by someone of substance, normally married, for his intermittent sexual enjoyment. This class of woman, if indeed she still exists, is not dealt with by the 1976 Act at all. The sub-section was included for the protection of families (households in which a man and a woman either do or do not bring up children), the man and the woman being, for whatever reason, unmarried.'[18]

Lord Salmon observed that 'battered wives' for the purposes of the Act included 'an unmarried woman, commonly but not very appropriately referred to as a "common law wife", living with her paramour in the equivalent of a matrimonial home'.[19] What puzzled him, and some of the other judges in the different courts, was how long a man could be excluded from his own home in favour of his mistress. Parliament had not laid down the exact maximum period; but it ought to be a short one. Lord Scarman made use of the phrase, 'unmarried family partners', in concurring with the rest of their Lordships in dismissing the appeal and allowing the orders against the man to take effect.

The very latest decision on this Act in its application to unmarried partners has been *Spindlow v Spindlow*.[20] The man in this case was

16. [1978] 1 All ER 1132, HL.
17. [1978] 1 All ER 821, CA.
18. At 1148.
19. At 1149.
20. [1979] 1 All ER 169, CA.

ordered to leave the joint home of himself and his mistress, even though there was no history of domestic violence. Could the court make an order excluding the man ('husband') from the joint home?

Ormrod LJ said that, if the parties had been legally man and wife, then, if there had been a divorce petition on the file, the court would have had jurisdiction to make this sort of order, excluding the husband from the home. Now there was no divorce petition here — there could not be! — but section 1 of the 1976 Act said that the unmarried couple should be treated on the same basis as husband and wife; even though there was no violence, therefore, the court had jurisdiction to make the exclusion order:

'the effect of the 1976 Act, combined with the decision of the House of Lords in *Davis v Johnson*, is for all practical purposes to equate a couple living together, with children, either their own or children of either of them, with the position of a married couple with children; and the court, in my view, should approach these cases with common sense in exactly the same way. It is said, of course, and it always is, that if this view is right a malicious girl with a child or children could oust her man friend from the house by merely walking out and putting up a bogus case. That may be the logical conclusion.'[1]

The exclusion order was upheld. The mistress marches onward, equated now in non-violent cases with the lawful wife. It is only one further step to order 'divorce' proceedings.[2] The courts will help the legislature to achieve this harmonisation of the law.

One other recent piece of legislation moving in the same direction calls for notice. By the Inheritance (Provision for Family and Dependants) Act 1975 a court is now given more extensive powers to make financial provision for the dependants of deceased testators or intestates who have been insufficiently provided for under the will or upon the intestacy. Relict mistresses do not benefit under the current law of intestacy; but such a person can now come in and make a claim as 'any person ... who immediately before the death of the deceased was being maintained, either wholly or partly, by the deceased'. So a woman who has been living with a man, and who has received substantial contribution from him in money or money's worth (and accommodation itself is money's worth), could make a claim. The principles upon which the courts proceed in adjusting and ascertaining the claims of those entitled are not unlike those under the Matrimonial Causes Act 1973 upon a divorce. The applicant can ask for 'reasonable financial provision' for her maintenance; the financial needs and resources of the applicant must be reviewed, as must those of the estate and other claimants. A mistress might thus compete against a widow for provision. Orders for transfer of property, settlements, and periodical payments can be made.

1. At 173.
2. Already possible in Japan: see p. 285, n. below.

Adverse dispositions or contracts made by the deceased to defeat the Act can be undone by the court – some interesting claims by thwarted mistresses can now be expected! In death, if not in life, the mistress and the wife thus come together in their entitlement.

The many other ways in which the fact of being a mistress may now come into the statute law cannot be explored here. They are admirably summarised in a helpful article by David Pearl, 'The legal implications of a relationship outside marriage' in the Cambridge Law Journal.[3] Put briefly, more and more housing authorities are now treating unmarried couples like husband and wife for the allocation of council property. In social security matters, the existence of a 'cohabitee' is taken into account when assessing the supplementary benefit entitlement of a woman. Whether the man she is living with is married to her or not does not affect the principle that her benefit will be reduced *pro tanto*. A mistress *may* be able to benefit under the Fatal Accidents Act.[4] But there are many other ways, notably in regard to income taxation and capital transfer tax, where a sharp distinction is made by the statute law between the married and the unmarried wife.

What shall we call her? The 'house-mate'

To call such a woman an 'unmarried wife' is a contradiction in terms. The expression 'cohabitee', which at least has the advantage of being genderless, is much used by the social services, but is otherwise unattractive. 'Mistress', as Pearl points out, can refer to (i) a woman living with a man in a stable quasi-matrimonial situation in a common home; (ii) a transitory encounter or relationship; (iii) a woman kept in a state of dependency, perhaps in a separate house (cf. *Horrocks v Forray*), the old-style Victorian mistress. 'Common-law wife', as I have already noted, is legally inaccurate.

It is essential, in my view, to have a new name for what is a new form of quasi-matrimonial relationship. The term should satisfy the following criteria: (i) it carries no opprobious overtone; (ii) it can be used in ordinary conversation by ordinary people without embarrassment or ambiguity; (iii) its meaning is sufficiently sharply defined to be useful for legal purposes, in indicating when a particular doctrine or rule is to operate; (iv) it should if possible be genderless and commutative, like 'spouse' and unlike 'husband' and 'wife' – this simplifies the statement of legal principle, and procures greater equality of treatment between the sexes; (v) it should have no existing legal or non-legal use or meaning; (vi) it should if possible be usable also in connection with regular marriage (which is why people use 'common-law wife' to show the functional connexion with regular marriage), if greater assimilation of the two states is desired – as recent decisions and legislation suggest.

3. [1978] CLJ 252.
4. See *K v JNP Co Ltd* [1976] 1 QB 85.

New institutions flourish when they acquire a new label – this is self-evidently so in the scientific domain, but it is also true in the social domain. A new and usable term would thus contribute to the definition and advancement of this form of relationship.

The existing usages fail one or more of these tests. So do Americanisms like 'live-in lover', 'constant companion', and so on. In England we are already familiar with the term 'flat-mate' – it is a person who shares a flat on a basis of equality with another. I propose the term *'house-mate'* to mean a person who shares a home on a basis of equality (it need not be a house, of course!) with another. The term has the advantage of already existing in the Oxford English Dictionary. It would cause no more embarrassment in conversation ('meet my house-mate!') than would 'meet my flat-mate!' It carries no necessary sexual overtones, but relates to the home-sharing function only – this is an important plus point, as it brings in households where two men or two women share a home, perhaps on a platonic basis.[5] The fact that the couple do or do not go to bed together should be irrelevant in the determination of

5. Contrast *Joram Developments Ltd v Sharratt* [1978] 2 All ER 948, CA, in which the Court of Appeal held that a platonic house-mate relationship did not make a young man, aged 51 years less than the old lady with whom he shared, at her invitation, a flat, a 'member of the family' of the old lady for Rent Act purposes when she died. If a generalised law of house-mates is developed, this decision requires reconsideration. This conclusion of the Court of Appeal has just been upheld by the House of Lords (see *Carega Properties SA v Sharratt* [1979] 2 All ER 1084). Lord Diplock, who delivered the leading speech, which was concurred in by the other members of the House, held that 'family' must be given its ordinary or natural meaning; he followed the dictum of Russell LJ in *Ross v Collins* [1964] 1 All ER 861 at 866, [1964] WLR 425 at 432, that there must be a 'broadly recognisable de facto familial nexus', and that 'two strangers cannot . . . ever establish artificially for the purposes of this section a familial nexus by acting as brothers or as sisters, even if they call each other such and consider their relationship to be tantamount to that. Nor, in my view, can an adult man and woman who establish a platonic relationship establish a familial nexus by acting as a devoted brother and sister or father and daughter would act, even if they address each other as such and even if they refer to each other as such and regard their association as tantamount to such'.
  If the test is what the ordinary person would hold to be a family relationship, then, with respect, the opinion of the present writer (or of any man in the street) must carry as much weight as the views of a learned Lord Justice. The argument that sexual intercourse must be at the basis of an imputed family relationship is immediately contradicted by the recognition, both'by ordinary people, the courts, and the legislation in many connections, that the relationship of parent and child can be created by such treatment and mutual recognition of a family relationship as are mentioned by Lord Justice Russell – a 'child of the family' is one who is treated as such. So much is implicitly conceded in the first paragraph of Lord Diplock's speech, in which he excludes in terms a connection by way of 'adoption (de jure or de facto) during minority' from the relationships he is examining. There is, with the greatest respect, no warrant for such an exclusion if one's point of reference is the practice, language, and mutual interactions of ordinary people.

their property rights. Husbands and wives by regular marriage would be house-mates on this basis; but transitory lovers would not. Kept women would not be house-mates unless the male partner shared a household with them. I shall use this term in the rest of this Chapter.

The future of the house-mate system

The inexorable movement of the law is towards an assimilation, partial rather than total, of unmarried and married house-mates. This movement is unorchestrated, chaotic and purposeless. I suggest that the time has come for a thorough look at the whole institution as it is developing, to define its constitutive characteristics, its legal consequences, and the degree to which the benefits and burdens of matrimony should be accorded to house-mates generally. 'Marriage' in English *Law*, as in other legal systems, means an interpersonal relationship between one man and one woman, recognised and protected by the *Law*, implying rights and duties as between the man and the woman which would not obtain if they were not married, and rights and duties towards any off-spring of their union. It further carries third-party implications both for traders who deal with the couple, the Inland Revenue when taxing them, and landlords when letting them property. All these character-istics, though not to the same extent, are now attaching to house-mates, especially, though not solely, where there are children of the association or children looked after by the couple jointly. Some of the implications, notably the attribution of equitable property rights on the basis of an implied understanding or of actual contribution of money or labour, do not depend on the existence of children. It would thus be wrong to see the work of courts and legislature as solely directed either to the protection of the children or the performance of the functions of a housing authority — though there are elements of both concerns in some of the cases.

What is the *Law* to do? It is undesirable in principle, I should have thought, to make no difference at all between (a) a union which is formally celebrated, intended to be lasting, accorded high social recognition, set about with mutual rights and duties of a clear-cut character, privileged tax-wise, and dissolved by a court after special procedures, and (b) one which is informally come to, carries no intention of permanence, not accorded much social recognition if any, carries no clear-cut set of rights and duties, is of uncertain significance in dealings with third parties, carries no tax privileges, is dissolved on an instant by the motiveless whim of either party, and where the property rights of the partners are not shared out by a court in accordance with defined statutory criteria. But there are also functional similarities, as the recent cases show. Maybe the answer is for the *Law* to recognise two forms of union, a more formal and a less formal, each with its own implications. Maybe the *Law* should presume the intention to form a house-mate relationship other than marriage whenever (a) the parties so signify by express words, or (b) it is an implication of law from their conduct, as by their jointly applying for housing, sharing each other's name, being together for a stated period (one year, say). Maybe the old Roman *Law* would thus be revived, or the developments in Tanzanian *Law* since the Law of Marriage Act 1971 imitated, under which there is a rebuttable presumption that, where a man and a woman have cohabited together for two years, and acquired the reputation of being married, they are duly married, and all the consequences of matrimony follow.[6]

Something has to be done; the present law is too uncertain and even dangerous for those affected by it. Landlords do not know where they are; a man who lets a woman into his home does not know where he may eventually find himself (*out* of the home, perhaps, under section 1 of the 1976 Act!). The only advice one can give to a man contemplating forming a sexual relationship with a woman is: (i) Make it and keep it transitory. Indicate strongly that there are no elements of permanence about it. (ii) Do not have the woman to stay longer than the weekend. (iii) If you are buying or building a house, and, contrary to the advice in (ii), have asked the woman to live in it with you, do not let her help pay for it or any part of it. Accept no contribution, direct or indirect, from her to the housekeeping or anything else. Specifically you must not let her start wheeling cement around, wielding a sledge-hammer, or decorating walls! (iv) Don't have any children: they pre-dispose the courts to find that a house-mate relationship is in existence, and to hold that, not just by leading her up to the front door but by pushing her into the maternity ward, you have granted the woman a contractual and irrevocable licence, or have constituted a constructive trust to look after her and her children. (v) If she has a child by another man, do not in any circumstances let that child come into your home with its mother; the courts may not differentiate between such a child and one that you have fathered.

6. The logical Japanese have reached this conclusion. Article 739 of the Japanese Civil Code provides that a marriage becomes effective only on registration; many unions are not registered, and hence not legally marriages. However, we are informed that 'the courts and the legislature, building on tradition, have given wide protection to the parties in what in positivist terms can only be a *de facto* union. The practice has even developed of granting *de facto* divorces': Anthony H. Angelo 'Thinking of Japanese law – a linguistic primer' 1979 XII Comparative and International Law Journal of Southern Africa 83 at p. 88, citing Coleman 'Japanese family law' (1956) 9 Stanford LR 132 at pp. 138 ff., and other references. 'Social custom in Japan however admits a properly celebrated [these words should be specially noted] unregistered union as a valid marriage'. What counts, in other words, is the gaining of social acceptance by following the forms and rituals prescribed by Japanese custom, and not the mechanical observance of the law. Japanese, says the author, have limited interest in law, do not much like it or attribute much importance to it – are the English so different?

All this is hard-hearted and cynical advice. It is made so by the chaotic state in which the law now finds itself. It is not right that people should be encouraged to be heartless, flippant in their sexual relationships, uncaring of their moral responsibilities. But neither is it fair that they should contemplate one form of relationship and wind up with quite another one. The people are making the new house-mate law; the legislature must now help them to define and regulate it. The work of people and law-giver is complementary in the making of new law.

Conclusions

What conclusions can be drawn from this necessarily abbreviated and imperfectly documented survey of the limits on the operation of law? (The imperfections of the documentation are, it is respectfully suggested, mainly due to the absence of appropriate in-depth field studies of the effectiveness of laws, studies which need the resources of the sociologist as well as the jurist if they are to be accurate and convincing.)

The first point which forces itself upon us is that laws are often ineffective, doomed to stultification almost at birth, doomed by the over-ambitions of the legislator and the under-provision of the necessary requirements for an effective law, such as adequate preliminary survey, communication, acceptance, and enforcement machinery. The more such laws there are, the less effective each cumulatively will be; weight of laws is not only oppressive, but ultimately self-defeating. The next point is that laws may become ineffective, even when they were originally achieving their object, because of changes in the social context of attitude and behaviour. The important point is to recognise such a resulting change in effectiveness, and to take the appropriate remedial steps, either by making the law more effective, or by repealing it as out of date and out of acceptance. Programmatic laws, as I remarked at the beginning of this study, are on the whole less effective than model laws; the reason for this seems to lie in the resistances of human nature to being told what to do, especially to change deep-seated practices and still more to change ingrained prejudices. Model laws offer a choice; if it is an appealing one, it will be taken up *if* brought to the public's attention. Much legal development is attributable to the acceptance of this choice.

Weak law invalidates the notion of law. Strong-sounding laws may still be weak because they are not complied with. The major reason for non-compliance seems to be resistance caused by the unacceptability of the law. This resistance can be overcome by careful persuasion and by winning eventual acquiescence, in other words, by a policy of consensus. Majority adoption or acceptance of a new law is not enough to ensure the viability of a law. There are two arguments for a consensus approach:

one is pragmatic – it is the best way to get effective laws; the other is moralistic – it is wrong to impose laws on people against their will, especially when the content of what is commanded is not a good in itself, but merely reflects the opinion of one person, or a small group of persons (an elite), as to what other people should do and should be forced to do. Customary *Laws* often relied on the consensus principle – supported by effective social sanctions – for their efficacy. They thus set an example which other and self-proclaimedly more sophisticated legislators can follow. The arrogance of the developed world which knows better – in technology, in finance, in law – is gradually proving itself inadequate to solve the real problems of tomorrow; humility, a willingness to learn from those one considers one's 'inferiors' in civilisation or education, is essential if the world is to be better ruled and better organised.

Some of the sharper of my comments are directed against 'elites', the self-appointed and self-selected arbiters of our social arrangements, who pretend to determine for us how we may think as well as how we may behave. Much discussion of political elites has concentrated on old-fashioned targets – the 'Establishment', the feudal lords, the big businessmen, the aristocracy, the military, the ecclesiastical authorities, and so on; these are no longer, in my opinion, the main threat or the main constituents of the ruling elites in the countries we deal with here. What we have instead (and they have been less discussed or pointed out) are *intellectual elites,* united by the sharing of common intellectual stances, consorting in the same arenas of power and debate, the new clerisy. In my employment as a teacher in a university I have naturally come across many representatives of this group busily at work imposing their ideas on others, treating only one opinion as acceptable or rational, controlling the lives of others on the basis of this sole opinion. There is a network of such elitists who support and advance each other. From them are drawn many of the 'experts' who advise on legislation or go out to a Third World country to impose on it some new economic or social strategy or structure. I would entirely accept and adopt the summary made by the American sociologist, Peter Berger, in his *Pyramids of Sacrifice,*[1] when he attacks the hardships forced on the inhabitants of Third World countries by 'experts':

'Policies for social change are typically made by cliques of politicians and intellectuals with claims to superior insights. These claims are typically spurious.'

To identify and seek to restrict the activity of elites is not to attack the notions of leadership and persuasion. Quite the contrary: a non-elitist society can only function if there is adequate leadership; and

1. London, 1976, at p. 13.

such leadership is a common characteristic of the customary societies I have mentioned. The effective leader, like the good committee chairman, has a multiple role; he collects, listens to and organises the individual opinions of his group; he articulates the inarticulate thoughts and conclusions which they may conceal; he is not afraid, on occasion, to try out some new idea; equally he is not afraid, if the new idea proves unacceptable, to withdraw. In his task he uses the arts of persuasion and not of compulsion. Persuasion means winning over, not trampling over, the minds of those who are ruled. All law persuades, as we have seen; good law is aware of this fact.

When I have tried out some of the ideas in this book on colleagues, I was amused to be met with a completely typical and predictable reaction from some of them — this was arrant populism, and only one step removed from fascism (the ultimate boo-word). We need not be frightened by this predictable reaction, usually coming from the intellectual elites who would be displaced or cut down to size if account were taken of popular opinion. Why should 'populism' be a rude word in the mouths of the elite, like 'fascist' before it? If populism means *proposing* policies which the people will accept, what is wrong with that? If it means *consulting* people before making decisions or acts which will affect them, what is wrong with that? As I said above, these practices are justifiable, not only on grounds of true democracy, but on the utilitarian or pragmatic ground that they are more likely to be successful.

There is a deep irony here. Populism was a powerful argument and appeal in the mouths of revolutionaries who sought to overthrow the established order, as with the French Revolution and its destruction of the *ancien régime*. It was a 'left' policy, and would be approved by intellectuals. Now populism is resented and attacked by intellectual radicals of the left as a conservative factor or tactic. Why this attack? Quite simply because the populist argument now threatens to overthrow the new established order, the order established by this same intellectual elite who are now in power! *They* are the *ancien régime* who resist change or the destruction of their powers and privileges; *they* are the reactionaries — whereas the populist programme is the *radical* one. Any strategy which involves going to the holders of power and asking them, 'By what authority or mandate do you exercise power?', is a subversive and radical one; naturally the powerful resist and attack such a strategy.

Populism does not say that the people are right, and that their will shall be law; people can be tyrants collectively as well as individually. What it does say is that the voice of the common people should be heard in deciding what is to be done to or for them; and that this consultation should not be an illusory or deceptive one, as in the pseudo-democratic system under which we now live. It is almost certainly correct that fewer changes in the law might be made if the populist approach were adopted; there would be disappointed reformers and intellectuals around; but, unless *they* have fascist or dictatorial tendencies themselves, they should learn to live with their disappointments. Their disappointment might lead them to examine more carefully what it takes to make an effective law, and then to put their humbler and more perceptive understanding into practice. They would not transcend the limits of law; but they would be able to use law to the limits which it imposes.

A guide to further reading

The main text has been written without constantly referring the reader to authorities for every proposition put forward. Some references have been made in the text itself; however, the reader, and especially the student enquiring after further discussion of the several topics, may find it helpful to have some indications on further reading, or where references to further reading may be found. These indications are *not* to be taken to be in any way comprehensive; there is a vast literature on many of the issues which this book raises, and to attempt a comprehensive bibliography of them all would be a life's work in itself. Thus writings about the sociology and anthropology of law, about legal theory in general, about political theory, about linguistic problems, about problems of development, about legal systems in Third World countries, about comparative law, and so on, are enormous in their scope. Some of these discussions go back to the dawn of western philosophy. Where discussions are thinner, as already remarked, is on the theoretical and practical aspects of the uses, uselessness, and effectiveness of law.

CHAPTER 1

J. Stone, in his various works, has accumulated a vast bibliography, and the student can do worse than refer to these by way of beginning. See especially his *Legal system and lawyers' reasonings* (London, 1964) and *Social dimensions of law and justice* (London, 1966). The book by R. W. M. Dias *A bibliography of jurisprudence* (3rd edn, London, 1979) is an excellent introduction, both for the starting student and the advanced scholar, not least because it is more than a list of titles, and includes short, crisp and critical assessments of each contribution.

I have obviously benefited greatly from H. L. A. Hart's *The concept of law* (Oxford, 1961) and from all the standard authors on jurisprudence cited therein. Writing about Hart has become an industry in itself; *Law, morality and society* (ed. P. M. S. Hacker and J. Raz, Oxford, 1977) is an example of this critical interest, consisting as it does of essays in honour of Hart (which manage to criticise his thought at various points, nevertheless!). There have been a number of such collective works in legal philosophy, such as *Oxford essays in juris-prudence* (ed. A. G. Guest, Oxford, 1961); *Essays in legal philosophy* (ed. R. S. Summers, Oxford, 1968); *More essays in legal philosophy* (also ed. R. S. Summers, Oxford, 1971).

Of the Scandinavian 'school', K. Olivecrona's *Law as fact* (2nd edn. London, 1971) and Alf Ross *Directives and norms* (London, 1968) have proved especially stimulating. G. Sawer's *Law in society* (Oxford, 1965) is a brief but pungent review of some of the themes of sociologically inclined legal theorising; it is most helpful in its survey of the main trends in this branch of legal thinking. See especially his chapter X 'Folkways, law-ways and state-ways', which touches on some of the main themes of the present work, and which inter alia is sharply critical of E. Ehrlich, the pioneer Austrian jurist, whose *Grundlegung der Soziologie des Rechts* (pub. in German in 1913, but translated into English by W. L. Moll under the title of 'Fundamental principles of the sociology of law', Cambridge, Mass., 1936) was one of the earliest attempts to look at the sociology of law in a modern sense. Sawer calls Ehrlich 'slippery'; I would prefer to call him 'difficult to grasp', which is not the same thing. He emphasizes the 'living law' of the people over against the juristic law of the courts and the jurists. Ehrlich comments:

'The immediate basis of the legal order of human society is the facts of the law: usage, relations of domination, relations of possession, declar-ations of will, particularly in their most important forms, to wit: articles of association, contract, and testamentary disposition. From these facts the rules of conduct which determine the conduct of man in society derive. These facts alone, therefore, and not the legal propositions, according to which the courts render decisions, . . . are of authoritative significance for the legal order in human society.' (at p. 192)

This line of thought, which stresses the primacy of what people do over what laws say they should do, is congenial to the present writer; though there are many ways in which our respective analyses diverge. Ehrlich's historical contribution to this theme merits special study.

R. M. Dworkin's work, now partly embodied in his *Taking rights seriously* (London, 1977) is also worthy of special note, as it pursues some of the problems with which my first Chapter wrestles in a way sufficiently divergent from that of other writers to be provocative of reflection.

I have found G. W. Paton's writing on jurisprudence clear, compre-hensive and fundamental for anyone wishing to get a general grasp of the field (and not only as it relates to my Chapter 1); the student who wants an indication of the main schools of thought and controversy in the history of jurisprudence cannot do better than begin with him; he is now issued as *A textbook of jurisprudence* (4th edn. by G. W. Paton and D. P. Derham, London, 1972).

On the general sociology of law and legal anthropology, it is difficult to know where to begin. The American *Law and Society Review* has been a prime source, and has included a number of valuable articles as well as bibliographies. Among these articles one may list Johannes Feest, on 'Compliance with legal regularities: observations of stop sign behaviour' in (1967) 2 Law and Society Review 447, as well as a number of articles in vol. 4 of the *Review* for 1970, notably those by R. S. Gerstein; M. Feeley; J. P. Levine; and J. T. Tedeschi, T. V. Bonoma, B. R. Schlenker, and S. Lindskold; all of which are concerned with aspects of compliance, the effectiveness of law, and power relationships mediated through law. Among vital works are L. Pospišil, *Anthropology of law* (New York, 1971) (written by a lawyer-cum-anthropologist); A. Podgórecki *Law and society* (London, 1974); S. Roberts *Order and dispute: an introduction to legal anthropology* (1979). These works contain many references to the classic monographs of legal anthropology, by such masters as I. Schapera, M. Gluckman, P. Bohannan, S. F. Nadel, P. Gulliver, and earlier by E. A. Hoebel and K. Llewellyn. It is sufficiently invidious to mention these out of many distinguished names who have worked in the field.

Studies of the uses and uselessness of law have, however, been relatively few, as the text says. Podgórecki (op. cit.) has shown a special interest in this area: see his chapter 11 'Anomie, conformism, legalism'; chapter 12 'Theories of the functioning of law'; and chapter 14 'Effectiveness of the law in operation'. See also the articles from *Law and Society Review* mentioned above. There are a number of essays, and extracts from earlier works, in *Sociology of law*, a selection of readings edited by V. Aubert (London, 1969). A number of these extracts canvass the relationship between law and public opinion, judicial behaviour, and the actual working of laws; and so relate to our field in one way or another. The fact that the extracts start with Sir Henry Maine shows the intellectual ancestry of this concern with the way laws function, and with the reasons law changes. There is an ASA monograph on *Social anthropology and law* (ed. by I. Hamnett, London, 1977) in which the editor's introduction, though brief, will be found a useful introduction to the relationship between the two disciplines. The case-studies by leading practitioners in this field usefully illustrate the working out of the principles in practice; all of them relate to Africa.

A special mention should be made of Sir C. K. Allen's classic *Law in the making* (7th edn, Oxford, 1964), which cannot be matched for its investigation of the role of custom and other formative influences in the shaping of English law.

Among the studies of legal effectiveness which should be looked at are *Law, its nature, functions, and limits* by C. G. Howard and R. S. Summers (New Jersey, 1965) (a series of readings at a relatively basic level); W. J. Chambliss and R. B. Seidman *Law, order and power* (Reading, Mass., 1971); A Podgórecki et al. *Knowledge and opinion about law* (London, 1973); L. M. Friedmann *The legal system: a social science perspective* (New York, 1975); M. Barkun *Law without sanctions* (New Haven, 1968) (note esp. his observation that 'legal rules are conditional statements' at p. 86, and his chapter 8, which discusses 'The uses and limits of law'), H. L. Packer *The limits of the criminal sanction* (Stanford, 1969); and J. Raz 'Legal principles and the limits of the law' (1972) 81 Yale LJ 823. Despite its title, *Beyond the limits of the law* by T. Bowden (London, 1978) is not of much assistance with our theme, as it is mainly concerned with police-work and social conflict on a major scale, which it approaches from a decidedly radical and committed point of view. See also R. Pound 'Limits of effective legal action' (1917) 27 International Journal of Ethics 180 = (1917) A. B. A. Journal 55; Harry W. Jones *The efficacy of law* (North Western, 1969).

As for France, a very recent long article by Roger Granger 'La tradition en tant que limite aux réformes du droit' (1979) *Revue internationale de droit comparé*, I, 37, should be consulted. Many of the themes canvassed in this work are also treated by Granger. 'Tradition' broadly defined is one of the limiting factors of effective law; law cannot distance itself too far from the 'times', the cultural values of the period, or it will fail; it is not only ancient traditions which create such resistances. Law is not a good instrument for realising the future. In Third World countries, legal change which is too violent, against tradition and drawn from western models, risks total disregard. One must put an end to what the author calls 'l'inflation juridique galopante' (galloping legal inflation). Self-management in Proudhon's sense must be the answer: '. . . la majeure partie des français ignore le droit qui les regit.' And this despite publicity through mass media, etc. Granger extensively reviews the situation in Third World countries, especially those of French expression — the story is the same as in the anglophone states.

Elizabeth Colson has recently published her *Tradition and contract: the problem of order* (London, 1975), which is especially concerned with the social contract, consensus, restraints on the exercise of political authority, legality — all topics with which the present work is also concerned (penetratingly reviewed at length by R. Abel in (1978) 16 African Law Studies 132).

On the linguistic side, the discussion of 'what is law?' involves a discussion of the meaning of words, phrases and sentences. The text rejects the view that there are essences lying behind words like 'law'; the argument further assumes that the meaning of a word is not defined by saying that it 'stands for' or 'represents' a 'concept'. The text plumps for the functional definition of utterances, by examining the function, defined and explained by reference to its 'context', of an utterance or a segment of it, such as a word or phrase. The word, etc, refers to and may be derived from experiences and occurrences in the physical world, as the text readily accepts; but this approach leaves no room for investigations of, say, 'The concept of law'.

There is naturally an enormous philosophical and linguistic literature on *meaning*. A good introduction to the philosophical side of this is provided by the slim volume edited by G. H. R. Parkinson *The theory of meaning* (London, 1968). The editor's introduction conveniently summarises some of the main philosophical approaches to this question. He discusses and rejects the 'concept' explanation of meaning at pp. 4 to 5. Either the 'concept' is personal to the user of the word, so that there is no shared 'concept' and thus no shared meaning of a word; or there is an inter-personal 'concept', 'in the sense that we speak of e.g. the concept of law', which he thinks is valueless:

'For to speak of a concept in this sense is simply to speak of the meaning of a word, so that the concept theory merely says that a word is meaningful in so far as it has meaning.'

This is perhaps to dismiss the use of the term 'concept' too harshly. It is not that someone has an 'image' in his brain when he utters the word 'law' — he would be hard put to it to have such an image! But there is a tangle of references in the real world which the user is trying to bring in by using the word 'law'; and that tangle of references, provided that it is not identified either as an image or as a shared idea, can be admitted as having existence in a certain sense. See the extremely clear and penetrating books by Palmer and Kempson respectively on *semantics*: F. R. Palmer *Semantics: a new outline* (Cambridge, 1976); and Ruth M. Kempson *Semantic theory* (Cambridge, 1977) — both take an anti-'concept' line.

See also the references under Chapter 5 at p. 299 below.

No special listing can be made of works on *communication theory*. There is an enormous literature on this, both on its physical and theoretical aspects (and on cybernetics, information theory, etc). One interesting attempt to marry the disciplines has been made by Walter Buckley, in his *Sociology and modern systems theory* (Englewood Cliffs, NJ, 1967). The most useful work by way of introduction to the theory of *general linguistics* will be found to be that by R. H. Robins *General linguistics: an introductory survey* (3rd edn, 1980).

For the use of words, and of political vocabulary generally, see T. D. Weldon *The vocabulary of politics* (London, 1953). He is especially strong against 'the illusion of real essences'. But see his comments on 'The State', pp. 46ff. (he rejects notions of the unique qualities of the state, or that the term has a self-evident meaning); 'authority', pp. 50ff.; 'law' and the 'Rule of Law', pp. 62ff. See esp. p. 67: 'The upshot of this discussion is that nothing but confusion follows from attempts to distinguish between "law" and "The Law". There are important differences between politics and games but the function of rules in both of them is the same. There is no point in attempting to distinguish between the laws of England and the laws of croquet from this point of view.' Generally Weldon follows an astringent, critical, nominalist line.

CHAPTER 2

For the African evidence derived from anthropological field investigations, and its theoretical interpretation, see the literature mentioned under Chapter 1.

CHAPTER 3

On the general, almost universal, ignorance or lack of conformity to law, see R. Granger, op. cit. at pp. 85ff., where for the Third World countries he puts the inapplicability of law at up to 80 to 90% of the national population. As for France, 'La présomption de connaissance de la loi n'est pas ici fondée sur les probabilités. La grande majorité de la population ignore la majeure partie du droit'. (at p. 93). Part of the problem stems from legislative inflation:

'Or l'inflation législative, chronique depuis un certain nombre d'années, s'aggrave jusqu'à frapper le corps social d'indigestion, dit M. R. Savatier, d'étouffement dirions-nous pour notre part.'

This 'suffocation' caused by excessive law-making in France has got to such a pitch that in certain parts of the law, such as the law of town planning, international commerce, building, labour law and social security law, even the specialists cannot be sure, says Granger, whether a particular regulation is in force or not without previous special study. The situation of the ordinary citizen is thus far worse (at p. 100).

Lord Denning's *The Discipline of Law* (London, 1979) reprints, with commentary, many of the leading cases in summary in so far as they deal with restraint of union power.

A study by B. Weekes, M. Mellish, L. Dickens and J. Lloyd, under the intriguing title of *Industrial relations and the limits of law; the industrial effects of the Industrial Relations Act of 1971*, does not have as much on our theme as one might expect from the title; but it is a very full survey of the industrial background, and chapter 8, 'Conclusions', is directly pertinent.

There have been a number of studies of *juries* and the 'jury equity' not to apply a law: cf. one recent study, M. R. Kadish and S. H. Kadish

Discretion to disobey (Stanford, 1973) at pp. 45–66 esp., and references therein. On the conflict between juries and the obscenity law, see G. Robertson *Obscenity* and the reported statement of a spokesman for the publishers that 'the police hardly ever use section 2 of the [Obscene Publications Act 1959], which is a criminal prosecution and gives the right to trial by jury, because they are just not likely to get a conviction in front of a jury on pornography nowadays'. Instead they use their power to ask for a destruction order before the magistrates.

On elites, see Geraint Parry *Political elites* (London, 1969), which analyses variant theories of elites. The most relevant chapter will be found to be Chapter VI, 'Elites and democratic theory', which discusses the broad question, 'Is the existence of elites compatible with the existence of democracy?'. In this chapter he reviews some of the celebrated thinkers who have tried to resolve the paradox and summarises their opinions. They range from such as G. Sartori *Democratic theory* (Detroit, 1962), who argues that the average voter is ill-informed and has no opinions of his own — 'Public opinion never originates ideas; it is influenced before itself attempting to influence. There would therefore be good justification for an elite of quality to shape and educate public opinion, especially where the elite is in competition with other elites' (summary of Parry at p. 148) — to Rousseau, who has been constantly criticised for utopianism, but who advocated a participating democracy in which government by the people is the goal, even if not immediately attainable. 'For Rousseau [writes Parry] the individual citizen found freedom in participating in making the laws of his community and then, in his capacity as a subject, obeying the laws he himself made' (at Parry, p. 150). It will be noted by the reader, firstly that the term 'elitist' in the mouths of political theorists does *not* mean one who advocates domination by an elite, but one who studies the role of elites in a polity; and secondly, that the argument of the present work tends rather to the Rousseau than the Sartori position. Sartori deals with what happens; Rousseau with what ought to happen. The two are thus not necessarily in conflict. Where they may conflict is in the prescriptions which they respectively issue for the future, and the approbation or lack of it which they express for a law-making and controlling elite. In the terms used by Parry, I would find myself largely in the camp of the 'radical democrats', who would seek to shape institutions so as to make the participation of the ordinary citizen in them 'normal, legitimate and desirable'. Rousseau and Burke are usually thought of as being at the opposite ends of the political spectrum; and Edmund Burke is remembered not least for his dominant articulation of the 'representative' theory of democracy, that representatives are not delegates of their electors, in contrast with Rousseau's championing of direct democratic participation. But, as David Cameron reminds us in his stimulating *The social thought of Rousseau and Burke: a comparative study* (London, 1973) the two thinkers were not as far apart as people usually suppose; and on this particular issue Cameron quotes Burke as claiming:

'that, although the "immediate and instrumental cause of the law" may be the governing power, "the remote and efficient cause is the consent of the people, either actual or implied; and such consent is absolutely essential to its validity".' ·

But, while Rousseau claimed that the people must be consulted before a law which affects them is passed on grounds of fundamental political morality − it is the duty of the governors to allow the governed to participate in making laws, Burke bases his advocacy of consensual legislation on expediency − it will make the chances of efficacious law that much greater.

The classic study of Somali society is that by I. M. Lewis *A pastoral democracy* (London, 1961).

On the general theme of the deprivation of legitimacy for a legal order or system by the withdrawal of obedience by its subjects, it is important to recall that this is no new phenomenon linked to modern constitutionalism and the problems of Pakistan or Rhodesia. An interesting historical example, might be presented by the collapse of the medieval and feudal system in England, conventionally dated from A. D. 1485, well explored by D. M. Loades in his book *Politics and the nation 1450–1660* (London, 1974), which is suggestively subtitled 'Obedience, resistance and public order'. His account of the collapse of the old order, detailed by Loades in his Part I 'The eclipse of the medieval monarchy', is preceded by a quotation from the complaint of the men of Kent, dated June 1450:

'The law serveth nought else in these days but for to do wrong.'

The courts did not provide the justice which men demanded; the law was ineffective to right wrongs, and itself became a weapon of wrong-doing in the hands of unscrupulous men.

CHAPTER 4

There has been a good deal of writing on what I call 'translocation' of laws, but which others discuss under 'reception of laws', or even 'legal transplants'. See, for example, M. B. Hooker *Legal Pluralism* (London, 1976), and the extensive bibliography appended thereto. On legal systems generally, their families and their translocation, the reader may find two synoptic works helpful: R. David *Les grands systèmes de droit contemporains* (Paris, 1966); and *An introduction to legal systems* (ed. J. D. M. Derrett, London, 1968). The latter is especially concerned with an outline statement of the characteristics of ancient and modern Asian and African laws, as well as of Roman law and English law by way of comparison. Each contains a useful bibliography which will take the reader more deeply into world legal systems. My own *Essays in African Law*, (London, 1960) and *New Essays in African Law* (London, 1970) have also been concerned with the practical effects of, as well as the legal mechanisms for, the transplantation of legal systems to African countries from Europe. A. Watson has written on *Legal transplants* (Edinburgh, 1974); and see also his 'Comparative law and legal change' [1978] 37 CLJ 313; 'Legal transplants and law reform' (1976) 92 LQR 79.

CHAPTER 5

On the equities and inequities of the tax system (pp. 15ff.), see for instance 'Law, justice and equity in tax' by G. S. A. Wheatcroft [in] *Law, justice and equity* (ed. by R. H. Code Hollander and G. Schwarzenberger (London, 1967)), at pp. 87ff. See esp. at p. 91:

'[without a long-term plan for simplication and improvement of the tax laws of the United Kingdom] ... unless this is done, we can give up pretending that "justice" or "equity" have anything to do with tax law in the United Kingdom.'

See also W. J. Blum and H. Kalven *The uneasy case for progressive taxation* (Chicago, 1953); and F. A. Hayek *The constitution of liberty* (London, 1960), chapter 20 'Taxation and redistribution',*passim*, which is generally in line with the argument here presented. See esp. p. 332:

'That a majority should be free to impose a discriminatory tax burden on a minority; that, in consequence, equal services should be remunerated differently; and that for a whole class, merely because its incomes are not in line with the rest, the normal incentives should be practically made ineffective – all these are principles which cannot be defended on grounds of justice.'

On the *right to disobey* laws generally, see M. R. Kadish and S. H. Kadish *Discretion to disobey* (Stanford, 1977). On this and many other related questions seen from the point of view of a political scientist, see *Freedom, anarchy and the law* by R. Taylor (Englewood Cliffs, 1973), a non-conforming approach to many of our topics which conflicts strongly with some of the points expressed here, but which at least recognises that no law enforces itself.

R. M. Hare, *The language of morals* (London 1952), is highly relevant and has been influential in determining the field upon which the battle is to be fought. See his Part I, *The imperative mood*, and esp. chapter 1 'Prescriptive language' as well as his analysis in Part III of 'Ought'. His clear style and persuasive argument should not induce us to agree with

him that commands are not merely attempts to persuade or get someone to do something. Hare's assumption that such persuasion in effect
denies rationality in the hearer seems misconceived; on the contrary,
one of the most powerful forms of persuasion is the clear demonstration
of the rationality of a prescribed course of action. (However, Socrates
and those who follow him were misguided in thinking that it was
sufficient to lay out the rationality of a particular course of action for
the hearer to be induced to follow it; that there are other forms of
persuasion is of course conceded; the position is conveniently
summarised by Damon Runyon's and others' use of the term 'persuader'
for a hand-gun.)

There are many respects in which one could take issue with Hare's
analysis; this is not, though, a textbook on moral philosophy, so that
one must resist the temptation to make a detailed commentary on his
seminal text. However, at p. 19, his discussion of agreement or assent
by the hearer of an utterance might have been clarified by a reference
to military usage, where the all-important distinction between the
hearer of a message indicating (a) that he has heard and understood a
message, (b) that he has heard it and will comply with it, is represented
by the two code words, 'Roger' and 'Wilco'. Correct use, by the
recipient of a message, of these words requires him to classify the
message as (a) one transmitting information only, or as (b) one requiring him to take some action, such as to move his force to Position
Q. What is more, the hearer does more or less than 'assent' to a
message, even an informational one, in the military context. To say
'Roger' does not mean that the hearer has asserted that he believes the
information contained in the message to be 'true'; merely that he has
taken the message into his consciousness. To use 'assent' for both the
Roger and Wilco situations can lead only to confusion.

At pp. 35ff. Hare deals with what we call 'hypothetical-conditionals',
or imperatives which are hypothetical in his terms. He categorically
rejects the conclusion that 'all non-moral imperatives are hypothetical',
but his following discussion shows some of the doubts which such a
brusque rejection of such a proposition inevitably provokes. His discussion is with respect made more difficult by an apparent failure to
distinguish the actual language used in an utterance cast in the conditional form – its surface grammatical structure – from its analytical
form. He discusses the apparent conditional imperative, 'If you want to
break your springs, go on driving as you are at present'. This, in my
view, can be analysed, *not* as an imperative, despite the surface form
of an imperative, but as a prediction:

'If you continue to drive as at present, you are likely to break your
springs.'

Legal/logical operations can only be carried out on the analytical and not
the actual or verbal forms of hypothetical imperatives.

Hare makes a fundamental division between 'descriptive' and 'evaluative' words or remarks: 'This strawberry is *sweet*; This strawberry is *large, red* and *juicy*' are quoted by him as descriptive remarks; 'This strawberry is *good*' (my italics) as an evaluative remark. But 'sweet', 'large', 'red' and 'juicy' *are* (*pace* Hare) evaluative words — they say that, compared with our inherent or learned standards of sweetness, largeness, redness and juiciness, and what we expect or demand from a good strawberry, this strawberry meets our criteria. Since laws constantly make use of standards in prescribing conduct — motor vehicles must have a braking system 'in good and efficient working order' (Motor Vehicles (Construction and Use) Regulations 1978, reg. 101); they must not have 'unsuitable' tyres (reg. 107), they must not make 'an excessive noise' on the road (reg. 114) — lawyers must be concerned with this question of words which imply or set a standard. 'Sweet', 'large', etc, express or set standards by which we judge strawberries which we would call adequate for our purposes. This is not to deny that there are many utterances which set no standard: 'There are no strawberries' might be one; but Hare's choice of examples may not help us in discriminating. (Reference may also be made on this sort of point — illustrated with a wealth of examples — to Stephen Ullman's *Semantics: an introduction to the science of meaning* (Oxford, 1962) especially his chapter 5 'Logical and emotive factors in meaning'.)

Standard texts on the relationship of law and morality (apart from numerous discussions in general jurisprudential works) include Lon L. Fuller *The morality of law* (New Haven, 2nd edn, 1969); Lord Devlin *The enforcement of morals* Oxford, 1959); H. L. A. Hart *Law, liberty and morality* (London, 1963). There are also endless controversial articles in legal journals which agitate the questions raised by these three gladiators of the law-and-morality circus. Needless to say, there is also a vast literature on each of the broad themes mentioned in this Chapter, notably on natural law, law and justice, and fundamental rights. No attempt will be made to guide the reader in these areas: reference to general treatises on jurisprudence should be made for starting materials.

CHAPTER 6

Although there has been much writing on codification from Bentham on, there has not been much discussion in the terms employed here of law as model and law as programme; though there is naturally a numerous literature on each of the examples cited. For India the writings of J. D. M. Derrett and Marc Galanter will be found most helpful in this context; see, for instance, Derrett's *Religion, law and the state in India* (London, 1968); and Marc Galanter 'The displacement of traditional law in modern India' (1968) 24 J of Social Issues 65. Other references sufficient to guide the reader to the sources and issues are given in the text in regard to Turkey, Kenya, Ethiopia, etc.

In regard to the *ujamaa* policy in Tanzania, especially as it relates to the originally voluntary and self-reliant, and eventually forcible, regrouping of villagers in *ujamaa* villages, a fair and full chronicle and assessment will be found in the work by Jannik Boesen, Birgit Storgård Madsen, and Tony Moody in their *Ujamaa – socialism from above* (Uppsala, 1977). *Ujamaa,* a Swahili abstract term, originally meant 'familyhood'; and it was alleged that the *ujamaa* policy of Nyerere's government reflected ancient legal and social values of African society, especially that tenure and exploitation of land should be community-based. Nothing in ancient customary law corresponds to or authorises the present policy and practice of *ujamaa* resettlement. Although the formation of *ujamaa* villages was in theory to depend on full democratic participation by those affected, the authors show that this has been far from the case. The result has been general failure. The number of *ujamaa* villages set up is no measure of the success of the new law and its administrative implementation. The policy has changed to mass resettlement by forcible means, accompanied by bureaucratic controls. Despite some superficial and peripheral successes, these are not deep-rooted and have not succeeded in achieving the basic aim of the policy, which is to produce a complete social transformation of the rural peasantry coupled with increased productivity.

The article by R. Granger, op. cit., will be found to discuss many of the resistances to law reform in the transforming sense considered in this Chapter. He also discusses such topics as the role of the mass media and government publicity in diffusing new laws.

CHAPTER 7

On Soviet *Law* generally, see, for example, R. Schlesinger *Soviet legal theory* (2nd edn, London, 1951); J. N. Hazard *The Soviet legal system* (2nd edn, Dobbs Ferry, 1969); id. *Settling disputes in Soviet society* (New York, 1960); id. *Communists and their law* (1969); E. N. Pashukanis *The general theory of law and marxism* (1924; trans. Babb 1951); and I. Lapenna *State and law: Soviet and Yugoslav theory* (London, 1973). W. E. Butler's general account of law in the USSR, *Soviet Law* (forthcoming), will discuss the 'Ideological foundations of Soviet law' in its Chapter III.

K. Grzybowski, in his book *Soviet legal institutions* (Ann Arbor, 1962), includes a discussion on socialist legality. However, the book, *Justice and the legal system in the USSR* (ed. Robert Conquest, London, 1968), provides perhaps the fullest documentation for our purpose. Chapter V discusses 'Party control and legality'. A few quotations will express the conclusions of this work:

'The primacy of Party control often works in a reverse direction to what is currently termed "Socialist legality".' (p. 114)

'Very little data are revealed about the actual executive control over, or interference in the work of the judiciary exerted by Party organs . . .' (p. 111).

The institutionalisation of new communal courts [*sic*] in competition with the judicial system is a 'new retreat from legal guarantees'. (p. 115)

See also the discussion by Dennis M. O'Connor of 'Soviet procedures in civil decisions: a changing balance between public and civic systems of public order' [in] *Law in the Soviet society* (ed. Wayne R. Lafave, Urbana, 1965), in which the author mentions the 'replacement of rules of law by principles of morality and social conduct' exerted through the acts of civic groups, including comrades' courts (p. 67). He says that there is a mass propaganda of norms and exemplary cases through the news media, 'and jurists are instructed to propagandize the law' (pp. 92–3).

On comrades' courts generally, the recent article by W. E. Butler 'Comradely justice revised' (1977) 3 Review of Socialist Law 325, will be found illuminating and thought-provoking. The observant reader may be stimulated to contrast the institution and its effects on the 'normativity' of *Law* with those of the jury and of justices of the peace in England. If it is a criticism, as it doubtless validly is, that comrades' courts function as much with the help of a general sense of rightness and wrongness as with a regard for the letter of the *Law*, and express community mores in legal form, then the same charge must be laid against jury justice in England, the United States and other common-law countries. This general theme – of the participation of the layman in the making and application of the *Law* – is an intensely important one for describing the limits of the operation of a law, and could have been further developed in the text. However, it is hoped to make a comparative study of this theme at greater length at a later date; meanwhile, the conference of the Commonwealth Magistrates Association at Oxford in September, 1979, has made this one of its principal topics of discussion on a pan-Commonwealth basis; and its papers should be consulted for further information. Some lawyers and legal systems officially reject any lay assistance in the administration of justice – the reasons for this rejection are predictable; but they have to meet the fact that most legal systems, on the contrary, rate it a valuable or even indispensable feature of their *Law* that laymen should help the courts and tribunals to administer it.

On the *Grundnorm* in constitutional cases, see Leslie J. Macfarlane 'Pronouncing on rebellion: the Rhodesia courts and UDI' (1968) *Public Law* 325 by way of beginning. There is now an extensive constitutional literature on this theme.

On *discretion* in legal systems, see the fascinating book by a professor of law and a professor of philosophy: M. R. Kadish and S. H. Kadish *Discretion to disobey: a study of lawful departures from legal rules* (Stanford, 1973), which deals with a large number of topics touching on various of the themes in this book, notably the role of the jury and 'jury nullification of unjust laws' (pp. 45–66 especially); departures by officials and citizens from the law, acceptance of a legal system, judicial discretion, the police discretion to prosecute; non-enforcement of laws and the reasons therefor; has a citizen a duty to obey laws? On the German *Legalitätsprinzip* see John H. Langbein *Comparative criminal procedure in Germany* (St Paul, 1977), which sets out the limits and the problems of the prosecutor's discretion or compulsion in German law.

As to *custom overriding law*, in classical Hindu *Law* custom overrides the written text of the Smritis; and this principle was recognised by the Privy Council in a number of decisions, notably *Collector of Madura v Moottoo Ramalinga* (1868) 12 MIA 397 at 436: '... clear proof of usage will outweigh the written texts of the law'. In Anglo-Hindu *Law* discontinuance of a custom repealed the validity of it if it was a *family* custom, but not if a *local* custom, per se, apart from difficulties of proof that it existed (cf. Mayne *Hindu law and usage*, chapter III). Today the role of custom is unimportant in the administration of Hindu *Law* (cf. Derrett, passim). The treatment in common-law Africa of custom was different from the Indian, and non-observance would invalidate a local custom, even if it had been proved in earlier proceedings; cf. *Eleko v Officer Administering the Government of Nigeria* [1931] AC 662 at 673: 'The native community may assent to some modification of an original custom ...'. But this problem is entangled with the role of judicial decisions in declaring enforceable customary *Law*, and once a court has taken judicial notice of frequently proved rules of customary *Law*, it may be difficult to convince a subsequent court that the custom has changed or been abandoned. In general, cessation of a custom means cessation of its legal effect – cf. the discussion in my *New Essays in African Law*, chapter 5.

CHAPTER 8

New decisions, and new learning, on the 'house-mate' and her rights may be expected daily. Since this chapter was written, for instance, two separate cases were reported on the same day (26 May 1979). In the one, a rich man died leaving (i) a widow, (ii) a 'common-law wife', (iii) a mistress (a combination I had not anticipated in the text). His will made no provision for the non-live-in mistress, though it did for the lawful wife and the 'common-law wife' (=house-mate). The mistress, who had been given a flat in Malta, an allowance, and a sports car by the deceased, claimed successfully under the Inheritance (Provision for Family and Dependants) Act 1975 on the ground that she had been 'maintained' by deceased. The High Court awarded her £19,000 from the £889, 000 estate. The case was said to be the first so brought by a mistress.

In the other case, a young father living with his 18-year-old mistress in a caravan and apart from his lawful wife was awarded custody of his two children (by the wife), aged 2 and 3, because the husband and his house-mate could provide a more stable home than could be provided by the natural mother, i.e. the wife, living with her own mother.

The general background can be ascertained by the student from the standard textbooks on family law, such as those by Cretney, Bromley and Stone, though none of them devotes special attention to the problems of the house-mate. Tony Honoré's *Sex law* (London, 1978) includes a good deal of relevant material, esp. in Chapter 2 'Living together'.

The need for legislative tidying up of the status of the 'common-law wife' (house-mate) was amusingly demonstrated in the following recent and authentic conversation in a Citizen's Advice Bureau; woman client to adviser: 'How long do I have to live with a man before I become his common-law wife?' (she had been living with a man for 3 months at the date of the enquiry)!

The Court of Appeal's decision in *Pascoe v Turner* [1979] 2 All ER 945, takes the position yet further. It was reported too late to be incorporated in the text, but requires careful study by way of supplement to the points and principles developed there. It adds yet another weapon to the armoury of the disappointed house-mate. There was no legal transfer of the legal estate in the house in which the plaintiff lived with his mistress as man and wife to the house-mate, because of want of form. There was no perfected gift of the house to her, though he told her it was hers. There was no express trust. There was nothing in the facts from which even a constructive trust could be inferred. And yet the Court was happy to hold that the man had created an estoppel by his words and conduct, standing by while she spent her money on improving the house; there was an imperfect gift, and in conscience equity required him to give the woman house-mate 'security of tenure, quiet enjoyment and freedom of action in respect of repairs and improvements without interference from the plaintiff'. The plaintiff was to be stopped from pursuing every legal means of evicting his mistress from the house 'with a ruthless disregard of the obligations binding on [his] conscience'. And so the Court of Appeal to this end made a declaration 'that the estate in fee simple in the property . . . is vested in the defendant'. This was certainly a short, sharp and ruthless way of dealing with the situation. It remains to be seen what new 'obligations binding in conscience' the courts will now discover in the house-mate relationship.

CONCLUSIONS

See R. Granger generally for *his* conclusions (op. cit. pp. 116ff.). 'Le droit est évidemment impuissant à lui seul à resoudre la crise mondiale de civilisation . . .' (p. 122). The ability of law to force social evolution, anticipating the future, is shown to be very weak, if not non-existent. There must be a fundamental re-adjustment of the relations between modern law and social reality. We must put an end to the galloping legal inflation (p. 123). There is a limit to what law can do, and the areas into which it should move. There must be a fundamental political shift in the incidence of power, following the lines laid out by Proudhon (p. 124). The all-powerful state is the main danger, in capitalist and socialist countries alike. Co-operation, mutual assistance, and other forms of voluntary association are the answer, coupled with a large measure of self-management on the part of citizens and enterprises. What I have called the 'Nanny-state' must be cut down; the subjects of the law must be treated as equal partners, Granger argues.

On populism, see G. Ionescu and E. Gellner, eds. *Populism: its meanings and national characteristics* (London, 1969); Theodore Saloutos, ed. *Populism: reaction or reform* (New York, 1968); Margaret Canovan *G. K. Chesterton: radical populist* (New York, 1977) (for the removal of doubts, I must emphasize that I do not subscribe to some of G. K.'s wilder prejudices, e.g. anti-semitism).

As to the 'consent principle' in democracies, see J. Stone, *Social dimensions of law and justice* (London, 1966), pp. 616–626, and references therein.

A very interesting article by Richard L. Abel, which came into my hands by the courtesy of the author only after this text was completed, dissents strongly from a number of the conclusions to which I have come in this study: see his 'Delegalization: a critical review of its ideology, manifestations, and social consequences' [in] E. Blankenberg, E. Klausa and H. Rottleuthner, eds *Alternative Rechtsformen und Alternativen zum Recht* (5 Jahrbuch für Rechtssoziologie und Rechtstheorie, 1979, Westdeutscher Verlag). Abel argues against the present trend, which he discerns, towards taking more and more matters out of the grasp of the *Law*, civil and criminal, and of the courts and legal professionals. This tendency he labels 'delegalization'. Clearly the conclusions of my study would lead to some diminution in law-making; however, not all of Abel's grounds for resisting this movement would, I think, apply to my statement here. I have rejected the 'romanticism' about early 'law' which he mentions as one element in delegalization, for instance; I by no means wish to extend the power of the big corporations; I seek more effective, though fewer, laws, but concentrate on the *process* by which such laws should be made; I blame the law-making elites for the excess of laws and overload of the system; I have expressly disclaimed hostility to the purposes of some of the liberalising laws, though regretting their ineffectiveness; I would not agree with Abel about small claims courts (in England, anyhow), which suit the individual small litigant better than the large creditor (or often, defendant); I would not agree at all with the contention that lawyers on both sides can equalise matters, which would only be true if each side could afford the lawyers in the first place; I would further argue, *contra* Abel, that informal means of settling cases and of imposing behavioural control are often more effective than formal; I support consensus as both a test and a condition of effectiveness, while Abel argues for dissensus and creative tension (which in its turn may well be effective in promoting final agreement and/or action, it is true).

It is, however, salutary to see the different construction that can be placed on what I hope we could agree are the same phenomena, though some further spelling out of the *objectives* of an acceptable legal system, and eventually of an acceptable political system, would be beneficial for the debate.

As to rule by elites and consensus generally, we may finish with a quotation from Dr Richard Price in his *Observations on the Nature of Civil Liberty* (8th edn, London 1778; reprinted in *Two tracts on civil liberty*, 1778), p. 7:

'Liberty, therefore, is too imperfectly defined when it is said to be a "Government by LAWS, and not by MEN." If the laws are made by one man, or a junto of men in a state, and not by COMMON CONSENT, a government by them does not differ from Slavery.'

Glossary

affirmative law	a law which requires positive action by its subjects – p. 48
anomia	ignorance or lack of *Law* among those members of a society nominally subject to it – p. 73
applied juristics	the study of the sociology of laws in operation – p. 45
articulated norm	a norm which has been formally declared ('emitted') in a normative statement – p. 10
catanomic	popular norm-making in accordance with existing law – *defined*, p. 119
compliance	action (or inaction) which implements the purpose of a norm – *defined*, p. 30
contextual interpretation	reference to the changing social context to modify the function of a statutory term – p. 103
crypto-norm	a secret norm actually followed by courts and people, contradicting the prescription of the overt norms – p. 255
effective norm	a valid norm which secures a high degree of compliance – *defined*, p. 30
framework law	a law which provides a framework within which a subject may make his own private catanomic law to create and control a form of association – p. 169
frustrate norm	a valid norm with zero or minimal compliance – *defined*, p. 30
institution	.. of a *Law*, comprises facilities and relationships identified and controlled by legal norms – p. 7
instrumental legal term	a specialised term employed by judges as a connection mechanism between the facts of a case and the applicable legal rules – p. 101
latent norm	a norm which has not yet been articulated, but which provokes what may be considered acts of compliance – *defined*, p. 30
LAW	the general idea or concept of legal institutions abstracted from any particular occurrence of them – *defined*, p. 2

309

Law	a coherent, total, particular legal system prevailing in a given community or country − *defined*, p. 2 SEE ALSO *legal system*
law	a particular normative provision of a *Law*; a rule or norm of a given legal system − *defined*, p. 2
legalism	the principle that a subject of a law should conform with it if it is validly made − p. 149
legality	the principle that legal rules should be regular, fairly made and fairly applied − p. 149
legal system	a system of norms, institutions and processes, made by a competent and legitimate authority, which control the behaviour of persons in an autonomous and legitimate political society or community − pp. 7−8
meta-norm	a norm which controls the operation of another norm (*also* super-norm) − p. 23
model status-relationship	a strongly permitted legal relationship, such as marriage − p. 168
norm	a form of imperative; ... of a *Law*, is expressed in a hypothetical-conditional statement, prescribing a pattern of behaviour assigned as a consequence of the occurrence of a particular hypothetical set of events − pp. 16−17. SEE ALSO *articulated norm, crypto-norm, effective norm, frustrate norm, latent norm, phantom norm, valid norm*
paranomic	popular subsidiary norm-making contrary to existing law − *defined*, p. 119
phantom norm	a norm? which has not been actually emitted by any authority − *defined*, p. 30
preventive law	a law which requires its subject not to do something − p. 48
process	... of a *Law*, describes the norms and institutions in action − p. 7
programme	the use of law to secure the transformation of a society in accordance with the plan of the legislator − p. 174
strong imperative	a norm or law which positively and strongly commands a particular pattern of behaviour − p. 47
translocation of law	the shifting of a legal system, or part of it, from its country of origin to another geographically distinct territory or community − p. 109
valid norm	a norm which is formally correct, having been made in due form − *defined*, p. 30
weak imperative	a norm or law where the legislator has no strong commitment to the pattern of behaviour commanded − p. 47; similarly with *strong prohibition, weak prohibition; strong permission, weak permission*

Index

[Terms marked with * are defined in the Glossary.]

312 *Index*